AF444164

Stories For Dad

Christopher F Bidwell
Bruce Eliot Bidwell

Printed in the United States of America
First Printing, 2024

Library of Congress Cataloging-in-Publication data available.
ISBN 979-8-218-48121-6
ISBN 979-8-218-48124-7 (eBook)

Cover Photo by Matthew Bidwell on Whiteface Mountain.
Cover – Christopher, Bruce
Back - Frederick (Grampa) Noss

For my loving wife Mona Lee Adams who was the impetus for this book. You make my life great every day.

For my awesome mother Lura Jane Noss Bidwell who I connected to during her Alzheimer's by reading aloud chapters from this book until she gave me a gleam of recognition in her eyes, the occasional snort of laughter and finally remembrance. I love you Mom.

Also by Christopher Frederick Bidwell
Cancer Insights: Chronicles of a couples journey through breast cancer

Also by Bruce Eliot Bidwell
Reflections: A Family Memoir

Special thanks to Lori Brooks and Mona Adams for editing the initial drafts of this book.

Table of Contents

Introduction

On December 15th, 2019, I was talking with Dad on the phone with my wife Mona. Dad was bemoaning the fact that he had not been around enough for us kids and he should have been there more for us.

Mona piped up and said, "What are you talking about Bruce. Christopher is always telling me stories about stuff that you guys did when he was a kid."

I went on to tell him a few things that I remember growing up that we had done together and it piqued his interest.

After hearing a couple of my stories, Dad asked me, "Chris do you think that you could write up a couple of stories of things we did together while you were growing up?"

"Of course," I said "I have a few ideas that I could get started on right away. I think I will start with a fishing story, since we have spent many happy outings on the rivers and creeks with our fly rods."

After the call, I started the first of six episodes of Stories for Dad, that I emailed to him as soon as I had finished each one. Once I had completed these first six stories, ones that I knew Dad would enjoy and perhaps be a bit eye-opening since it was from my perspective, I wrote another 4 stories of family vacations that we took with Dad and the family. I just continued with my stories of growing up, with antidotes of things I found interesting or entertaining and continued sending them out. They became more Life with the Family, since Mom was a big part of most of the stories as well as my siblings and friends.

Dad passed away on November 9, 2020 at the age of 91 just 2 days after Joe Biden was declared the winner of the 2020 presidential election. Six months earlier, Dad had told me that he wanted to stick around just long enough to see Biden win the election. I told him in that case I was voting for Trump so he would have to hang on for another four years!

I wrote all these stories during the last year of Dad's life and he got to read them all including the final two chapters that were read to him by Robin, his loving wife while he was in hospice. His comments are at the end of each chapter. I never got to see my dad during this time because of the Covid-19 Pandemic lockdown. This was my way of saying goodbye to him.

Please note that the Ridge Road chapters jump around and are not totally in chronological sequence, since we lived there for eight years from 8yo to 15yo. I told the stories as I remember them and not in strict order.

The final chapter was written by my dad as thoughts of his impending end of life were occupying his mind and the writing was cathartic for him. Dad had previously published a family memoir called Reflections and this last chapter is a coda to his book.

01 Time with Dad - Fishing

Some of my earliest recollections of fishing was the excitement surrounding opening day of the fishing season. I would build up to that day by going through all the lures in my tackle box, organizing my creel and reading articles about fishing in Sports Afield. Matt and I would trade lures, flies and gear as we were sorting through all our stuff.

Dad was strictly a fly fisherman, but he was not against us simply putting a hook and a bobber on our fly rods so that we could use worms. We were young, so getting a fly out to a sweet part of the brook was a bit out of the question, plus most of the other kids and adults would be fishing with bait also, so we did not want to be at a disadvantage.

When opening day would finally arrive, we would go to an area where there would be lots of fisherman (including fisherkids, really just fishers) which meant a lot of shared excitement. Probably my favorite place to go was a little brook on the other side of Firetown Rd. The state would stock a lot of the bigger streams and rivers, but a guy that owned the property would stock his creek himself, since he loved having kids fishing on opening day. Dad, Matt and I would go down there tromping around looking for a good place to drop a worm amongst all the other fisherkids doing the same. We always caught several trout each that we would put in our creels to take home. Dad would be wearing all his buff-colored fishing gear and would be tromping around the forest helping us find likely spots to land another trout. Sometimes we would go to a bigger stream or even a lake for opening day, usually a place where the state had recently stocked with fish. There would be lots of other excited people getting their first fishing fix since the previous Fall.

Dad would take us fishing during the season, usually to secret spots that he knew about and almost always a brook or a stream. The only time we fished rivers was when we were up in New

Hampshire on summer vacations. One time just Dad and I were fishing a stream in Connecticut in the early Spring, Dad was wading, I had my sneakers on, fishing from the bank. The mosquitoes were particularly bad and I was spending more time slapping the bugs from my face and neck, generally causing a little ruckus. Dad was getting annoyed with me for scaring the fish, although he did not say anything.

Finally, Dad called to me, "You know a true fisherman learns to ignore the bugs!"

At that moment, I knew in my heart of hearts that I would never be a real fisherman.

It did not mean that I would not love fishing for the rest of my life, but that if the bugs were out, I would happily go exploring around, slapping the bugs with my fishing gear lying by the bank.

Dad would take us fishing along the bigger granite boulder-strewn rivers in beautiful New Hampshire. Dad, my younger brother Matt and I would fish, usually with Dad wading and Matt and I fishing from the top of the boulders scattered around the river. After about an hour, I would start to get bored and would put down my rod, creel and net to head upstream, jumping from boulder to boulder to boulder, exploring what was around the next bend. I would eventually come back, pickup my gear and continue fishing with them. As a result, they would generally catch more fish.

In the winter, Dad would teach Matt and I to tie our own flies. He had a vice, yarn, hooks, hackles, feathers, fur and all the gear to create the patterns that we had seen in the magazines. He showed us how to wrap the body, how to wrap the hackles around the hook-eye to make a dry fly and tie it off. He eventually gave all this gear to us boys and we would spend time making up our own fly patterns and trying to make the famous ones such as a Royal Coachman. We would tie up all the flies that we would need for next year's fishing season.

As a family, we would spend August up in New Hampshire at a big old house called Kinderheim that was not far from Pond Brook, that we always called Swift River. Matt and I would take these flies that we had made and we would bushwhack down from the big house to the beaver ponds down by the creek. We always had great luck catching the little brookies on our hand-tied dry flies down there. We would fish them until the thread would start coming apart before retiring them for a new one.

In later years, when I was living in Colorado, Dad would come out for fishing trips with us. One of our favorite trips was to fish the headwaters of the North Platte River in Wyoming. We camped at Six Mile Gap one time with Matt, my sister Julie, Dad and myself. We setup a tent by the truck and fished the river for a couple of days. Julie slept inside the Ford Bronco, snug in her sleeping bag. We would eat our fish around the campfire at night, feeling like self-sufficient woodsmen (woodsperson) as we consumed the day's catch.

There was a limit that you had to throw back any fish under 18", since this was a "Blue Ribbon" fishery and they wanted to protect the breeding stock. I was up near the top of Stovepipe rapid, which was just above our camp, fly fishing from a boulder that I had jumped to from the bank. I hooked a good-sized trout and played it until I got it close to the rock. I got my net off my back and put it down next to the water as I was pulling the fish in. When I put my foot down at the base of the rock to scoop up the fish, my foot slipped and I slithered into the water. I swam the top part of the rapid, hanging onto my net and rod and managed to get out of the current into an eddy. Miraculously my fish was still on the end of my line and I pulled him in and caught it. Pulling out my measuring tape I saw that it was only 17 inches. I had gone through so much to catch that fish, I went ahead and kept it, with just a slight twinge of guilt, and we had it for dinner that night.

Another time Matt, my son Colt, Dad and I were camping back at the headwaters of the North Platte River, but this time we came in from the East and were camping at the Pickaroon campground down a jeeping trail. We had the camp to ourselves since it was August and the river was low and wadeable all the way across. This made the fly fishing easy, since we were out away from the trees and bushes along the bank and casting was clear. It was a fun and relaxing trip. Matt setup his floorless pole tent while Coulter and I slept in a dry bathtub-floor pup tent. It rained the night we were there and, in the morning, the sun came out and there was a rivulet of water that went right through the center of Matt's tent, but Dad and him stayed reasonably dry on both sides of the water. Coulter was probably 10 and we had brought his bike with us. We were sitting around the campfire the dusk of our first day fishing there. Colt came flying down the dirt road towards the camp on his bike when his front tire slid out and he went sliding face-first into the dirt. I jumped up and could see that he might have a scrape or two, but that he was OK, and he was getting ready to cry.

I immediately said to him in a loud and concerned voice, "Is your bike OK?"

It was enough to take his mind off his scrapes and look at his bike to make sure that it would be rideable tomorrow. No crying needed. We were catching numerous trout on this trip, but one afternoon we were in a bit of a fishing slump.

Colt looked at me and said, "Grandpa is a great fisherman, so why is he not catching anything."

I replied to him, "Colt, Grandpa is a true fisherman. A true fisherman learns to continue fishing, even when you are not catching anything."

This is great stuff! I think that you should keep on since you obviously enjoy writing. The memories are important to be shared. Perhaps this could be included with the Addendum as another mini-book. -Dad

02 Time with Dad - Paper Route

When I was 8, we moved into a 50's style house on 2 acres in Simsbury. Just like Christopher Robin, there was a good 100 acres of woods, swamp and a creek that went all the way to downtown. It was a kid's paradise. This 50's - 60's style is still my favorite for living in, in fact my current house is very similar, just updated with double-pane windows and better insulation

Both of my parents, especially my dad have a love of books that I inherited. I would read library books from home, but my favorites were my parents childhood books. My Mom had books such as <u>Wild Animals I Have Known</u> by Earnest Seaton Thompson (1898) a naturalist that would write about animals in the first person, so it was very easy to relate to them especially Raggylug the Cottontail. In fact, I have a special love for bunnies to this day. I also had Dad's complete childhood book collection and would read all of the same books that he had read as a young boy. I had been reading dad's books, such as <u>Ken Ward in the Jungle</u> by Zane Grey (1912) and <u>The Lone Woodsman</u> (1943) by Warren Hastings Miller. The stories captured my imagination with the tales of traveling into the Mexican jungle by rowboat or up into the wilds of Canada and traveling by canoe. I had decided at the time that I wanted a canoe. The only way to get this canoe would be to purchase it myself, so I needed a steady source of income in order to save the money to purchase a full-sized boat. Dad was more a sail-boat type of man, not a canoer, but he drove the perfect rig. A V-8 Plymouth station wagon with a built-in roof rack that I knew he would be willing to transport the canoe with.

In 6th grade, I arranged with a kid at school to purchase his paper route from him, since it was in and around my neighborhood. At the time, that was really my only option to earning money. My parents took me down to the Simsbury Bank and Trust and set me up with a savings account and I got my SSN at the same time.

The Hartford Courant truck would come to the house at 5:30 every weekday morning and drop off the 30 papers for all the customers on my route. My parents, knowing of my plans, helped me out by purchasing a 5-speed fat-tire bike that we outfitted with baskets. The first month of work, all my profits went to the kid I bought the route from, as payment. Then, after purchasing a little Sylvania transistor radio to listen to in the morning on my bike rides, I started saving for the canoe. When I was a child of 6 or 7, our paperboy would come to the house and always had an earphone plugged into his ear, so I knew that was the standard kit of any paperboy worth his salt. The funny thing is that I always thought that it was plugged into his ear for power.

The paper route changed my life in several ways. I used to watch Saturday morning cartoons with my brothers and sister. Now Saturday mornings were "collecting day", where I would go around to all the houses and collect the weeks subscription from every customer. I would rip off a little square from my collection book as a receipt, and if I was lucky, I would get a tip from the home owner. These tips were the money that we were allowed to keep, typically a couple nickels or a dime, but occasionally a quarter from the people that wanted me to put the paper between the door and the screen door. The rest of the money I would pay to the local paper office after riding my bike downtown, or getting a ride from my dad.

The other life-change was that I could no longer sleep in. The weekday papers had to be delivered to all the houses by 6:30 AM. On Saturday they would be delivered in the morning just before I would go around later to do my collecting. I would enlist my dad to help me on cold days that were snowing if he had time, otherwise I would ride/push my bike in the snow to the houses. I had much better luck getting help from him on Sunday, when he did not have to get up so early to help me and he did not have to go into the office. That was also the day that I needed the most help since the Sunday paper was so thick. Often, I would load up about half the papers into my baskets, deliver them, then ride home, get the rest of the papers and deliver the remaining papers. Where we lived on the top of Ridge Road was good for delivering papers, since it was downhill to Firetown Rd. Then just a slight uphill on Firetown Rd to Ray's Barbershop, and downhill again on Plank Hill Rd to the end of my route at the ballfields. I would ride back to the barbershop and push my bike up a trail in the woods back to the "Circle" that we lived on.

In the second year of my paper route, I had noticed that one of my houses had a rusty old barbell lying on the ground. One day, when I was doing my collecting, I walked past this barbell that had never moved in over a year of delivering papers to this house. I asked the man if he was interested in selling the weights. I offered him a small sum of my cash and he just gave it to me. The best tip I ever received in all my time delivering papers. Later in the afternoon, Dad drove me down to the house in his Plymouth and we loaded the barbell with the rusted metal weights still attached into the back of the car. We brought it home and cleaned it up with a wire brush and some oil and WD40. It always had the brown patina of rust on it, but to me it was a thing of beauty. I put it in my bedroom and would workout with it several times a week. In my mind, I had discovered the secret of weightlifting, like joining a secret club, since back then, weightlifting was not ubiquitous. I did know about it since I had two friends, Mike from Science academy whose dad was a lifter and Mark, a friend whose dad had a bench and weights in their basement. It was definitely better than the isometrics I had been doing from the book <u>How to Be Strong</u> by Charles Atlas that I had ordered from the back of the bubble gum package at Ray's barbershop after one of my haircuts. This led to a lifetime of lifting weights that I still enjoy and helps to keep me young at the tender old age of 64.

I never played baseball at the ball fields at the end of my route. Instead, we would call and roundup neighborhood kids to play ball at the "One Way Sign". We always followed the pros, by playing baseball in the Spring and football in the Fall.

Dad never pushed me into signing up for Little League baseball in the summer. He was not a big sports fan and never pushed me into sports which I was glad of, except for the after work catch, we would do sometime in the back yard, him with his old soft glove and me with a harder newer glove that smelled so strong of good leather. I just hated the idea of playing such a fun game as baseball, but being bossed around and yelled at by the adults as would happen in the organized leagues. I did not see the point in it since we would have such good games at the circle. Later on in the summer, my best friend Jerry had signed up for little league with the encouragement of his dad. I would swing by the ball fields on my bike to see him on my way off on some little adventure. He was SOOO envious of me, since his favorite thing was to ride his banana bike around town with me and our friends, me on my paper bike of course.

One time, on a snowy morning, I was bundled up and pushing my bike up our steep driveway to the circle. About halfway up, I had the first real epiphany of my life. I realized with absolute certainty that there was no God. I don't know if I came to this realization because all the childhood falsehoods finally coalesced in my brain. That there was no tooth-fairy, there was no Easter Bunny, there was no Santa Clause and those other little falsehoods told to you by your parents to make life more like a fantasy and more magical around the holidays. I think the real reason was a little deeper than that. All my Monday School classes at the church after school with praying and stories of biblical characters having conversations with God were proving to be false. I never heard back from God when saying prayers, he never talked to me and everything about him was so abstract. The grown-ups would just dance around the subject with non-specific answers about God when I asked about them. Whatever the reason, I had lost all faith in God, something I would not regain for almost another 40 years. During this godless period of my life I eventually came to believe in a higher power. In fact, I had another little epiphany 30 years later when I was sitting in my kayak in an eddy above a long class V rapid on the N Fork of the Poudre. I was listening to the water in the pool I was sitting in, watching the aspen trees quake, looking up at the deep blue sky behind the huge Sherman granite monolith of Turkey Rock and I realized that there was indeed a higher power. At the time I just knew there was a force in the universe that had to create such unbelievable beauty. This force at the time was not God, as the father of Jesus, just something I knew existed.

Eventually I had saved up $125 and I started scanning the Yankee Flyer want-ads, looking for canoes. It paid off when the Avon Marine & Lawn Mower shop out on Route 44 was getting out of the boating business and was selling a 15' Permacraft fiberglass canoe for the same amount that I had saved up. The whole family went out in the Plymouth and we looked at the boat. To me it was a thing of beauty and not only that, but it was brand new as well. I purchased the boat and we tied it on top of the car and brought it home. Success! Mom gave me several vinyl flowers that I stuck on both sides of the canoe and remained there for the entire time I had it.

We would take the canoe when we went on family picnics, when we would go out to the lake, when we would vacation up to New Hampshire and whenever I could talk my dad into going paddling. A lot of the time he would drop us off at a place like Great Pond. Matt and I would go off paddling and fishing from the canoe. One time we were dropped off at Bear Camp Pond in NH with the canoe, camping and fishing gear. Matt and I paddled around the big pond up into the marshy areas exploring. We finally beached on an island and setup our pup tent and spent the night there catching pickerel, frogs, and chasing the water snakes. It was a great time. We loaded up the next morning and paddled back to the parking area and our folks picked us up.

It truly was the vehicle I was hoping for to get out and have little adventures, go fishing and just enjoy paddling.

The paper route was not always a smooth-running operation. I had some kids that I would occasionally encounter on my delivery or collection rounds that would give me shit. Now we lived in the rural-suburbs of Hartford in Simsbury where there was little crime, but like any town we had bullies.

They might run across the street and grab my bike and confront me, saying something like, "Hey Bidwell" (back then calling someone by their last name was the ultimate insult!), "Do you think you are a tough guy, or just a bad ass".

I know that of the two possible answers, they would all lead to a fight. I would say something stupid like "Both", and jump off my bike. The papers would spill across the street since I could not be dorky enough to put down my kick stand. Generally, we would wrestle around on the dirt on the side of the road until we either wrestled to a draw, or I got him in the ultimate 12-year old's submission hold, The Headlock. Either way, they would later perhaps yell an insult, but would leave me alone after that. I just considered it a necessary hazard of having the best job in the neighborhood. I was lucky that the older teenagers would only mess with me, but never confronted me physically.

I kept the paper route for another year after the canoe. It was nice to have a little pocket money. I would purchase mini-bike frames, and look around for engines to put in them. Grandpa Bidwell was one of those rare people that would mow his lawn with an upright power mower. These were ideal for mini-bikes, since they were horizontal shaft motors that could be bolted into the bike frame. Put on a centrifugal clutch, hook up a chain and we would be off. These motors were hard to find used and I would ask grandpa if I could have his engine when he was done with his current lawnmower. Somehow, I got an engine every year it seemed. Grandpa was really helping me by retiring the mowers before they had worn out, just to provide me with new engines. Dad was not much for working on engines, but he did run the Bidwell Hardware Company that had every tool a young aspiring mechanic could want. Socket sets, flywheel pullers, screwdrivers, wrenches, pliers, etc. I would get a discount on these tools, and Dad would just bring home a tool for my toolbox occasionally when I was stuck on a build. It's funny but my parents never wanted me to have a motorcycle, but they were fine with these mini-bikes. We would ride them down to the railroad tracks on the other side of town and follow the tracks clear out to Granby and nearby towns. If we ran out of gas, we would fill up at the gas stations, where the guys working there would tell us that the hoses contained gas the people that filled up their cars left in the hose. Emptying one hose was always more than enough to fill up the little tank.

When my paper delivering business had run its course, I eventually sold my business to a fellow classmate. I had thought that after I quit delivering papers, I would resume my Saturday morning cartoon viewing but I never cared for cartoons after that. I had a better paying job lined up with better hours and a much better boss working for my dad during the summers at the Bidwell Hardware Company.

This is so good! Your discovery of a higher being in the rapids is so human and believable. I was bullied in elementary school as a shy skinny kid by a red-haired boy in sixth grade. You are more open in your stories than I was. I should have learned to box. I never discussed this with you boys but some boxing would give you needed confidence since it doesn't take much to make most people back down. Hope you are healing well. love Dad

This is wonderful. I didn't remember you getting the lawn mower engines from Grandpa. You must have had more relationship with Grandpa than I realized. That gives me a warmer feeling for him. Thank you. Love Dad

Great stories. I remember going collecting with you once in a while, I would ride on the back of your bike sitting on the basket with my feet in the baskets. Also, I remember playing baseball on the circle. When you guys would let me play. I learned how to paddle and got my love of paddling with your old Canoe. -Julie (My sister)

03 Time with Dad - Bedtime Stories

We lived at Carver Circle when I was little and my parents would read to me. I really remember them reading stories in the living room before we went to bed. Lots of Dr Seuss books, EE Milne, and others. I remember one book that they read to me before I started Kindergarten. It was a Dr Seuss book called <u>One Fish, Two Fish, Red Fish, Blue Fish</u>. In fact, they read it to me so many times that I actually started memorizing the entire book. Eventually, I could read the entire book cover-to-cover. I was convinced at this tender young age (before kindergarten) that I could read. It was not until years later that I realized that I was not really reading, but just reciting the words that I had memorized. It was easy to recite the entire book, since each page had cool drawings that would prompt my memory for the words to recite. Now in later life, I can only recite the title, such is memory; you don't use it, you lose it.

I know I was a difficult child back in those days. I could not read yet, so going to bed was boring. If I was not sleepy, I would generally just wander back downstairs when I needed to stretch my little legs. Usually, my parents would put up with this, perhaps scold me and walk me back upstairs and put me back into bed. If it happened enough, and they were fed up, they had to resort to extreme measures. This would be tying a rope around my bedroom door knob and the other end to the banister across the hall. Then If I got up later to come back down, I would tug on the door and it might give a little, but it would not open. In my memory, I would then resign myself to my fate and climb back into bed and go to sleep. I'm sure my parents have other memories of that.

Later on, when Julie was born, Matt moved into my room and took the lower bunk on the bed. Our parents would come into the room and read us stories together. Sometimes we would lie there thinking about the story after they had left and gone downstairs for some quiet adult time. Sometimes we would not make it awake until the end of the story. Sometimes we would have questions about the story that Mom or Dad would answer before heading down. The best end to the "Goodnight story time" was when they would hang out a little longer to answer a question or two about the story.

We moved to the 50's house on Ridge Rd when I was 8 and that is where I really start remembering bedtime stories. As a little background, when bedtime came around, us kids would go upstairs, brush our teeth, change into flannel jammies and climb into bed. Before I fell asleep, one or another of my parents would come around and step into the room to say goodnight to me before actually going to sleep.

Actually, the title of this little remembrance should be "Questions before going to bed". I would ask questions, sometimes philosophical, religious or scientific questions before bedtime. There were really 2 reasons for this.

One was that if I could ask a deep question, that might provoke some thought on my parents' part, I could have them in the room a little bit longer as they would answer the question and perhaps any follow-up questions that arose. The other reason was that I was a very curious child and had so many questions floating around my head, especially at bedtime when I would relax and reflect on some issue that would be in the back of my mind.

I don't remember too may bedtime stories during this period of my life, since I could already read, I liked reading and I generally had a book that I was into, but I'm sure they read me a few. Part of it was that by this time I had a sister and two other brothers that would each get a visit from my parents before going to bed. I'm sure that many times, Mom and Dad would want to get together so Dad could talk with Mom about some guy he had to fire at work, or Mom would want to talk to Dad about something that would be inappropriate with the kids around. These would be the times that no matter the question, it would be a short talk before they would say "Good Night" and close the door. Sometimes I would not have a handy question floating around my head, so when I went to bed, I would wrack my brain for a suitable question. I could not say "Dad, I have a question." after he came in to say goodnight to me, since I had to actually have a question, otherwise my window of his attention would be gone and he would close the door on his goodnight rounds for us kids.

My parents shared these rounds and some nights it would be Mom coming to say goodnight. I would need to have good questions for her, so that she could not just blow me off with

"Good question, we can talk about it later", and close the door till the morning.

When Dad would come into the bedroom to say Goodnight, I would ask him something that puzzled me like, "If the Universe is infinite, then what are the boundaries, where are the edges? How can it not be inside of something bigger with no boundaries? Where does space live? I don't understand."

This would have been a good question for an Astrophysicist. Dad did his best to answer this question, but it still puzzles me to this day, so I guess he was a little puzzled by this as well.

One time I was very sick for a week with nausea, throwing up, and feeling like crap. My Mom attempted to cheer me up by giving me a book called <u>The Duck on the Truck.</u> I would read this book over and over again the whole week while I was nauseous, just to take my mind off the flu. I had read it so many times that I basically had it memorized, just like the old Dr Seuss book. When I got better, I put the book up on the shelf and forgot about it. Then perhaps a year later, I was scanning my book shelf for something to look at and saw The Duck on the Truck. I picked it up and started reading it. The funny thing is that almost immediately I had the creeping feeling of nausea, like a black form of déjà vu. I put the book down since it made my head feel achy. Several times in later years, I would peek at the book and the reaction was always the same, I would experience the crappy feeling in my stomach and head starting to build. I wonder sometimes if I still had that book if I would get the same black déjà vu if I were to start reading it now. My guess is that I would.

I was playing in the backyard down in the woods when I spotted a young crow that had jumped out of the nest and could not fly back up into the trees from the forest floor. I chased this young crow around until I caught it and put it under my arm. I brought it up to the house in the warm Spring afternoon thinking that I would tame it and make it my own pet bird. I did not have a cage, so I just let it go in my room. It just sat there on the floor looking warily at me. I grew bored and decided to leave it alone and I ran out to play till dinner-time. When I came back, no one had noticed the bird in my room, but what I noticed was that there was white bird shit on everything in the room, on the floor, on my bed, on my desk. It was a mess. I was still determined to keep the bird as a pet and it was not cawing and crowing, but was just flapping around and still had not attracted any attention. I had learned from the stray cat Willow that I found after playing baseball at the circle one time, that Dad would immediately say "No" to a new pet, but if I kept it around, fed it on the sly and made it stick around, then he would soften up and we could keep it. After dinner I went upstairs and hung out with my new crow friend in my room. When it was time for bed, I got my jammies on and the crow was still a secret to the household. Well Dad came into the room to say Goodnight. I had the lights off, but he immediately sensed something was amiss. He may have spotted the white crap on everything, might have smelled the bird or may have heard it flapping, but he turned the light on.

The secret was out and in surprise he said "Oh my God Chris, what is this bird doing in your room?"

He did not really say it, but yelled it out. Soon Mom and my siblings were all at the door looking at the cool bird. After the initial shock of excitement and wonder had worn off, Dad told me in no uncertain terms that I could not keep a wild animal as a pet. It probably had a mom crow outside worried about this bird and I had to let it go right now. I caught the crow and took it out back and tossed it in the air and it glided off down the hill and up into a White Pine tree in the forest below. I never saw that crow again, and I never got in real trouble with my folks over this little adventure, other than having to clean up my room and scrub the bird crap off of everything. It did allow me to stay up past my normal bedtime that night, so it was really a win-win situation for me.

One time that I remember, my mom came in to say Goodnight and I asked her the question, "Mom, do buffalo believe in God?"

Well Mom's Dad, Grandpa Noss to me, was a Protestant minster with a congregation up in Andover Massachusetts, so Mom's answer to me was "That's a good question for Grandpa, I'll ask him."

That did not work too well for keeping Mom in my room and talking for a few more minutes before I had to go to sleep, but he did write me a nice letter with a thoughtful answer to my question.

I did not know before Mom asked him, if Buffalo were part of God's creatures and they were content knowing that there was a god looking after them, or if God's creatures were put on Earth for the benefit of mankind and did not think of God like people did. He had a more philosophical answer. I felt good that an adult had taken my question seriously and that meant more to me than anything.

Oct 15, 1959

Dear Christopher,

"Do buffaloes see God?"

Yes, they do. Buffaloes do not need to go to school to learn to be buffaloes. They know how already. Buffaloes never make war, or complain, or gossip, or say that life is not worth living. Buffaloes eat grass and are happy to have it. They don't think they need caviar and steak. Buffaloes don't worry or fret. When they are tired, they lie down and sleep without any fuss. They know that everything belongs to God, and that with him they are forever safe. Not one of them falls without him. All this is true of them because they see God. They wouldn't know what they know if they didn't see him.

I am glad you asked this question, Christopher. I don't think I would ever have thought of it all by myself. Good night and God bless you.

Grandpa.

I sure wish he were around so I could ask him some questions about his Buffalo story in the note, just like my questions to my parents at bedtime, just to spend a little more time with him.

I love your memories of bedtime stories. That is precious to have and I feel so lucky to have them. Can you use larger type? I have just finished the" Pelican Brief", an early John Grisham which reads like it is happening today. Love to you and Mona. Dad

04 Time with Dad - Pets

We had a little beagle when I was a kid around kindergarten age. I remember nothing about this dog, but it was enough so that I learned that we were "Dog People", and it started my love of dogs.

When we moved to my favorite Ridge Road house, we no longer had that beagle and we were a dog-less household. It was not long before my parents decided to get another dog since both of them were dog people and liked having one around. My parents looked for a dog in the local classified in the Yankee Flyer. I don't know if they had a specific breed of size of dog in mind, but they searched until eventually they found a German Shepard that belonged to a couple that was moving to England and they could not take the dog with them. The dog was named Rodnick. Dad brought Rodnick home just at dusk after picking him up from the couple. We were all excited and met Dad outside when he arrived. Rodnick jumped out of the station wagon with his 6-foot leash on, so that he could acquaint himself with his new surroundings and his new family. We really lived in the perfect place for a dog with all the open woods for him to run around as I knew from spending most of my time out exploring in the forest. Immediately we all fell in love with this big dog and were petting him and hugging him and looking at him and basically just showering him with affection. It was a family party outside and we were all so happy until, in the excitement of the moment, Rodnick slipped his leash. Actually, he just tugged when we just had a loose hand on the end of the leash and like a dog, he bolted off into the woods behind the house in the gathering dusk.

I don't know what the rest of the family did, but I took off after him running like I had done when chasing raccoons around the woods when they were unlucky enough to be spotted by me. Rodnick took off down through the woods to the bottom of our property with me chasing him, yelling his name and crying. I managed to keep an eye on him as he bounded to the wet swamp at the bottom of the hill below the house. I splashed through the mud and shallow water, running and trying to keep an eye on him and terrified that if I lost him, we would never see him again. He continued on through the pine forest on the other side of the swamp. I was determined to follow him, even though it was starting to get dark. Eventually he started slowing down and sniffing and wandering a bit, no longer in a straight line. We were now in the woods behind the Bergman's house. They were a family that I would eventually work for as a babysitter for their little boy occasionally. They also had a dog and Rodnick was sniffing and peeing since he caught the scent of their dog. Anyway, this was my chance to catch him. He had his nose buried in a bush, busily sniffing when I grabbed him in a bear hug around the neck on my knees and held him tight, sobbing and heaving for breath from our sprint from the house. It seemed like I held him for 5 minutes like this and I think that is when the two of us bonded. I slid my hand down his leash, grabbed the end and he walked back home with me like this was part of our daily walk. For me it was an exciting and very emotional introduction to our new dog.

We had no fence at our house so Rodnick would mostly just wander around the house outside, but several times a week he would explore in the woods for an hour or two, just like I liked to do. It was a good environment for a dog. Sometimes Mom would make Dinty Moore beef stew. She would add my favorite vegetable, peas. Whatever we had left over after dinner we would put in a bowl for him to finish. I remember he would eat all the stew, just leaving a licked clean little pile of peas at the bottom of the bowl.

Some of the neighborhood kids and I were playing baseball late one nice Spring Day at the "One Way Sign" which was the start of the circle where we lived. It was a perfect place to play ball because the street was doubly wide there since the road came back through on the other side, making the infield really wide for our bases. The outfield ran for about another 100' before going down a steep hill. Any ball that rolled down that steep hill was a home run. I was playing center field when Jimmy connected hard with a pitch that went over my head. I ran after the ball as it was rolling down the hill. The crown of the road would cause the ball to eventually go to the side where I caught up with it. When this happened, it was always a little intermission in our game, like a 7th inning stretch that could randomly happen during any inning.

As I was walking up the hill, I spotted a white cat off in the woods. I walked into the woods to check it out. I knew all the pets in our neighborhood and this was definitely a newcomer. Immediately I knew that I wanted this cat as a pet. I turned around and walked back to our home plate and told everyone about the cat and that I wanted to try and catch it as a pet. We ran back to my house and got a can of tuna fish. I opened the can and we ran back to where the cat was. Luckily the cat was still there. I grabbed a pinch of tuna tossed it to the cat. He immediately wolfed it down. We managed to lure the cat all the way back to the house with the tuna. By this time, it was just Matt and I, the other kids having gone home since our game was on a cat delay. When we got home, I put the mostly empty can under a rhododendron bush next to the front door to keep the cat around. Matt stayed outside to keep an eye on the cat and I went inside to announce to my parents that we now had a cat.

Mom was a little wary, but accepting of the idea of a cat.

Dad however was definitely not very open to the idea. "What about Rodnick? He does not like cats. What if this is some neighbors cat that just wandered away? What are we going to do with a cat?"

Eventually we came to a compromise.

Dad said, "If the cat really wants to be part of our family, then he will stick around the house. If the cat is still living outside at our house after a week, then you can keep him.

Notice that he did not say "we". I knew at that moment that I had won, since all I needed to do was keep food outside next to the house for a week. That skinny tomcat was craving food and I was pretty sure that he would not be going anywhere. I did not tell Dad that I was feeding the cat, although Mom was in on it, since I needed to raid the pantry for the next seven days and she would give me food suggestions after the tuna fish was gone.

During that week, I named the cat Willow. The big skinny cat was pure white and I named him after the white buds on the Pussy Willow trees that looked just like his fur. Plus, the tree had pussy in the name, it was perfect! After the seven-day waiting period was over, Willow was still hanging out around the house and he officially became part of the Bidwell household! He transitioned to an indoor/outdoor cat and everyone in the family became "cat people", and all grew to love him. In fact, Willow started a family tradition for us, always having cats after that, which is a very good thing.

Willow and Rodnick were very wary of each other and kept their distance. Willow would hiss whenever Rodnick would come near. One day we were all outside in the front yard, including the pets. Willow was walking close by to Rodnick, when Rodnick suddenly lunged at Willow, teeth flashing and growling. As quick as you can blink your eyes, Willow jumped and grabbed Rodnick with his claws and latched onto his back. Rodnick ran around in circles, yelping, whimpering and scared as Willow hung on for a few seconds of a canine/feline bareback bronco ride, before jumping off. Rodnick had learned his lesson about Willow. Willow was a full grown un-neutered tomcat and was very capable of taking care of himself. It was like when two boys fight and then after the fight the mutual respect causes them to become friends. That is what happened between the two of them and they never got into a fight again and became friends. Dad and Willow never got into a fight, but they eventually became friends also.

Now, later in life, when all us Bidwell's are out living separately in our own homes, the true cat lovers in the family have become clear. Jeremy is the biggest cat lover. He has always had a cat and in fact named his business Rex-tech after his favorite cat Rex! I am also a cat lover although there was a period when we just had dogs and no cats. I do currently have two cats, Beemer and Red and they love our dog Dillon as I know, since they will all sleep together on the floor. Dillon is very much like Rodnick. The third cat-lover in the family is Robin. She had a cat when Dad and her were living on Laurel Street in Hartford. The cat was named appropriately Laurel but I think they cannot have cats in their current house and it must bug Robin, at least a little bit.

Years later, after Willow had passed away, we got another calico cat. Willow had always stayed home when we went on vacations but we decided to take this cat with us on our vacation to Meredith Neck in NH. I cannot remember which cat this was since we had several after Willow. It was one of either Cinnamon, Ginger or Bok Choy, since these were some of the cats we had after Willow, but I blocked it out of my memory. Most likely the cat was Ginger. Dad and I were heading up to NH ahead of the rest of the family to open up the house and out-buildings for our vacation. We were bringing Ginger with us in Dad's new Oldsmobile Vista Cruiser, definitely my favorite of all of Dad's vehicles. Ginger definitely did not like road trips and was extremely agitated and edgy on this ride, so much so that Dad was having trouble concentrating on the road and I could not keep the cat calm. Ginger was jumping around all over the car and making agitated cat noises. Eventually I came up with a solution. This was definitely my solution. Dad agreed to give it a try.

We had an empty cooler in the back of the car. I crawled into the back of the car and managed to get Ginger into it. I took a piece of 1x2 pine board and put it in the cooler to wedge the top open so that Ginger would have good ventilation. We drove on for another 40 minutes when I wanted to check on Ginger and make sure she was OK. We pulled over and I climbed into the back and the cooler was just as I had left it and the cat was doing fine.

We continued on to the lake house and parked the car in the driveway. I jumped out and opened the back to let Ginger out since she had been cooped up in the cooler for the last half of the trip. When I looked in the back of the car, my heart just dropped into my sneakers. The lid to the cooler was closed, the piece of wood had fallen into it. I opened the cooler and I could immediately see that Ginger was dead. I was all shaky, knowing that it was totally my fault that the cat had died. It was my idea to use the cooler and prop it open with a stick. I walked up to Dad and told him what had happened. He was upset that we had so foolishly transported the cat in such a manner to kill her. He immediately took total responsibility for the accident. I know that he was just being a good dad, but I knew in my heart that it was all my doing. We had a couple of hours before Mom and the rest of the family would arrive, so Dad and I dug a grave in the trees in the front of the vacation house and buried poor little Ginger. Of course, the rest of the family was very upset when they arrived to find out that the cat had not survived the trip. At least they did not have to see the dead cat. I told Mom that it was all my fault for killing the cat. I thought I had a good idea, but it was in fact a very bad idea. I'm sure that no matter how much mom listened to me about it being my fault, she took it out on Dad, but this is just speculation on my part.

I felt bad about it for the whole vacation, but I did learn a valuable life lesson. Never trust yourself when just checking on something that you may have a doubt about in the back of your mind. In fact, anytime that I check on something, I know that a single check may not mean anything. A single check never sets my mind at ease anymore. Either resolve the situation so that checking on it is NOT required, or keep checking often until you are completely satisfied that the situation is past the "checking on it" stage. Examples of this are putting out a campfire. I'll sit with it until the fire is just embers and go get ready for bed. Then I'll check on the fire. It usually looks exactly the same with just some glowing ember at the bottom. I cannot just say to myself "It looks OK, I'm going to bed". I will either have to grab a beer and a chair and sit with the fire until it is definitely not a fire hazard, or just get a bucket of water and put it out once and for all, no checking on it required. Something as simple as writing these notes, when I'm done, I'll check on it by re-reading what I wrote. This is just a single check and means nothing, I probably missed something. I need to have someone read it back to me as well and then wait a day to see if I may have missed something. Otherwise, I'll just check on it when I've mailed it out and look at it then. I'll probably find something missing, but by then it's just too late.

To this day, whenever I check on something, I'll flash back to poor little Ginger and question why I'm just doing a check in the first place.

I remember taking Rodnick with us when the family went hiking into an overnight at the cabin. You tripped over Rodnick, spraining your knee and we hauled you out on the sled. He was starting to lose strength in hind quarters. As far as Ginger goes, I have always felt guilt at her death. I take the blame rather than you because I thought that the lash up was risky. Love Dad

05 Westledge

When I was in Jr High School, my parents were getting tired of life in the suburbs. This was the late 60's and there was a trend afoot for moving back into the city. My parents wanted to be part of this movement. They were thinking about moving into the city and had concerns that they would move just before I would start High school. I thought at the time that they were worried about throwing a white suburban kid into the tough inner-city school system and it would be hard on me.

So, in my last year in Jr High, my parents gave me a brochure about this new private school in West Simsbury called Westledge. The school sounded interesting. It was situated on a campus in a couple hundred acres of woods, with cedar buildings scattered around like a mini-college. There were no grades, even though this was a college prep school, in the hope that we would not be motivated by getting the highest score on tests but would study whatever interested us. This meant that almost all the classes (except Math) would have written exams and the teachers would supply us with written feedback. The kids could go hiking in the woods between classes, there was an Athletic building with sports fields for soccer and Lacrosse. It was a small school with only 240 kids, unlike the much larger schools in the city. The school even had a ski hill with a rope tow if you signed up for Skiing as a sports elective! The school had Outward Bound classes with rock climbing, camping and marathon running. The school was all about diversity and 30% of the kids were from the inner city, basically the North-end of Hartford. They would take buses into Westledge every day to get to school. The school sounded amazing, so of course I was all about it. We applied for admission and I was very excited when the brown envelope came to our house with the acceptance letter. I would be going to Westledge! That also meant that we were moving to Hartford although we did not move until after my freshman year.

For my freshman year at Westledge we still lived in Simsbury. Often, I would ride my bike the 4 miles to school, sometimes my dad would drop me off on his way to work, even thought it was in the wrong direction. I also car-pooled with a teacher at Westledge who had two kids Carrie who was my age and her older brother Mark that went to the same school. I would bring my skateboard to school and would often ride down the hill from our house to Firetown road where they would pick me up. Once at school I could ride the long, steep and smoothly paved road down from the school to Westledge Road between classes. I have always been a surfer at heart, just riding on pavement and surfing later in life on the big waves in the rivers of Colorado.

In the summer between my freshman and sophomore years we moved to a house in the City of Hartford. Our move to Hartford was like dipping a toe into the pool to test out the water. We dipped our toe into Hartford by moving just 2 blocks into the city from Prospect Avenue. Prospect Avenue is the street that separates the wealthy West Hartford from Hartford, serving as the city line. This was a common way for suburbanites to move into the city without having to live in the inner city. My parents found a very nice house that was priced perhaps a third the price of a house across the city line. In fact, one of my friends Adam lived in a house on Prospect Ave where his dad had his dental office. They were literally on the city line, but on the Hartford side of the street as well. We were fairly close to the Governor's Mansion up on Prospect Ave. Our house on Terry Rd was huge and in very good condition, no real upgrades other than carpeting were needed when we moved into the house. My brother Matthew and I took the two bedrooms on the third floor that had a big bathroom separating them. There was a separate back staircase, originally for the kitchen staff and/or maids that went from the third floor to the kitchen on the first floor separate from the main staircase. Deeper into the city, there were many big houses like ours, but almost all of them had been converted into apartments with three or four units in a single house.

The school bus would stop at the end of Terry Rd and pick us up. It was a coincidence that just next door to us lived a family that had two kids, Jill and Jeff that also went to Westledge. The three of us would get on the bus on its way out of the inner city and we would squeeze into whatever seats were remaining for the 40-minute ride to school.

I made friends in the first week with Steve, a fellow freshman as we were cleaning out the French Room. We did not have janitors, but the students and teachers would spend an hour after classes vacuuming, mopping, scrubbing and cleaning. I still remember the strong smell of ammonia in the cleaning buckets. I started talking with Steve and we became friends for the remainder of our high school years.

The school was progressive in that the students were given a say in the running of the school. Every morning there would be an all-hands assembly in the main administrative building where Lou Friedman, the Headmaster and founder of the school would bring up issues, concerns, news, atta-boys. The teachers and students could do the same. We did experiments such as chewing gum in class, which I liked. We also did an experiment with smoking in class. It sounded pretty cool and progressive as we raised our hands in the school assembly but it only lasted a week. Most of us were non-smokers and it was very annoying. As a concession we allowed smoking outside.

I loved Physics. We had a teacher from Ghana that spoke precise English and was a Physics Wiz and an excellent teacher. Since I was so interested in Physics, I would pay close attention in class and he would explain the concepts very thoroughly and it made it easy for me to soak everything up. I was just an average student since I could take the tests and pass them without studying. This backfired on me in an embarrassing way one day in class. The teacher was explaining a concept, but was having trouble getting us to understand it.

He said, "Chris, let me see your book, I'll show you what I'm talking about with some examples."

He took my book and opened it up and immediately his focus turned from the point he was trying to get across to the condition of my book. As he opened my book, the binding made the cracking noise that a brand-new book makes when you open it up for the first time. He picked up the book to head level and examined it as he opened and closed it several times.

He said, "This book looks like it has never been opened."

He then looked down the pages with the book closed and exclaimed "The ends of the pages are completely white with no trace of discoloration from fingers turning them."

He then proceeded to lecture me about the importance of reading the textbook to support the things he was teaching us in class. I was mortified, since I was not an outgoing student in class and now all this attention was focused on me. Eventually his focus turned to the entire class as he angrily lectured us on the importance of study skills. I was spared his direct wrath but I'm sure the other kids in the class that actually were reading the textbook, such as Jerry were mad at me. I did start reading the textbook after that, not because I wanted to enforce the concepts that we learned in class, but because I did not want to be humiliated in class again.

My favorite classes were creative writing ones, which were taught by Ann Levine. I liked her and she really helped foster my love of writing. She taught me valuable lessons on writing techniques, such as not using so many run-on sentences. I remember having a writing assignment and hanging out in the student center when the other kids were relaxing together discussing school work or studying. I would just be sitting there looking up aimless at the tall ceiling like I was zoning out. In reality I would have a creative writing assignment and would be searching for a good idea for something to write about. This was the most difficult part of the class. Often Mrs. Levine would give us a difficult topic to write about which could make coming up with a good story difficult. I usually liked to write stories with vivid descriptions, as I would see it in my mind. One time she gave us an assignment with a topic that I absolutely could not come up with a story idea about. I did a terrible job on a short paper that I turned in. She asked me in some comments on my paper about why I had done such a poor job.

I wrote, "Because I thought the assignment sucked".

Well, this created a shit-storm of attention among the teachers. Mrs. Levine was extremely upset and it was up to my advisor, Mac Cheney to give me a talking down and resolve the situation.

He said to me, "Do you know what you wrote to Mrs. Levine?"

"Yes", I replied, "I meant that I did not like the assignment."

"Actually, what you told Mrs. Levine is that you want her to suck your dick!"

I was flabbergasted. Suck meant something that you did not like, not that you wanted a BJ! That had not even occurred to me when I wrote that. I really liked Mrs. Levine. Mr. Cheney had me apologize to my favorite teacher. I had to tell her that I was extremely sorry for my comments on her assignment and that I never meant that I wanted her to suck my dick. Such was the direct openness of my high school. I sure learned my lesson, but it was not really a life lesson, since I continue to use that phrase and nowadays no one gets their nose bent out of shape when I say something "Sucks".

I met with Mr. Cheney every week for 30 minutes for our one-on-one conversations. I liked my advisor and he had to really work to get me to open up to him. I know that a lot of the kids would open up about their problems and just dump all their issues and challenges to their advisor. I know this because my advisor in my freshman year was Mr. Levine (Ann Levine's husband). He was one of those cool teachers and he used to be a forest ranger up in Maine.

I would meet with him and he would always ask me at the start, "What problems are you dealing with? What is bothering you?"

I would always answer, "I don't have any problems and nothing is bothering me".

Part of this is that I really did not have any serious problems that needed to be discussed. The other part is that I would not discuss it with him even if I did. After my freshman year, Mr. Levine told me that he was dropping me as advisee since there were so many other students that had serious problems. He would rather talk and advise them, rather than the problem-less me.

Mr. Cheney, my second advisor was very interested in my girlfriend situation. I liked Mr. Cheney the chemistry teacher, since this was a favorite subject of mine and we had a connection, probably why he agreed to take me on as an advisee. He would ask me why I did not ever ask the younger Cooper girl out on a date, or Carrie since I had carpooled with her to school so many times and it would be easier. I would just shrug it off and say I was not interested in them. He always had ideas on other girls that I should ask out. I appreciated that he was looking out for me, probably trying to get me out of my shell with girls and adults, but I just did not know how to answer him. My solution came later on when my friend Mac told me something his girlfriend Ruta had told him.

As I was munching on my baloney and American cheese sandwich with mayo and white bread, Mac said, "Karen thinks you are cute."

About this time, I bit into the heel of the head of iceberg lettuce that Matt had put into my sandwich as a joke. I threw my sandwich on the plate which Mac took to be shock and dismay about the prospect of Karen. Mom had setup a system where Matt and I would make both of our lunch sandwiches on alternate days. He got me good with that "lettuce". He would pay when I got home, ha-ha.

Actually, I was surprised and pleased. I thought that Karen was probably the cutest girl in school. I asked him why he thought so and he told me that Karen had said this to Ruta, Mac's girlfriend who had told him. I had my eye on a couple of girls in school that I liked, but was a little intimidated by girls and especially by asking them out. With the knowledge that Karen thought I was cute and fortified by thinking that she probably would not turn me down, I asked her out on a date. I actually asked her out on a double date with Mac and Ruta and she agreed and became my girlfriend for most of my sophomore year. We went on lots of double dates, since Mac had his driver's license and I was only 15 and could not yet drive. Now when I would meet with my advisor, my dating life was no longer a topic of conversation.

I had French class, the only language that was offered in my high school. Spanish would have been better, not only since i had started learning it in 2nd grade and really liked it but there were quite a few Puerto Rican and Bolivian kids that I knew in school. They got to talk together in their own secret language that even the teacher could not understand, but worse yet I could not talk to them in their native tongue which would have been very cool. So, I was in French class with a good-looking young teacher that spoke to us almost exclusively in French to help us learn faster with her sexy French accent. The class was OK, but the part that

I did not like was that we would be sitting there and she would randomly call on us to standup and answer a question in French and the class could help if we were stumbling on the words. At that time in my sophomore year I had a little case of boner-itis that would happen periodically, but especially in French class.

Boner-itis is what I always called it, nowadays it is called "Triple B" (Boner Before Bell). I wish I had known that this was a ubiquitous thing among high school boys, but at the time I thought it was my own personal affliction. My solution to the problem was to just wear my coat in class so that I would be covered up for those Impromptu recitals. My heart was not so into class to begin with because of the Spanish-thing. At the end of the semester, I got my review, a page-long writeup on how well I did in class that semester, basically a long-winded grade. In her review, she said that I did not seem to be excited about learning French and that I always kept my coat on in class like I did not want to be there. I never took off my coat and sat down and really immersed myself in the classroom experience. If only she knew...

A bunch of us students came up with an idea for a class. It would be creative writing, but it would be self-taught by all the students in the class. We would meet occasionally with our remote teacher Mr. Holdt, who would monitor our class work and look at the papers that we had written. It was an excellent class. We would decide on a topic and then have several days to write a paper on that topic. In class we would swap papers and read each other's papers out loud to the rest of the class. Sometimes we would just comment on them after reading them individually. The other interesting thing about the class was that I was the only boy with about 7 girls. Since there were just us students in the class, we could write about sensitive topics although they always knew my papers, since they were not so touchy feely, but were more about concrete things. I learned a lot about the inner thoughts of girls in this class, but I think they probably learned nothing about the inner workings of boys from my papers.

On one of our assignments, I was having trouble coming up with an idea to write about. I was sitting in the cafeteria staring off into the distance at the lunch counter and half-watching the school Mom, Mrs. Weber. An idea formed in my mind as I was sitting there and I wrote my entire short paper sitting right there in the cafeteria. Here it is.

The Life and Death of Mealine Cardo

Mealine was sitting around with a bunch of his peers, all of them frustrated and bored. He was trapped in the same rut. A big mysterious stranger came and bought him. As soon as he was purchased, he was stamped on the back and punched around. All the rest of the week he was punched around and by the end of the week he was really worn down. Mealine's owner was mad at him because Mealine was now worth hardly any of what he had been paid for. The big mysterious stranger hauled off and punched Mealine one last time with all of his might. Mealine fell to his knees and died. The big stranger walked off wishing that he had someone else to knock around.

This did not go over well with the girls in my class. They said that boys were violent and uncaring and this story was proof of that.

I gained no points with the girls except for Jen, a very cute girl, that commented on my paper "It took a while to sink in but I got it. It's good if you wanted to write a riddle."

Most of the other comments were like "I still don't get it".

I remember signing up for just a fun class about Macramé. To me it would be learning about knots, something that is always useful. I could also make cool rope ladders, learn to tie a noose, or even better, make a rope bridge. Perhaps make gear like belts, nets and backpacks. In my brain the possibilities were endless. When I actually got to the class, once again I was the only boy in the class with a bunch of girls. I was a bit surprised but should not have been, since we did nothing with rope, it was all twine. Twine is good for plant hangers, wall hangings, bracelets, perhaps a dress. In light of all these uses for twine, I lost sight of why I had even signed up for this class. I did get to hang out with the cute girls, but I could never ask any of them out, since it would be too embarrassing. My Mom did have a couple of pieces of pottery that I made in art class, but I don't remember her ever having some twine knickknack that I made.

I took a poetry class with Mrs. Levine. In hindsight I don't know why I never considered pursuing a career in writing or journalism. I was just always interested in science and that won out. I really liked all of her classes. Here is an example of a poem I wrote from my class.

Pigged Out
Tuned in, turned off
Speak up, you're out
How come?
Who knows, who cares?

Do this, do that
Come here, now scat
Stop dead, burn out
Who's next?
He's next
Who me, ya you
Why me?
Don't ask, be quiet
Watch this, It's over
Get out

What's next?
Shut up, turn in
Freaked out, fucked up
Turned in.

My other two favorite teachers were Val Hart and Mr. Golden. Mr. Hart was a disheveled stringy haired hippy dude and taught a class called Future Changes. His parents played a cruel trick by naming him Valentine Hart although it probably helped to make him the good man that he was. It was a great class. We would have discussions about scenarios on what the future might be like. We talked a lot how the world was going to be different in the future and that we had better be ready to embrace change since most of the rest of the population would always want things to remain the same. This was a valuable life lesson for me and was one of the few classes where I could open up and just be myself as part of our lively discussions.

Mr. Golden taught English literature and introduced me to the writings of Ken Kesey and James Dickey among others. I devoured all the excellent book choices he made as our reading assignments in class and it opened up an entire new genre of books that I continued to read well after High School.

In my underdeveloped adolescent brain, I had a chip on my shoulder about the entire Outward-Bound program at Westledge. For one thing, I just did not like authority. To me authority was Adults. I never liked Adults telling me what to do. I could deal with it in class, but I usually kept my mouth shut in class since I did not want to bring adult attention to me. Many of the teachers at Westledge were excellent instructors and would get to me and pull me into their teaching in a way that I would really enjoy the class. That would usually not be enough to open me up to being a big participant in the in-class discussions, unless I was called upon. This led to my not wanting to participate in Outward Bound. In my mind, I did not want a bunch of teachers from the school, that perhaps took a course or two in Outward Bound to be teaching me (basically telling me what to do) about woodcraft, living in the woods, camping, surviving. In hindsight I could have learned a lot about rock climbing but that was not enough to deter me from never signing up for the Outward-Bound classes at school. I had grown up with miles of woods behind our house and spent most of my time exploring the woods, creeks, and swamps. We would camp out there, often hunting squirrels with slingshots. All the clothes I wore when my parents would take me out shopping would be the green and brown camouflage colors that would allow me to blend in when creeping up on animals or hiding from "teenagers" that were the most dangerous animals in the forest for a pre-teen boy. I thought that I knew more than the instructors and did not want them telling me, teaching me differently. There was a good thing that came out of my misguided notions of not taking Outward Bound, something that I'm sure I would have enjoyed. That is that I played on all the sports teams instead.

The good thing about playing sports for a small school, when all you have going for you is being a scrawny tough little kid, is that eventually I made it on all the varsity sports teams. I was a late bloomer and did not really fill out and mature until a year or two after high school. I did lift weights and that was my other edge, a slight edge granted, but still an edge. My favorite sport was Lacrosse. We had a good coach and a couple of ringers on our team. I made it onto the varsity Lacrosse team since we just had enough kids to have a second string, which is where Steve and I played. We had a couple of ringers on our team. Ben was a year or two older and Ruta's older brother was the other. They had played for a year or two already, so they really knew what they were doing and they were both very tough players, never backing down. I liked this sport because although I was not the speediest player, I was quick and the big defensive players on the opposing teams could never get a clean check on me with their sticks. When Steve and I were juniors and we were just starting to get good, Westledge cancelled our Lacrosse team and switched to baseball.

Between playing soccer, baseball and Lacrosse, I got to know and be friends with a lot of the kids that I rode into school with in my freshman year. One of the goals of Westledge was to make us comfortable in a diverse, multi-cultural environment. This was much more effective for me by playing sports, since we had Blacks, Bolivians and Puerto Ricans on our teams and this is where I got to know the other kids. We learned how to cuss in Spanish from our teammates and would shout out curses. The other teams never knew what we were saying. In fact, our team soccer picture had most of us smiling and laughing as we all said "Puta", one of our words instead of "cheese". These words were the only Spanish in my vocabulary.

One time we were playing a baseball game against the town of Avon. Normally we would play against other prep schools, but Avon was close and the coaches arranged this game. I was playing second base and Mark was pitching. He had a hell of an arm and we were beating the Avon team. Around the seventh inning, the townies started yelling threats and insults at the players on our team. This escalated to saying they were going to kick our asses after the game. I don't know if it was because we were a bunch of privileged white kids or that we had blacks and Puerto

Ricans on our team and they were prejudiced. Either way they did not like us, but it helped to bond our team together in an us vs. them way. My advisor Mr. Cheney and Mr. Gifford, our very tough other coach managed to get us unscathed into our vans where we celebrated together all the way back to school as one big happy family.

It wasn't until 30 years after I graduated from high school that I learned the real reason that I went to Westledge. My Mom was visiting from Connecticut and we were talking and the subject came around to me and Westledge and what my parents were going through at that time. This is what really happened from piecing together my mom's recollections and my remembrances. My Parents were called into Henry James Jr High for a consultation with the school guidance counselor, someone I had never met. Now my parents are very much into higher learning and I was raised with the expectation that I would be attending college after high school. Mom had graduated from Oberlin with a degree in Psychology and Dad had graduated from Harvard with a degree in Economics. School was very important to them. The reason that the Guidance Counselor had called them in to talk was to help them decide what track I should take in High School. Of course, my parents expected that I would take a college preparatory curriculum. The counselor told my parents that I was NOT college material. My aptitude and IQ tests were showing that this track would be well beyond my ability and that I should follow a track that would lead to trade school and to just graduate from high school might be a challenge for me. My parents were very shocked and upset. They would not accept this as an answer. They knew that I was very smart and creative and this had thrown them for a loop. I had always done very well in math classes and was an excellent reader. They thought that if I were to continue in the Simsbury school system that I would not be able to flourish intellectually.

I was puzzling over this fact after Mom told me this story and the light came on for me as to why this was. There was a class in Jr High that all the students were required to take. It was called Study Skills with the teacher Mr. Scully. A lot of the class was learning how to organize assignments using a little notebook. In it we would write things like assignments given, when they were due and when tests and quizzes would be. Basically, using the notebook as a calendar to keep track of schoolwork. The biggest part of the class however was taking tests. We took aptitude tests, tests to determine our reasoning, mechanical ability, IQ tests, placement tests and on and on. None of these were tests that we were graded on, we just took them, often several a week.

Well in the first week or two into this class, I was sitting at my desk and all of a sudden, I had to go to the bathroom really bad. I mean I did not know if I could hold it. I raised my hand and told Mr. Scully that I had to go to the bathroom. We were probably taking a test or something at the time in class and he refused to allow me to leave until the class was over in another half hour. I spent the rest of the time just concentrating on holding it in and could not concentrate on the assignment. I was so angry at Mr. Scully that I had to extract revenge on him. After that, for the rest of the semester and the rest of the Study Skills classes, I decided that I would screw up all the tests that we were given. In my mind, it was a good way to get back at Mr. Scully and it did not matter since we were not being graded on any of his tests. I would totally get even with him by giving silly answers, wrong answers, writing things that had nothing to do with the question on a written answer. I would even write bogus things in my study notebook, making up assignments and tests right before class. He would check our notebooks once a week and was fine with my made-up schoolwork. This is where it backfired. The Guidance Counselor gathered most, if not all of his information on the students from the results of the tests in Mr. Scully's class. Using this information, he would make recommendations to the parents about what track the students should take next year in High School. Like I said, I never talked to the guidance counselor. I'm sure my IQ test showed that I was about on par with Forrest Gump.

Well, my parents took matters into their own hands and decided to put me into a private High School. Westledge had just opened up and seemed like a perfect fit for a struggling boy like me. My parents never gave up on me. They knew that I would go to college, but I can't help but think that this must have thrown some doubt into their minds about my future potential. My Mom would always tell me how creative I was and I wonder if that was why she gave me that compliment so often. The silver lining for me was that I got to go to probably the best High School in the state, rather than Simsbury High.

Just last year in 2019, John Scully passed away after teaching for 26 years in Henry James Jr High School. I found this out from his son's posting on the Simsbury Facebook page and learned that he was much loved by his students. He had over 400 glowing comments on this page, almost all by former students about what a great teacher he was and how much he helped them. I also wrote a condolence to his son about how much he helped me, just in a roundabout way that I did not go into. This just goes to show how much the direction of your life is determined by random fate and that I am a really luck boy!

P.S.
Here is a hint about the story of **Meal**ine **Card**o.

Mom and I were shocked with the statement by the guidance counselor, who was a neighbor on Ridge Rd on the circle. He obviously didn't spend any time except to make a decision based on your skewed test results. His name will come to me, but we always thought he was not very bright. I never had any doubt of your intelligence and have always admired your physical daring in the natural world. Mom and I knew this story very well. - Dad

06 Bidwell Company

The Bidwell Company was known as the Bidwell Hardware Company for the first 80 years of its existence. It was started in 1893 as a little storefront hardware store. It grew and grew over the years until I was old enough to start working there. I worked there for five summers, starting after my freshman year of High School. When I started working there it was a pretty big enterprise. There was a storefront on North Main Street in Hartford. The building stretched back for an entire city block all the way back to Ann Street The back was a warehouse with a truck loading dock. The company mostly catered to commercial contractors, but anyone could walk in off the street and purchase anything the company had to sell. There was a front office upstairs where my dad, the President worked in an office behind a front anteroom with a secretary.

The main floor off the street had a large counter with smaller hardware items in aisles of shelves behind. Across from the counter was a large open area where the salesmen worked. That was also where Mr. Lee Holcomb the VP worked. In today's parlance he would be known as the COO, the Chief Operating Officer. He handled most of the day-to-day operations of running this large business. I don't know the exact count of employees, but I would estimate about 25. Mr. Holcomb always had a thick soggy cigar in his mouth and would talk loudly on the phone out of the side of his mouth giving his speech a little swagger. Most of the salesmen would do the same, but with cigarettes. In fact, I believe that everyone in the front office was a smoker.

My dad upstairs would also smoke cigars, but was more refined and would put his cigar on the ashtray when speaking on the phone. Dad would be working with the Accountants, Lawyers, bookkeepers and suppliers keeping the financial part of the business running smoothly. The only women that worked there were the secretaries that worked upstairs on the "Executive Floor" as I called it. Dad would dress in a suit, with starched white shirts from the dry cleaner. We would use the cardboard from his clean pressed packaged shirts at home for school projects and artwork.

The only time I ever worked upstairs with my Dad was when I was a little kid and he would bring me into work with him, like a "bring your kid into work day". He would have the secretary makeup some job for me. The secretary would make up some nebulous task, make it sound very important, and put me to work with a pad and pencil. I never understood exactly what I was doing, but I tried my best. I would be a little bit worried afterward that the important task I had finished was not completed to satisfaction and I hoped it would not be the demise of the company. In an office next to my dad's was my grandfather's office. Elliot Bidwell had been the President prior to my dad. He still worked there but was semi-retired. He spent most of his time working on the Bidwell Company catalog. This was a catalog the size of a small city phone book with thousands of products that could be ordered over the phone or by mail/FAX.

Besides the store front, front office and executive floor, there was a large warehouse that did shipping and receiving of large trucks, a welding area for putting together commercial windows and doors, a mail-order area where the mailed-in and called-in orders from the catalog would be filled, packaged up and sent out in the mail, by trucking company or with the small fleet of Bidwell Company trucks.

The store was a couple of blocks North of Interstate 84 and was 3 or 4 blocks outside of the main downtown. Being North of I-84 was like being on the wrong side of the tracks. It was not a ghetto, but it was definitely an economic re-development zone. This was probably why we did not get a lot of "bird-housers" walking in the front door to work on their home projects.

I started working in the back of the warehouse near the loading dock doing receiving with Frank Cilley. The truck drivers all called him Red on account of his red hair. Not just on his head, but he had red hair all down his thick arms as well. He was a big guy, but not fat, who always had a twinkle in his eye. When we were just hanging out together after unloading a big truck, he would tell me stories of his exploits in World War II. He was well respected by everyone and was a hard worker. He drove a dodge camper van that he and his wife would take on camping trips. His favorite destination was Arizona.

I asked him one time if he worked out, since he was strong and in good shape. He told me that he gets all the exercise he needed moving the stock around in the warehouse, some of it was very heavy and bulky. He told me that in WWII, there were soldiers in his platoon that were muscle-bound guys. He said that when they went on long treks with heavy loads on their backs, the guys that would gas out and be panting at the side of the trail would often be these body-builder types. That was his incentive to never workout, a life lesson for Frank. I was interested in this since I worked out with weights and was getting stronger, but I was not interested in being a body builder, although I wanted to have big arms like Frank.

Sometimes the work would be slow and I would get bored. I'd ask Frank what I could do. He might send me upstairs in the warehouse to organize insulation, or to straighten out nails. One day after lunch, we walked over to look at the nails that I had been straightening out in the morning. He pulled out a 12-inch steel spike nail from an open box and looked at it.

He asked me "Do you know how to throw a knife?"

"Of course."

"Show me how you do it."

So, I picked up one of the big nails, held it by the pointy end over my shoulder behind my back and made an overhand throwing motion. That is how I always did it and how they did it on TV as well.

He proceeded to tell me "The problem with your technique is that it attracts attention to you. When throwing a knife at an enemy, they will see you if you throwing it so you need to be stealthy and throw it underhanded."

He then demonstrated the underhand throwing technique. Frank got an old box and put it about 25 feet away, then threw a nail that went straight into the box pointy end first with enough force to kill a man for sure.

Frank continued, "The other problem with throwing a knife overhand is that the blade is spinning in the air and has an equal chance of hitting with the handle end. The trick is to throw the knife so that it spins for a half a revolution in the air so that the blade that is pointing towards you when you let go will be pointing directly towards the German when it meets its target."

That skill has served me well for the rest of my life! Just kidding.

I did however learn a valuable life lesson later that first summer working with Frank. I would be working in the warehouse and would get bored and ask Frank what I could do. Frank was always busy in the warehouse doing what had to be done, catching up on the books, cleaning and straightening out the inventory or something. He would come up with some task for me to work on. Towards the end of the summer, after I had asked him for the thousandth time what I could do, he came up with the perfect job for me.

Next door to the warehouse was the warehouse for the old Bidwell Rubber Company. This was a spin-off business that was successful for a while, but had been shuttered for many decades before I was on the scene. Frank led me to the back of the warehouse, then out the door to an alley. Down the alley was an old door. Frank opened it with a key and led me in. He found the light switch and turned it on. It was a wonderful old wood office area covered with dust; we walked down a wide ramp. The left side of the ramp led to the front of the store, which was shuttered up with plywood and had not seen any people in years. The right side of the ramp led to some wide stairs that went down to the basement. We walked down into the basement and got some of the lights on. There were old shelves filled with dusty stuff that no one would be interested in purchasing. Just leftovers from the Rubber Company and some old hardware that had become obsolete and was being stored down there. Frank gave me a clipboard and a pencil and told me to clean up the shelves and make notes of anything that might be useful. I was a little leery of this job, but it would definitely keep me busy. It was a huge basement and was filled with things for which I saw no use.

Frank left me there and said to just work on this for a few hours, until 4:30 and then come back to the loading dock to cleanup for closing time. I was wandering around the basement trying to figure out where to start. There was water dripping over towards the street. I could hear the patter of the occasional rat running behind the shelves since I was invading their territory. Now I'm not scared of basements and in fact not scared of most things. I would shower with one eye open all the time however after watching the shower scene in Psycho, something I did until the end of my High School years since I had enrolled in a student-led class called Hitchcock, where we watched it a lot.

I could feel the hair on the back of my neck prickle up when I would hear some noise while counting widgets and writing down a count of them and tidying them up. When 4:30 rolled around I put down my clipboard on a shelf and walked calmly toward the stairs. When I got close to the stairs fear kicked in and I bolted as fast as I could taking them 3 at a time and not stopping at the top but sprinting faster to the door out into the alley. I grabbed the door and pivoted as fast as I could out of the building, immediately stopping and then walking casually down the alley as if nothing was wrong. I opened the door to the Hardware company, my heart beating out of my chest. I don't remember if I ever went back down there to retrieve my clipboard, but I learned my lesson. It made me a better young man. I learned to just do what needed to be done. Rather than just standing around, I would keep busy, just cleaning up the stock, sweeping, and doing whatever was needed to keep the warehouse functioning optimally. This is a valuable life lesson that not everyone has learned. I've been on rafting/kayaking trips where we are setting up camp and I can keep busy helping the rafters with the kitchen, the groover, strapping down things on the raft, and being generally helpful. When I see people just standing around aimlessly looking for something to do, or sitting down with a beer because no one is telling them what needs to be done, I know they have not learned this lesson.

Customers would come out to the warehouse from the front desk. Benny or another of the counter guys would send them back when they needed the larger items that were stored there. If Frank was busy, I would greet them as they entered the warehouse, take their receipt and get the items that they were looking for. From working in the warehouse and from doing inventory, I eventually learned the location of almost all the stock in the huge warehouse and could get the items the customer was looking for. I always had Frank as a backup, since he knew the location of absolutely everything and I could yell over to him, asking where in the warehouse was a part or tool I was looking for.

Frank and I would do inventory in the warehouse. Once a year, we would need to count all the stock and write down the count of everything in the entire building, including all the smaller tools up in the front of the store. This was before POS registers that would take items out of inventory as they were being sold. We would climb around the entire warehouse with little red circle stickers to mark the items after we had counted them. A lot of this work took place up on big ladders, since so many of the shelves were 12 feet or more above the floor. This was a very labor-intensive task, since everyone except the sales and executives would be involved in counting all of the tens or hundreds of thousands of parts, tools, fasteners and equipment. An accurate count was very important to keep stock up to date so that customers driving into the store could count on getting everything that they needed and we would have the needed parts when filling catalog orders.

The sales guys would walk past while I was up on the ladder counting inventory and they would always say, "I see that you are getting up in the world".

They would say that over and over whenever I was up on the ladder, never tiring of the same phrase, or even changing it a little bit. I think that was part of the game, to be as annoying as possible, like they did not remember ever saying it to me in the past. I just hope they were not that annoying to the customers that they were trying to sell to.

I spent one summer working with Dana, the COO's son in the order-processing department. We would fill the catalog orders from customers, package it up and mail it out. This job took me out of the large warehouse and into a part of the building closer to the front office and counter. I needed to learn the location of thousands of smaller parts that would typically be what we would be shipping out. Things like smaller power tools and hand tools like screwdrivers, wrenches, pliers, etc. There were also thousands of fittings, fasteners, screws, nails, etc. as well. Some of this was in the shelves behind the front counter. Others were in the basement storage. There was nothing scary about the basement of the Hardware Company since it was accessed every day and was just another part of the warehouse. Dana taught me the ropes. This included gathering all the items in the order and updating a packing list. The packing list was important, since there would often be items that would be back-ordered (remember the archaic inventory system) and would be listed as such on the packing list. We would need to keep a file of which items were back-ordered for which customers. We would periodically check the list when new stock came in to send out the remaining items on the list. Dana had a stereo setup in our order processing room, mostly playing Cat Stevens and the like. Once we got the inventory together for an order, we would select a box of the appropriate size, staple it together, fill it with the items in the order, add some packing, slap on a shipping label and put on the cart to take out to Frank in the warehouse to send out to the customers.

There were several employees behind the counter that would help the walk-in customers. The guy in charge was a little Armenian guy named Benny. Benny had an encyclopedic knowledge of all the parts behind the counter. If you were looking for an obscure tool for example and did not know where to look, Benny would always know. He had worked for the Bidwell Company for years before I started working there. This was his career and he really loved it. I think part of it was that everyone that knew him totally respected his knowledge of the location of all the parts. He also knew the function of each and every tool as well. He could make recommendations to customers about similar parts or tools that might be better, cheaper or better quality as well as hints as to the best way to use them for maximum efficiency. I was in awe of his ability and he often helped me when I was filling orders and did not want to waste time searching for a part I knew nothing about. I'm sure I was a pain in his ass, me the boss's son, asking him where parts were all the time, especially when I was learning the inventory up front. This was interesting work, but I preferred the work out back in the big warehouse where I could also interact with the customers and truck drivers.

Sometimes over lunch I would walk up North Main St and get a burger at the restaurant up the street. Usually it would be a cheeseburger, fries and an orange Fanta to go. I would bring them back to the warehouse to have lunch with Frank. He would make fun of me, since the brown paper bag would be falling apart at the bottom from the grease of the soggy fries. It may have been greasy, but it was darn good! A few times my brother Matt would stop by. I don't know if he ever worked there, but we would walk down North Main Street and check out the stores. We would purchase things like little plastic TV sets where if you pushed the bottom, a different picture of a naked girl would pop up on the screen. One time we went into a shop with lots of knives in the window. We were looking at the knives and a couple Puerto Rican guys sitting in the back asked my very blond brother if he would like a free hair cut with a knife. We politely declined and left, although there were several sweet knives that we would have probably purchased. I always liked exploring the little shops along Main St, since this was my neighborhood where Dad's store was located. Speaking Spanish probably would have helped, but I did not mind.

In later summers, after I had my driver's license and was bigger, I would start helping with the deliveries. We had two truck drivers, a big black guy named Joe and a redneck guy from Granby named Carl. They were both good drivers, but I always preferred working with Joe, since he had a good attitude, liked his job and liked to talk. Carl was moody and not very talkative and I think had a chip on his shoulder because I was the boss's son and would have a built-in career and easy life because of it. I would tell him that I did not plan on working in the Hardware business when I was an adult, but had other plans. He never did believe me. I think Frank knew this because when there was a heavy delivery and the driver would need assistance, he usually sent me out with Joe.

I mainly did deliveries when something had to be shipped right away with some small parts that were holding up work for an important customer. I would get the address from Frank or one of the drivers and they would show me the location on a map. I would backup one of the company cars, usually a Plymouth Satellite to the loading dock, load the delivery items into the trunk and head out. I always drove the V8 sedan like a bat out of hell, since I wanted to give myself time to find the address. Usually, the truck drivers would know the location of the business from past deliveries, but it was almost always a first time for me, so driving fast was my edge. Carl would be amazed that I could do the delivery and get back to the warehouse in the same time it would take him, but he did not know about my edge. Perhaps that was the reason that he never really warmed up to me.

The two summers after I graduated from Westledge I often got to drive the large split axle delivery trucks. You would shift up into gear, then do a second shift into the high range of the axle using a pull-button on the shift knob, effectively making a 4-speed transmission an 8-speed transmission. I just loved driving these big trucks and could really enjoy it, in part knowing that this would not be my career for the rest of my life. The down side to the big trucks is that I could not use my edge of driving fast, but would need to search for the address from the cab of the truck driving slow down the street. To this day I still love driving big trucks, tractors and Bobcats although I usually have to make do with my pickup truck, the perfect mountain vehicle.

I never did work up on the "Executive Floor" with my dad and grandfather. I really liked the jobs that I did at the Bidwell Company anyway and don't know what I could have done there, just working summers. Dad liked his job from what I could tell, but if he had the choice of career after college, he would not have chosen to be a hardware man. I know that his dad Eliot had asked him to join the company and he felt some obligation to work there. Perhaps he did not want to pass that obligation on to me, or he could see that I wanted to work in some science field after school. Either way, Dad and I never sat down and discussed if I would like to work at the Bidwell Company after college. I never saw it as an option for myself. In my mind the world is a big place with unlimited possibilities that I wanted to explore and really find my niche. After I moved out to Colorado in the International Scout that I had purchased from my Grandma Noss, using money I earned at the Bidwell Company, the company started hitting hard times. Eventually Dad had to close the store and I know that it killed him to have to lay off all the employees that had made it their life's work. They were all like family and the family was breaking up, most never to see each other again. I would never set foot in the warehouse again to see Benny, Frank and the others.

My Dad would lose his life's work as well as a big part of his identity. It's too bad that none of them had the opportunity to take a class like I did at Westledge about dealing with change in the future to help make the transition easier.

Thank you for your great description of your five summers at the BHC. It was a mistake to buy the Rubber Co. I never knew what they did. I did not have the right aptitude to run a retail/wholesale operation. Interesting my Harvard honors thesis was a description of why such a diversified retail operation could survive. I got cum laude but the company did not survive. Dad

07 Family Vacations – Cape Cod

When I was growing up, we always took family vacations in August. I really enjoyed these getaways, and would know during our summer vacations from school, that I would be going on a cool family vacation towards the end of the summer.

The first vacations that we took while I was in elementary school were to Cape Cod. When at home in the early part of the summer, I would often run around in just shorts. The good thing about this is that my feet would toughen up and I would tan and brown as a nut. These were two good things for a vacation at the ocean, since being barefoot was the best way to be in the sand outside and being tan already was good since the sunscreens at the time would not filter out a lot of the Ultraviolet rays. Coppertone was the most popular, but even with that on, going in and out of the water would eventually wash it off of your body.

We would rent a cottage in Eastham on the bay side of the Cape where the water was warmer and the tides would go out for a quarter mile. They would have cool beach names like Sea Watch, but no street numbers, so accurate directions from the realtor would be essential. Dad would drive us up with his station wagon. Sometimes Mom would drive separately in her little Karmann Ghia. Often Dad would not stay for the entire vacation, but would drive back to Connecticut to go to work for a few days. Usually, our vacation would last for 2 weeks. We could generally walk to the beach, but we would often drive to bring our umbrellas, beach towels, sand toys and stuff. The cool thing with the bay is that at low tide, you could wander way out on the sandy flats and explore the muddy tidal pools where horseshoe crabs, minnows and other sea life would be trapped there for several hours. We would build big sand castles with walls and wait for the tide to come in and see how long our castles could withstand the onslaught. When I was a little older, Matt and I would go out to the edge of the sand flats and skin dive with just a mask, snorkel and fins at the edge of where it dropped off a bit into the bay. We would explore there, searching for Blue Crabs and the occasional scary but harmless sand sharks. The scariest thing we ever came across was a big creepy-looking Spider Crab with a small body and long legs. Good thing that we were floating on the surface, looking down.

When we were back at the cottage, we could fly plastic bat kites with the fairly steady breezes, often running around trying to keep them in the air. This was difficult sometimes with the tough bushes that would grow around the cottages. One time the wind was so steady, that we tied off my kite to the deck railing, went in for dinner and the kite was still flying after we had finished!

My birthday was in the middle of August, so I got to have my birthday while we were on vacation. It would always be something beachy, such as a kite, some swim fins or a boogie board. I would be bugging my parents to take me to the beach even more often than normal, so that I could use these items before our vacation was over. At the time, all I ever wanted to eat for my birthday was steamed or fried clams and a chocolate cake. It's a good thing that everyone in our family (except Jeremy) loved clams. My parents got a watch for me on my birthday on one of our early trips. I was very excited to get it and would look at it all the time and feel good. I always wanted to be an Oceanographer from spending time at the Cape, so my parents knowing this, got me a very nice Caravel diver's watch good to at least 300' depth. I think the main reason that I always had a watch was so I could be home by 5:00 in time for dinner at 6:00.

The other cool thing about Cape Cod was when we would drive over to Coast Guard Beach or Nauset Beach to spend a day at the huge sandy beaches off the North Atlantic. The water was much colder here, usually in the upper 60's. There would be huge sand bluffs overlooking the ocean. As kids, we could run off the bluffs and jump down to the steep sand below, tumbling head over heels, laughing and screaming all the way down. Those were the days. If fact those were the days before the bluffs were protected and this sort of activity is no longer permitted. There would actually be surf here that was perfect for body surfing and boogie boarding, both of which are tremendous fun. I learned to body surf from my dad. We would wade out into the surf together. When we got out to the waves, he would crouch down and I would climb onto his back, grabbing him around the neck. It was a bit like riding a greased pig, since Dad would be sweaty and have some suntan lotion on. He would dive into the wave and I would ride along like dad was a big flesh boogie board. That got me used to riding the waves and tumbling after they broke over you and also to get my timing down for doing it on my own later. When I finally got the hang of body surfing, I would walk back to the beach after a surfing session and my tight swimming shorts would be filled with a couple of pounds of sand. They had not invented board shorts yet!

At low tide, there would often be sand bars protecting the beach from the pounding of the surf, where the little kids could play safely. Beyond this there would be shallow water going out for several hundred feet for playing in the surf. We never worried about undertows, since they would typically be in the deeper channels heading out from the beach, where we would not be playing. Eating sandy sandwiches and chips for lunch on the beach was part of the experience, although it seemed like ages before the hour after eating was up and we could go back into the water to safely swim without cramping up. This seemed like a ruse that our parents made up so that they could relax after lunch without needing to keep an eye on us kids in the water, but all the families I knew did the same.

Dad would take us to the Town Cove in Orleans to rent a rowboat. They would supply us with stringers of line wrapped up in a square wooden "spool". We would have a little cardboard bucket of red worms. These worms had pincers and were a little scary to put on a hook. The worms would be dropped to the bottom and we would check our lines for a little tug, meaning that a flounder had taken our bait. We always caught several of the flat flounders, enough to bring back for a yummy fish dinner. That was the only time I remember Dad fishing without a fly rod!

On one of our drives up to Cape Cod, we were all packed into Dad's Station wagon, Mom and Dad in the front, Julie, Jerry in the back seat, with Matt and I in the far back seat looking out the back window, surrounded by all our vacation clothes and gear. I was 8 and Matt was 6. We had stopped at a gas station in Massachusetts. After a bit, I climbed out of the back of the car and went into the gas station to use the bathroom. When I came back out, our car was gone. Dad had driven off down the highway, oblivious to the fact that I was no longer in the car. I panicked since this was the first time I had been alone in a strange place. I did not cry; OK I may have. I did not know if they would be able to find a way back to me. It was always a mystery as to how we ever got where we were going in the first place. I did not understand how we found our way to the cottage. Even more mystifying was how we found our way home after the vacation was over. Dozens of different highways and roads, many intersections with left turns, right turns, even going straight. It was something that grownups understood but was lost on me. I wandered into the Gas Station office and there were two men and a woman inside. I told them that my family had left me there. I may not have had to tell them, but either way they knew I had been left behind. I remember thinking that the odds of Dad finding his way back here were slim and that the people in the gas station would most likely become my new family. They were nice and reassuring, positive that my mom and dad would be back. I was not nearly as certain. It turns out that my "new family" was correct and my family did return and pick me up so I got to go to the beach and not spend the month of August in a highway gas station.

Much later, when I was in high school, we went up to Orleans to stay for a few days at a cottage that was being rented by our family friends the Alcovelins. They were just at the end of the town cove where the estuary leaves and goes out to the Atlantic. The tide would flow up the estuary and fill the Town Cove at high tide and empty it at low tide. I was looking at the tide charts and saw that low tide would be at 2:00 so I came up with an idea that Mark and I could skin dive the current going out to sea for the almost 2 miles to the outlet. Mark, the Alcovelins oldest son was an athletic kid, I was the adventurous kid. Mark was a bit hesitant about this but eventually acquiesced and we were a go! We came up with a plan that we would take a little K-mart raft to put our lunch, towels and beach gear in. The little raft would also be good so boats could see us, especially the very sea-worthy fishing boats would use the estuary to punch through the surf at the mouth to get out into the Atlantic. At noon we hiked with our gear down to the estuary, put on our skin-diving gear grabbed the end of the line to the raft and swam off into the ebbing tide. The water was about 6 to 12 feet deep down to the sandy bottom, with a pretty strong current. We could dive down to a few feet above the bottom and watch it stream past us, with the occasional crab or fish zinging by. When we got out to the inlet, we swam off to Nauset beach on the right and pulled our raft onto the sand. We relaxed, swam, body surfed in the ocean while I kept time on my divers watch. The watch was handy, since Mark and I waited until about 4:00 to swim back home up the estuary on the flowing tide. In fact, we got back home just in time for dinner!

The vacations were family bonding. Your writing brings a new dimension to our family memoir. We got a big map from the US Navy showing that John's ashes were buried at sea from a US Destroyer with full military honors in the Baltic Sea. Jeremy has just been to Estonia and would have flown near the site. love Dad

I really loved that one with you being left behind. So funny! An adventure with the "Home Alone" kid! -Corrine

08 Family Vacations - Cabin & Kinderheim

The Cabin

My grandfather was the pastor at the South Congregational Church in Andover Massachusetts for most of his working life starting in 1930. He, my grandmother Emily, and their infant daughter Tish, moved to Andover at that time and had two more daughters, Jane (my mother) in 1931, and Gussie (my aunt) in 1934.

In 1944, Grandpa was interested in purchasing some land in New Hampshire, and he wrote to a realtor in Tamworth NH.

In his letter he said, "I am looking for a property within sight of the Sandwich Range. About ten years ago I spent 2 months with my family at the foot of Chocorua Mountain. We have never got over it. It should be a hundred acres or more, secluded. An old tote road is enough. Let there be woods."

The realtor responded and they looked at a nice property in North Sandwich which they really liked, but that deal fell through. The realtor finally found them a property further up the same road as the original property, at the top of the Ox-Bow as it was called. It was an old summer place that had burned down quite a while before and was now all forested with a nice meadow to the North. Across a stream to the south of the meadow was the entire North side of Young Mountain, also part of the property. The only problem was that it was five times larger than the original one hundred acres that he was looking for. They met the realtor and the whole family with the three little girls hiked and explored every inch of it, marveling at the diversity of hardwood, birch and pine trees. Even camping on the property to spend a couple of days there. The property was so beautiful that the family fell in love with it, so a plan was made to finance the 80% that the down payment would not cover.

Grandpa walked the property with the official State Forester from the government Timber Cruising service. They found about 200 acres on the West side of the property that was dense with hardwoods, some of the trees over three feet in diameter. The forester estimated about a half million board feet of lumber could be logged out of this area. They tried contracting with several lumber companies to harvest the timber on this portion of the property in exchange for helping with the mortgage. The first problem was that the banks were not willing to finance a timber operation that was not mostly pine and birch, which were in high demand at the time. The other problem was that the lumber companies did not have any timber crews to work the property because of the draft and enlistment of World War II.

Finally, they hit on a plan to have a furniture company finance the mortgage in exchange for harvesting all that hardwood. Grandpa Noss and my mom boarded a train up to West Ossipee NH to meet the realtor and then examine the property with a couple of men from the furniture company. When the train arrived at Mt Whittier Station, the realtor lady was not there to meet them. They took their luggage and sleeping bags and walked to the realtor's place in Tamworth about 4 miles away.

As my mom said to me, "Grandpa was much too impatient to wait and wanted to be off to the realtor lady's home, so we went walking along the road with our packs and sleeping bags since we were planning to sleep for the weekend up on the property".

The realtor arrived from a meeting out of town while they were waiting in the living room and saw Jane reading a book, all braids and legs.

Grandpa said, "Jane is a Participator in other people's feelings. She is worried about you, worried about the wife of the couple selling the house and the lumber man that wants to purchase the property". *This is probably why she became a psychologist, counseling people at New Britain General Hospital later in life.*

The realtor talked them into spending the night in an actual house and not on the ground. The next day, Mom and Grandpa met the two furniture men up at the property and they walked part of the two hundred acres of hardwood. The men were not too excited about it, and not very confident about putting together a crew to harvest it. It looked like this deal was going to fall apart. At least mom got to spend some quality time with her dad and go hiking in the woods.

Grandpa and Grandma had a discussion back in Andover and they decided to sell their house. They were worried that other people might make an offer on the property and a lumber company was already making overtures to the owners about purchasing all the land themselves. It is almost unbelievable the amount that they loved that land and that they were willing to sell their home for property several hours away without a dwelling on it. They put the Morton Street house on the market and it sold very quickly. They used the money to purchase all the land outright, without needing a mortgage. *

That was the good news. The bad news, for the girls at least, was that for the next 18 months they had to put all their furniture in storage. My Mom Jane, stayed with a couple on Central Street, Tish stayed with an uncle and his wife on Chestnut Street and the youngest, Gussie stayed with her parents at some friends, the Ripken's, on Abbot Street. My Mom often talked about how difficult it was to be separated from her family during this time. Gussie concurred this to me as well. They then moved in for two more years with the maiden Harriet Carter, using the upstairs bedrooms and a "second living room" on the first floor. Eventually the church purchased a parsonage house on Elm Street and the family was back together.

This is the house that I remember visiting as a kid. Grandma Noss always had a box of Nilla wafers that I never had anywhere else. I loved those little golden cookies. I was so little that I remember little else. My mom told me a story of when I was four, I climbed up the stairs, then over the banister and onto the tall grandfather clock and sat there on top while the family was running around the house looking for me. That's one story I wish I remembered! The church later bought a smaller parsonage house, but by that time we would mostly visit them up at Valley Farm.

That first summer up at the North Sandwich property, here on called "The Cabin", Grandpa put up a roof on the pagoda, the one remaining structure on the property. In the ensuing years he, Emily, my mom and her sisters helped him to build a cabin with a big wood burning stove. The cabin had a nice view of Young Mountain off to the southeast.

One time, before I was born, Grandpa and my mom went up to the cabin in the winter time after the cabin was built. They had parked well below the Joes Footbridge and had hiked in through the snow. At the footbridge, Grandpa scrambled down to the river to fill a water container. As he was reaching across the ice to the open water patch, he slithered into the water getting soaking wet. Mom looked down in horror, since the water was extremely cold, the temperature outside was also quite cold and they had yet to cross the footbridge and climb the trail to the cabin through the untracked snow. Grandpa stood up in the water, his winter coat heavy and dripping with the soaked in water. He still managed to fill the water jug and climbed out of the creek. He just toughed it out and they managed to make it up to the cabin where they fired up the large cast-iron stove and warmed up and dried off their clothes. Mom had told me this story multiple times and I know she thought Grandpa could have died when he fell into the creek and that she was worried that they might not make it up through the snow to the cabin. That just shows me how close she and Grandpa were, not only the worry about this epic snow hike, but also that he often took her on little bonding trips like this that really helped to define my mother as well.

My parents would take us up here often for little vacations. It has a rough double track road up to the cabin that Grandpa Noss would use his 4WD International Scout to access. There was an outhouse called the Hedi Lamar after Grandpa's favorite actress. We would just say we were going to the Hedi, whenever we had to do our business. There was even a picture of her tacked to the inside.

We never had comic books at our house, in fact our parents insisted that we read actual "chapter books". This rule was out the window at the cabin, since there were dozens and dozens of comic books in the bookcases. Almost all of them were Archie comics. I have no idea where they came from, but I was really glad they were there and I read every one of them. This would keep all us kids entertained until bedtime. During the day, we could play outside, there were lots of garter snakes in the foundation of the cabin to chase and catch, plus we could chase each other and play catch with a baseball or a frisbee. In the summer we could continue down the road past the cabin on foot down to Pond Brook, which we always called Swift River. At the bottom of the road was the Joe's footbridge which was the reason for hiking. The creek flowed over smooth New Hampshire granite outcroppings and boulders and was great for exploring, fishing, catching leopard frogs and bullfrogs, swimming, rock hopping and picnicking. One of our favorite spots is Picnic rock where the creek slides over the rock and we could slide down the rock in the water as well.

We skied into the cabin one winter with my family. We were skiing on the hill outside when Rodnick crossed my path and knocked me down, spraining my knee. We spent the night, snug in the cabin with the wood stove burning brightly, hoping my knee would get better. It did not. The next day my Dad had to pull me out on a sled back to the road. My Mom was busy carrying Jeremey out since he was so little, Matt and Julie were skiing. It was an ordeal since my sled kept sliding sideways off the trail. We ended up going to Joe Fogg's house, the local sheriff, where he and his wife warmed us up with hot chocolate and water basins to soak our cold hands and feet. My feet were about as cold as they have ever been. So cold in fact that my knee was just an afterthought. After we got home, the doctor just said to give it some rest and I would be fine. This was only the first of three injuries I have sustained skiing and snowboarding. This was an epic, but an adventure none the less, and would not spoil me on adventures.

It was a happy coincidence that the octagonal pagoda looked like it was styled after a Japanese pagoda since Grandpa Noss had grown up in Japan before he came to the US to continue his schooling before college. This was where the chopped wood for the stove was kept as well as the axes, grinding stones, mowers and yard tools. There was a refrigerator in there as well that ran on kerosene. I always wondered as a kid, how that refrigerator, that was burning kerosene could create anything other than heat. Perhaps that is why I was so interested in science as a kid, to find the answers to these types of questions.

Kinderheim

We started going up to Kinderheim when I was in Jr High school. This was a big old house about a half mile from the cabin. Our cousins John, Fred and Susan with their parents Uncle Rudy and Aunt Tish (Mom's older sister) would stay at the cabin every

August, so we stayed as close as we could, since the area was home to us and the forest and mountains were very beautiful. Kinderheim has a big wrap-around covered porch with a nice view of Young Mountain off to the South. In German, Kinderheim means "Children's Home". I don't know if it was ever an orphanage or if it was just a big house designed for families with lots of kids, which would define our family of 4 when we would have family friends and their kids staying with us. There were a couple of bedrooms downstairs and the upstairs was a huge open space filled with single beds. All the kids would sleep together in this room. The house was old when we were staying there 50 years ago. The open rafters of the ceiling were home to several bats that would fly around the room after dark. It never bothered us, perhaps since we were sleeping in their home and they were pretty much out of sight. At dusk we would go outside to toss pebbles up into the air and the bats would swoop down to check them out, thinking it was some kind of big insect. The kitchen had a big marble table with pots and pans hanging above, a real country kitchen with room for everyone.   On the porch was a four-foot-long megaphone, hanging from a rafter. We could yell into it to try and talk to the Mutters over at the cabin. I would play taps on my trumpet after the sun went down and it would echo across from Young Mountain. There was a big open area in the front of the house and the rest of the area was dense forest.

If we headed down the dirt road to the East, it crossed a creek not too far down. We walked down there one time when the Westons's were visiting us with Lissie and Laurie. This creek was in the woods and was leaf-filled. We would usually fly fish here, but this time we went swimming, since it was hot outside and the creek was handy. We were splashing around when Lissie stood up and looked down at her legs. There were a couple of leeches hanging off. She screamed "LEECH" at the top of her lungs and ran all the way back to the house screaming with the leeches hanging off and the rest of us kids chasing after her. Luckily for us there were very few ticks in this area in August.

One time the Mutter boys walked over from the cabin and we decided to hike to the top of Flat Mountain. We could see the mountain off to the North from Kinderheim, but there was not a trail from this side. We had a compass, plus we could see which way to go, but it was pretty heavily forested on the way up, with a couple for granite outcroppings along the way to get a view.

Well on the hike up, Fred called out as loud as he could, "Shit".

We looked at him and he said, "Well we are out here in the middle of nowhere where no adults can hear us".

We all agreed with his logic and started yelling all the cuss words that we could think of at the top of our lungs. We spent a good 10 minutes yelling and laughing and having a grand old time. A couple of years earlier, when our family was visiting the Mutters down in Westport, Matt, Fred, John and I decided to create a club. We were the Bidwells and the Mutters, so we decided to name our club the BM club which we thought was extremely clever and funny. The BM club was in fine form on this mountain climbing expedition. We eventually made it to the top, had our lunch and water and enjoyed the summit. Dad always told us to just drink the minimal amount of water when hiking. Just take little sips every once in a while, so you don't cramp up. I don't know why our parents were so worried about us kids cramping up, but the current logic is to chug as much water as you can when exercising to keep hydrated. We made our way back down the mountain to Kinderheim without getting lost. Our parents met us outside. It turns out that on the ledge where we were shouting "Fucking" and other cuss words, the sound was carrying down to the house and our parents heard some of what we were yelling. They were upset in a joking sort of way that made us feel that what we did was OK since we were just boys letting off steam.

Matt and I decided one day to hike up the road to Joe's bridge and then follow the creek up to Great Falls. This was a waterfall, not too far below Flat Mountain Ponds which is the headwaters of the Whiteface River. We brought our skin-diving gear with us so that we could dive in the large pool below the falls. When we got to the falls, the pool looked pretty deep. We swam in the pool and did several dives before we could touch the bottom even though it was probably only 12 or 15 feet deep. The problem was that the water was extremely cold down towards the bottom and it kept repelling us before we started getting a little used to it.

When we had finished our little diving expedition, I had the bright idea to just skin dive back almost a mile to picnic rock which was just above Joe's footbridge before hiking back home to Kinderheim. We floated down with the current, stopping to check out what the creek looked like below us especially where it dropped out of sight in a little cascading rapid. We were unfamiliar with the creek this far up and we did not want to swim into something that would beat us up, especially since we were swimming head first. In several places we had to wade through some shallows or steeps, but we made it all the way to picnic rock, adding to the exploration of the creek. Mostly it was just rocks and bubbles that we saw along the way. The only fish I remember seeing were up in the pool below the falls.

We took a family picnic up to the Kancamagus Highway which was on the real Swift River. This was actually a river that flowed through the granite like our little "Swift River" which was only a brook. We found a nice spot by the river for a picnic. We were wading and swimming, enjoying the summer day before lunch. During lunch, we were all sitting there looking at the river when a spider floated over head on a long strand of silk that was glistening in the bright sunlight. We all watched this spider float down over the river. Immediately when the spider touched the water, a big trout jumped up and swallowed it down. Well Dad saw that and decided he was going to catch that trout. He tied on a large dry fly and did a perfect cast out over the river. We could all see the large dry fly floating down towards the water. When the fly was a foot or so above the river, the trout jumped out of the water and grabbed that fly before it ever had a chance to get wet. Dad played that nice trout for a while before landing it in the net. We brought it home for a trout dinner to complement our nice lunch on this fine day!

We would shoot archery outside in the field next to Kinderheim. We would setup a little target and shoot at it, keeping score like darts. One-time Matt and I were getting bored and we decided to shoot the arrow straight up to see how high it would go. I took the first shot and it went up surprisingly far before turning sideways and dropping back down. We would follow it down with our eyes. We had fun seeing who could keep the arrow up in the air the longest. This was all good clean fun until I took my hardest shot up into the sky. Matt and I watched it up to about the time it reached the apex of its flight, when we both lost sight of it.

"Run" we both shouted as we ran as far away from the shooting spot as we could. I remember the top of my scalp tingling the whole time I was running, expecting an arrow to stick straight into the top of my head. Needless to say, we stopped playing that particular game after that big scare. Right across from where we were shooting was a big barn containing an old horse-drawn covered carriage that we always called the caravansary. That is what we called it although that term actually means a roadside inn. We would sit in it and look around the barn at all the other old equipment like we were scanning a museum to see what was most interesting. There was nothing in there to play with other than sitting in the carriage, but it was a cool place to just hang out, especially when it was raining and we did not want to be in the house with the grown-ups.

The only time we saw the townie kids from the town of North Sandwich is when our parents would drive us down to the potholes. This was an area in a creek outside of town, where there were round potholes carved into the granite by the water. You could climb up on the rock above the pools and jump into these potholes from any level up to about 12 or 15 feet up. If you were really brave, you could jump off the bridge that was about 25 feet up. There was a pool below, but there were several boulders in the pool that you had to avoid. This was always a good test of nerve when sitting on the bridge railing with other kids. It was like a non-verbal dare when the kids would look at you. Of course, you had to accept the dare, and the thrill after jumping was just icing on the cake. It was a little addicting and you would want to go back up to the bridge and sit on the rail again, warming up in the sunshine. We were so far up a private dirt road at Kinderheim and the cabin, that there were never any chance encounters with outsiders. In hindsight, that is the perfect place for a vacation!

It is great to have these stories to remind us. Do you want to share this with the family and ask for comments? What is your thought about developing a book.? I am conscious of my time becoming more limited. Dad

You did a lot of valuable research with Gussie. The story of financing the land is something. I never knew. You could title your book "A Boy's Life." I subscribed to Boys Life magazine as a boy. Dad

* Many of the details of purchasing the cabin was paraphrased from Chapter 5 "The Hardwood Timber Mortgage", from chapter 5 of <u>A Brook of Our Own</u>, by Marjory Gane Harkness ©1945.

09 Family Vacations - Meredith Neck

My parents rented a nice lake-house on Lake Winnipesaukee out on Meredith Neck in New Hampshire for several wonderful August vacations. It had a wrap-around sleeping porch, a garage with an apartment, a boathouse and a fish house. It was an older property in excellent condition with lots of character, in an area where many newer lake-front homes had been built. This is exactly the type of place that Mom loved. We started coming here for the full month of August during my high school summers.

When we arrived at the house for the first time, we were exploring the house and property. When we got to the little fish house, I absolutely loved it. It was on big wooden sled runners with metal bottoms. The house itself was not much bigger than the bed. It had a couple of round hatches in the floor, where you could fish from, when it was pulled out onto the ice in the winter. It was all paneled in wood and was snug and very cool. This became my private bedroom for August. I really loved it. The porch around the main house was screened in on the East side for use as a sleeping porch. When the August nights got too warm, we could sleep out on the porch to stay a little cooler in the breeze. It was fun when our parents had friends over with kids and we could stay up talking together until we fell asleep. On the weekend evenings we could sit out on the dock after dark and watch the fireworks display across the water in Weirs Beach. The fireworks would flash and we would count for 15 seconds until we heard the boom after the sound had traveled across the water.

When I was in Science Academy, we would catch butterflies, beetles and other insects, but never spiders. The lake house had spider webs all around with big garden spiders waiting patiently for a fly to get stuck. We got jars, perforated the lids and caught several of these spiders. We would catch flies and watch the spiders kill and eat them. We would catch yellow jackets and put them in the jar. The spiders always won these battles. Sometimes we would put 2 large spiders into the same jar and watch them battle it out to the death. I was never really scared of spiders, but watching all these little gladiator games inside the jar made me a little scared of them. They had big pinchers with some poison to incapacitate bugs, and I did not want anything to do with them outside of a jar. I think it just increased the creepy factor for me. It put an end to any ideas I had of becoming an entomologist in the future.

There were mailboats, the Doris E. and Sophie C. that would ply the waters delivering mail to the larger islands in the lake. Often, we would paddle the canoe way out close to where these large boats would cruise by and surf the large wakes back towards shore. Now the lake is deep and the wakes would be just steep swells and not breaking like they would do if it was shallow water. They were large enough however that we could catch a surf a nice surf, ruddering in the back to keep the canoe straight and speeding along for a little thrill for 100 yards or so before they would fade off. There would be two or three more that would be behind and we could catch those as well before they petered out.

One time I was hanging out with the women on the porch. My Mom, "Aunt" Gussie and Grandma Noss. They were discussing the letters that Uncle Bob, my grandfather's brother had written to his wife. I don't know how they came across these letters, but letters were never thrown away. People back then did not have time to journal, since they would write these long letters to each other and it would serve as a journal later. Anyway, they were talking about how Bob was just so in love with his wife that it must be suffocating for her. He would write her love poems and dote on her. They were in agreement that this kind of love was too over the top. There was always a girl I had a crush on in my class from kindergarten till, well till I graduated from high school. The type of love that Uncle Bob had was exactly how I knew our love would be if I ever had any of them as my girlfriend. I remember thinking that if I ever fell in love, that is exactly the type of love that I would want. Loving someone so much that you just wanted to write them poems and tell them of your love for them. I always greatly admired my mom, I thought she had great ideas and always knew what was best. This was the first time that I can remember thinking that I did not agree with her on something, if you discount what time I should come home or what time I should go to bed. Those last two things are trivial. Love however, well Love is the meaning of life, what life is all about and what makes life worth living. I don't know why so many people obsess and wonder what the meaning of life is, when it is right there in front of them all the time!

Speaking of Gussie visiting us, she was there when I had a birthday coming up on Sunday. They were all having so much fun just being women together that my birthday slipped their mind until Sunday came around. Gussie went into full panic mode. She wanted to bake a cake for my birthday, but we had no ingredients for a cake, no cake mix, nothing. Well she went down into Meredith looking for a market, but all she could find was a gas station mini mart. She got angel food cake, whipped cream and powdered chocolate. She got home and made this cake with a chocolate whipped cream frosting for my birthday party. She was very apologetic about the cake, but I remember this so well since I liked the cake so much. I think half of it was the creative energy she put into it and the love that made her worry that it was not good enough. That was my best birthday present.

I went to the YMCA camp Morgan in NH for a couple of summers and learned to sail on a sailfish. That is a sailboat without a cockpit, with a center board and a single mast that could be sailed single-handedly. I learned how to run downwind and tack back to the starting point, just the basic sailing skills. Well Matt and I decided we wanted to try sailing with my canoe. We built a mast from a 10' wooden pole and anchored it to the front seat with rope and anchored the base to a piece of wood on the bottom of the canoe. The sail was made of a polyethylene plastic sheet from the Bidwell company. We made dagger boards out of 1x6 pieces of lumber that hung down into the water from both sides of the canoe. We setup everything on the dock, then slid the "sailboat" into the water. Matt sat on the floor between the mast and the dagger boards hanging onto the halyard, I sat in the stern as the helmsman, ruddering the boat with a canoe paddle. Matt pulled the rope to extend the sail and it immediately billowed out and pulled us away from the dock. We managed a couple of easy tacks to test out the maneuverability. On our third or fourth turn, the Dagger boards fell apart and we lost the ability to tack upwind. We were out pretty far from land and could not get back as the breeze was heading South away from our summer house. We decided to ride it out heading into the big open water between Governors

Island and Timber Island. Just past these two islands is an area known as the Witches. This is a scary area of rocks just below the surface that has sunk quite a few boats. We knew it was off of Timber Island, so we fought with the rudder to keep as far away from the island as we could. We finally saw little whitecaps marking the witches far off the port bow and knew we were OK. We sailed all the way to Glendale on the South side of the lake and to a public dock there, dropped our sail and tied up. We had sailed about 4 miles across the lake from our house! We walked up the dock, found a pay phone and called Dad. We told him where we were and asked him to come get us. He had to drive the 30 miles by car to the dock. Dad was not upset with us; in fact, I think he was a little impressed that we had such an adventure. It was not long after that dad bought a Sunfish, a slightly bigger version of the boat that I had learned to sail on, but with a cockpit. He knew that we would continue our little adventures and he wanted to make sure that we could sail safely and actually tack back home.

Us kids would fish from the dock for small mouth bass using Mepps spinners. There was a little breakwater between us and the house to the East where the fish liked to hang out. This was in the days before fish finders, so one of us would skin dive over to the breakwater and point out where the bass were. We could give input as to the depth and if they showed interest in the lure. It was always fun to be watching the fish through the face-mask when it darted out and grabbed the bait and fought its way away from the dock. We would paddle the canoe to a secluded little cove a half mile up the lake. It had a channel through a lot of underwater rocks into the nice fishy cove. We would fish there and use the same technique. One of us would slither into the water with our diving gear and look for bass that we could point out to the person fishing from the canoe. This was great for me, since fishing would sometimes get boring and I could break it up by diving. That's part of the reason that I liked fishing from the canoe, when the fish were not biting it was always fun to paddle and explore in the canoe.

We made friends with a neighbor kid named Kip from Boston, several houses down. His favorite term was "pisser", but pronounced "pissa" with a strong accent.

He would even use it several times in the same sentence such as, "Did you see that pissa Donzi speed boat that just went by, it would be really pissa to take a ride in it!". We became friends when my parents rented a little Alumacraft boat with a 9 1/2 horsepower outboard. My brother and I were tooling around heading to the Cattle Landing public docks and Kip was doing the same with a little plastic outboard that he had and we got to talking. Earlier, Matt and I had found some water skis in the boat house at our lake house. For a lark we hooked the tow rope up to the boat and got in the water with the skis on, just to see what it would feel like to try water skiing. Much to our surprise, we would be pulled in the water for a little bit, and then bingo! We would pop up to the surface and would be actually skiing! We were going just barely fast enough to actually get up, but up we were. That was our total experience with skiing so far. Well Kip's dad had a huge ski boat moored on the dock. When we would hang out with him at his house, his older sister would be, cranking Iron Butterfly out the window, but only the song In-A-Gadda-Da-Vida. She was much too cool to hang out with us. Eventually we went water skiing with Kip when his dad would come up on the weekends and we got to do some real water-skiing, even learning to use a single slalom ski. I never listened to Iron Butterfly after that, having had my fill of that repetitive song on his dock and I never picked up using the term pissa either.

This lake house was not too far from my grandmother's house In Tamworth, called Valley Farm. We would see her often at her house or she would come out and visit us at the lake. She had been living there alone since I was 12 when my grandfather passed away.

Great memories that you are remembering. You definitely have a book... Dad

10 Family Vacations - Valley Farm

My grandfather inherited some money back in the early 60's when one of his 11 siblings passed away and he used that money to purchase a retirement home for him and Emily. They found a house that they named Valley Farm in Tamworth NH, which was about 10 miles from the cabin where they would be visiting a lot. They used it as a vacation house until Grandpa retired in 1967, coincidentally the year that he also died.

The house was built in 1860, on 40 acres and was already over 100 years old when I first visited it with my family. It was about a mile down a narrow dirt road from the Whittier Cash Market the local country store just across the Bearcamp River. The main thing I remember about it was the smell, especially in the breezeway containing old tools and firewood that you walked through to get from the house to the newer garage. It had a huge Sugar Maple tree just outside of the front door that usually had a syrup bucket on it in the Fall.

We would occasionally visit in the Spring, mud season in NH. This was the least preferred time to visit because of the bugs so we would liberally douse ourselves in Old Woodsmen's Fly Dope, a concoction that would keep the flies and bugs away using its sheer bad smell. We would put it on bandanas around our neck, to help keep the bugs away from our face. That smell brings back memories of childhood so it is now a good smell for me. There would be mosquitoes, black flies, deer flies, horseflies and no-see-ums, we would see Grandpa out with his brush cutter trimming back the forest from the road to the house so we would have more room to drive the car through. There were woods behind the house and below the house was a large grassy, swampy meadow. Grandpa would bundle up and go down into the meadow to trim back the grass and would come back covered with ticks that he would pick off his clothes before walking across the grass back to the house. We never went down there except in the winter when the ticks were absent. We could take a walk about a half mile up the road to a sweet spring on the side of the road where we would fill up our water bottles. The water in the house was from a well, but the smell of mineralization was so strong that I had a hard time drinking it.

One summer we were all outside drinking Grandma's lemonade and running around. There was an oversized swing set frame, but it was missing the swings. I was 8 or 9 and shinnied up a leg to the crossbar and stood up. I then reached up to the top pole which went twelve feet across to the other side where the chains for the swings would be attached normally. For my 8-year-old self, it seemed pretty high from the ground. Even so, I reached up and put a hand on the top bar and swung out, my goal was to reach the other side, swinging with my hands. I was doing pretty well and was about halfway across when I swung my hand out, grabbed the bar and was immediately stung on the palm of my hand by a hornet. I screamed bloody murder, let go and hung there by my other hand and a couple of other wasps flew out and stung me just for good measure. I was too frightened to let go since I was so high up, but just as my good hand was about to slip off the bar, my grandfather who was running over to the swing set grabbed me by the legs and carried me off. The stings hurt, but my grandfather who fancied himself a TOMOA was impressed that I hung on while being stung, rather than panicking and dropping to the ground far below.

He told me one time that he never liked those angelic pictures of Jesus that lots of people have hanging on their wall. He said that the type of man who would confront the tax collectors and turn over their tables had nerve and toughness. Perhaps he said that, since that was the way he was as a minister. Besides being an empathetic paster, he was also a tough outdoors man and would always test my knowledge of fighting.

"Double them over" he would say as he mocked an exaggerated punch to my stomach with his right hand.

"Straighten them up" he would growl as he pretended to hit me in the jaw with a left uppercut with enough force to stand me up.

"Put them away!" he would yell as he feigned a strong right punch straight into my nose.

I never put his advice into practice except once, as I generally preferred the tried-and-true headlock.

I have read my grandfather's notes about him and my grandmother backpacking together back in the 1940's up in Glacier Park. He had an 80-pound pack and was carrying most of the load so his wife could enjoy the hike. He called himself her superman, which I thought was cool. Hey, now that I think back to all the Archie comics in the cabin, I bet he had read some Superman comics, since he would not have seen it on TV or movies and was probably the source for the Archies! I guess he needed some light reading to offset reading the Bible so much.

Dad and Grandpa Noss decided to hike Whiteface Mountain one time with Matt and I, when I was 11. Grandpa Noss died of a stroke when I was 12. I remember being in the Ridge Rd house in CT when we got a call from Grandma that he had passed away from a heart attack. My Mom was surprised and shocked and crying as was the rest of the family. I processed the news and could feel myself starting to laugh. I remember thinking at the time that I should be crying and what's wrong with me, I loved Grandpa Noss with all my heart. I worried about this for years later, never telling anyone until I was an adult. I realize now that crying and laughing are similar responses, in fact I have seen my dad and Uncle John laughing so hard that they started crying with tears running down their faces at Dad's bachelor party at Jeremey's house. I never cried after that until years later when my wife died and crying was the natural thing to do and I did it a lot, even when just hanging out with my dog Dillon.

We drove to the trailhead just off the Wonalancet River, not too far from the cabin actually. We loaded up our packs with our supplies. I had lunch, a canteen, a light jacket and a rock pick, since I liked rock collecting and was thinking that being a geologist might be a desirable occupation. When we were geared up, we headed out on the 4-mile trail to the top at 4000 feet, 2800 feet above where we were. We were hiking along the river for a way before crossing and beginning the ascent. We hiked through the blueberry ledges, but were too early for any berries. I would look around on all our little hiking breaks and would chip out little quartz crystals or other rocks that caught my eye with my rock hammer for my collection. We stopped at a rock ledge on the way up for lunch and to enjoy the views. It was really nice to just hang out with my brother, Dad and Grandpa. I wandered off looking for rocks and found a nice specimen with the outline of a bigger quartz crystal that someone else had already pried out of the rock. We continued across some steep ledges near the top, but we made it up and took a nice break, being sure not to chug too much water. We took some pictures, but the best pictures are the ones with people in them, such as the ones we took at our lunch break. We hiked back down, for me going down was much easier.

When we got to the car, we were standing there, me in a little trance of elation when Grandpa pulled my pack off my back. "Holy cow, what do you have in here, rocks? "

I looked at him sheepishly and nodded affirmatively.

He opened my pack and under my pick was a pretty good pile of rocks. I don't know if he thought I was foolish to be needlessly carrying such a weight in my pack or if he was secretly impressed that he had another little Superman in the making. I like to think the latter. Dad was just used to me doing this kind of thing.

Grandpa Noss had an International Scout with a little fiberglass cab over the front and a pickup bed in the back. All of us kids loved riding in the back of this truck. He would take us around on his errands with us in the back. We were at the store one time and my sister Julie asked him if we could take a "Long-cut" on the way home. Grandpa thought this was hilarious and without saying so, took a long and circuitous route back home to Valley Farm. On the way, every time we came to a hill, he would cut the engine, put the truck into neutral and coast to the bottom, then starting it up again. He would do this since the Scout only got 10 miles to the gallon and he did not want to waste gas. A true environmentalist before his time.

Another time the BM club (John, Fred, Matt and I) were in the back of the Scout when we drove through Sandwich as they were having a large auction right off the street downtown. We put our heads together since John had a funny idea. He always had something funny banging around in his head, and could keep us laughing. As we got closer, we could hear the crowd and the auction going on louder and louder.

We could hear the auctioneer shouting out, "I've got 10 dollars, who will give me 11, 10 dollars, who will give me 11"

The four of us shouted out as loud as we could as we were passing by,

"We'll give 10 dollars and ONE PENNY!"

Grandpa never stopped the Scout to see if we won the bid.

I was helping Grandpa weeding the garden one time and we had the back of the Scout loaded with greens, weeds and other garden stuff that needed to go to the dump. He and I jumped in the truck and drove out to the Tamworth dump and unloaded. When we had the truck unloaded, Grandpa noticed a huge pile of hay that someone had dumped off and Grandpa wanted it to cover his garden. Well one of the redneck guys that worked at the dump, really wanted to light this pile on fire, since it would make some good flames I suppose. While Grandpa was loading hay from the huge pile into the back of the scout at the same time the guy working there lit the other side of the haystack. Grandpa had the Scout about half loaded when the flames were getting pretty big and coming around to our side of the pile. We had to pull the truck away with our unfinished load. That was the only time I had ever heard him bad-mouthing anyone, but he was sure mad about that guy.

We had driven up to Valley Farm with the family and had tied my canoe onto the roof of the station wagon. We could paddle around the many lakes near the house. I was outside exploring in the woods South of the house, but West of the swampy tick-filled grassland. In those days I usually had a hatchet strapped to my belt. I would walk through the forest and chop a little marker in the bark of a tree every once in a while, to see the route I had taken to help me find the way back. I had not gone too far when I came across a sweet little brook. It had minnows swimming in the clear water. I followed my markers back to the house and told Matt about the creek. We pulled my canoe off the top of the car, put the paddles in it and drug it through the woods on the leaves and pine needles to the creek. We decided to paddle down the creek as far as we could, to explore. About every 100 feet we ran into a tree that we would have to slide the canoe across, then hop back in and paddle to the next obstruction. In several hours we did not get too far, but had a great time doing it. We eventually turned back around, since we knew how many trees we would have to drag it across to get back to our starting point. This was the first time that I ever had it on moving water, even though it was just a little brook, I was hooked. Matt later built and paddled a kayak at Loomis school and became an expert kayaker from this humble little beginning.

I was very interested in trapping, from reading stories of the woodsmen up in Canada trapping beavers. I had tried my hand at it at home, setting beaver traps at a pond of one of Julie's friends, Beenie. Her parents gave me permission to trap a wetland behind their house that had beavers. I set traps and checked them, but never caught a single beaver. My Mom mentioned that Grandpa Noss had a friend Mr. Thompson that trapped in the winter when he was not farming. Grandpa setup a meeting with me and Mr Thompson for a time when we would be visiting that winter. My dad dropped me off at the Thompson residence, which was just several miles down Whittier Road from Valley Farm. Mr. Thompson had long dark hair and was a big husky man, but not fat. He was a Flathead Indian and had moved here from Montana when he was a young man. He had a large vegetable farm with the Bearcamp river right behind his fields. In the summer, his wife and he would sell the vegetables from a road-side stand to passer-buyers. Well Mr. Thompson threw a large basket into the back of his truck with a lunch and we took off deep into the forest. It was quite cold out when we got to the first stop. We got out of the truck and walked through the snow into the forest for quite a way to where he had set a trap for fishers. A fisher is like a very large mink, but mostly hunted squirrels in the trees. They were viscous and would kill anything close to its size. We got to the trap and it had not been sprung, it was just sitting in the tree with some musky meat as a bait. The trap was a square body trap that the fisher would climb through to get to the bait. The trap would spring closed on its body and would swing out away from the tree, holding the animal in the air until it died. If the trap was set incorrectly, the fisher would hold onto the bark and try to pull itself out of the trap so hard that it would pull it's nails off.

We trudged back through the snow to the truck and headed off to the next trap location a few miles away. This was a beaver trap in some ponds. As we were trudging through the snow, my feet were getting very cold. I was wearing thick socks under my rubber-bottomed, leather-upper LL Bean boots. These boots were good for mud, but had almost no insulation from the cold. They were lacking the thick felt insulation that the warmer boots had. They had always been good-enough for Connecticut, but were not New Hampshire quality. I kept my mouth shut about cold feet and we got to the beaver pond. Mr. Thompson got down on his knees at the pond and brushed the snow off the ice where he had set the trap and peered down through the ice looking for the trap. He saw that the trap was missing and most of his green sticks that he was using for bait were gone. He excitedly told me that we had a beaver! I think he was extra-glad since he was taking me, a neophyte trapper along and wanted to have a successful trip. He took off his big basket that had straps like a backpack and pulled out an axe that he used to chip through the ice. When he had a big enough hole, he pulled off his gloves and reached down and pulled out the end of a long skinny log. He had taken the log and attached a wire to one end, then twisted a piece of wire pointing out towards the pond every several feet towards the end of the 12-foot log attaching the other end to the log as well. He had attached the ring from the chain on the foot trap to this wire. The idea was that if the beaver stepped into the foot trap, it's first instinct would be to swim to deeper water. The ring would slide along the wire to the end of the log when the beaver could go no farther. When the beaver would be running out of breath, it would try to swim back, but the twisted wire pieces would prevent it from going back, drowning the beaver. He pulled the log out from under the ice and at the end was a big fat beaver. He threw the beaver down on the ice, took the trap off and we looked at this magnificent creature. I had never seen a beaver this close before. Mr. Thompson put on his large basket backpack, then picked up the 60-pound beaver and lifted it over his head and dropped it into his backpack. I imagined that his hands had to be as cold as my feet, but he never mentioned it either.

We drove back to his barn and unloaded his catch. Inside he had numerous beaver pelts all stretched out and hanging. He also had about a half dozen large fishers also stretched and hanging that were fascinating to me. I never went trapping after that, having seen the skill and difficulty that the task entailed, but also seeing these beautiful creatures dead and imagining what the last few minutes must have been like for them. I did go back to visit Mr. Thompson the next summer and he took time off from his work to walk me back to the river and show me a huge snapping turtle that he had caught crawling up the bank towards his corn field. The turtle was alive but had a pitch fork stuck firmly into the dirt bank with one tine squarely through the center of its neck. It was still alive, but would be in his stew pot in the evening. Mr. Thompson was truly living off the land, just like his ancestors before him. I had a real respect for him and liked him since he treated me like an adult and not a kid. I realized that his normal life was an adventure that I was just not ready for and that he had a toughness that I would never know.

One summer day Mom took us down to the Whitter cash market for lunch. She bought each of us a hotdog. We walked across the street to the Bearcamp River and had our lunch there. We could see trout swimming as we were eating and Mom remarked that they would probably like a bite of hotdog also. We went back to the store and she bought another hotdog this time for bait, and we pulled our fishing rods out of the back of the car. We broke off little pieces and put them on our dry fly hooks. We immediately caught a couple of good sized Brookies. It was one of the best lunches ever. It's little things like this that make New Hampshire so special. No wonder it is my mom's favorite place.

Mom told me years later that Grandpa Noss discovered two things when he retired. One was music, he had a phonograph and would listen to classical music on it. The other was beer that he would enjoy after a hard afternoon in the vegetable garden or relaxing with Grandma in the shade of the sugar maple tree.

TOMOA - Tough Old Man of Action

Chris, these memories keep getting better. I do not remember Mr. Thompson and your beaver trapping... Your book will have a more personal story than mine. Dad

11 Carver Circle, Simsbury CT

We moved to a brand-new subdivision on Carver Circle when I was too young to remember. Before that, my parents had an apartment in East Hartford. I was probably 3 years old when we moved and we lived there until I was 8 or 9. This was a colonial style house. My best friend was Paul, who lived just down and across the street.

I actually went to pre-school for two years at our church in Simsbury. I remember Mom dropping me off and I would walk in with my little braided wool rug rolled up under my arm which we used for sleeping on the floor at nap time. At story-time, the teacher would have us all sit down on the floor Indian-style to listen. I was good for about 5 minutes when the cross-legged position would be too much for me and I would squirm and stick out my legs and move around much to the chagrin of the teacher. I did like playing with the large blocks.

Dad would come home from work in his suit and I would often ask him if he had any gum. He had chiclets in his pocket sometimes and if he did, he would pull out the pack and offer me one. If I asked him and he said he did not have any, then I had a plan. I would run up to my bedroom and get my favorite little blanket and come down and stand in front of dad.

I would twirl the blanket around in the air over my head and say the magic words, "Abracadabra, please and thank you."

These being all the magic words that I knew. I would then search all of Dad's pockets for gum. Sometimes it would be in his inside jacket pocket, sometimes in a pants pocket, sometimes there would not be any gum. It never discouraged me if there was no gum, I probably just said the incantation incorrectly. All it took was finding it occasionally and I would keep the faith in this magic. I gave up this practice when I started going to school, not consciously, it just faded away, like so many childish things that I've since forgotten about.

We had a TV, but only got 4 stations, ABC, NBC, CBS and PBS so we did not watch a lot of television, just our favorite shows. If you missed an episode, then you would probably never see that one again. I do remember seeing an ad on TV for PF Flyers. The ad promised that you would run faster, jump higher and basically be the fastest kid in the neighborhood. I bugged my parents for a while before they bought me a pair. When I strapped on the sneakers, I was sure I was being transformed into a super-kid. I went around the neighborhood, running everywhere and racing all the kids I could find. I was so fast it was amazing! When I was in kindergarten, I had a huge crush on a girl in my class. I managed to invite her over on a Saturday to hang out. We were outside playing, doing kid stuff. Paul came over to play with us which was cool with me. I don't remember if I was wearing the PF Flyers, but the three of us decided to race around the house. We started on the driveway and took off for the race. Paul and I were in front and my crush was right behind. As we approached the 3/4 mark, I slowed down a bit so she could catch-up. By the time we got to the driveway, Paul was first, she was second and I came in last. I really wanted her to like me, so I let her win. In hindsight, she was probably much more impressed with Paul, since he was so fast. I think it was another 10 years before I ever asked another girl out on a date. They became much more mysterious and perhaps dangerous in the sense that if they said no, I would be crest-fallen. I peaked very early in the dating game!

We had some neighbors, the Mogers, down and across the street that had 3 boys. The middle boy named Steve was my age. Their dad had been a big basketball player in college and fancied himself the neighborhood athlete dad. He had poured a large concrete pad in the backyard with a basketball hoop so the boys could follow in his athletic footsteps. I was over there on Steve's birthday when we were pretty young, in fact I had not learned to even ride a bike yet. Well Steve got a bike for his birthday. We were out in the garage and playing with the bike after the party and trying to get the hang of it. Steve just could not ride the bike. I tried and after several times, got the hang of it and was riding it around the garage and down the driveway. Steve's dad came out to see how we were doing. I just knew that he was quite upset that the neighbor kid, was riding the bike, but his kid could not. Bruce Bidwell's kid was a better athlete than his own son, and it really bugged him. When I came home and told dad, he was proud of me and probably was proud of himself just a little bit, since his little prodigy has bested Mr. Moger's son in an athletic endeavor.

A little later, my sister Julie had a crush on the littlest Moger boy. Matt and I would tease her about it.

You know, "Julie and Jonnie, sitting in a tree, k-i-s-s-i-n-g", type of stuff.

Dad came up with a solution. He made up a fictional girlfriend for both Matt and I called Sonia Heiselman. Whenever we would tease Julie, he would tease us about Sonia. It eventually worked and we stopped teasing Julie, at least about her "boyfriend". To this day, Sonia Heiselman is still occasionally in my thoughts, especially when I see someone being teased. Perhaps Dad had a crush on a girl named Sonia when he was a little boy, but where he came up with the name remains a mystery. I bet my mom wondered the same thing.

Even though our Carver Circle neighborhood had storm sewers, all the houses were on their own septic systems. I remember the backhoe being in our back yard when our septic tank needed to be replaced. It was basically new, as my parents had this house built for them before we moved in. We had storm sewers along the street. The street was not paved, but was oiled. Every year the oil truck would drive slowly down the street spreading oil, followed by the sand truck to cover the oil to keep from getting on cars, bikes and shoes. In several days it would harden like pavement and would be good for riding bikes.

Across the street from us was a steep wooded hill dropping 60 feet down to the Owens Brook at the bottom. Paul and I were exploring just below the street at the top of this hill. There was a storm sewer pipe just sticking out of the ground. In case of a big rain, the water would accumulate in the storm sewers and come blasting out of this pipe, flow down the big hill and into the creek. We were there on a nice day and were peering into the cement pipe. It was about two feet in diameter, just big enough to fit our skinny little bodies. We looked at each other and talked about how far we could crawl into the pipe on our bellies and elbows. We made some exploratory crawls in about 10 feet then backing out. Eventually we made it in about 20 feet before backing out. The backing out was much slower. We would play at this on subsequent days. Eventually I crawled all the way under the street to the storm sewer on the other side. I knew that if there was a pile of sand or something blocking the way, it would be very arduous to crawl backwards and out. Apparently, I did not have any claustrophobia and I did make it to the light coming in to the sewer junction, with a metal grate above.   Paul ran up and looked down at me at the grate and we were so happy to make it. I was happy since I could crawl straight back out fairly easily. Paul never made it all the way to the junction, since it scared him to be confined in that narrow tube, but he did crawl in pretty far. We knew that we could not tell our parents about this, since they would probably be more scared than us about their children being under the street. They knew we had been on some type of adventure, since our clothes would be filthy. Eventually they did find out when some kid climbed up our pipe to the junction and got turned around, not being sure which pipe he climbed out of. The grate had to be pulled off and he climbed out exposing our secret underground playground.

We would climb down the hill in the summer to the creek which snaked its way through the trees, wading up, chasing the minnows and seeing little trout under the cut-banks. Across the creek was an old abandoned orchid which was cool, since the apple trees were much easier to climb then the tall white pines that lined the steep hill that we climbed down. There was tall grass around the trees and it was a great place to explore as a little kid. If we waded down the creek a quarter mile, we would come to Eno's Pond. Here there would be turtles and frogs. Paul, Matt and I would walk down there with our fishing gear and fish for sunfish and the occasional bullhead. The bullhead catfish had spines on their fins so it would be tricky to get your hook out of their mouth to throw them back. One time we brought a bucket down with us and threw our catch into the bucket, about a dozen of the little sunfish. We brought them back to the house and dumped the bucket of fish into our little wading pool in the back yard. This was going to be our own personal little fish pond, not really thinking about how creepy it would be to splash around in there with the fish. The next day Matt and I went out back to check on our fish and they were all floating on the surface. After that, we always threw whatever we caught back. We were the original "catch and release" kids, well before it was cool!

In the winter, this same hill was amazing as a sledding hill, it just required some skill. We had sleds with metal runners with a T-handle in the front. You would lay on your belly, hands on the T-handles, knees bent with your boots up over your body and slid down the hill. There were so many White Pine trees that it would be like a slalom course dodging them. The good thing is since these were fairly old growth trees, the branches did not start until about 20 feet up, making sledding easier and not having to worry so much about poking your eyes out. We never wore goggles or helmets. I don't think helmets had been invented yet for kids. As we sledded down, we would build a track to follow. The track would eventually get a little icy and get much faster. If you veered off the track, the best thing would be to roll off your sled into the soft snow to stop as the sled kept on until eventually flipping or crashing into a tree. We would get really good workouts just hiking back up our track to the top. Today's kids just have plastic sleds that would never work on this type of track. Sometimes progress is really regress.

There was a girl my age, Susie, that lived down the street past the Mogers. We would play together and sometimes she would invite me in for lunch with them. The lunch was good but the best part by far was that her mom would serve Tang as a drink. In my house, mom was health-conscious and we would only have orange juice, with full pulp, as the no-pulp version had not been invented yet. I would drink this orange juice and gag as the thick pulp would go down my throat. I hated it like I hated Lima beans, but it was a daily thing with breakfast in our house. Susie was so lucky to drink the sweet, pulp-free Tang, just like the astronauts. I asked my mom for Tang and she actually did buy it once for me, but when it was gone, we were back to OJ. My parents were Democrats, I always knew this since my mom was fairly political and my parents would talk politics. I learned that Susie's parents were Republicans at lunch one day when her mom was saying something about John F Kennedy, who both my parents loved. Now Susie was pretty cute and I liked her, but I knew that we would not have a future together and could never get married, since she would be a Republican and I would be a Democrat. What could have been, if I had had an open political mind, but at the time I was a staunch Democrat of course, since I was what my parents were.

I would walk to Central School which would be just under a half mile or Beldon School, just over a half mile while we were living on Carver Circle. It seemed like every other grade; we would switch which school I was going to. At Central School, we would play 4-square mostly at recess. In second grade, my class was down in Beldon School and my teacher was Mrs. Palin who, against the school curriculum, was teaching us Spanish. I loved it and we picked up the basics of the language pretty quickly. I thought we could use it as a secret language to talk to each other and our parents would never know what we were saying. Alas, that 2nd grade class was the only time in my life that I was learning Spanish, so I never mastered it.

I remember one time, putting my head down on my desk in the middle of class and falling asleep. My friend Mary woke me up so I would not be such a slacker. It turned out that I had Mononucleosis and I had not even had the pleasure of kissing someone! I knew Mary since our parents were friends and we would visit them up in Granby and run around and play at their farm before having dinner with our families. In 3rd grade, we moved back up to the Central school.

My parents never watched the Ed Sullivan show and one day I was at school and all the kids were talking about the Beatles, who had just been on the show. I did not know what they were talking about, I had not seen the show. Eventually, the first album I ever got, several years later was Abby Road. Actually, that was the 2nd album, I really got Led Zeppelin II as my first album, but you could not sing along to it. I could sing along with almost all the songs on the Beatles album so I liked it the best. At Beldon school, we would play football and kickball outside and that is where I made friends with kids from the other classes, and a few not friends, ha-ha. In 4th grade, we were back in Beldon School. We would trade baseball cards outside, really, we were playing for baseball cards. I would compare decks and pick out a card from the other kids deck that I liked. He would pick out a card he liked. If we thought they were both the same quality player, then we would flip for them. You would flip the card to the ground and the other player would call "match" or "dismatch". If you called correctly you got to keep both cards. This game was fun but there was no skill involved, other than knowing which player was more valuable than the other. I would walk up the trail to Central school with the other kids. Often Steven, a kid who fancied himself tough, would sneak up behind me and knock my books onto the ground, sometimes the other way around. He was probably 10 pounds heavier than me, with an always red ruddy complexion. We would fight every time wrestling on the ground, trying to get each other in a head lock or get him to say uncle. We were very evenly matched and would not hesitate to wrestle each other on the way home as the other kids would give us a little berth on their way home up the hill. Afterwards, we would both pick up our books and papers off the ground and continue up the hill. Often, you became friends with the kids you fought with, but never with Steven.

Speaking of fighting. I was going to school up at Central and I got into a fight with Scott, a bigger bullet-headed kid in my class. We were actually fighting in the classroom, while the teacher and most of the class was out, just a few of us boys. We fought and wrestled each other to the ground and were banging on chairs and desks and wrestling. In hindsight, this would now be considered a "ground game" in MMA rules. We fought with the other kids looking on, breathing heavy and we were both getting tired. We finally wrestled to a draw. This is where I discovered my super-power. Govain, who was the toughest kid in school, was there watching the fight. He decided to have a little contest to see who won the fight. We were going to hold our hand out to the other kids and see whose hand was shaking the least, that would be the winner. I was out of breath, exhausted and knew with certainty that my hand would be shaking all over the place. So, Scott held out his open hand palm down towards the ground. His hand was shaking all over the place, since he was just as exhausted as me. Then came my turn. I just knew this was going to be a tie. I held out my hand and to my astonishment, my hand was completely calm, not moving a bit. I was declared the winner, but most importantly, I discovered my super-power. Keeping calm, even while I was in the middle of turmoil. Good to know. I guess it is a little true that boys tend to be friends with the kids we fight with. Scott is the boy that I ended up purchasing my paper route from a year later.

Ricky's family moved from Texas into a house down across from Paul's house. Ricky's dad built him a tree house in a large Maple behind the backyard. We would go up there and hang out since it was the closest thing to a fort that we had. We were all about 9 at the time. One day we got together up in his tree house and he had a Playboy magazine that he had "borrowed" from his dad. He pulled it out and we all went "oooh". I just did it because the other kids did. I did not know what Playboy was, but the other kids seemed to. Perhaps they were just going along like me. The only time in my life when I felt any kind of stirring down there was when I was walking through the toy department at Leaders Department store. I would be looking at the boxes of model cars and planes, the footballs, board games, and would be on toy overload and I would get a little chubby. Ricky opened the magazine and flipped through the pages until he dropped down the centerfold for us all to see. This was different. We all went crazy over this sexy topless photo of the bunny of the month. I was just feigning crazy because I did know what all the fuss was about. It was not erotic, but a curiosity to me since I don't remember ever seeing a naked woman before. Perhaps this is something that teenagers would get excited over. I had always had crushes on girls, ever since kindergarten, but I just wanted to hang out with them, wanted to perhaps put my arm around them. I would see my current crush walk into the classroom and know that she was the one I liked the best, not someone that I wanted to bone.

Sometimes in the summer, Dad would say, "Kids, get ready, quick like a bunny, we are going to Lincoln Dairy."

We would bundle into the station wagon and head up to the nearby town of Hoskins where there was an ice cream shop with the best quality and best tasting ice cream. We would all go in and get our cones and eat them back in the car. Matt and I would usually scarf ours down as fast as possible, since mom would generally only eat half her cone and offer the rest to the whichever kid in the back had already finished theirs.

Dad would also say, "Variety is the spice of life."

I don't know why this was one of his favorite sayings, since we would always go to Lincoln Dairy for ice cream. This IC parlor was right at the junction of Hopmeadow Street and the County Rd that led to the huge McLean Game Refuge. Mom would pack up a picnic basket and we would drive out to Salmon brook in the Game Refuge. We would walk through several large corn fields to a trail in the woods that would lead back to the brook. The brook flowed down rocky ledges through the trees with clear cool pools about 3 or 4 feet deep that were perfect for swimming and wading. We would have our lunch there and frolic in the water, chasing the trout and having a great time. We were always the only people out there and would have that part of the brook to ourselves. I'm super glad that this wild area is still there, unlike the wild area across from us on Carver Circle which is now developed with townhouses. It is things like this that make me a strong environmentalist.

Chris, your memory amazes me. I remember Lincoln Dairy ice cream but not the chicklets. I did not realize you had so many fights. You were tougher than I was growing up. Dad

12 Ridge Road, The early years

When I was eight, we pulled up roots and moved across town to a 2500 square foot contemporary house on Ridge Road. It was built in 1956, but was ahead of its time with a '50s style split-level open design. It had a large living room with lots of natural light coming from the wall of huge single-paned East-facing windows, an exposed wooden cathedral ceiling and a floor to ceiling fireplace. The upstairs had a balcony looking down into the living room keeping the house open. This house would have been the perfect passive solar house, if the windows faced South and it had better insulation. Despite that, I loved the sun coming into the house in the winter where I could lay in the shag carpeting in the morning sun in the living room.

I was still going to Central School after we moved, just three quarters of a mile South of school rather than North. There was still bus service but by the time I walked to the bus stop, I would be halfway to school if I had walked. There was a "marble season" at Central meaning that us kids would bring marbles to school and shoot for "keeps". I don't know how we knew when the season was, but for about a month, we all shot marbles, then not for another 6 months or so. I would take an old sock to school with a few marbles and come home with a sock full of marbles, almost every day. These marbles would be my ammo for the year.

I had a slingshot and would often go hunting squirrels in the woods with it. I used glass marbles for ammo. They would shoot straight, but did not have the mass to kill a squirrel like lead shot, but could knock one out of a tree. One time I shot at one near the house that had a crab apple in its mouth and knocked the apple out.

Mom would be amazed that I would consistently bring home a full sock of marbles, after going to school with a nearly empty sock. Remember my Super-Power, well it came in handy again shooting marbles as well. I would find a kid out on the playground and ask them to shoot. If you asked, then they got the first shot. I would toss one of my marbles five or ten feet away. After it landed the other kid would shoot his marble to try and hit mine. If he missed, then I would shoot at his (I don't remember girls playing this game). If I hit his marble, I got to keep it, and so on and so on... It was very entertaining and profitable at the same time.

When we would go clothes shopping, usually just before a new school year, I would always want camouflage colors. I was always playing in the woods, hiding from teenagers, hiding in the bushes in "the circle" if I heard people coming, so my colors were browns and greens, the most likely to blend into the natural surroundings. That all changed several years later after the Beatles influence had pervaded my young life. Those young rockers with their British style and long hair were the definition of cool. Besides wearing a "Beatles cut" haircut, longer all around with bangs to my eyebrows, my style had changed, as it had for most of the boys in my school. The cool thing to wear in 6th grade was "skin-tights", meaning pants that just hugged your legs tightly, penny loafers that never fit well on my skinny feet and a CPO (Chief Petty Officer) wool jacket. It took me quite a while to put the entire outfit together, since Mom would not just go out and pick this stuff up. The stores where we got clothes did not carry tight pants and the loafers were not practical. It seemed like an eternity before I got the entire kit together. Grandma Bidwell would tell me that wearing my hair so long down just over my eyes would make me blind someday. So far so good on the vision!

The other real fun thing was the school fair. The teachers and parents would setup games that you could play such as trying to get a ring on a peg, fishing with a magnet in a bucket and other equally entertaining games for kids. Mom would always bake a cake to donate to the cake walk, my personal favorite thing at the fair. There was no skill involved as it was like musical chairs, but the winner could choose from dozens of cakes. Usually my family would be there, but on those occasions when they were not, I would walk home through the woods, up Plank Hill Rd, then up the woods behind our house carrying the cake and whatever little trinkets I had won. We would eat the cake at home later and that was the pièce de résistance.

Sometimes Mom would take me on outings, just the two of us. One time we went out in her little Karmann Ghia on a boys/Mom-day-out. We were tooling around in Western Connecticut, no real destination in mind and Mom was excitedly talking about things she was thinking about and encouraging me with talk about how I could be anything I wanted to be, how creative I was and how much fun life could be. I was enjoying looking out the window, trying to keep my elbow on the window sill feeling cool. We passed over a good-sized brook on a bridge that had been reinforced with dark traprock to prevent erosion and pulled over on the other side. I jumped out to go rock collecting and exploring on the upstream side of the bridge and Mom said she would explore for rocks on the downstream side. I was scrambling down the rocks towards the water looking around and loving just being on a little adventure. Near the edge of the water, I spied a little bit of green and pulled out a rock, rinsing it in the water. It was clear and green and embedded in some of the road-fill basalt, brought in from a nearby quarry. I brought it back up to the car and showed it to Mom and she was ecstatic, really. She went on and on about how beautiful it was. This was the crowning glory of my little rock-collecting career and the first time an adult had ever really shown true interest in my finds. When we went home, she placed the rock on her dresser and it remained there for the rest of the time that I can remember. We identified it as prehnite, a gem mineral. Whenever we would go to museums, I would look at their display specimens of prehnite and they were never as large, clear and green as the one I found on our little day out.

I was walking with several friends and we were talking about girls. I liked girls, almost always had a crush on a girl in school, but I really knew very little about them. We were talking about what it would be like when we were married and had kids. Jimmy, who had two older sisters and knew more about sex than the rest of us was explaining exactly what we would have to do with our wife to get a baby. I did not believe it and was a little flabbergasted. One of the other kids agreed with him and provided the additional information: that you would have to do the deed every time you wanted another child. I was processing this information and thought it must be true, if it was concurred by another kid. I knew that I would want to get married, even at this young age, but thought that we just might not have any kids. That way I could enjoy being married and in love, but would not have to deal with that! As we were talking about this I began to come around and eventually thought that I would probably do it once or twice, just to have a kid or two. That was so far out in the future that I could think of this problem abstractly, not in concrete terms. I processed this information and talked about it with my friends over the course of several weeks. During one of these talks, trying to make more sense out of girls and having babies, one of my friends broke my bubble. He told me that he heard that once might not be enough to have a kid. He heard that sometimes you might have to do it hundreds of times! Hundreds of times!? Is this a cruel joke, is he trying to trick me into freaking out? I did not know.

It's funny how timing is everything. Not too much after this my dad asked me if I knew about the birds and the bees. I said that yes, I knew all about it. Really much of it was still a mystery, but I did not want to admit that and I would be way too embarrassed to discuss this sensitive topic with Dad. Dad said OK, probably as relieved as I and handed me a book on sex and reproduction. He told me to read it and we could talk about it later with any questions I had. I never did have any questions for him about the book. In hindsight, I should have handled this differently. All the little and big questions I had, I could have saved up so I could ask him when he came up to say goodnight, rather than having to think of questions at the last minute. I could have stayed up later every night having these discussions with dad, enjoying not having to go to bed immediately and I would have been the most sexually literate kid in the whole neighborhood!

I could tell what kind of day Dad was having when I would come home from playing ball, exploring in the woods, building forts in the snow or whatever. If he showed interest in me, then he had a good day and would focus energy on us and our day. It was Mom's job to ask him about his day, not ours. If he had a tough day, then he would blow us off like we were not even there. Luckily, he had mostly good days. I had been working on climbing a big oak tree down below the house overlooking Plank Hill Rd, named for the planks they would put on the road back in the day when it was muddy and the road was quite steep where it came into downtown Simsbury. The tree had tough oak bark with no branches until about 20 feet up where there was a huge forked branch that looked like the coolest place to sit. I had been working on bringing little pieces of pine boards and nailing them into the trunk with common nails from the Bidwell Company. I had to build a ladder up the trunk to the big branch, but had to be careful to put in enough nails to anchor it firmly to the trunk. I would climb the ladder many times with wood, nails and my hammer to get the tree ladder up to the branch. After a couple of days, I finally got the ladder done. I climbed to the top, scooched over to the huge thick branch and made my way out to the fork with legs on both sides of the branch. Where it forked was perfect for sitting, since the branch to the left was higher than the branch to the right, but they were still pretty close together. I settled down in my spot and was relaxing, my back resting on the upper branch, kicking up my feet and looking up through the leaves at the sky and happy with my handiwork. About then is when I heard a cracking sound and looked over to the right just as the big branch was cracking and separating from the trunk. I had not realized that this lowest branch was rotten, it was so thick and healthy looking, but my little 90-pound weight levered out towards the end of the branch was enough to make it fail. I fell backwards with the large branch as it was breaking and pulling away from the trunk. That is what saved me since it pulled the branch out from under me and I landed on the soft oak leaves flat on my back, knocking my breath out. I laid there like a carp, opening my mouth and trying to breath, but no air was coming in or out. Eventually I got a little wheezy breath, so I knew I was not going to die. Finally, I caught my breath. I laid there breathing in the beautiful air, looked over to my right and there was a bowling ball sized rock not a foot away. I looked to my left and there was a watermelon sized rock about 2 feet away. I was so glad, surprised and thankful that I had not smashed my head in, had not died and had not even got hurt. I gathered my wits and walked up to the house and walked in the back door.

Dad had just got home and I said, "Dad, I just about died!"

He replied, "That's nice Chris, now wash up for dinner."

I knew right away what kind of day Dad had at the office and we never talked about it again.

I don't know if I exaggerated much when I was a kid, or if my parents were just used to me doing crazy stuff and it did not phase them anymore. We had thick blue wall-to-wall shag carpeting in the living room like was popular in the 60's and I loved to roll around in it. I was fooling around in the living room one time and fell down on the carpet and felt a prick on my wrist. I looked and there was a little tip of a splinter sticking out. I grabbed the little tip and pulled but it did not come out. I then pulled harder and out came an entire toothpick, all red and bloody and I almost threw up. It must have been sitting upright in the carpet when I fell on it, so it drove almost all the way through my wrist. I was slightly traumatized when I found my parents and told them what had happened, thinking it would be something bad, that I would need a tetanus shot, or some type of x-ray to see if my wrist was OK. They just said, it was fine and not to worry about it. I showed them the toothpick, but they were still not concerned, perhaps they just saw the little red spot on my wrist and it looked like nothing. It eased my mind a little bit, but I was not convinced that they fully understood the seriousness of the situation. Well, parents know best and if they thought I was good, then I suppose I'm good. The only lasting effects of this is that I dislike and don't trust shag carpets or toothpicks to this day. I still think about that toothpick and always pick one up off the floor, even if it is lying flat on a floor flashing back to the little stabbing.

I was sitting in the kitchen one day with Mom and she was scolding me saying, "Christopher, you had better straighten up your act and start cleaning your room and not just stuffing stuff under your bed."

I looked at her and with a little emotion, said to her, "TS mom."

She took my sorrowful emotion to be disrespectful indignation and immediately got mad jumping up and yelling, "What did you say to me?!"

I replied "TS mom" and she got into a bit of a rage and picked up a big wooden kitchen spoon about the time I bolted out to the living room.

She was running after me chasing me around the family room and back through the kitchen before I sprinted up the half-stairs to the front door and ran outside before she could catch me. I had never seen her so mad at me and I was scared of getting a wooden spoon spanking. We yelled back and forth, I knew she was really upset, since Dad was the one that dealt out spankings in our family.

She angrily asked me "Do you know what TS means?"

I replied "Yes, Terribly Sorry."

To which she replied "Very funny, it means Tough Shit".

I was very surprised, not being familiar with that phrase and she was not consoled much, thinking I was just pulling a fast one on her to get away with being so disrespectful of her. Eventually we came to a truce but I did not go back into the house for a while until I was sure that she had put the wooden spoon down. TS Mom!

I never enjoyed going to church, Sunday school was a little better, but it took such a big chunk out of my Sunday. The Congregational church that we went to offered a Monday school that you could also attend, so that you could keep your weekends free. I signed up for that. So, every Monday after class in 5th grade, a small group of us would walk down from Central School, through all of downtown Simsbury to the church. The best part of Monday School was the walk. After school me, Steven and a couple of girls would walk downtown. We would stop at Doyle's Drug or Leaders department store or a little market across the street for gum, drinks and candy. We would talk and eat and wander towards the church. For this whole school year, we got to wander the downtown together which was always a good time. Steven and I had made our peace and were close to being friends. We would have our class in the little chapel and would sing and read bible verses and talk about Jesus. This was around the time of my epiphany about God. Apparently, this was not enough to strengthen my faith.

This was also the church where Mr. George Weston was the associate pastor and lived in the parish house with his wife Ann. They were good couple friends with my parents and had three daughters, Lissie who was Matt's age, Laurie who was Julie's age and Meredith who was Jerry's age. Our families would get together quite a bit. Lissie was the tomboy and would try to hang with Matt and I. Inevitably she would get hurt, but she never ever gave up. That girl has grit. We were jumping off the old tool shed one summer. We would climb up the back-side and jump off the front onto a pile of sand that my dad had dumped there for a sandbox that was not built yet. When Lissie tried it, at the last second, she dropped onto her butt before jumping and got about a million splinters from the old wooden roof. She limped into the house and her mom spent a half hour pulling all the splinters out with tweezers. Mom and Ann were the best of friends and would laugh and talk and have the best time together. Us kids were free to do pretty much anything we wanted.

I bought a wooden go-cart off of the Yankee Flyer. It had a flat seat and a covered space in front for your feet. The wheels in front were on the ends of a 2x4 with a rope attached to each end that went inside the covered area so you could steer by holding a rope in each hand. It was a bit tricky to hold it steady and on course. When we were getting the hang of it, you could put your feet down on the road between the seat and the foot well to drag the soles of your sneakers as brakes although the idea was not to ever do that for the maximum speed and a fun ride. Well Lissie, Matt and I pushed it to the big hill that led down from the top of Ridge Rd. You could gain some serious speed and really get a thrill riding it. Matt and I did a couple of rides and Lissie wanted to try her hand at it. With a little bit of trepidation, we literally gave her the reigns to the go-cart. She got on the cart, feet on the ground, grabbed the steering ropes, lifted her feet and started off down the hill. About halfway down, just as she was getting some serious speed, she panicked and jammed her feet down, like slamming on the brakes to slow down. Her feet immediately got pulled under the low seat of the cart and her ankles were dragging on the pavement as she careened off the street into the trees crashing into a large bush. We took her limping and bleeding from her ankles, back to the house so her mom could bandage her up. She was probably the only girl that went on our adventures. Getting hurt on an adventure is called an epic, and I have had plenty of them myself, so Lissie should hold her head high.

We had a utility room that we called the "dark room" since the family that had the house before us used it for developing camera film. It had no windows and was completely dark when the door was closed, and the back of the room behind the furnace and water heater was a little scary. There was a long workbench on the back wall and I used it for my chemistry kit. At the time I had decided that I wanted to be a chemist when I grew up, working in a chemistry lab inventing cool stuff like my friend Jerry, who's dad had invented Loctite adhesive. That stuff was what kept Harley-Davidson motorcycles from falling apart and becoming more reliable among other things.

This was after my phase of wanting to be an Airforce pilot when I would spend many evenings putting together model airplanes, my favorite being the X-15 which was a cross between a rocket and a jet.

This was before my phase of wanting to be an oceanographer where every evening around dinnertime I would argue with my dad who wanted me to set the dinner table when my favorite TV show Sea Hunt with Lloyd Bridges was on. He was a professional scuba diver in the show and I was convinced that watching this show was like training for my future career.

Anyway, I would do experiments like making gunpowder which is equal parts potassium nitrate (saltpeter), sulfur and charcoal where the saltpeter was the oxidizer and the other two are the fuel. The problem was that my chemistry kit did not have any potassium nitrate, so I had to substitute sodium nitrate. I combined these ingredients into a mixture that I hoped would be similar to gunpowder. I was not sure how explosive this mixture would be so I dropped a match into it as I ducked down under the counter. Nothing. I did it several more times but nothing happened. I had some strips of magnesium in the kit and knew that it would burn very bright and hot when held in a flame long enough to catch on fire. I took some of the chemistry tongs, lit the magnesium strip in a match flame and when it caught fire and was burning impressively bright, I dropped it into the mixture ducking under the counter. The dish with the mixture went WHOOSH and proofed up in smoke and flame and was out. Not exactly an explosion, but still pretty impressive. I had invented something that was worthless, but it was not discouraging to an aspiring young chemist.

Most nights, after dinner my parents would watch the CBS Evening News with Walter Cronkite. He sounded like the voice of authority, if Walter said it, it must be true. There was no chit-chat or idle banter between the news anchors, just a straight shot of the news, in a very serious delivery. I was not too much into the news with the images of helicopter crashes in Vietnam and stories of national importance that I had no interest in. There was another show however that I really liked called the 21st Century with Walter Cronkite. It was all about how cool the future would be with automated houses, working from home, flying cars, computers and other stuff that I would get excited about. The only problem was that I would be 44 years old when this next century started. Forty-four years old! I would have one foot in the grave, I would be over the hill, I would be old and in the way, my time would be past! I went into the bathroom to figure out how bad 44 would be. I stood in front of the mirror and scrunched up my face as hard as I could making it all wrinkled up. Aaaargh! I was going to be so old! Why can't the future get here sooner? I would just have to be content with the present, since this would be too far off in the future to enjoy. This is actually a good philosophy, living in the moment. Rather than waiting for things to get good in the future, live your life right now! This is still the way that I enjoy my life, but part of it might be that I'm very lucky to be living in the 21st century!

One time Matt and I were lying on the floor upstairs and looking at maps in an atlas of the United States. We were trying to decide where we wanted to live when we were grown up. We both knew that it would be out West somewhere so that is where we concentrated our search before settling on either Wyoming or Colorado. We marked the map with little 'X' marks where our houses would be, both high up in the mountains of each state. It must have stuck in the back of our little brains since we both ended up there. I wonder if that is part of the reason that I knew from an early age that I did not want to follow in Dad's footsteps as the president of the Bidwell Hardware Company. Probably that and the fact that working there was not Dad's true dream job either and he did not want me, being the oldest, to be burdened with the expectation of having my life career planned out for me. I was free to have the world as my oyster for places to live, carriers to dream about, and girls to meet.

A week before Thanksgiving, I was with Paul from my old neighborhood and he was talking about a turkey shoot that he had heard about. We discussed it and wondered if they would allow twelve-year old's to participate, especially since neither of our parents had any guns. We decided to just go and find out for ourselves. On the day of the shoot, we rode our bikes past downtown, across the Farmington River and up to the base of Talcott Mountain where the State Police had their firing range. We watched a couple of rounds to see what it was all about. They would put a target about 40 yards away which was just a square of paper with an X in the center. Whoever got a pellet closest to the X would win the round. There were a dozen hunters per round. The winner would get a live pheasant. We walked up to the table where you signed up. The table was where all the hunters would place their shotguns when they were not shooting. We asked if we could shoot, the guy at the table was all enthusiastic and said that not only could we shoot, but we could use one of their guns as well. We paid our dollar for a round and Paul and I each picked out a gun. Paul and I had no gun safety training at all, although Paul had a pump action pellet gun that we would practice with so we were not total neophytes. My idea was that the bigger the gun, the more likely it would be to get a pellet close to the target, since there would be more pellets. I chose a sweet looking side-by-side 12 gauge and Paul did the same. When our group was called to shoot, we walked up with the other 10 hunters and each took a single shot at our target. When my turn came, I held up that heavy gun, pulled the stock hard into my shoulder as the guy at the bench had suggested, lined up the sights on the little X, exhaled until I was steady on the target and squeezed the trigger. After we had all shot, they collected the 12 little targets to see who had won. I won! My Super-Power had come in handy once again. Paul was a little upset that he did not win anything since it was his idea but such is competition. They gave me a coupon to go to a farm nearby and pickup my live pheasant. Dad drove us all out to the farm and I got a beautiful Ring-necked Pheasant. We took it home and let it free in the closed garage. It was really a magnificent bird. The idea was that the next weekend, you would bring your pheasant back to the shooting range. They would release the bird up into the air and you would then shoot it like shooting skeet. I could not bear to shoot the bird, so we eventually just opened the garage door and watched it hop and flap out into the woods behind our house.

All was not lost however. Paul and I went back the next year and luckily, I won that year as well. I had hit the bullseye directly in the center with one of the little shotgun pellets as had another hunter in our group. We had a shoot-off and I won that as well, winning a coupon for a frozen turkey at the Finast Supermarket in Simsbury. Mom and I went to the grocery store a few days later and chose our turkey. I was very happy and proud of myself for providing the turkey for Thanksgiving dinner that year.

Between Benjamin Bunny, Raggylug, Peter Cottontail and Bugs Bunny, I have always loved bunnies. Granted I would go out hunting squirrels with my slingshot, but I never went out looking to hunt for a rabbit. Until… Paul came over to hang out and brought his pump-action pellet gun. We had used it for target practice behind his house and it was fun to handle a rifle, rather than a slingshot which was my usual hunting weapon. We headed down into the 100-acre woods to go exploring and target shooting away from the house, perhaps try shooting at frogs in the swamp. As we were entering the swamp, we spotted a cottontail on the bank over by some pine trees. It was perhaps 150 feet away, so Paul decided to shoot at it. He took aim and hit it dead center, knocking it down. We were both surprised and a little shocked as we were pretty sure that we could not hit it being so far away. We walked around to see what we had killed and it was a perfect little rabbit. Perfectly dead.

We both kneeled looking at the rabbit and we both felt bad about killing it. It was such a waste and we could not take back what we had done. We had to make the rabbit's death mean something. Our little 12-year-old selves were discussing it and we decided that we would eat it. I was reluctant to take it back home and hand mom a dead bloody rabbit and ask her to prepare it for a nice family dinner. I did not know how she would react. She did not like guns and I did not know how she would think about a freshly killed rabbit, especially since it was killed by a gun and she would have to skin it, pull out the guts and cook it.

OK plan B, we would cook it ourselves. We took the rabbit away from the trees a bit, gathered some rocks and snapped the lower dead branches off of the white pine trees. Even at that young age, I carried a little white folding pocket knife from the Bidwell Hardware Company and a book of matches in case I got lost in the woods, and we were in the woods. With a bit of trepidation, I cut into the belly of the rabbit and worked to get the pelt off, like I was one of those French trappers that I had read so much about. It was messy work, trying to hold onto the slippery knife and cut up the belly. We took turns cutting the head off the rabbit since the knife was not serrated and it was slow going. Eventually we got the head off and peeled back the skin to the tail and pulled the pelt off, me holding it and Paul holding the bloody body of the rabbit and playing a little game of tug-of-war. We fell back as the pelt ripped free of the body. I reached into the body cavity, grabbing the guts of the rabbit and pulled them out like I was cleaning a fish, just that this was a rabbitfish. We threw the guts and head into the swamp where the turtles could eat it. We started a fire in our little fire ring and when it was going pretty well, then took turns cooking the rabbit like we were roasting marshmallows on a thick stick. We did not know about waiting for the fire to create coals for a nice even heat, but it took so long with our primitive cooking technique that towards the end we did have a better cooking fire. Eventually it was browned and pretty blackened on the outside since we wanted to be sure to kill any rabbit disease that could make us sick. Paul sat cross-legged on the ground and I sat on a rock and we took turns pulling off little stripes of meat and eating it. Just tiny little tentative bites to get a taste of the rabbit, and see how stringy and chewy it was. We ended up eating quite a bit of the poor little bunny, tiny bites at a time until we had had enough that we could consider we had killed it for food, and not just for sport.

We put the rest of the rabbit on the fading coals of the fire and headed back up to the house, Paul with his gun and me with the rabbit pelt. We must have made quite a sight, two bloody boys with a gun and a pelt, but no-one ever saw us. We hosed off in the back of the house and I stashed the pelt in the tool shed. Paul headed home on his bike with his gun over his shoulder and I went back into the tool shed. I stretched the pelt onto a board with the fur side down and nailed the edges to the piece of wood. I then used some of mom's salt and poured it all over the pelt to dry it out. I did not know how to cure a pelt, and this is not the way to do it. After a week, the pelt was dried out, but it would crinkle like parchment paper when it was picked up, not soft and supple like a pelt should be. If you laid it down and ran your hand across the fur, it felt good, it just was not quite perfect.

I never did kill another rabbit after that. It always seemed to me, just shooting an animal would be the hard part of the hunt. I now realized that the real work actually happens after you have killed your prey. I also discovered that I have an affinity for bunnies and would not be killing them again. I would rather read about them by an excellent naturalist author like Earnest Seaton Thompson who would make them real, like little kids having their own adventures.

Paul and I would hang out, mostly building and racing each other on our mini-bikes at a new development behind his house where we used to play in the abandoned orchard. They were preparing for a large townhouse development down there, but all they had built for a year or two were the roads. These roads had no traffic and we would ride around them on our bikes, tuning them and adjusting them to be as fast as possible. We even took my wooden go cart and bolted an engine to the seat next to where we sat and tooled around on that. We slowly grew apart and I had a new best friend, Jerry who lived down off of Hopmeadow Street right next to Beldon School. Jerry and I mostly rode bikes around town. He had a sweet banana bike and I would ride my "basket bike" from my paper route. I would visit his house for lunch sometimes when we were cruising around town. His older brother had Coca-Cola signs and paraphernalia all over his bedroom and his mom would always serve Coke to us with sandwiches. We never had any type of soda at my house so when I drank the Coke, it would make me burp up my nose and it would burn like hell. I never got used to it, I liked the sweetness and fizz, but the burps were too much for me. When we started 6th grade, Jerry and I were in the same class together, but were assigned to seats halfway across the room from each other. Whenever we would glance in each other's direction, we would start giggling and could not stop. Eventually Mr. Burbank separated us by putting Jerry into a separate classroom.

Jerry's dad worked for Pratt & Whitney Aircraft. After 6th grade, his dad was transferred to Palm Beach Gardens Florida and the family moved away. That summer, when I was still 12, my parents bought me a plane ticket to fly down to visit Jerry and his family down in Florida. It was my first time away from home by myself (except summer camp) and I was excited to be on a trip totally by myself, fly in a jetliner, see Florida and hang with my friend Jerry. The flight was fun. He and his parents picked me up at the airport. They had a cool ranch house with a screened in swimming pool separated with a wall of sliding glass doors that could be pulled to the side, making the pool area just another big open area in the house. We could play in the pool all day and catch all the little lizards crawling on the screens. Jerry's Mom dropped us off at the inland waterway with his Florida Skiff, which is a tough fiberglass skiff with a 9.5 hp outboard motor on the back. We pulled each other all around on skim boards behind the skiff. At one point I was behind the skiff in about 3 feet of water and the bottom was just teeming with sting rays. If I fell off the board, I would have to float on my back to keep from standing on the bottom, but we made it through. At one point I got mad at Jerry for padlocking my belt loop to a wire garden fence when we were out in the yard screwing around. We would do this stuff to each other all the time, but this time it bugged me. I realized when I ripped off my loop to free myself that this was the first time I had ever experienced homesickness. I felt much better afterwards knowing what was wrong with me and that was the only rough patch. We would go to the beach spending hours skim-boarding in the backwash from the surf. I really liked Florida!

Another time his parents dropped us off on a boat launch in a lush river that was emptying a mangrove swamp into the ocean a mile or two away. We tooled up into the swamp exploring the big roots sticking out of the water and looking for Alligators. We never saw any. We then turned around and tooled back down towards the boat launch and pulled out. We walked down to a highway bridge going over the river and walked out to the middle and sat on the rail, looking down into the water way down below, probably

20 or 25 feet, but it was pretty far for a couple of twelve-year-olds. As we were looking down building up our nerve, Jerry jumped, I jumped while he was still in the air. The river was pretty big, so I knew it would be pretty deep as well, but when we hit, my feet hit the hard clay bottom about 8' down and I ended up squatting on the bottom to take up the force of the fall. Jerry popped up and a moment later I popped up as well, surprising Jerry who did not know I had jumped. We swam the hundred feet or so to the muddy bank. As we got close to the bank, we saw that it was just covered with crabs everywhere. We brushed the crabs aside with our hands while climbing the bank on our hands and knees, getting covered in mud by the time we got back up to the road. We must have been a sight later when Jerry's mom came back to pick us up.

It was with a mixture of sadness and excitement when I flew back home when the week was up. I had a couple of pictures in my Instamatic, but mostly just memories.

I did see Jerry after that visit when a friend Tucker and I took his Z28 Camaro down to Florida on Spring break from College at FDU. We never discussed exactly what we would do when we got there. It turns out all that Tucker wanted to do was to go to Disneyland, and other tourist attractions and I just wanted to spend the time at the beach with other kids and probably lots of girls. We got into a big fight, just yelling at each other and decided to split ways. I called Jerry who was home on his spring break and he invited me to stay with his parents again. Jerry and I spent most of the week at the beach swimming and hanging out. We would walk up to the swimming pools from the big hotels to swim and use their diving boards. No one ever escorted us out or even looked at us like we did not belong there. It was a great break. Tucker and I reconnected for the ride back up to school but we were no longer friends, so we listened to lots of music. I had reconnected with Jerry, but it was the last time I ever saw him.

There was a family that were friends of my parents since my mom went to Oberlin with Joy, the wife. They lived at the bottom of the hill on Ridge Rd. They had two kids, Jed who was Matt's age and Kim who was a year older than I. Kim was a tall, good-looking girl and by far the fastest runner in the whole neighborhood. Jed mostly hung out with Matt. I was standing in their driveway one day and there was a crow sitting at the top of a tree not too far away. I put a cat's eye marble into the leather pouch of my wrist rocket, took careful aim and shot at the bird. Simsbury had a bounty on crows and if you shot one, they would pay you. I liked crows, and sometimes like this, the bird was so far away that I was pretty sure I could never hit it, but I wanted to see how close I could get. The shot was right on target for a clean hit. The crow had been eyeing me and he saw that marble in flight heading towards him. I remember watching with amazement and relief when the crow squawked and jumped up with its wings as the marble whizzed past right where he had been perched just a second prior. That bird not only had amazing eye sight, but could accurately compute the trajectory and time it would take to hit him to leap out of the way. I think they had evolved that way so they could be eating a critter on the ground and be able to stay to the last possible moment when a hawk was bearing down or a fox was running towards them. That was the last time I ever shot at a bird, since God or my blind good luck had prevented me from killing it and I wanted to stay ahead of the game. We were at their house playing a water balloon war on our bikes. We would ride bikes and would throw balloons at each other. I was in the garage on my bike while a couple of neighbor kids waited outside with balloons waiting to attack us. I circled around in the garage a couple of times to build up a little speed and sprinted out of the garage as hard as I could. At the same time Jed yanked on the garage door rope to pull the door shut. The edge of the door hit me right at my hairline and knocked me head over heels backwards off my bike and onto the pavement. I got up and all I wanted to do was stagger the couple of feet to the grass and take a nap. That was the closest I ever came to passing out (if you discount the time after Corrine was born and I got a vasectomy, but that is another story). I had my hand on my head and when I pulled it away, it was covered in blood going down my forearm and dripping off my elbow. That totally shocked me out of my fainting slumber. We went into Jed's bathroom and Matt took a look at my head. He was looking at the gash on my head, thinking he was looking at my brains. I asked him how bad it was and he said we better get a grown-up to take a look at it. All of our parents were gone out somewhere, so we walked down to the bottom of road where the Smiths lived. Mr. Smith was Scottish and had a strong accent. They were friends of my parents also. Mr. Smith took me to the little medical clinic across from Henry James Jr High school where the doctor gave me 22 stitches. I had always hated needles and would cry bloody murder, fighting to get away when my parents would take me in for a doctor checkup and I found out that I was going to get a shot. Just the thought of that long needle slowly puncturing my skin, then sliding through my muscle tissue was way too much for me to endure. This time was different. I knew that I was hurt and I knew it would be better when he finished stitching me up. I was basically resigned to my fate. The other factor was that I could throw a fit in front of my parents, but I was reluctant to do so with Mr. Smith and this strange doctor. I was lucky that the scar was basically hidden at my hairline, but a dozen years later I had a blaze of white in my otherwise dark head of hair, most likely from the loss of blood in this area weakening the hair follicles there.

You were quite the marksman, with the crows and the turkey shoot. Great memories of your friends. You are cooking! Dad
PS Mom. No wonder Jane chased you with a big spoon!

13 Lloyd Joseph

In the summer after 5th grade, my parents arranged for a kid my age to come spend part of the summer with me.

Lloyd Joseph was from Harlem; it was a little awkward at first as I was showing him around. He had never been around dogs much and was scared of Rodnick, but he got over that in the first week. At first, we wandered around and met the neighborhood kids and got a pickup game of baseball started. Where we lived, there were no Black people around so none of the kids had any preconceived notions about race and everyone accepted Lloyd as just another friend. Lloyd was just as accepting of my friends as well. My parents integrated the neighborhood, at least for the summer.

Sports is always a good way to hang out, having a good time and getting to know each other, plus we could use more kids on our teams. We played ball quite a bit and Lloyd got to know my friends around the neighborhood. We would go exploring in the woods behind the house, catching frogs, turtles and snakes in the swamp, climbing trees, hunting squirrels and just running around outside.

My parents had joined a beach club up in New Hartford and we would go up there and go canoeing and swimming. The lake only had a beach at the club, the rest of the lake was just a cut-bank with lots of trees. We would paddle around the lake looking for beavers and turtles and diving with our masks from the canoe.

Lloyd and I were the same size and both very skinny. We would compare our chests to see who could count the most ribs and it was always a tie. There was a cool A-frame beach house where you could get drinks and food right on the beach. We would go upstairs to the tiny room and play Foosball and hang out like it was our fort. On the way home, my parents would stop at a diner that we liked for burgers and fries, but I always got a scrambled egg sandwich, since I loved them there. It was like having a twin brother and we were never bored.

The winter after he had stayed with us, our family drove down into New York City and we met Lloyd and his mom. I had been in the city before when dad took me in to see a Yankee's game where I got a ball cap which I wore for most of my childhood. We had to cross the street to get over to the cafe where we were meeting the Josephs. I told my dad I would run ahead and do the crosswalk light. I ran down to the crosswalk pole, stepped up on the base of the pole, reaching up to pull the crosswalk lever and jumping back down all proud of myself.

My Dad walked up quickly and pushed the crosswalk button looking down at me and saying, "You just pulled the fire alarm!"

I was mortified! So much for being a city slicker. We walked across the street to the café, meeting Lloyd and his mom. As we were sitting down for lunch, a firetruck pulled up across the street with lights on. We never said anything to the Josephs, not wanting to seem like a bunch of country bumpkin yahoos. It would have been fun to hang out with just Lloyd for a while and see his neighborhood and meet his friends and really connect again.

Lloyd came out the next summer as well. We just picked up where we left off a year ago, just buddies sharing everything. One time we were standing up at the balcony in our house overlooking the living room. I was showing Lloyd how to make a zirk. I took a chunk of plastic from some packing material and we lit it on fire leaning over the balcony. The plastic would burn until it started dripping burning plastic making a 'zirk' sound all the way down. To protect the tile, we put newspapers on the floor which was a mistake because the burning plastic of course started a paper fire. Lloyd and I panicked and ran downstairs kicking the paper together and stamping it out. The whole house smelled like burning plastic and burning paper and there was ash everywhere. We gave ourselves a bit of a scare.

Lloyd and I were in the "dark room" and were playing with the chemistry kit. We found a formula for making lots of thick dark smoke from testing a little batch. We decided to make a larger batch and fill the entire dark room with smoke, then when we could not take it any longer, we would open the door and walk out trailing smoke like it was nothing, just to freak out my parents.

When we had the room completely smoke-filled, we opened the door and walked out nonchalantly together towards the kitchen with the smoke billowing out behind us when mom and dad both yelled out, "What on earth are you boys doing?"

We replied, "Just doing some experiments, but we wanted to get something to drink.", like we were serious chemists on our way to developing important new substances.

In hindsight we should have been working on a better formula for zork.

We were never pen pals and I had no way to get a hold of him and I never saw him again after my 6th grade summer. Perhaps it is just that I was 12 and living in the moment all the time and did not have the skills to maintain contact. Aside from the kids I played sports with at Westledge and Tracy, a girlfriend, I've not really had any black best friends since then. The people that you rub elbows with in your day-to-day activities are the people that become your friends. It would be weird to go out just to make a friend that was black, friends just happen, although that is what happened when I was 12.

These are great memories of your days with Lloyd Joseph. You are really saving the family memory. Thanks Dad

14 Ridge Road - Dogs, Westledge, phys ed

Matt and I were at home on summer vacation and decided to go up to the orchards about a mile west of our house. We took my bike and pushed it down the trail to Ray's Barbershop. I got on the bike and Matt climbed into my baskets. They were heavy duty that you could sit on with a leg in each basket. We peddled out Great Pond Rd and got off to push the bike up the hill that led into the orchard. There was a house near the bottom of the hill with a big lawn that reached out to the street. They had a mean German Shepard that would run out and had bitten me on the calf before. We did not see the dog on the way up the street, but he was usually outside. At the top of the hill, we rode a bit more to where there were some trees hanging a bit over the old stone wall by the road. We pulled the bike off to the side, climbed over the stone wall and picked a couple of red delicious apples. There was a cider house on the other side of the orchard that we would go to with our parents occasionally to get apple juice and the really tart cider. You could also pet and feed the goats that lived there. We were just in the "back 40" where it was always quiet. After wandering around the trees for a while, we decided to head back. I was pretty sure the German Shepard would be outside, we just lucked out coming here that the dog was not around. Matt and I discussed the dog and we decided we needed some defense for the cruise down the hill. We selected a rock about the size of a cantaloupe that Matt could handle easily in the baskets and headed off on the bike. We picked up pretty good speed coasting down the hill but the dog could hear the clicking of the gears and came sprinting across the lawn towards us as we approached the house. He ran out onto the street as we were coasting by and was running alongside, attempting to nip at us. Matt dropped the rock squarely on the dog's head knocking his chin down and skidding onto the asphalt. We kept going and I peddled fast as the hill let up, but the dog had had enough. We were high on our racing adrenaline all the rest of the way home.

I had been bitten another time delivering papers down on Plank Hill Road. I was near the end of my route coming towards the Vincent's house. The house had impressive white pillars in the front, showing off how well they were doing from the proceeds of their funeral parlor downtown. There were Vincents all around town, and on summer days, Jerry and I would visit Mark and play in the pool in the backyard of his house several blocks away. The Vincents on my route had a blue-tick hound chained up in the backyard all the time. This had made the dog mean and on this particular day he had broken his leash and came running around the side of the house, jumped up and gave me a nice nip on the knee. I skipped delivering to them that day and finished my route. I could see a little blood where he had ripped open a hole in my jeans. It was just an accepted part of being a kid in those days. I mentioned it to my dad when I got back. He chalked it up to bad luck that the dog broke its leash. No one had fences anywhere in our neighborhood and a lot of the neighbors had dogs, but we knew them all and they were mostly friendly. We never put Rodnick on a leash and he was a big German Shepard, but was only aggressive to other dogs that happened to wander into our yard.

One time two large Black Labs were walking through the trees in front of our house when Rodnick bolted after them growling with the hair on his back standing up. I was certain there would be a big dog fight but when those labs spotted Rodnick coming, they turned tail and ran off. Rodnick was a good dog. He finally succumbed to the bane of German Shepherds, hip dysplasia. He gradually lost the use of his back legs until my parents eventually had to send him to "The Farm". We were cat people after that, at least until we moved to Hartford.

In Jr. High, we started taking Phys Ed doing basketball and flag football with wrestling in the winter. The school suppled us with shorts and a tee shirt since we would be doing sweaty exercise-type stuff which to me was funny since I had been doing recess twice a day in elementary school and we played all these games, even wrestling in the dirt and got sweaty, but they never cared about that. Well at the end of class one day, a bunch of us boys were in the big tiled shower room and were all taking hot showers when one of us sat down and slid on his butt toward the drain. It looked cool so we all soaped up our bodies and the next thing you knew, we were sliding across the floor from one side of the room to the other. We would put our feet up on the tiled wall and push off and slide all the way across the floor to the other side. We had just made up our own sport, soapy-butt-sliding. Well, the Phys Ed teacher heard an unusual amount of yelling and laughing and came out of his office to investigate and found a dozen boys all zinging back and forth in the steamy shower room having far more fun than we ever had in his organized games.

The next thing we knew we heard him bellowing, "What on earth do you think you are doing? I should call all your parents. Don't you know that you could all get athletes ass!"

We did not know if he was kidding or not, but our fun was over and we never did it again. In retrospect, that is the awesome thing about being a kid. A group of grown men would not see the potential of a good time in a shower room sliding, laughing, yelling and having a good time. Adults would act like adults, but sometimes you just need to let the inner child out to really express yourself.

One of the cool things about my high school Westledge, is that we were free to wander the woods between classes. It was a very wild area, in fact the last half mile of school property bordered on the McLean Game refuge that stretched for miles and miles more. I loved the woods and would often grab my club, which was a root-ball with a 5-foot trunk just big enough to easily carry with one hand. A boy cannot go out exploring without a weapon. I would go exploring up the creek, climb around the cliffs to the top of the ridge and just be one with the world. Often, I would hike with friends, we would roll rocks off the top of the ridge and over the cliffs. When I was by myself it was always much more peaceful.

There was a reservoir down behind the school to the West that was a drinking supply for the town of Simsbury. I was exploring down there with my friend Mike. Mike and I had been friends years before when our parents had sent us to Science Academy. We would do lab experiments, go on field trips, play soccer and learn about all things Science, mostly about the natural world. We would catch and mount butterflies and beetles. Mike was a tough kid whose dad was a marine and had Mike workout with weights ever since he was little, even before I started lifting. I became friends with Mike when he would drink chocolate milk from the machine. I had never had it before and tried Mike's, then got one of my own and we were friends from then on. At the time I really wanted to be a scientist studying things in a lab which is probably why I liked chemistry so much at the time. It just happened that we both ended up at Westledge years later. I suppose that the type of parents that would send their kid to Science Academy are the type that would also send their kids to Westledge which is probably why we were back together.

Mike and I passed the No Trespassing signs, waded across the top of the dam and went exploring across the shore on the far side. There was a very steep bank leading down to the water. Eventually, several hundred yards up from the dam was a huge Ash tree, growing about 30 feet back up the bank from the edge of the water. It had a nice large branch hanging out towards the water with a rope dangling down. The rope was quite thick around, like something you would use to tie a yacht up to a dock. On the end was a large frayed knot. Apparently, some of the local West Simsbury kids would hang out here as well. We grabbed the frayed rope end and carried it up to the trunk of the tree. We were a good 15-20 feet up from the water at the obvious launch point. There was a second smaller knot about 7 feet above the large knot at the bottom.

Mike and I looked at each other with the thought, "What do you think?".

I knew what I thought and took the rope with my right hand and had my left just above the upper knot and jumped. I grabbed above the upper knot with both hands, squeezed the lower knot with my thighs and swung down rapidly towards the water, then swung back up in an exhilarating arc and back to the launch point where I jumped off and Mike grabbed the rope. Then he gave it a try. We loved it and swung there for another half hour before heading back to school.

After we had crossed the dam and were walking past the little water supply building a truck pulled up into the little parking lot.

A guard jumped out and yelled, "Hey, you kids! Stop right there!".

Well stop we did not. Mike and I sprinted off up the trail towards the creek that ran into the reservoir. We did not want to run straight East toward school, then the guard would know where we had come from. We ran like the wind all the way up the creek a bit before heading uphill to the other trail that led from the school to the game preserve, doubling back to school.

I had used tie wire when working on the mini-bikes and go carts and knew how useful it was. Mike and I went back swinging often during the Fall. On one of our excursions, we tied some wire about 10" off the ground from one small tree to another across the trail in several places from the dam parking lot up towards the head of the reservoir. Our thinking is that if we were having fun swinging way out across the water and a guard was waiting for us back at the parking lot, we could sprint back up the trail. If the guard was fast, we would skip over the wires and the guard, not knowing about the wire would trip and not ever catch up with us. I know we got chased at least one other time and we were never caught.

Later, in the winter, Mike and I were talking about the swing and Steve wanted to check it out. When we all had a good break between classes, we took Steve down there. It was snowy out and we tromped down there in our boots, gloves and jackets, across the dam that had hardly any water flowing across and up to the tree. We slipped and slid up the bank with the rope in the snow to the launching point. The reservoir was frozen over, except a foot or two along the bank. We took off our gloves and Mike and I each did a swing out over the water, hanging onto the icy upper knot. It was even more exciting going out over the ice. It was Steve's turn, he grabbed the rope like we had, stood there for a while thinking about it and jumped up, grabbing the knot and swung out over the water. About halfway up the arc on his swing out, his hands slid off the knot. Mike and I looked in horror as he careened down and hit the ice flat on his back, bouncing off the ice and sliding another 15 feet past where he hit, which was now just broken up ice. Steve just laid there and moaned. Mike and I both yelled to him to get on his stomach and crawl towards shore where we were. Instead, Steve slowly just got up and walked towards us like a zombie around the open water where he hit. We could hear the ice cracking and making noise all around him and we expected him to fall through at any moment and possibly drown. When he got closer to shore, he did break through. Mike and I waded out as Steve was flailing towards the bank and we managed to grab him and pull him to safety. Steve was in shock, he was soaking wet, cold and getting hypothermic. We each grabbed an arm on both side of him and managed to walk him back to the dam, across the dam and up towards the trail. We were all three exhausted at this point.

We heard, "Hey, you kids, stop right there!".

I knew that we were caught, Mike and I were worn out from carrying Steve. Steve was obviously in shock and could not run, or so I thought. Steve just bolted up the trail like a rabbit. We followed him up the trail, expecting to be caught at any moment but the guard gave up the chase fairly soon. We followed our tracks back up to the sports fields and went into the Athletic building. The three of us pulled off our wet clothes, putting them in the large industrial dryer and hung out talking about our near disaster. We had had quite a scare, all three of us thinking Steve could have died. We missed a class or two waiting for our clothes to dry. We were never caught, either by the guards or by anyone at school. At one of our school assemblies a week or two later, it was announced that we should stay away from the reservoir since kids had been spotted down there. No blame was directly laid on our school however. After that day, I don't think the three of us ever talked about our epic adventure. It was not really a bonding experience like you would think, but we did continue to hang out, play sports together and remain friends.

Mike would talk about wanting to go to Vietnam and fight. We would talk to him about what a bad idea that was, how war was not this romantic idea of some grand adventure, but would be a scary time that could warp your mind forever, definitely away from anything good. On the evening news, Walter Cronkite would be talking over images of soldiers pushing through the jungle and wading through rice paddies, carrying M-16s with green helicopters flying overhead. It just looked like a good place to die. When I was 12, the whole war seemed very abstract and far away, but at 17 it seemed very real and close. We all had draft cards and the draft did end when we were 17, several years before the war actually ended, just a year before any of our numbers could have come up. Mike never did have to go there and a weight was lifted off all our minds.

On Halloween evening when I was 15, I was waiting for my friends to come to the house and pick me up. They were late and I decided that they had blown me off, so I just headed out on foot down Ridge Rd. I don't know what we were going to do, but on my way out of the house I grabbed a couple of eggs and put them in my pocket. I was walking down the street, down the steep hill and was heading towards Beldenwood Road when I spotted a car coming. I was watching the car and playing with the egg in my right pocket. I could see that there were three or 4 people in the car. On impulse as the car was driving by, I threw the egg at the car. Well the egg was right on target to hit the passenger side rear window only it turns out that that window was rolled down. The egg flew through the window and hit the large person in the back seat squarely in the head, splatting egg through the rest of the car. Well, the car slammed on its brakes and 3 teenagers jumped out, looking for blood. I immediately turned and ran into the dark woods, my safe haven. They chased me into the woods and I ran in as far as I could. I could hear them searching for me and yelling at each other as I was hiding behind the trunk of a large pine tree. They searched for a while as my heart was pounding before they gave up and headed back up the road. I stayed in the woods for a while, before heading home, having had more of an adventure already than I had planned for.

The next day, at lunch I was sitting outside with my friends talking and I was a little pissed that they had forgotten about me.

Mac said, "We were running late, so I took my parents car instead of my little VV bug since there would be 5 of us."

Jody piped up and said, "We were heading up to your house and were on your street in fact when some asshole threw an egg that hit me in the side of the head."

I could not contain my emotions, laughing a bit and the cat was out of the bag. Jody was one of the bigger kids in school and he jumped up, pulled me out of my chair and was pushing me back towards the windows into the cafeteria.

I had been taking a really fun class in school called hand-to-hand combat by a teacher that was a Vietnam vet fairly fresh from his deployment. He taught us the stuff that he learned in the army about fighting, blocking punches and a lot of Judo. In fact, we would put on demonstrations during the school assemblies of our skills. A lot of it comprised of running to a six-foot-high pile of hassocks, stepping onto a block and jumping over the hassock head first, doing a tuck and roll while slamming your palms onto the mat while rolling to help cushion the blow. I remember him telling us that when someone punches you in the face, your instinct is to immediately quit the fight, but a grown man can take three hard punches to the face before going down. I'm glad I never had to test this theory, not just because I was not quite a fully-grown man, but who wants to get hit three times in the face.

Well Jody was pushing me backwards and I held my ground, leaning backwards with him. I put my Judo training to work. The first part of a flip is to get your opponent off balance, then it is much easier to throw them especially if they are bigger than you. I grabbed his shirt and threw Jody over my hip and shoulder which probably would have been enough to stop this potential fight. Instead, I threw him into one of the large cafeteria windows and he smashed the glass with his body, getting a pretty good cut on his arm. That ended the fight right there. We put a bunch of napkins on his cut and I walked him to the administrative offices where we saw Mr. Friedman, the Headmaster. I felt bad about it since Jody was my friend and I did not want to hurt him. Well Mr. Friedman's solution was for me to drive Jody to the hospital and have him sewn up. That was really a great idea, since we talked on the drive and I hung out with him while he got his stitches and we remained friends. He later became an excellent policeman due to his good temperament and intimidating size. This creative solution by our Headmaster showed me how he managed to raise funds to pursue his dream of creating this one-of-a-kind school, Westledge. His dream had created a dream school for me to attend, thank you.

I'm glad that you are out walking. I remember Centennial Cone Park as a very interesting loop trail. Always watching the bushes for snakes. Did Dillon every get bitten? We get regular postcards from Coulter, from exotic places like Thailand!   I never realized how much you got from Westledge. We made the right choice. Dad

15 Ridge Rd Misc. Stories

When I was in the 4th grade at the end of the year, a survey was passed around asking about musical instruments. I always had liked the trumpet in the old westerns when they would play reveille or taps and checked the trumpet box.

At the start of 5th grade, we were in class and the teacher had a bunch of us leave to go to the music room. I was a little puzzled and when we got there the teacher told me that I would be playing the trumpet. The light came on and I realized that that checkbox survey about instruments was a sign-up sheet to be in the band. I must have had my mind on summer vacation and was not really paying attention to what I was filling out at the time. I brought home a form for my parents to take to the music store in Hartford to rent a trumpet. My parents were all about it and I had a trumpet the next week. We learned the musical scales in music class, learned the different keys and practiced simple songs together, eventually as a band when I got to Jr High School. We were not an orchestra since we did not have any string instruments, at least not in that first year. I quickly got the hang of it and had no trouble blowing out strong notes; the hardest part was learning all the different fingerings for the notes in the different keys. Smell is one of the strongest senses for bringing on déjà vu memories, and whenever I smell the mineral oil that we used to lube the trumpet, it brings back memories. I played all through Jr High and we played several concerts during that time. I ended up walking to school with my books and my trumpet during this time which made it hard to be cool, but it was worth it.

When we moved to Hartford, my mom did not want me to quit since she thought I had real talent and potential, I was not so sure. She found a private tutor at the Hartt School of Music at the University of Hartford with a professor that was also the 2nd trumpet for the Hartford Symphony Orchestra. We played lots of classical music and pieces that he would teach by playing different tempos in different keys. More like working on drills. I enjoyed playing while learning entire songs, which we did occasionally. In my spare time at home, I would play fun contemporary music like Herb Albert, the Muppets Theme song and even Christmas carols that I could jazz up. I enjoyed it and probably would have liked to play with kids in a jazzy rock band just for fun. I had to take a break from playing when I got braces and could not blow into the mouthpiece without making my gums bleed. This break was for at least a year and when they came off, I just never played again.

In my bookcase at home, I have a full top shelf that only contains helmets. It seems like everything I like to do requires a helmet. There are always gaps in my helmet collection when I take them down for snowboarding, bike riding, motorcycling, kayaking and other athletic endeavors. It will be a very sad day when my helmet collection no longer has any gaps during the different seasons. I still have that Olds trumpet, but it is relegated to being a bookcase ornament below my helmets. It never leaves its spot and it is a reminder of something I no longer do, like those helmets will be someday.

When I was 11, our family went up to Boston to meet Mom's parents at Harvard for the annual football game with Princeton; my dad's and grandfather's alma mater respectively. We were enjoying the game at halftime, eating hot dogs and pretzels waiting for the 2nd half to begin. My grandfather took me to walk around the stadium with him to stretch our legs. We wandered around and he took me into a shop with memorabilia of mostly Harvard jackets, caps, banners, mugs and a little bit of Princeton stuff. My grandfather announced that he wanted to get me a football banner and it was up to me to choose which one. He held up the crimson triangle-shaped banner with a pilgrim in knee socks and a hat with a buckle. Then he held up the square orange and black banner featuring a large tiger. Well of course the tiger was better than the nerdy guy and who does not like orange and black. My grandfather had sandbagged me. We made it back to our seats and I ended up flying that banner for the rest of the game, much to the chagrin of my dad, who knew that the Harvard mascot could not compete with a tiger. I suppose if my dad had taken me to the shop, he could have woven a story about how cool the Yankee pilgrim was, what a good fighter, eater and all-around good guy he is and how the tiger epitomized the evil of human-eating carnivores or something. Then I may have selected the Harvard banner. I'm sure there was some subtle manipulation going on with my grandfather as well. When we got home after the game, I got some thumbtacks and pinned it up on my wall for the next several years until we moved to Hartford.

Robert was one grade above me in school. The kids his age generally did not like him and would make fun of him. He rubbed them the wrong way and was a bit of an asshole. He lived just a neighborhood away and I gave him the benefit of the doubt. The kids his own age would not hang out with him and my friend Jimmy, who was also a grade above me, advised me not to be friends with him. I did not take his advice even though my own instincts were the same as Jimmy's. I suppose if I had women's intuition, I would have ignored him. I knew he was a little creepy, but kids are sometimes a little weird anyway. For me he was always more of an acquaintance, never rising to the level of a true friend, because of stupid little things he would do.

For example, occasionally when we would go to the bus stop, he would try to impress the other kids and call me BiddyBoy, like that was the worst insult. I would call him Baldy. He did not like getting a taste of his own medicine and he would get very upset, but he never learned his lesson to just shut up. I think the reason I hung out with him was just the convenience of him living semi-close when my other neighborhood friends were not around. We would get along, until he would do some stupid thing and I would not hang out with him for a month or two. That should have been a red flag to me to just not have anything to do with him.

An example was when Robert was working on building a tree house in the woods below his home. For about a week, I would go over and help him. It was way up in a White Pine tree with no branches for the bottom 25 feet, so he had nailed 1x4 boards to the trunk of the tree to act as a ladder. This was always a bit sketchy to me, since the boards would get looser every time you used them and if one pulled out you could fall backwards. I used the 3-point contact method like climbers use when 4th classing a route. Never have more than one limb of your body out of contact with the ladder (Rock for 4th classing) to minimize the chances of having a fall. When we got up to the tree house, there was a trapdoor with a hasp and a padlock for security, not that there was anything valuable up there. Well one day Robert and I were up working on the fort, nailing up boards and building a roof on it. Robert got a call that Jimmy and another kid from his class had stopped by his house. I kept working while Robert climbed down. He was excited that kids his own age were at the house to see him. I kept working on the fort for another 5 minutes and decided to climb down and see what was up. For whatever reason, when he left the tree house, Robert had locked the trapdoor, locking me in. I was immediately pissed off that he had done such an assholey thing. Robert had not used his head, since the tools we were using could also be used for non-building tasks, such as getting out of the tree house. I think he thought I would just quietly sit up there like I was in prison, but he did not know me well enough, since we had never risen to the level of being friends. I pried open the trapdoor with my claw hammer and pried off the hasp with the lock, dropping it to the ground. I pulled open the trapdoor and climbed down the ladder. At each step on the way down, I pried off the rung that was nailed to the tree until I was at the bottom.

Now the tree house was 25' up with no rungs to climb up to it. There was no lock on the busted trapdoor either, but it did not matter, since no one could now get up to it. He had proven himself to be a creep once again and being an asshole has consequences.

I wandered home and was doing my own thing when about 40 minutes later I could hear Robert shouting, Bidwell, I'm going to kill you!"

Back then, calling someone by their last name was an insult. Sometimes, calling someone by their last name could even lead to a fight. I ignored Robert. Yeah, he was a little bigger than I was, but I was tougher so I knew he would just make threats, but would not back them up. I did not hang out with him for a couple of months after that.

We did not have a basketball hoop at my house and Robert did. One day I was walking down the street and Robert was out shooting hoops by himself and I wandered over to have a game of horse with him. We were shooting and Robert was bragging about something he had done to a girl that I knew. It was basically a type of low-level molestation. It sickened me and I looked at him with eyes that finally saw him for the person that he really was. I never was his friend again, never had anything to do with him again and wrote him out of my life. He had proven for the final time that he was not only a creep, but a pervert on top of that to abuse a sweet innocent girl. I should have listened to my instincts like Jimmy had advised, that Robert was a creep and not worthy of anyone's friendship. I just made sure that my sister or any of her friends were never around him.

Often, when I meet a person for the first time, I make a snap judgment. I subconsciously assess if they are someone that I would like and would want to hang out with. For me, these snap judgments are correct about 50% of the time, meaning they are totally random. The real test is after knowing a person for a while, are they still behaving like my initial snap judgment. Are they behaving like someone I respect? Do they share my values? I know this about myself and when I meet someone and I make a snap judgment, I'll temper it by waiting to make a final judgment until I know them a little better. I'm not saying friends need to be just like you, that is a mistake. It is a mistake that a lot of church-going Christians make by only making homogeneous friends with like-minded other Christians with the same type of jobs, living in the same type of neighborhoods. They never meet and make friends with people from diverse backgrounds that can open their minds and expand their horizons. Robert kept doing things over and over that pushed the boundaries of my friendship. Giving someone the benefit of the doubt is one thing, but ignoring your instincts after a person has proven the type of cloth they are made of is grounds for keeping them out of your life.

Our family friends the Alcovelins came over for a family visit one weekend. Mark and I decided to go on a bike ride and I had just the place, Barkhampstead Reservoir. It was over 10 miles away, and we could go swimming there, plus it had a cool dam. We loaded up our gear in my baskets and headed out on our bikes. It was a nice warm summer day and we made it there in about an hour on the hilly roads. We found a place by the water where the shore dropped straight down about eight feet to an underwater ledge. I had been reading how a normal breath only takes about

1/8 of the oxygen from the air in your lungs. At this time, I wanted to be an oceanographer and read up about the ocean, learned the names of most of the fish in the area, both freshwater and in the ocean. I even had a subscription to Skin Diver magazine which talked about scuba and re-breather gear. I had brought a Bota bag with us, basically a soft wine flask that I used for a canteen, just for the purpose of trying it out as a rebreather. I put my mask on, put the end of the bag in my mouth, picked up a rock with my free hand and dropped into the water holding my breath until I hit the bottom. I sat there for about 10 seconds, then exhaled into the bag and then breathed back in. That was the first successful breath, no water leaked into my mouth and I was good for a few more seconds till I took my second breath. The same thing, I was not running out of breath, I was not light headed and I was still underwater. I took 7 total breaths, saving the 8th breath as a safety margin before swimming back up to the surface. Mark had been watching me down there and could see that I had been moving and was OK. He was a little reluctant to try it, since it looked a little sketchy, which of course it was. I did another dive with our homemade rebreather just to show him that it was safe. He finally decided to give it a try and his dive went fine. I was ecstatic that our little test was a success and we had successfully used our own self-contained-underwater-breathing-apparatus or SCUBA as it is known, although technically this would be classified as a rebreather.

We then rode our bikes to the top of the Seville dam. There was a road across the top and a small building rising out of the water that led down to the bottom where the water could be let out from the base of the dam. The building is cool since it is a masonry cylinder with a cone-shaped roof made out of stone. In fact, the roof was built by my Grandma Bidwell's father C. G. Bostwick. He had a roofing company, specializing in slate shingles that were used in a lot of the older homes in Hartford and unique structures like this. The dam itself is 135 feet tall and over a third of a mile across with a spillway on the far side. We were on the middle of the dam where the backside was a grassy embankment leading down to the bottom in a steep slope. Mark and I were enjoying this beautiful place that we had all to ourselves. I was looking down below the dam and asked Mark what he thought about us riding our bikes down the backside. We could ride our bikes at a diagonal so we would not reach the high break-neck speed that going straight down would do. I had been riding my bike over pretty good jumps back at the ball fields near home. There was a steep trail leading down through the woods and at the edge of the ball fields was a large pile of dirt, used for keeping the infield in shape that just happened to be at the bottom of this trail. We would ride our bikes down the trail, over the pile of dirt and catch pretty good air on our bikes before landing. I figured that I had the experience needed to tackle a hill of this size. Mark was not so sure, but he was game.

We positioned our bikes about 30 feet apart at the back edge of the dam. That way we could start off at the same time, just parallel to each other. Mark was off to my right and we were heading to the right going down the dam. We pushed off at the same time, going through the 18" high grass that covered the backside on our bikes. I was immediately surprised at how quickly we picked up speed, we probably had chosen too steep of an angle but at this point we were committed. I could see Mark speeding through the grass out of the corner of my eye, as I was concentrating hard on maintaining control of my bike. The dam builders were not just concerned in holding back 8 miles of water behind the dam, they were also interested in keeping the dam from eroding. As part of this, they had constructed cement sluices, basically half pipes about 2 or 3 feet in diameter, going diagonally across the back of the dam, but in the opposite direction than we were heading on our bikes. Neither of us spotted them until the last second. I saw Mark jump off his bike before hitting it as I attempted another approach of riding it out. My front tire hit the backside of the sluice, throwing me over the handlebars. The good thing about the steepness of the dam is that when I hit the grass, it was not brutally hard, but was at a steep enough angle to soften the blow. The bad thing is that it caused us to roll and roll and roll to a stop. We were a bit bruised and scraped up but were otherwise OK. I hiked back up to my bike and the front wheel was bent in a few inches, but it had not punctured the inner tube. Mark's bike was ok other than the handlebars being twisted, but we bent them back straight. Mark was annoyed at me for suggesting that we ride down that dam. I did not twist his arm and he could have just watched me go for it. It was what it was and I did not understand his annoyance, especially since it was after the fact and we were not hurt. I was high on the adrenaline rush from the ride, but it seemed to have the opposite effect on Mark. I calmed him down as we were walking and sliding our bikes down to the bottom of the dam by telling him that I was going to have to ride home on a busted wheel.

The ride back took a few hours, since my wheel went thump, thump, thump as I was riding so I could not go very fast. We got home before dark. I always thought Mark had the advantage on our little adventures. He was more of a natural athlete than I was, I was just more fearless than him. In fact, we both went to Camp Morgan for a couple of years up in New Hampshire, but at different times. When I went, we played a type of rugby called murder ball with the other kids, in addition to all the other camp activities. When Mark went, they had the camp Olympics. Many of the kids there were from the inner city of Boston and would be there for the entire summer, we were just there for a couple of weeks. The next year when I went back to camp, Mark had set records in many of the Olympic events, that is how good of a natural athlete he was. I on the other hand was quite good at the rugby game, since when the other team came running at me, I would just growl and run and fight harder to get towards the goal. We had different approaches to athletic endeavors and they were both effective in their own ways.

The interesting thing is that years later, when I was married and had two young kids, we were at my mom's house in Avon for a baptism for Coulter and Corrine being performed by George Weston. Dad was there (they were divorced by then), as were my grandparents Bidwell and Grandma Noss. Our family friends the Westons and the Alcovelins were there also. After the ceremony I was talking with Mark who I had not seen for several years and he still had a little angry chip on his shoulder towards me. I asked him what was wrong. It turns out that on our many young adventures together, he told me that he could have died on almost all of them and that it was only by good fortune that he had survived. I was shocked. These adventures that the two of us had shared were cherished good memories for me. They were the opposite types of memories for Mark apparently. I guess the adrenaline rush that I love or even just the thrill of doing something exciting, was the same feeling that he did not like and the thrill was just something that frightened him. I don't know for sure. I just hope he was having a bad day, that perhaps his girlfriend had dumped him or he got a demotion at work, or being a lawyer was not the awesome career he had hoped it would be, just something he was upset about life and was just venting on me. If that was the case, I was helping him out by allowing him to get his frustrations out. When we were together, we always had a good time. It is just that we were thrown together as friends, since we were friends by virtue of our parents being friends. Perhaps we were not as good friends as I thought, but I know I would have sensed that and would have just gone off on my own. I definitely do not have "gadar", but I definitely do have "friendar" and he was a good friend. I'm sorry to have scared Mark, I love him and hope after more reflection that he feels the same!

I enjoyed your story of Grandpa Noss and the Princeton Banner. He was a real supporter of Princeton. Loyalty long term is precious. Robert is a puzzle. Mark is an enigma. I am so lucky with my family and to have Robin whose support is vital. - Dad

16 Ridge Rd – More Misc. stories

When I was 11 our family decided to take a road trip up to Massachusetts for the State Fair. I had never been to a State Fair before and was pretty excited, it would be like a big carnival or perhaps like our school fair where I could win something cool, like a chocolate cake or a Chinese finger trap and go on a bunch of rides. We bundled into the Plymouth station wagon in our normal configuration with Matt and I in the back facing out the rear window. I remember the curvy back roads that we took on our way up to Springfield, watching the road and trees fade into the distance as I daydreamed about how on earth, we would ever find our way back home. I am a map enthusiast and can spend entire evenings just pouring over paper maps, zooming in with digital maps and exploring this amazing earth from my armchair. I had not yet discovered maps at this young age.

Today everyone uses their GPS and smart phones to get them to their destinations and are just as clueless as to exactly where they are as I was sitting in the back of the car. God forbid that their phone dies on a trip and they might have to ask for directions.

I have also always been in preparation for wilderness survival since I was 11, just in case I got lost. I've been carrying the three things needed to stay alive if stranded out in the wild. In fact, I still carry them with me to this day. That is my one habit that will never die, I even carry them into the office and if I survive this life long enough to need full-time nursing care, I'm sure I'll have my compass, knife and lighter with me then too. I've never been a GPS guy. I did get a Garmin pocket GPS one time as a birthday present from Matt when I was 40. I took it hiking up in the foothills with Corrine to get some exercise, spend time with my daughter and try out the GPS. We loaded up our daypacks with lunch, water and a camera and headed up into Golden Gate State Park for the day. I set the GPS to track our path so that we could just follow it back to the car when we were done. I told Corinne that we would just hike out and get lost, then spend the rest of the day trying to find our way back. The two of us set out on the trail and just wandered through the woods and rock outcropping, taking side trails where they looked interesting and just exploring, not caring where we were going, since the GPS was going to guide us back. We arrived at a lovely grassy meadow in the early afternoon and had our lunch. Corrine and I talked about the wonder of the natural world and she was very interested in what we could do to protect it. She was concerned that someday it would be developed and civilized and no one would ever remember how magical it used to be. That was a concern I've had my whole life as well, but she wanted to take it a step further and actually do something about it. I was very proud of her, not just her adventurous spirit, but the urge to protect the wild areas as well. We decided to head back to the truck so I pulled out the GPS and we looked at it. It had all the paths and side trails mapped out and the distance. It was pretty awesome compared to a compass and a map and I might have been a convert to this method of navigating. As we were admiring how easy it was going to be to just follow our track back with this device, it ran out of batteries, literally right there, just as we were going to need it. I knew the general direction that we would need to head back to the truck, but once we got down into the forest and rocks and intersecting trails, things would get a little dicey. We headed back, I have a good sense of direction, but in the forest, it is easy to get turned around. I was not worried about getting stranded out here overnight as just heading South, we would arrive at a road miles from the truck, but after dark. We did take a wrong fork and I was totally turned around and I had a mini-panic attack that we were actually lost. We discussed which way would be best and we back-tracked a little to get on what looked to be the correct trail and eventually made it back to the truck. I never used that GPS again and it is still sitting in a drawer in my desk.

Back to the story… Matt and I were enjoying the ride up to MA in the old Plymouth. Dad had cracked the back window a bit so we could get some fresh air. After about a half hour, I was starting to feel queasy, as was Matt and we yelled up to Dad to pull over, we were not feeling well. Matt and I got out and stood next to the car on the embankment. Matt started retching and throwing up and the sound and smell of it immediately made me do the same. Soon Julie and Jeremy were out of the car to observe the excitement and Jerry started retching, just from the sound, smells and images of his brothers doing the same. Julie managed to hold it together, but I'm pretty sure she did a little retch as well, with a slight bend at the waist and her mouth closed to help prevent anything from happening. We cleaned up got back into the car and made it up to the Fair.

The Fair was awesome, the best I had ever been to with rides, music and people laughing and having a good time. We wandered around doing most of the rides. Any ride that one of us kids wanted to go on, my parents stopped and we did it. We were going to get total fair overload and it was all right with all of us. We walked by the house of mirrors and it was extremely entrancing to me. I had to go in. I walked into the house by myself as the rest of the family waited outside. It was surreal, like a Salvador Dali 3-D interactive experience to my young inquisitive self. It was hard to navigate since the openings and the mirrors looked exactly the same. At some points, I saw images of myself going on and on to infinity getting smaller and smaller. If you walked into at mirror, you were just looking at yourself from inches away. At the back of the mirror maze was a room of distorted mirrors to make you short like a toad and tall like a giraffe and just plain distorted. It was cool to see what contorted shapes they would put your body and face into. I headed back out through the maze and was having trouble finding the way, probably since I had a destination and was not just slowly soaking in the wonder of it all.

Eventually I saw the outside and my parents standing there and ran yelling "Mom, Dad", just as I crashed headfirst into the diagonal mirror that was reflecting the outside.

I'm sure my parents looked up and saw their oldest son running headfirst into a mirror and wondered what was wrong with their kid. At least they had three others that were more normal! Eventually we got to my favorite ride, the bumper cars. I had always been intrigued with driving, and this was as close as I had ever had to doing it. Dad showed me the basics, really just two things.; How to steer with the steering wheel and how to press down on the accelerator to make it go, no brakes. I think I rode that car on three separate rides, I could not get enough. In my mind, I now knew how to drive. It was SOOO easy! All the way back home in the car I was happily daydreaming about driving, not even worrying about how my parents would find their way back.

When I was 15, I got my learners permit and could drive as long as there was an adult in the car. I did a lot of drives with Mom in her Ford Maverick. It had a little 6-cylinder engine, but to me it was a powerful, sporty machine and I loved driving it. Mom liked it for the same reason that I liked it, perhaps not as much as her Karmann Ghia but a little more practical with kids. The hardest part was knowing when the car was centered in the lane and she gave me a good tip. Just line the front center of the hood to the edge of the road and that car would track right down the middle of the lane. I still occasionally use that tip when I want to check myself on the road. We would practice when dad was at work. The first-time dad took me out was in his new Oldsmobile Vista Cruiser, the best car dad ever had. It was sporty looking for a station wagon, with lots of power and the latest in technology, fun to drive and comfortable. We were driving back home from somewhere and Dad pulled over at the bottom of Ridge Road and let me drive the rest of the way home, not too far but just a taste of his sweet ride. Matt was in the back seat and Jerry was in the third seat in the way back. I was enjoying the power steering and ease of control and headed up the "homerun hill" towards the circle. I got to the top going probably a little faster than I should and hit the brakes. That was the first time I had ever driven with power brakes. I hit them a little too hard, OK a lot too hard and I'm sure I laid a little rubber down on the road. Jeremy flew over the back seat, landing head first in the foot well next to Matt. I scared the crap out of dad and myself.

Westledge had a little rope tow and a ski lift that we could ski on after a good snowstorm. It was good to practice at school. On the weekends we would meet at Ski Sundown in nearby New Hartford for night skiing and it was a much better ski hill than school since it had longer runs and a chair lift, plus there were no grownups to boss you around. It was great fun being out at night and skiing under the lights. My friend Jody came with us one time and he was just learning but he wanted to go up to the top with us since there was an intermediate run down from the top. He was not an intermediate skier however, more like a rank beginner but what better way to learn than to jump into it with both feet. We got to the top and skied down a bit. Jody followed and we could see that the big guy was having trouble. As we were watching him come down, he was careening toward the side of the hill where the snow-making gun was blasting over the slope making snow. The gun was on a tripod about four feet off the ground. Well Jody skied by right in front of the nozzle and was blasted off his feet with the cold water that had not yet frozen into snow. His frozen hat was blown out into the middle of the slope and it looked so comical that we could not stop laughing. When we got to him his face was wet, his hair was starting to freeze, his parka was completely saturated and he was cold. We were near the top of the hill and worked with Jody to get him to the bottom without succumbing to hypothermia.

On another trip, I was on a Westledge school ski trip to Butternut Basin in Western Massachusetts where the bus dropped us off for a day of fun. An hour or two into the day of skiing, I was going down just an intermediate hill when my ski tips crossed, sending me head over heels onto the slope. I had some Tyrolean ski bindings that we had picked up at a garage sale and the bindings did not separate from my ski boots. I sat there on the ground, but my right leg was pointing upslope at an unnatural angle. It hurt like hell, but the endorphins were already starting to kick in, dulling the pain. I was loaded onto a sled, taken down the hill and then transported to the local country doctor who worked out of his house. He had no X-ray machine although he did have a nurse, that was probably his wife. She told me that this was going to hurt, and boy was she right. She took my foot and pulled it hard away from my knee, twisting it to the proper upright position. Man did I groan and yell. She continued to hold it while the doctor wrapped my leg in plaster from my groin to my toes.

The next day my parents took me into Hartford Hospital for an X-ray of my leg. They declared that the leg was set perfectly and that I had a spiral fracture of the right tibia, which would keep me in a cast for the next three months. I was hobbling around home and school in a cast for this entire time. I wasn't too mobile at this time to do fun stuff with my girlfriend and we ended up breaking up.

We actually broke up on the phone. I had prepared a statement that I read to her on the call and in the middle of it she stopped me and said, "Are you reading this to me?"

I stammered and said a white lie, "Of course not!" She did not believe me and it was awkward. I found out first hand that breakups are hard to do.

When I finally got the cast sawn off, I had one normal leg and one skinny little monkey leg covered in long dark hair. I was freakish. I was on crutches for another several weeks before I could start walking and then I gained strength fast. I had this large knot of muscle at the top of my skinny little leg from holding the heavy cast out in front of me for three months. When I was healed up enough to play on the soccer team, I discovered that I now had one of the more powerful kicks on the team due to my new huge muscle. I had a follow-up appointment with Dr Scudder, our family physician and he informed me that my right leg was now an inch shorter than my left. During the time I was in the cast I had a growth spurt and my right leg was putting all its energy into healing rather than growing. He just told me to keep active for the rest of my life so I would not have problems with my back and spine. This advice fit in well with my personal philosophy of just doing things all the time and not sitting around inside.

I used this excuse years later when I would want to go kayaking and my wife René would balk. I would tell her, "I don't just want to go kayaking, I have to do it as therapy for my back", which was not a lie, since the torso twisting from paddling and the hip snap when rolling up were the best exercises to keep my back flexible.

In my back pocket, I had a copy of the Connecticut DOT Drivers manual with all the rules of the road. I carried it with me everywhere and I knew that book like I knew One Fish Two Fish Red Fish Blue Fish. Of course, my dad gave me a book about driving that I had also read cover to cover. The main thing I remember about the book was using the armrest on the door to steady the wheel for a smoother ride with your elbow. I wish I still had that book, and the Sex Ed book, and the Duck on the Truck book in my collection.

On the Sunday of my 16th birthday, the thing I was most excited about was getting my driver's license. The next day Mom took me to the Simsbury town hall and I took my written test, then the driving test in her Maverick and got my paper driver's license that day. Now I was mobile, as long as I could borrow a car. I was well on my way to becoming an adult, a very immature adult but still...

About 6 months later, I enrolled in a driver's safety class at Westledge, since passing that class would lower my parent's car insurance on me. When I took the class, I had already been driving for half a year on my own. Most of the other kids did not have their licenses, so my instructor decided that with me, we would do errands rather than the by-the-book drivers ed. The instructor was a cool younger guy and a newlywed and would take me to downtown areas in places like New Britain that I was not familiar with. He would point out a parking space and I would parallel park in the spot while he would run into a shop and get something for his wife as I waited in the car. It was actually a brilliant strategy by the instructor, since it made it an advanced class and I really learned a lot about driving and how to treat your wife.

I am really impressed with your preparation for wilderness survival. You have survived a lot more than I have. I am glad you survived drivers' ed. Your journal has morphed into a best-selling book, at least with the family and friends.
Dad

17 Terry Rd - The Scout

In the summer after I turned 16, I talked to my Grandma Noss about purchasing her 1964 International Scout. I had figured out the market value of the truck and she agreed to the price of the 7-year-old truck. It had been sitting neglected in her garage up at Valley Farm in New Hampshire for 4 years. When I got there the dusty truck looked so good to me. I spent a couple of nights with her, catching up in the old farm house that I had always loved and working on getting the truck ready for the 200+ mile drive back home to Hartford. On Sunday morning, we had it ready to go and I headed out in the truck.

The Scout was built by International Harvester which primarily made farming tractors and semi-trucks. The Scout was about as close to a tractor as you could make an automobile. It had a cab like a pickup with a bench seat and an open back. It had a 152 cubic inch slant 4, which was basically the 304 CI V8 engine just cut in half with almost 100 horsepower. It was only a 3-speed manual transmission, which meant that it could only cruise comfortably on the highway at 55 miles per hour and the gears would whine like a tractor. You would think that it would get excellent mileage, but it only got 10 miles to the gallon and had a 10-gallon gas tank. None of this deterred me, since I just loved driving it, I liked the sound of the gears and it reminded me a lot of Grandpa Noss.

Grandpa Noss was an outdoorsman and did a lot of exploring of wilderness areas with a backpack and a tent in his summers, much of it with his wife Emily. His love of wilderness had made him an environmentalist and the lousy mileage bugged him, but the Scout was perfect for getting into the cabin on the muddy two track and hauling stuff around the farm. In fact, during most of my childhood, for my birthday I would get a membership in Save The Redwoods Foundation from Grandpa Noss and perhaps a little something from Grandma. I am still a member, not just in honor of my grandparents, but because they are truly magnificent and awe-inspiring trees growing in huge groves. The last time I was in Northern California, Mona and I hiked for a quiet day in the Montgomery Woods grove which was purchased and now protected by the Save the Redwoods Organization. It is very satisfying to see some tangible results from our donations.

I said goodbye to my grandmother, living alone in that old farmhouse and drove the Scout South towards home. When I was getting close to Keene, the truck's clutch stopped working and I could only shift by matching the engine speed to the gear speed as best as I could. I managed to make it to a truck repair shop, but there were no mechanics there since it was Sunday. I knew a little about cars. I had taken a class in auto mechanics with Mr. Weber at Westledge. He was the school handyman; his wife Helen ran the school cafeteria. He was also a mechanic and taught this class out of the garage of their house right on campus. We found an old Volkswagen boxer engine and for a semester I took it apart and put it back together. I learned about carburetors, distributors, points and plugs, coils and condensers, pistons and valves, crankshafts and bearings and exactly how a four-stroke engine works. This was all valuable knowledge, but it did not help me in figuring out why my clutch had failed.

As I was mulling over how to get the rest of the way home, a big truck pulled up and parked. The driver was also looking to get some maintenance. I talked to him about my predicament and he offered to look under the hood. Immediately he noticed that the clutch fluid reservoir was completely empty explaining why my clutch pedal no longer functioned. I don't know if clutch fluid is something that truck drivers routinely carry with them, but he had a can of it in his truck and together we filled the little reservoir. That was enough to get me going the rest of the way. I always carried extra clutch fluid with me after that.

I continued on through Massachusetts on my way home when I ran out of gas. Between the small gas tank, the lousy mileage and the busted gas gauge, it was just a breakdown waiting to happen. Once again, I was stranded on the side of the road when a state cop pulled in behind me with his lights on. He was mostly interested in my four-year-old expired plate, my lack of current registration and my lack of insurance papers. It had all the earmarks of a stolen car and he was a little bit excited to catch a car thief in action. I explained the entire situation to him and he gave me a stern warning and told me that if anything I had told him was a lie, he would hunt me down before I reached the state line and haul my ass into jail. I wasn't too worried. The best part of talking to the cop was that he had a gas can in his trunk and gave me enough gas to get to the next station. Saved again by the kindness of strangers, a public servant, but a stranger none the less. I also started carrying a spare can of gas in the Scout from that time on.

I made it home safely and cleaned it up making it mine. The tires were pretty old and shot so I got some cheap retreads from the tire shop across Main Street from the Bidwell Company. I upgraded the radio to an FM stereo so I could listen to the rock stations WPLR and WHCN. This truck was rock solid with its manual steering and manual brakes. I could take the top off in the summer and fold the windshield down and make it like a dune buggy. The doors would even come off by removing a couple of hinge pins. It was the most fun thing to drive.

One time my friend Adam and I were four-wheeling in East Hartford down by the Connecticut River. We were driving down a muddy track and the trail looped around close to the river into a large mud bog with water on top. We could see the 4wd trail going into the bog and coming out on the other side a couple hundred feet away. We drove into the wet bog and were about halfway through when the Scout just quit moving. I gave it gas and it was like a muddy paddle wheel. It was muddy on the bottom with a foot of water on top with the water splashing out of all the wheel wells. The truck was just not moving. I worked it back and forth to no avail. I had it in four-wheel-drive low range and we just sat there with the truck in gear and the tires slowly spinning discussing who was going to wade out of the bog to get some help. As we were talking, the truck gave a little shudder and started moving forward on its own. I did not have my foot on the gas, basically we were just idling in gear with the tires slowly turning. We could not get the truck out, but the truck was getting itself out. We did not dare touch the gas as the truck slowly inched towards the other side of the bog. When it got to the other side it slid to the side for about 10 feet before it got a grip and pulled out of the water. I was amazed. The truck had saved us. It was our hero! We headed back out onto the road with the extremely muddy vehicle and two very relieved teenagers.

Another time I was four wheeling with my friend Mac in the wintertime outside of Farmington CT. There was a snowmobile trail that we started going down since it was very well packed. We made it about a half mile down the trail to where it came back out onto the road. The snowplows had created a snowbank about 4 feet high at the edge of the road. The trail we were on just stopped there. It would have been very tough to get back out the way we came so we decided to just blast through the snowbank. The scout had a very beefy front bumper made from an I-beam looking piece of iron. We got a little head of steam to blast through and headed to the road. When we hit the bank, it was frozen solid. Luckily the Scout just rode up the snowbank and over the top where it stopped with all 4 wheels in the air. It was a semi-rural road that the truck was perched above. We got out and stood on the road looking at the truck sitting four feet in the air, partway over the pavement. It was funny and worrisome at the same time. At least we were not stuck down the trail where the truck would be hard to get to, but at the same time it was stuck in such a way that we could not make it budge. We stood there talking about our situation with the frost from our breath smoking out of our mouths.

Eventually an older gentleman in a pickup truck came down the road and stopped rolling down his window chuckled a little bit and said, "Looks like you boys did a pretty good job of high-centering your vehicle. Would you like a little tug to get you off?".

We gladly accepted and with a length of tow rope and a little pull from his truck, the Scout slid off that bank and right onto the pavement. It did not hurt the truck at all, although that Spring my exhaust system and muffler were very loose and swinging around. I climbed under the truck and tightened up everything under there with tie wire. It worked well and held for several years after. Most likely the exhaust was jarred pretty good when the truck slid over that big frozen snowbank but it was fixed for next to nothing with a little wire and some pliers, both of which I kept stored under the front seat of the truck for future emergencies. The kindness of strangers came through once again.

In my sophomore year of High School, Jill and Jeff, my next-door neighbors sat in the front seat of that wonderful Scout with me when I drove them to school and back for the rest of our high school years. It was much handier than taking the bus, plus they paid for my gas making it economical for me to drive to school. Gas was only $0.33 per gallon and it is 45 miles round trip from Hartford to Westledge, so they saved me $7.50 per week in gas money or about $30 per month. The funny thing is that I would have to fill up that truck after only 2 trips to school. The other funny thing is that I never got really close to either Jeff or Jill even though we lived right next door to each other. Jeff hung out with a different crowd at school and Jill was very quiet when I was around her. It was definitely a win-win for all of us however.

I was a little shy around Jill and Jill was a little quiet. One day after school, Jeff was getting a ride home with friends and it was just Jill and I. It had been snowing for most of the day at school. We were driving home in about 3 or 4 inches of fresh snow on the road. I was in 4WD and was confident in the traction ability of the Scout when all 4 wheels broke traction going around a very gentle curve. The Scout did a total 180 degree turn in the middle of the road and stopped and stalled. Jill looked at me with wide eyes, I acknowledged that with raised eyebrows and my own wide eyes. I started up the truck, turned around and headed home, this time a little slower. We had communicated about the near disaster without either of us uttering a single word. Such was our relationship.

Mom and Dad were having a dinner party and they were talking about swearing. It's funny, but I had asked Dad if he ever got drunk and he told me that he never did, although they always had a lot of fun in adult get-togethers like this which in my mind was pretty close to being drunk. I suppose that it is just what they called "tipsy" back then. Anyway, their conversation made me think of my friends and I having lunch at school and discussing the best string of swear words and we came up with a good expression to spit out whenever we needed it. Well I was walking through the living room and one of the guests asked me if I ever swore and what a high school kid would say if he was swearing.

I said "God-damn mother-fucking cock-sucking two-timing son-of-a-bitch" as I walked back out of the room.

Everyone was just a little shocked that this spew of profanity came streaming out of my young mouth like I talked that way all the time, and when I glanced back into the room, I saw a faint little expression on my dad's face that he was just a twinge proud of me.

Adam had a friend whose older sister worked for the D&D Speed shop down on the Berlin Turnpike. This was a stretch of highway straight out of American Graffiti. There was a stop light every half mile for several miles on a straight stretch of the highway where kids would drag race. There were fast food restaurants, car part stores, restaurants with car hops, speed shops and kids hanging out along the side roads. The sister was a few years older than us and was "Miss D&D", just the type of hottie you would see on an auto parts calendar. She managed to get Adam the keys to the shop's hot rod, a Dodge Super Bee 426 hemi with about 500 horsepower. He, Paul, Mac and I spent the evening tooling around in that amazing car. I was surprised that it had an automatic transmission as I thought all drag cars would have a manual transmission, but the car was so fast that a normal person could not physically change gears faster than the auto tranny. We took it up to West Hartford Center where we would meet and hangout on the weekends in high school. We cruised down South Main Street at about 25 MPH when Adam hit the gas and that car laid down about 50 feet of rubber. We raced a Triumph Tiger motorcycle and left it in the dust. It was that kind of exciting. We were the cool gearhead kids for just a couple of short hours.

Later Adam, Mac and I were back down on the Berlin Turnpike sitting at the McDonalds with the jacked-up Camaros, Mustangs and other muscle cars. My boxy square Scout looked a little out of place, until Adam took the top off of a square McDonalds trash can and put it on the hood of my truck. Now we had an 18" high hood scoop on the front of the new Muscle Scout. It was a truck of a different color that could fit into any social situation now rubbing elbows with the other race cars. Perhaps we were posers, but for another 30 minutes we were the cool gearhead kids again until we finished our burgers, fries and shakes. Of course, when we were done eating, all my friends and a stranger or two threw all their trash into that 'scoop' on the hood of my truck!

I had no idea of your history with the Scout. I never knew you were such a mechanic and how you kept getting out of trouble. Jane and I must have had a blind eye to your weekend activities. At least you never got injured or arrested.
love Dad

18 Terry Rd Wait and See Pudding

When I was 16, the drinking age in Connecticut was still 21. This was about the time that the states were lowering the drinking age to 18, since there was a draft going on for the Vietnam war which had been raging for 8 years already. They could not with good conscience draft boys to kill people, but not let them have a refreshing alcoholic beverage. I'm pretty sure that if I killed someone, I would need a stiff shot afterwards. Coincidentally, this was the same time that the 26th Amendment was passed (1971), giving 18-year-olds the right to vote in federal elections, for the same reason. In fact, the Army had a drinking age of 18 at this time as well.

The drivers license in Connecticut was just made out of paper, without even having a picture on them, so switching the birthday was a simple matter of changing 1955 to 1953 without any obvious signs of manipulation on the license. Now 1953 would still only be 18, 3 years shy of the Connecticut drinking age. Rhode Island however had already lowered their drinking age to 18. That and the fact that a 16-year-old that looked like a 14-year-old would have a much easier time sneaking into a bar with a drinking age of 18, than a drinking age of 21, meant that the only place we could drink was in Rhode Island.

We would meet at West Hartford Center on the weekends to gather with friends. One evening there was a party at the house of a friend that went to Hall High. The party was in the basement of his parents' house. His parents were home but were upstairs and they provided the keg of beer. Their thinking was that they would rather that the kids drink at the house and not out in a park or sneaking into a bar somewhere.

When we arrived at the party, a friend of mine says, "Hey Chris, you've got to play catchup, I'm already on my 4th beer!"

I was impressed with his drinking prowess, but I knew that I would be nursing the same beer for the entire evening, since I really hated the taste of beer. It was not until I was in my 20's that I acquired a taste for it, but it was really when I was in my 30's and would get off the river after a hard day of kayaking that beer really came into its own for me.

I was in Elizabeth Park in Hartford on another night with my core friends from high school. We had a couple of bottles of Boone's Farm apple wine and a baggie of Mexican pot. The pot was typical of the time with a good deal of stems and seeds. This was the first time any of us had smoked. We started by sharing the bottle of wine. The wine was sickly sweet, but sickly sweet and bad was a little better than just bad. Together we managed to roll a crappy joint that we lit and passed around. We passed it around three times before accessing our situation.

I looked at Mac and asked, "Are you feeling anything?"

He said, "I think so".

I replied, "I think I feel a little something, I'm not sure".

We waited a while, had some more of the sweet wine and did another round of hits on the joint. We all sat around on the grass trying to enjoy the high that was not there. We told ourselves that we were a little high, but it was not that much different than looking out the window as a little kid on Christmas Eve and telling yourself that you think you saw Santa flying over. The only buzz that we felt was from the wine. None of us understood why all the hippies were so jonesed on pot.

On one warm summer evening we were standing on the sidewalk at West Hartford Center, just hanging and chatting, getting a little bored watching kids cruising by and decided to go to a bar for a real drink. We ended up getting into Adam's Land Cruiser and headed out on Highway 2 for the 90-minute drive to Misquamicut, a beach town in Rhode Island that we were all familiar with. We parked on the sand parking lot and found a bar that backed onto the beach that looked accommodating. I handed the doorman my altered driver's license with my heart beating out of my chest and a tough look on my smooth young face hoping it would make me look a little older. I needn't have worried; the doorman was relaxed and gave our IDs a cursory glance as we entered. This was my first time in a bar and I had the feeling that everyone in the bar had stopped what they were doing to look at us, or at me in particular. As I was walking over to the bar, I was feeling very self-conscious like someone would yell out, "What the hell is HE doing in here!" I was also a little worried that the bartender would have the same thought and demand to see our IDs, again, I needn't have worried. We slid onto the bar stools next to each other and stared at all the bottles on the wall, so many choices. I knew I would not have a beer and wine was also out of the question, since I would not order strawberry or apple wine. I was an adult and needed an adult beverage. Adam, Mac and I talked it over and decided on shots of tequila. That way the nasty liquor would be down fast, like holding your breath when taking medicine plus it had the added benefit of being tempered with salt and lime. It made it kind of festive with the three of us all in this together. The shot glasses, salt shaker and lime wedges were lined up in front of us. We licked the back of our hand, shook some salt on it, gingerly took the shot glass in our other hand, looked at each other barely containing a little smile since we wanted to look like veterans at this process. We quickly licked the salt, quaffed the shot and sucked on the lime. I think I kept my lime in my mouth for a full minute to help hide my shock, surprise, excitement and satisfaction that I did the whole shot, did not start coughing and did not barf on the bar. I was high on life at that moment, not even needing any more liquor. Of course, that did not happen as we continued doing shots, probably another 3 or 4 during our time at the bar. When we had had our fill, we walked unsteadily out of the place and around to the beach, finding a soft place to sit in the warm dry sand. None of us were in any shape to drive, so we decided to sleep right on the beach. The three of us fell asleep pretty quickly on the sand and very surprisingly none of us got sick. We woke up with the sun and drove back to Hartford. In hindsight we were probably still a little drunk, but we made it safely. Adam dropped us off at our cars in W Hartford Center and we all drove home. When I arrived home, I coasted quietly in the Scout and parked in back of the house, let myself in the back door into the kitchen. The house was quiet, no-one was up yet. I was elated. Our big house had a back staircase and I quietly walked up to the third floor taking wide steps with my feet next to the floor molding to prevent the stair treads from creaking. I made it to my bedroom and crashed for another couple of hours, no one the wiser.

Adam, Mac and I were on campus at Trinity College smoking a joint before going to my first concert with Sha Na Na in the school auditorium. I was not familiar with this 50's band and was not sure what to expect. The show started with Bowzer walking out on stage, introducing the band, then running a comb through his slicked back hair and flicking the comb at the audience, spraying us with some of his hair grease. Then the band started up and rocked my world, the music was so good. I must have felt the pot a little bit this time, since I thought it was the best music I had ever heard!

In later years my youngest brother Jeremy had come up with what he considered the Bidwell family drink. Matt, Jeremy and I would sit at the kitchen table in his old farm house with his wife Sue looking on. The drink that he came up with was an Orange Whip, otherwise known as a B-52. It is a layered drink of sweet liquors in a tall shot glass with Kahlúa on the bottom, Baileys in the middle and Grand Marnier on top. Jeremey poured these drinks with a little spoon to ensure a perfect layering. We would do the shots. The first time we did this we were up for the entire night; Jeremy's wife Sue went to bed as the laughing and joking got to be too much for her. At about Midnight, Jeremy had the bright idea to get a "family photo" with Sue. The three of us went upstairs and Jeremy woke up sleepy Sue. The three of us climbed into bed with her and took a selfie, before selfie's were invented. Three of the four of us had a great time getting that shot. Jeremey and I were later sitting on the couch, Matt had wandered off but neither of us noticed. We later heard what sounded like a coyote outside which was not too uncommon since the house is at the base of the Talcott Mountain ridge. We decided to go out and have a look-see. The coyote turned out to be Matthew, straddling the top of the roof of the tool shed out back. He had his hands splayed out behind him, his head turned up to the night sky looking at the moon and howling. I think he may have been drunk, haha. We watched him up there in awe, not just at the howling, but at the fact that he managed to climb up on top of the roof in his state. Jeremy and I joined him for another few minutes of delightful howling, like a full pack of coyotes. We managed to wake up Sue again as she asked us about it the next morning.

This is only the first part of the Orange Whip becoming our family drink. The second part of this story takes place during Dad's bachelor party before his wedding to Robin. We were again at Jeremey's and were again doing our layered shots. After several hours of male bonding, fun and festivities with Jeremy, Matt, Uncle John, Dad and I, Jeremy poured a round for everyone.

Uncle John in a fit of just being himself and enjoying life picked up a shot glass, held it high in the air and proclaimed a toast, "To my brother Bruce and his wonderful bride, may they enjoy a long and happy marriage together".

With that he took his shot, slammed the shot glass down on the table and yelled, "Outstanding!".

We all looked out on him, very impressed and held up our shot glasses and repeated, "To Dad!", downing our shots, slamming our glasses on the table and yelling, "Outstanding!".

At this moment, the official Bidwell family drink and the proper way to quaff it was born! What a wedding present for Dad.

When I was 17, Connecticut lowered the drinking age to 18, meaning my altered driver's license would now almost work in my home state, but at least the age discrepancy was only a year now. It was time to try a bar right here in Hartford, so Adam and I headed down to the South end of Hartford and cruised down New Britain Avenue, looking for a likely bar. We passed one, just a little run-down with several people outside and a bouncer at the door and decided that looked perfect. We walked up the short stairs to the front door and the large doorman checked our IDs but was not fooled one little bit and promptly turned us away and told us not to come back. So, we were headed back to the car when we noticed people going into the bar via a side door, so we decided to try that. We walked up to that door and there was another big Italian guy standing at the door. We showed our drivers licenses and he let us in. Sweet! We walked into the place but I did not feel as out of place as I would coming in the front door and wandered over to the bar which was at the back. We slipped onto our bar stools and did a shot or two tequila and were enjoying the atmosphere and music at the bar, taking our time between shots.

As we were looking around the bar, I locked eyes with the burly bouncer from out front.

"What the fuck you little bastards" he growled as he rushed over, grabbing Adam and I by the scruff of our shirts, pulling us out to the front door where he literally tossed us down the stairs. We were young and a little loose from the tequila so tumbling down the concrete steps barely phased us. He shouted at us threatening all kinds of things if we were to ever come back. This bar was not nearly as accommodating as the beach bars we were accustomed to. In hindsight, we got free drinks that night plus we got several scrapes and bruises as badges of honor to show our friends, so there was a silver lining to our evening.

A couple of years later, when I was home for the summer after my freshman year at FDU, I was talking with my brother Matt. He was 17 and asked me to take him to a bar like Adam and I used to do at his age. I quickly agreed and we decided to find a place in Hartford, the usual way, just by cruising down the street until we found a place that looked good. I asked to see his license, and he had done a fair job of changing 1957 to 1956. He had just scraped off the top of the 7 and completed the loop at the bottom to make a 6. We headed out that night in the Scout and drove along the city line of Prospect Ave to Park Ave, hung a left and headed into the city looking for an appropriate place. Just a few blocks into the city, we spotted a bar on the right, so I pulled into an empty parking lot just across the street. We walked across to the bar and half the signs in the window were in Spanish. This time the bar itself was filled, mostly with Puerto Rican men and a few women with no free bar stools. I ordered a couple of beers from the bartender and we sat down at a table, both looking out towards the street. The bartender had never checked my ID or asked to see Matts so we were in like Flynn. I had obtained a little taste for beer in college and was OK drinking it now. Matt never had a problem with it.

When we were younger, I did not like flavor. I mean if I had a hotdog, there would be no ketchup or mustard on it, if I had a salad there would be no salad dressing on it, if I had spaghetti the marinara sauce would ruin it for me. Matt on the other hand was the family gourmet. New foods and exotic cuisines were just fine with him. He loved the intermingling of different flavors that would be torture for me. My parents always viewed him as the kid that would grow up to be high-class, unlike the rest of us. Well, that is probably why Matt was good with beer as a teenager, since the bitterness of the hops, the sweetness of the malt and the bite of the alcohol was pleasing to his discriminating palate.

We were on our second beer enjoying ourselves when there was some loud yelling coming from the bar. Before long there were several people yelling at each other, and the most belligerent fellow that seemed to be causing the problem was hit in the face, being knocked back and knocking another fellow from his bar stool. It was like in the movies where the entire group of guys erupted in a mass melee of yelling, punching, shoving and fighting. Two guys were wrestling at the table behind us and bumped into my back. I pushed back and stood up as they fell to the ground behind me. I yelled to Matt that we needed to head out NOW. We headed for the door before my little brother and I got drug into it. Unlike my little brother Jeremy whose mottos is "Don't mess with me, I rile easy", I am slow to rile since I need to be pushed to the tipping point to get into that angry fighting mode. The two guys that fell into my back were nothing but an annoyance, nothing to get upset about. In fact, the entire argument that started this bar brawl was in Spanish, so we had no idea what they were all fighting about in the first place. Matt and I went out the front door onto the sidewalk and crossed the street to the Scout. We sat there talking about what had just happened. Not two minutes later several cop cars came careening in, lights a blazing and stopped in the street right in front of the bar. Four or five cops exited their cruisers and went running in. I was super-glad that we had got out of there. Matt got the bar experience that he was looking for, we had a little adventure followed by a show of force by the cops to watch as a grand finale.

Jane and I certainly had no idea of your weekend bar activities with your buddies. I do remember the B 52s on my bachelor party. Now I enjoy Becks non-alcoholic beer with my supper. It helps the digestion. Robin does a wonderful job getting food that I love like cranberry sauce and piccalilli and marmalade. Since I now love

soups, Maureen and Sue keep us supplied along with Trader Joe's Tomato. My needs are few and simple now. Although not so simple for Robin who helps me with my shower and other physical needs.
    Dad

19 Terry Road

Life was different in the city without having the woods and open spaces to explore. The woods behind our Ridge Rd house was changing with development. They had drained the swamp and re-routed the stream that flowed through the heart of the woods into a pipe that was part of the storm sewers for the new housing development that was under construction. That house was being changed from rural to suburban so moving to the city was less of a burden. I loved the 50's - 60's style of our old house with the big open windows looking out into the back yard from the living room. That is still my favorite architectural period. Westledge was in West Simsbury and was still very rural with lots of woods and ridges and brooks to explore, so that was a saving grace for me.

The Terry Rd house was also quite different being that it was in the heart of the "Historic West End" of Hartford, surrounded by hundreds of other well-kept large homes and separated from the run-down part of Hartford just across the N Park River to the East. It was a 1929 three story brick Georgian Colonial style house with a slate roof built by my great grandfather Bostwick on Grandma Bidwell's side. It had six bedrooms and four baths all packed into 4325 square feet that my parents got for a steal at $52K in 1972. My parents felt like royalty walking up the grand staircase with rich red carpeting to the large double-sliding pocket doors leading into their big master bedroom with a sitting area in front of a large fireplace and a separate "changing room", master bath and a walk-in closet. Julie and Jerry were just down the hall also on the second floor like a prince and princess, while Matt and I were up on the third floor like the help. I'm not complaining since I loved the privacy of having our own floor, plus the convince of having our own separate back staircase that lead down to the kitchen.

We settled into the house, I put a large bookcase that dad had built to his specifications to fit into our old house, into the big dormer window of my bedroom that faced out to the West. I painted the walls dark blue and the ceiling black to highlight the black-light posters I plastered on the walls that a friend of Jerry's called "scary maps". There was an attic that was filled with old newspapers where us kids would go up and read stories about Al Capone. The house had hot water radiators in all the rooms powered by an oil-fired burner in the basement that had been converted from the original coal. In fact, there was a filthy room behind the furnace with a coal chute that would be used to store the fuel for the original furnace. In the winter, Matt and I would take a radiator key to bleed the air out of the lines so that we would get some heat into our rooms. I would fall asleep at night in the winter to the uneven tapping of the water lines creaking under the pressure. Even Rodnick found his favorite spot in the entryway at the front door which was like an air-lock to keep the cold air from entering the house when guests arrived. There was a missing pane of glass at the bottom of one of the French doors that he would squeeze through so that he could lay on the cool tile floor with his back against the door to catch any cold air leaking in. This was his happy place, plus the perfect spot for a guard dog to hang out.

The four of us kids would go into the back staircase from the kitchen and see who could climb all the way up to the third floor without touching the floor, just by chimneying along the walls, then mantling around the first landing where the staircase would turn 180 degrees with a window to the East, then working up to the second floor to that landing and grabbing the molding at the door that lead to the second floor hallway, then working up to the next landing where the staircase opened up with a railing to the third floor. Eventually we all made it, scuffing up the walls with our sneakers, bare feet and hands. This back staircase was basically a kid's playhouse. After I moved out to go to college, Mom had the other kids paint the staircase like a mural with whatever images, colors and patterns that suited their fancy.

Dad finished the basement adding a carpeted workout room with a little bathroom where Mom would have friends come over to do Yoga and exercise to music.

Jeremy was surprised the first time he saw the women working out through the big sliding glass window in the walkout basement and came running up exclaiming "There are ladies downstairs doing crazy stunts!"

Jeremy had a room in the back of the basement where he kept his collection of rusty iron relics and where he also learned about the inner workings of various household appliances by taking them apart and puzzling on how the contraption worked. That is probably why he is so good now at putting together the complex gas chromatographs and sampling equipment for his company RexTech.

I learned at an early age that part of keeping things in good condition was having a good case for them. Be it a camera, or school books or anything that needed to be protected. I was getting more serious about the sport of archery at this time and purchased a Bear Victor Super Grizzly 50-pound hunting bow, made and designed by the legendary Fred Bear. Before that I had been shooting with Dad's longbow that he made out of a piece of yew when he was a kid in summer camp. I learned to shoot with it and we got many good years out of that old bow. Since we were in the city, I would usually shoot at the archery range. My new bow was a beautiful yet simple recurve bow. That meant holding the bowstring back required holding the fifty pounds of pull steady as you aimed for the target. I also knew that I would need some good protection to hold this piece of archery equipment so I got a soft protective case. I still have that same bow, still in excellent condition almost 50 years later, just because of that case. Now I can shoot outside since I live in a remote area and I can still hold that bowstring steady. I guess that is thanks to my super-power!

I was sitting on my bed looking around my room and thinking about nothing in particular, just about doing stuff. I thought that there are so many things to do in life, things I wanted to do, but have not done yet, things I wished I could do many of which were within my means, some which were not. A big part of doing something new is to just go out and do it. I could just get off my butt and do something, even if it was something I already liked to do like shooting a bow. That's the thing, I could just get off my butt, but at times like these I would just enjoy musing about life. I thought that 90% of doing something was just getting up, getting excited and doing it. This is when I came up with my motto that I have tried to follow for the rest of my life.

"There's only one way to do it, and that's to do it!"

I think I was basically thinking about not procrastinating since there are so many things to experience and life is so short. Really, the longer you live, the shorter you think life is. This advice has come in handy for many things not just trying something new or going on an adventure but for practical things.

Later, when I was a Geologist and the Oil boom died, I was thinking about what I could do instead. I could wait it out, I could get a job doing something else, or I could go back to school and get a degree in something else. Going back to school had the best chance for a long-term career in something that I liked, but it was the most difficult choice. I thought about this for a long time before I decided that there's only one way to do it and that's to do it.

I applied and was accepted into the CSU Computer Science department where I spent the next two years getting a degree. I'm so glad I did since I really enjoy writing software. It is good to work at something you like and I have spent many years working at that since graduation. I'm glad that I did it. This is also good advice for keeping a wife or partner happy. She will often want to do something like shopping and it would be easier for me to just stay at home while she is out, but I will think, "Just Do It!".

Damn, Nike stole my 13-word phrase and distilled it down to those three magic words. My motto in a nutshell. It's a good thing that I did not decide on a degree in marketing!

A very puzzling thing when I was in high school was talking with the Career Counselor.

We would meet and talk, but always about one subject. "What do you want to be when you grow up?"

Westledge, for being a crazy, open, experimental school was at its heart a college prep school and what the counselor was trying to figure out was what I should study in college, what my major should be and where I should go. You would think this would be such an easy decision since there had been many different careers that I wanted to be when I was younger and many other things that I enjoyed doing. I could have been a chemist. In fact, I was glad that Westledge had a chemistry lab when I was looking at the school before I went there. I had also wanted to be an Air Force pilot when I was in elementary school and studied all the military and commercial jets, learned how an airfoil worked to generate lift and would dream about flying. Collecting rocks had been a hobby of mine. I would collect them on hikes, we would chip tourmaline crystals from the local outcropping. I loved exploring outside and looking at maps so being a Geologist would also be an obvious choice. I had also wanted to be a lab scientist from being in Science Academy and really enjoying it. I remember sitting in the lab at Science Academy and thinking about what it would be like to be an adult scientist working in a lab just like the one I was sitting in. The obvious choice would be to work for the Bidwell Hardware Company and get a degree in Business Management, but I knew that would not be a career for me. Part of why I enjoyed working there was that I knew it was not going to be a long-term career, so I would go full balls-out enjoying myself and working hard in the warehouse since I did not have to pace myself to do this for the rest of my life. I could be an auto mechanic, since I enjoyed working on engines, mini-bikes, my truck and had even taken a class in it already. I almost forgot; I had also wanted to be an oceanographer/marine biologist from my days skin diving in Cape Cod. Ever since I had been younger and attended Science Academy I had been interested in science. My parents would get the Sunday New York Times. It was not delivered, but we would stop by after church at Doyles Drug Store in downtown Simsbury and Dad would pick up his paper. They would always hold a copy for him and he might pick up a cigar or two when going in for the paper. We would get home and my parents would read the paper in the living room, discussing the articles that they were each reading. I would ask for the science section and they always pulled it out of the huge newspaper for me to read. Many of the articles were over my head, but many of them were aimed for the lay person and I could learn cutting edge things in the world of science.

There were so many choices for a future career, but when the counselor would ask me about it, I would just come up with nothing. I think the problem was that I was expected to make a life decision when I was only 16 and I did not want to screw up. My motto to 'just do it' only applied when there was something that I was thinking of doing, not when I did not have any idea of what to do and my mind was blank. Eventually I came up with nothing other than I wanted to study some type of science probably. There are so many fields of science that it really did not narrow down my choices much. I could even be a pilot or a mechanic and still study science.

After high school I went to college at Fairleigh Dickenson University with a major in psychology. I had taken a psychology class at Westledge and liked it, plus my mom was back in grad school in Vermont to get her Master's degree to be a psychologist. She ended up being a counselor at New Britain General Hospital for many years helping some seriously crazy patients. Psychology served several purposes for me since I could use it to help figure out who I really was, as well as being a scientific career, even if it was not a career that I had dreamed about. In college I enjoyed the abnormal psychology classes and things like the self-actualization pyramid. I took quite a few classes in child development which would be good for raising kids, in fact most of the students attending these classes were women. I was learning about Freud's psychoanalytic approach based on the libido with the id, ego and super-ego, Jung's analytical psychology approach based on differences between a person's conscious and unconscious mind, Pavlov's classical conditioning approach made famous with his experiments of dogs salivating and Watson's behaviorism approach which focused on the external behavior of people, all which were about different ways of understanding and applying psychology. Some of these theories were sexual, some conditioned, some from upbringing, some from their environment and some from just how you were born. I was studying science and I wanted to know which approach was the "correct approach". I wanted the hard science approach of using the scientific method to determine which was right and which had been proven wrong. I wanted one answer, one approach that I could focus on. I went to my advisor, who was a professor in the Psychology department and asked him this question. He basically told me that the approach that I should follow was the one that I believed in. That was the crux of my problem, I was trying to figure out which one to believe in. This was no help. What helped me was a fellow student. He was also a Psychology major and was telling me that he could not wait to graduate and start helping people. I remember thinking at that time, "I don't give a fuck about helping people". I mean, I do like the good feeling you get from helping people, I just did not want to do that as my career. That is when I knew that this is not what I want to do for the rest of my life.

I had even taken a career assessment test in college which was multiple-choice. Westledge had taught me that often there are many choices that could not boil down to just a simple multiple choice. You often had to write a little paragraph to answer the question. A good example is "would I rather read a book, watch TV, go on a walk or ride a bike". Well, if I was tired, I might just want to watch TV, if I was feeling like just hanging out, I would want to read a book, if I was restless, I would want to go on a walk, or if I was feeling adventurous, I would want to ride a bike. It would take a paragraph to answer this simple multiple-choice question. I needed a structured approach to follow when taking this test. I decided to always take the adventurous choice, if there was no adventurous choice, then take the answer that had to do with reading somehow. I took this test with this approach and the results were a little puzzling, but also expected. For a career it suggested either an author or a farmer. For my personality, Adventure was almost off the scale. I discounted any of these answers because I had skewed the results with my approach. Again, my career approach was stymied. It would be great to go on adventures and write about them, but how is that a career choice and who would want to read about it anyway. I actually did work as a farm hand for a year, about 10 years after taking that test. I totally enjoyed that year of working on the farm, since farming was nothing like I envisioned and I learned a lot and really liked the work. Being a farmer requires having a plot of fertile ground however and usually it is part of continuing the family business when you inherit the farm. Even if my dad was a farmer, I'm not the type to just take the easy path of being in the family business. What I ended up doing was switching my major to Earth Resources, the closest FDU had to a real Geology program. I really enjoyed the classes in this major but it was a bit "soft", learning mostly about how the earth's geology affected the environment and how to write environmental impact statements. There was no mineralogy, structural geology or the emerging plate tectonics.

What I needed was a tougher and more rigorous path that a Geology degree would have. I knew that I would need to go to a university that could offer that, which eventually led to me driving my Scout out to Colorado.

On Independence Day one year, Adam and I headed down to his parent's summer cottage in Westerly RI, to hang out on the Misquamicut beach for the weekend. We took my Scout down there and his cute older sister Julie was already there. That evening we were hanging out talking and Julie had an idea that on the 4th, we should enter the parade. We all talked about it and decided that the Scout would make the perfect parade float. The next day Adam and I prepared the Scout to be a float by taking the top off of it, folding down the windshield and taking the doors off. Now it was a blank float ready for decorating. We mounted flagpoles with American flags that we picked up at the hardware store. We wrapped the whole truck with red, white and blue tinsel rope, painted the truck with colored soaps and basically threw anything festive we could find on the "float". The next morning, we got dressed up in Americana and painted our faces and Adam, Julie and I got in line for the parade. The line started moving and we cruised down in the middle of the parade procession, Adam and I smiling and laughing the whole time while cranking tunes and Julie sat on top of the bench seat throwing candy at the little kids with a basket she had prepared. It was a great time. Afterwards we all went swimming in the ocean to clean the paint off, cool off and just enjoy the beach. The three of us headed home on highway two. When we were a few miles out of Hartford, Julie recounted a story of a time when she was driving back on this same highway and spotted a cute guy hitchhiking in the other direction. She had a wild hair and turned around and picked him up, just to meet him. I was in love with her from then on.

Mac and I decided to go hiking one weekend and we drove out to the Berkshires in western Massachusetts in his beetle. I knew his beetle well since we would cruise around in it and go to the B movies at the drive-ins with our girl friends when we were double-dating. We did not find a hiking trail, but did stop at Catamount Ski area and decided to hike up the slopes to the top. The ski area was closed and we just hiked up the empty ski slopes to get the view and just hang out. On the way down the hike was getting a bit tedious and I spotted a cable draping down close to the ground from between 2 of the lift towers below us. This looked like it had potential for some fun so we stopped when we got to the thick steel cable. It was like a zip line that was not a zip line but had the potential to be a zip line. We looked at it and thought if we got a stick, we could hang onto it on both sides and go sliding down the cable. We looked around and could not find anything suitable. Then we hit on the idea of using our belts, looped around the cable. I pulled my belt off, looped it over the cable and wrapped the ends around my hands to get a good grip. Mac looked apprehensively at me, not so much that I was crazy to be trying this, but that he thought I would just hang there on my leather belt and not go anywhere. I bent my knees up, putting my weight on the cable and lifted my feet off the ground. I actually started sliding slowly and whooped that it was working as I started picking up a little speed, soon I was careening down the cable at a pretty good clip and approaching the next tower. I decided to drop off into the grassy slope below. I hit the ground and took one step before diving down the hill into a tuck and roll. This was just like the tuck and roll that we practiced at Westledge as part of Hand-to-Hand Combat class. I was just a little scraped up, but otherwise fine. I looked up as Mac came walking down the hill towards me, not trusting himself to drop off without injury. We had a hike and a little adventure, a perfect day!

My Scout was no good for hauling my canoe, so we would use dad's station wagon. Usually, we would use it up in New Hampshire, but occasionally we would take it out to a lake in CT. Matt had taken a class at Loomis, his high school where they learned to build their own kayaks out of fiberglass and then paddle them on the Farmington River next to the school. I saw his kayak instructor one time at the races in the Tariffville Gorge and he looked like what I envisioned that Lewis, the jacked outdoorsman looked like in Deliverance. An expert boater with a rugged face, athletic body and big arms like Frank from Dad's warehouse. Someday I would be like him, paddling well into middle-age and passing my skills on to less experienced paddlers. Although I wanted big arms like those guys, I now know the truth that a solid core is much more important than strong arms for kayaking since the whole idea is to paddle with proper form using your torso. At the time, I had never been in a kayak, just a canoe and that was mostly in lakes.

Matt and I took his fiberglass kayak out to the class III rapids on the Farmington River in Satan's Kingdom. Matt explained the importance of leaning downstream when peeling out of an eddy facing upstream and turning 180 degrees downstream into the current. To me it seemed easier to just paddle straight downstream out of the bottom of the eddy, but Matt assured me that paddling out of the top of the eddy is the best way to do it. Matt executed a nice peel-out into the current and ran the rapid while I looked on. He carried the kayak back up and I gave it a try. I sat in that tippy round shallow arched hull in the eddy with an alien two bladed paddle quite unlike the single bladed canoe paddle that I was accustomed to. I gathered up my strength, wits and courage and paddled out of the top of the eddy into the river. Before I could even catch my breath, the rug was pulled out from under me and I flipped upstream as quick as a bunny. I wet-exited, swam the rapid and pulled out at the bottom in the slack water after gathering the boat and paddle. Matt gave me another demonstration and then I followed suit with the same result, a quick swim. We had fun playing in the water with the boat, however I did not get into another kayak for a dozen more years.

My friend Mac had a little Kmart raft that we took up to the same rapid in Satan's Kingdom in his VW bug. We pulled off on the dirt near the rapid and were working on blowing up his raft with our breath. About a quarter of the way we were both out of breath and our jaws were aching. This was not going to work. Mac came up with the idea to fill it up with the exhaust from the tailpipe of the bug. We wrapped a towel around the pipe and into the raft and actually managed to get it filled up. We were not planning to breath the air inside the raft so everything was hunky dory. We had no problem paddling that little raft like a big inner tube through the rapids in a mostly uncontrolled manner for a fun time on the hot summer day. It was not enough to make me want to be a rafter however, since I liked the better control and speed of my canoe.

Graduating from high school was a big deal for me. School was not particularity difficult, although the only studying I really enjoyed was reading the assigned books and writing papers for English class. Math class had homework that I did not mind, although we did not have any particularly gifted math teachers, so I had to work a little harder that I should have to grasp some of the concepts. Mr. Gifford was the main Math teacher and he was also the assistant soccer coach to Mr. Johnson who was English and was an amazing soccer player in his own right. Mr. Gifford was also a good co-baseball coach with my advisor, but he was a great wrestling coach, even though my high school did not have a wrestling team. He would teach algebra and trigonometry classes but would describe the concepts using descriptions that I found convoluted and not straight-forward. In the first part of my freshman year, he was teaching stuff I already knew from Jr high and I was frustrated that he was not teaching it properly. I mean it was correct, just not the way I would have explained it. I knew then that our brains worked a bit differently and I would have my work cut out for me in his classes. The girls in math class would talk about how they were distracted watching his arm muscles flex as he was writing up on the blackboard. None of us boys could ever best him when we were training in the wrestling room. In the end he did keep my love of mathematics alive as I became accustomed to his teaching style.

Mr. Vibert, the history teacher that I had carpooled with during my freshman year had become the headmaster. Mr. Friedman, the founder, school visionary and original headmaster was in a wheelchair from a bad car accident as a passenger in a speeding Porsche. The two of them gave us a great send-off at the graduation ceremony and I had all the skills needed to go out into the world, using a "Westledge" perspective that served me well for the rest of my life.

After graduation and hanging around getting pictures taken by our parents we wandered off and our parents went home. Most of us ended up in the parking lot and were drinking beer, someone even brought a keg. I was straight-up sober, since all those things were so nasty tasting to me, I might have done a slug from one of the whiskey bottles being passed around as I nursed a beer that I probably did not finish. After an hour most of us decided to move the party to a little swimming pond on the other side of Hedgehog Mountain. I did not have a car since I was dropped off by my parents so I hooked up with Jerry. Jerry was a big kid, in fact a little bigger than my friend Jody but I really knew his brother Skip better. Skip was a year younger, but was very open and funny and I really liked him. Skip had died the winter before graduation when he drove his car off the road into a pond and drowned. Jerry had not gotten over this of course and that was probably part of the reason that he had been drinking so heavily at our after-graduation party here in the parking lot. Jerry and I got into his car and headed down the long school road and I immediately realized that I had made a mistake. Jerry was totally intoxicated and was talking loudly, veering down the road from side to side. I shouted right into his face to pull over, again and again but he was ignoring me, just ranting gibberish so I reached over to the steering column and pulled his keys out of the ignition. The car was no longer running, but the drunken Jerry simply took it out of gear and we continued down the road at the same speed down the hill. He careened onto the main road without even looking for traffic, screeching the tires as we made the turn and I was terrified, having no way to get to the brake pedal or even the emergency break by the driver's door. We were heading around the end of the mountain and Jerry, drunk as he was, continued on the path to the pond where we were meeting. The problem was that the next turn onto Hedgehog Lane was a sharp one that I could see that we were not going to make. Jerry screeched around that corner and right into a telephone pole, smashing the entire front end of the car and banging my knee on the dashboard. Jerry was so drunk he did not feel anything. I got out of the car and stood by the side of the road, Jerry was still in the car ranting about something in the driver's seat, when Adam pulled up in his land cruiser. We discussed the situation and Adam's advice was for me to hop in his car so I would not be taken to the police station with Jerry, since I had done nothing other than getting the shit scared out of me. It was common knowledge that the house at the corner where we crashed was the chief of police in Simsbury, so there would be cops showing up soon. I weighed my options, stay with the drunken Jerry who I could not help or go with Adam and try to calm my nerves with my friends. I chose the latter. I heard later that the police had to restrain Jerry to get him down to the police station since he was being so belligerent and aggressive. I had made the right choice, but I never felt totally right about it.

The BM club was back at it the summer after I graduated from high school. This was my last vacation up in New Hampshire. Matt and I were in the Scout, John and Fred were following us as we were heading into town on the dirt road leading down from the cabin and Kinderheim. Just as we got to Bennet Street a station wagon with two cute girls drove past on the dirt Bennet Street. We pulled in behind them and followed for a bit before the girls took off in a cloud of dust. I did not follow them too closely because of the dust, but I then started fishtailing the scout in second gear to kick up a good cloud of dust to our mutter cousins behind us as an annoyance. Soon we got to the pavement on Bennet Street as I saw the girls pull into the house just down the street from Joe Fogg's place, an officer with the Sandwich Police department. We continued on and just before we got to the end of the road, Officer Fogg came flying up, lights a blazing and pulled both our cars over. He was livid that we had the gall to go speeding past his house kicking up dust and wanted to give us both speeding tickets. He asked where the station wagon was, but we were not going to rat on the girls that had pulled into their house just past Joe's own house. If he was an officer worth his salt, then he should have known exactly where the station wagon went. Joe threatened us with speeding tickets and reckless driving and told us we would have a court date next month. My cousin John and I would both be out of state in college and Matt and Fred would be out of state in high school, so that was out of the question. I told the officer that yes, I was kicking up a little dust in the Scout, but I was in second gear and the truck could barely do 30 MPH so there was no way I was speeding. The only car that was speeding was his next-door neighbor that he did not catch. He could not prove that we were speeding, and kicking up dust on a dirt road was not an offense, so he let us off with a verbal warning. He never remembered that I was the little freezing boy that he and his wife helped to warm up after our skiing epic years earlier. Perhaps he did, but neither of us acknowledged it and that may be why we were let off with just a warning.

Wow! It was 202 Terry Rd. So many stories that I never knew about. Did Mom? I forgot you studied psychology at FDU.

20 The FDU College Years

In my senior year when I was applying for colleges, we went down to Madison NJ to take a look at the Fairleigh Dickinson University campus. The campus was on the almost 200-acre grounds of the old Vanderbilt estate. The 100-room English-style country mansion was built in the style of my parents' much more modest house in Hartford, just on a much grander scale. It housed the administrative offices and many of the classrooms. The mansion had large terraces and beautifully manicured grounds in the back, the library was out in front and the athletic building was off to the side, both of which were also some of the original beautiful buildings. There was a new student center and dormitories as well as some new classroom buildings, and the campus was beautiful. I loved the campus and decided that this was where I wanted to attend college.

My parents drove me down to the school at the start of my freshman year and we got situated in the dorm. I was up on the third floor and shared the room with Woody, who was on the school basketball team. We were friends, but ran in different crowds. I did not know it at the time, but there were two dorms for the incoming Freshmen. The dorm I was in was the "hippy" dorm and the other dorm was the "jock" dorm. This was not entirely true, since my roommate was a jock but the dorm you were assigned to was based entirely on a questionnaire the school had sent out earlier. It looked like if you checked the box that you sometimes smoked pot, you were in the hippy dorm. The first month was similar to the week I had spent in Florida with my best friend Jerry, where I got a touch of homesickness, but I got over it as soon as I started making friends. I took the basic introductory college classes during this first year which were basic, but challenging requiring some serious studying to understand and comprehend the concepts and to pass the midterms, quizzes and final exams. Since I was a psychology major, I had a fair share of psych classes but had the leeway to choose electives in the other colleges that sounded interesting.

I took one class that Freshman year called Modern Novel. I had really liked Mr. Golden's reading class in high school where we read <u>Deliverance</u>, <u>Sometimes a Great Notion</u> and other contemporary novels and wanted to continue. This class was not anything like my classes at Westledge where we would sit around in a circle on the stepped carpeted floor and have group discussions about the book, with the teacher leading and guiding us. In this class we were reading what I considered archaic books, mostly written around the turn of the century. We would read these older classics, such as <u>Zorba the Greek</u> and do a little discussion of the books in a more formal classroom setting, but the professor would go off on what I considered tangents to what we were reading. He would talk about what the book was a metaphor about and what was the symbolism of the different parts of the book and even the characters in the book. I thought he was full of shit, just trying to be an academician and read meaning into things that had no meaning, just to justify his job. We read Zorba the Greek but I had a hard time enjoying the read. It is a tragic story about an introverted Englishman that inherited an old unworking mine in Crete so he goes there to inspect it and hooks up with a very colorful local peasant miner that assists him. The pair inspects the mine, after both try making it work and fail. They are both interested in different women in town and their affections causes one of them to be killed and the other woman gets sick and is robbed of all her possessions by the towns people. It was a straightforward tragedy, the business venture fails, the romances both ended badly and in the end the Englishman decides to run home. Well, the professor pulled the book apart looking for hidden meanings, deeper messages, analogies to contemporary life, what the lovely woman symbolized, etc. I was wondering why he could not just enjoy the book for what it is. A tragedy with a little adventure, a little romance, and a sad ending.

We read many other books, and would write papers on the symbolism, the deeper meanings, and the metaphors. I really wanted to write about what parts of the book I enjoyed, how descriptive the prose is and what pulled me into the story making me want to finish reading the book and if it was really good, why I did not want the book to end. I forced myself to write about what the Professor wanted and was looking for in our papers, searching for what I called "the story within the story". Perhaps that is not what the professor called it, but it described perfectly what he was looking for. Eventually, towards the end of the semester, I was starting to come around and thought that perhaps the professor was onto something. It was looking likely that he actually knew what he was talking about and I had been wrong about him all along.

Some of these books were more interesting with the symbolism and were much more than the sum of their parts. If the book was really good, then it could be enjoyed after I had finished reading it, thinking about the parts and what the deeper meaning is that the author is trying to get across. Perhaps it is a serious contemporary topic that was too sensitive or even dangerous to write about directly at the time so the inner story had to be hidden inside the main story of the book. That class turned out to be probably the best class that I took in my two years at FDU, although I did not realize it while I was taking the class and never did change my major to English.

It is easy to just relax in your dorm room between classes, or study in the library but I wanted to keep working out and be active. We would throw a frisbee out in the grass outside the dorms and I started going to the school gym. I had always worked out at home with my barbell set and now I had the luxury of a gym within walking distance, just across campus in the athletic building. All I was looking for in a gym was to be able to lift weights, frisbee would take care of my cardio. There were a few free weights scattered around, but what interested me was this new state of the art Universal Machine. It was setup like a cube with one workout station on each side. There was a bench press with a stack up to 220 pounds, a leg press, a military press, a lat pull and an arm curl. These were all the basic exercises that I did with the barbell, just in a much more convenient package using a pin to select the workout weight on the weight stack rather than putting weights on and off. I loved working out here, in fact some of my new friends were guys that I worked out with, most of which were playing varsity sports. I put on 15 pounds of muscle my freshman year with that machine.

Across the hall in the dorm was a kid from Massachusetts, Kip, that became my best friend during my freshman year. He had been in prep school for high school, so he was accustomed to dorm life and was very comfortable with it. We would hang out smoking pot and shooting the shit about life. He had played lacrosse in high school, like I did and had his lacrosse stick with him. I borrowed his extra stick to throw and train outside, doing sprints and catching the ball over our shoulder, running in circles throwing the ball to each other and taking breaks to just throw the ball back and forth. I had another friend in the dorms, Jon from Maryland, that had played lacrosse in high school and was on a lacrosse scholarship to FDU. He eventually became one of my 5 roommates when I moved into a "Suite" in the upperclassmen dorm my sophomore year. I was outside with Jon later on in the winter and we were in a snowball fight with some kids from the other dorm and I noticed that Jon could throw a snowball much farther than I could. It is just a natural athletic skill that is hard to work on, unlike lifting weights. That is one thing I liked about lacrosse; I could throw with the best of them using the leverage of the stick to launch the ball. Between playing catch with the two of them outside, I decided to join the FDU lacrosse team. This was a big sport at my campus of 3000 kids. I knew I probably could not make the varsity team, since Westledge had cancelled our lacrosse team for baseball in my last 2 years of high school so I was out of practice. I tried out however and made the JV team. It was very good for keeping active and in shape and I also got to know all the players on both the JV and varsity teams since we worked out together. We would take the team bus to other schools to play their JV teams, or in the case of Steven's Tech, we played their varsity team since they were a smaller school. I scored my first goal at that school in dirty Hoboken NJ on a field without a single blade of grass, just dirt so that game stands out in my mind. We were happy on the bus ride back, all dirty from our win and I was glowing inside knowing that I was getting better faster playing midfield with the team and could probably make varsity when I was an upperclassman.

Towards the end of my first semester at FDU, I had a couple of good friends, Kip and Pete. We were sitting around and I was talking about spending summers up at the cabin in NH and how one time my family took a winter ski trip up there. We were smoking a joint and discussing what we were planning to do over the upcoming Christmas break. One thing led to another and we decided that the three of us should do a winter adventure and go up to the cabin in January after Christmas, or Hanukah in Kip's case. We would meet at my house in Hartford. Kip would drive down from his dad's place in Ipswich MA and Pete would come over from Bristol CT which was quite close. We loaded up the Scout with all our winter gear and headed up to North Sandwich. There was quite a bit of snow when we got up to New Hampshire and even more when we got up to where Bennet Street turned to dirt, or in this case, unplowed snow. I got out and locked the hubs, put the scout into low range 4WD and we slowly worked our way up the road in a good 15" of the white stuff. We crawled our way up into the trees and the Scout was working hard to stay on the road. We were perhaps a quarter mile from the Joe's footbridge when the Scout slid off the narrow road to the right and into the snow below, piling it up onto the passenger side. The three of us piled out my driver-side door with a little effort since the truck was listing at a pretty good angle. We stood there in the snow and debated about what to do. It was getting a little late in the afternoon, I decided that we should just leave the truck there, unload all our gear, posthole our way up to the cabin and worry about the Scout later. It was a plan. We pulled our packs out of the Scout and worked our way up to the bridge in the snow. The footbridge was a little sketchy with the snow and the log hand-rail fairly high across Swift River. We made it across like Everest adventurers crossing a crevasse on an aluminum ladder, but I digress, err exaggerate. We slogged our way up the trail to the cabin and we were sweaty and tired, so I knew we had better heat up the cabin soon before we got the chills. I found the key to the cabin and the pagoda where Uncle Rudy had hidden them. We opened up the cabin and went inside and fired up the big wood stove with some handy split wood in a basket inside. In about an hour the cabin started heating up and we took off our hats, coats and boots and settled in, making ourselves at home. We each chose a bed and unpacked our gear to make this home for the next few days.

Kip and Pete had never done anything like this before and were quite amazed that my grandfather had managed to acquire such a remote and beautiful place and build such a snug and comfortable cabin. We cooked dinner on the large wood stove of Dinty Moore beef stew with bread and rum & cokes, my preferred drink at the time. We relaxed, smoked some pot, broke out the backgammon game which Kip had taught me to play back in the dorms, and had a comfortable evening betting on things. There is just something extremely satisfying about being out in the wilderness in harsh conditions, but being totally comfortable at the same time. We all felt this although none of us put it into words. I enjoyed the nostalgia of reading the old Archie comic books and the knickknacks that reminded me of my grandparents. Pete was going on about what a cool adventure we were having in his jovial loud voice while Kip was just talking excitedly about our trip so far. It made me feel good to turn some friends on to this little piece of heaven that held a special place in my heart and that I got to share.

We chopped firewood, went on exploratory hikes in the snow, used the ice-cold Hedi Lamar, made water from the snow and were just being woodsmen for the days that we were up there. When it was time to go, we cleaned up the cabin, loaded up our packs, locked everything up tight and hiked back down to the Scout that we had not thought about for four days. I was thinking in my head about what we could do to get the Scout pulled out of the snowbank. It was a long way off the road for a tow truck, but we could hike out to Sheriff Fogg's place and ask to use his phone. As I was musing about these things, we saw the Scout up ahead just sitting in the middle of the road like nothing had happened.

We walked up to it and there was a note under the windshield wiper which read.

"You have been helped by the Wonalancet Four Wheelers Club!".

That was so awesome. It was a final perfect cap to our little adventure. You have to love the folks that live up in the North country. I wished I had a way to show my appreciation, but I hope their payment was just them feeling good about themselves for helping out a fellow four-wheeler. Thank you! That was the last time I ever stayed up at the cabin, but it was a very good final memory of the place. Thank you, Grandma and Grandpa Noss!

Back at FDU that Spring, I decided to play Rugby. It seemed like a good sport for me, kind of like the murder-ball games that I had excelled at during my time at summer camp. I figured a fearless and aggressive attitude would make up for my lack of large size. I tried out for the team and made it onto the squad. I got to know the team during our practices and liked the rowdy bunch of hard-drinking guys that all fancied themselves as tough guys, mostly by virtue of playing this game. The best guy on the team was a big very long-haired Native American guy that would have been an actual tough guy whatever he was doing. He was fearless, muscular and tough and we all aspired to be as good as him someday. There were several things about Rugby that I liked. It was really a social game, not just getting together after practice to hang out. After an actual game against another university, no matter who won the game, both teams would get together with a keg of beer and sing bawdy rugby songs, enjoying the company of the other team. In fact, the song The Ten Days of Christmas has forever been ruined forever for me by the extremely crude Ten Days of Rugby. I don't know any other sport that does this type of socializing after the game with the other team. Another aspect of the game is that there are really no substitutes. If you are hurt during the game, then you are sent to the "blood-bin" while your substitute plays for you. Once you have recovered, the substitute must return to the bench while you go immediately back out onto the pitch. Just the terms that the game uses make it sound like a sport for real men! You get to wear these really tough jerseys which is really the only part of your uniform and is the only Rugby-specific gear that you wear, other than a pair of cleats on your feet. The other team can grab your jersey, unlike football and use it to throw you to the ground.

I was just getting into Rugby and had played three or four games when my shining moment came at a game against Drew University.

During the kickoff the ball went flying high into the air and right towards me. I held up my hand yelling "I've got it!".

I caught the ball and was determined to just run so fast and fearlessly hard towards the opposing team that they would take pause before tackling me. As it turned out, there was a player on the Drew team that had the same attitude. We ran towards each other in opposite directions and smacked our heads together during his tackle attempt. I just lay there on my back in the field and literally saw stars and birds circling around in the sky above just like in the cartoons. Somehow, we did not knock each other unconscious, but we did knock ourselves out of the game. The game just continued playing, as players lying on the field was fairly commonplace. The other player and I eventually got up and staggered off the field into our respective blood-bins since we were in no shape to continue on. As I was sitting there thinking about this game in a semi-concussed state, I decided right then and there that this sport that smashed heads together without a helmet was contrary to higher-learning in a university. This was the last Rugby game that I ever played although I had a couple of heavy-duty jerseys as a reminder of the glory I never attained.

Kip and couple of our friends and I were sitting around in his dorm room talking when another kid in the dorms came in and said that he had some acid and would we be interested. I had never done it, but apparently Kip was a veteran from his prep school days. We ended up getting hits for everyone in the room and dropped the LSD that weekend. It was on a little square of paper with a little dried drop of acid in the center. We each took our little square and put it on our tongues and hung out. It did not take effect immediately. I was sitting in the room looking at the cable spool that served as a table with a candle in the middle when the entire candle and table started melting down into the floor like it was just one giant candle. That was weird, like a daydream when I was wide awake. I looked up at a poster on the wall of a horse and the horse then trotted off the poster, across the wall and out of the room. OK, no doubt about it now, I was tripping. Everything was surreal, we walked around the dorms and outside marveling at the new reality of everything. Nothing was as expected and the normal laws of physics were out the window. One of our friends was going into downtown Madison and a couple of us went with him. I don't know what happened to Kip at this time. We were wandering around downtown and I was enjoying the weird scene when we went into a little college market. I grabbed some sucker candies since my mouth was dry and went up to the counter. The guy behind the counter looked at me and I looked at him. He said something that I didn't quite understand about the price and I reached into my pocket and pulled out a couple of bills and just dropped them onto the counter. Figuring out the change was outside of the realm of possibility at the moment. We went back to campus and later that evening the trip started to mellow out a little, but just a little. It was probably 6 or 8 hours since the horse ran off and I was not aware of time, but it seemed like I had been tripping for a very long time and that this would be my new reality. I thought that I might be like this forever and wondered that if I could not count out change, how I would be able to ask questions in class and be lucid. Everyone would look at me like I was "out there". We eventually wandered up a bushy hill behind the cafeteria where there was a manhole cover that we pried off and climbed into a semi-secret underground bunker that one of us knew about. There was graffiti on the cement walls and we all hung out in there in that cool secret cave until it was light out and we wandered out one at a time into the bright sunshine like some primeval cave dwellers. That was an interesting and eye-opening experience for me, how my reality could be so totally different with just a little hit of a very potent drug. I enjoyed the trip and I also knew that I would never do it again. I think I was still a little scared that if I did it again, I could end up being that "out there" kid that no-one could relate to since I would have an alternate reality from everyone else.

I ended up visiting the "jock" dorm quite a bit to hang with my friends there and determined that there was almost as much pot smoking going on there as in my dorm. Kip and I would go over and hang with our friend Pete that lived in that dorm. Pete was a full-on pot smoking hippy from Manchester CT that was always talking about something. One time I was over there, most of the lacrosse team was in his dorm and one mean little jock with broad shoulders that was on the varsity team his freshman year was outside Pete's door. He never smoked pot and was giving us shit and I started giving him shit back, like we were going to fight. When he left, Pete warned me not to rile him up because although he was smaller than me, he was very tough and everyone gave him a wide berth. I knew from practicing with him out on the field that he was one of those people that respects you more when you give him shit back, if you don't, then in his mind he just won. Won what, I don't know, but that is just how he was.

There was an intramural wrestling tournament at the school that I entered since I had wrestled intramural before and was feeling strong from working out. In fact, by the time the tournament was announced, I had worked up to benching the entire stack on the Universal machine bench press station, my personal gauge as to how strong I was getting. There was a friend of Woody's on the basketball team that would workout in the weight room and I got to know him there. I was getting pretty muscular at the time and he was still a tall skinny kid, but a good basketball player. He was musing with me one time when we were working out that perhaps it was that smoking pot was what made me so much more muscular than him. I told him that he was nuts, it was just that I worked out hard three days a week and almost never missed a workout. I'm just lucky I guess that I have always enjoyed workouts. He never did believe me, but he obviously had his doubts since he never resorted to smoking pot to test out his theory. When the wrestling tournament came around and I was wrestling the other 160 pounders. I used the moves that Mr. Gifford had taught me at Westledge and managed to win all my matches. I was feeling pretty good about this, but I am exaggerating since my last match was with a wrestler on the FDU varsity team who made quick work of me on my last match, pinning me. I like to think that he was fresh and was waiting to just wrestle the tournament winner in his weight class but that is just my speculation.

The next day I was changing into my Lacrosse gear for practice when that tough little broad-shouldered kid walked by and said, "Hey I heard that you pinned Ferd (another player on our lacrosse team) yesterday, nice work".

I just looked up at him with a little smile but did not say anything, since I was not used to us not giving each other shit. We were never friends; we just had a mutual respect.

Towards the end of my freshman year, five friends and I decided to sign up together to get a suite in the upperclassmen dorm. Jon and Tom would share a bedroom, Jeff and I would share a room and two other friends would share the third bedroom. This was a step up from our current dormitory since we would share a bathroom and not share it with the entire hallway of rooms, plus we had a nice little living room and we were all friends that got along. Kip was not part of the group since he was transferring to another university for the next school year. I also changed my major to Earth Resources so that I would have a new curriculum when I came back in the fall. The family came down to pick me up with my stuff from the dorm, not that I had accumulated much. My favorite part of the drive home was crossing the Hudson River on the 3-mile-long Tappan Zee bridge and looking East toward the city 25 miles away.

That summer I worked at the Bidwell Company, helping Frank in the warehouse and driving the big split axle delivery trucks. Having a little spending money was good at school, although my parents were paying for my schooling. I took a class in Geography at CCSU to get a few more credits and I was very interested in the geography of the US since I planned to explore it after college. I was sitting in this class one day and the professor was talking to the 8 of us guys that had enrolled in his class and was talking about how he was glad that there were no women in our class since it would change the chemistry and affect the in-class discussions. I thought this was a very weird thing to say, but then he went on to say that some of us had not written enough on our last essays on the piedmont and we had better pick up the slack or he would not be able to give us all "A''s in the class. We looked around at each other thinking "Cool!". It was very handy to have the use of my Scout again since freshmen were not allowed to have cars.

Matt and I borrowed Dad's Vista Cruiser and took it up to Tamworth NH to visit Grandma Noss who had been living there alone. It was early in the summer and Grandma had opened up

Valley Farm and we were her first houseguests. We hung out with her, reading books and exploring around in the woods behind the house and helping her with chores getting the house ready for the summer. She made us dinner one evening and when I dumped the Parmesan cheese from the shaker onto my spaghetti, there were as many mealworms falling out as there was cheese. Grandma took it in stride saying they were just dead bugs from the winter and picked them off my plate. Grandpa had purchased a phonograph, but all he had was classical music, so Matt and I went into town and got some music for it. I got a Led Zeppelin album and Matt got an Iron Butterfly album which I'm sure was like running fingernails down a chalkboard to Grandma, but she was glad to have the company. We put lots of Old Woodsman's fly dope on our neck bandannas and using a hatchet made a trail way back into the woods by blazing marks on the trees so that we could get back.

We drove Dad's station-wagon home after our visit and were in Massachusetts when the car started running very rough and sputtering so I pulled into a gas station that had two garage bays, so I was pretty sure that it was owned by a mechanic. I was worried since this Vista Cruiser was my favorite car ever, probably even more than my Scout and I hoped that it was not something serious. It turned out that the oil had not been changed in quite a while and was below the dipstick. Also, the points were corroded and were not connecting solidly enough to provide a strong spark for combustion. I was relieved that these were such minor problems and the car was fine. They changed the oil, replaced the points and condenser which was just part of a minor tune-up and we made it home fine. What I did not realize that this breakdown with a couple of his boys made Dad lose all faith in that wonderful car and he traded it in the next year, much to my dismay.

I told my mom before I went back to school that I was tired of waiting for my life to begin, being in college. She told me that it is still life and to enjoy it since I might find it was one of the best times of my life. She was right about it just being life and it is a good lesson to learn to enjoy being in the moment, enjoying life, instead of waiting for some goal or time period to pass to start enjoying it. Mom always had a positive outlook on life! In fact, mom had a motto to "be flexible". This meant that if you were planning to do something and the shit hit the fan, just go with it and change your plans. It does not mean to just agree with someone with a different point of view than yourself and be wishy washy, but to stick to your convictions, but if things turn out different than you were expecting, just go with it. This was the same as some of the lessons that I learned at Westledge as well. I would ponder this philosophy sometimes in my bedroom at Terry Rd since it was at odds with Henry Stamper's motto of "Never Give an Inch" in my favorite book at the time, <u>Sometimes a Great Notion</u>. I decided that I liked mom's more upbeat motto better than Henry's confrontational and stubborn one.

When I went back to school, I took the Scout since that was a privilege of being a sophomore. I was pretty gung-ho on Geology (actually Earth Resources) and asked my professors about the local quarries and pegmatite outcroppings and would go there on the weekends rockhounding. My favorite place was collecting fluorescent minerals at the Franklin Mine not too far from school. I would collect specimens and view them back at school under an ultraviolet light to see how I did. Some of them were pretty beautiful in just normal sunlight as well.

I took a class in philosophy that I really enjoyed since it made me think about things from different angles. It was eye-opening just like my Modern Novels class had done the previous year. It is the type of class that would make you a more interesting human being and keep the wheels of your mind turning all the time.

I could see why Grandpa Noss had enjoyed his Philosophy studies so much in Theology school, although he said after getting burned out working on his PHD at Harvard, "You learn more and more about less and less", before dropping out.

I was thinking this second year that I was wasting my parent's money, changing majors, getting high fairly often with my roommates and playing sports. I also wanted to travel after my geography class and I wanted to go to a more rigorous hard-core geology program. My roommate Jon was talking about how fantastic the skiing was in Colorado with blue skies and snow so powdery that it just evaporated into the air rather than melting. I was thinking about much more than skiing, but it sounded pretty good anyway, plus my friend Mac had just moved there to be with his girlfriend that was going to the University of Denver. I made the Dean's list during my Earth Resources studies and that was a good indication that I was on the right track. Taking a break from school to spend time in Colorado was growing in my mind as a plan after my sophomore year.

We would play awesome Capture the Flag games in the grounds behind the admin building at night, running around the terraces with dozens of kids in the semi-darkness. Jim, a friend of mine and awesome lacrosse player was running with me towards the other team when Jim jumped over a hedge that was in front of a low sculpted concrete railing protecting against a twelve-foot fall to the grassy terrace below. I saw him disappear into the dark and ran around down the stairs to the lower level, expecting to see him moaning on the ground. He was up and standing there with just a little scare from jumping into space essentially. Being young and athletic has its perks, since that fall would have killed most normal human beings. Mom was right that life was still good at school and there were many fun activities, other than studying for midterms and finals.

I was impressed with your interest in the modern novel. You have a pent-up need to write obviously. Your story is unique. How will it translate to a larger audience is the question? We have been watching CNN a lot. Governor Cuomo is very knowledgeable and a vital counterpoint to Trump. Our family adventure to the cabin set up your return trip with friends. Rugby is a dangerous sport. I have just watched Governor Cuomo's daily briefing on NY state and the virus. He is becoming a national authority.
Love Dad

21 Boulder part 1 - Cloud 9 & Shannons

I had decided during my sophomore year to take a break from college for a year or two and head out to Colorado. I wanted to see the Rocky Mountains, I wanted a break from college, mostly I wanted to go to a school that had a good Geology department and I thought that if worked there for a couple of years, I would be able to pay for the rest of my college with an in-state tuition. I had a friend from FDU, Bob that was going to accompany me for the travel adventure.

I loaded up the Scout with mostly clothes, hiking and camping gear. My family stood in the driveway as I backed the scout down the driveway as I had done many times, but this time I backed right into the hedge. I pulled the Scout forward and made it to the street on my second try. My mom was hoping that this bad early start to my trip was not fortuitous. I headed down to New Jersey to pick up Bob and we headed out on the Interstate for Colorado at 55 MPH since that was the comfortable cruising speed for the utilitarian old truck. We slept next to the truck in Grandpa Noss's old floor-less waxed canvas pole tent in Western Pennsylvania the first night. Grandpa had sewn much of his own gear since he was backpacking before there were camping outlets like REI and this was the one piece of his gear that I had. The second night we pulled off to a state park in Indiana and setup camp. There was a guy camped next to us that was very excited that he had found quite a bit of wild marijuana and had filled up his car trunk with it. We tried a bit of it with him and decided that it was just wild hemp, but he could not be convinced. We took none of it and could not understand why he had not come to the same conclusion, since the empirical evidence clearly proved that there was no THC in it. The third night we pulled off the highway in Nebraska at lake McConaughy looking for a camping spot. We pulled off the road into a tall grassy meadow and had not gone 10 feet, when the field exploded with grasshoppers. They poured into the truck over our elbows that were leaning out the windows and dozens of these large insects filled the truck before we could get the windows rolled up. We backed out of there and headed towards the lake with the bugs crawling all over us, on the windshield, in our hair and on our gear in the back looking for a bug-free spot. We headed out past a boat launch onto the beach and drove down on the sand in 4WD for a quarter mile before stopping in the middle of the beach to camp in the sand near the water. We shooed out most of the bugs and setup camp on the soft sand and went to sleep. Sometime after midnight we woke up with strong Westerly Nebraska winds blowing the sand onto, into and under the tent. It was a little less than miserable, but a lot better than grasshoppers crawling all over us, so we just made the best of it.

I was pretty excited the next day, since we were going to arrive in Colorado and get our first peek at the Rocky Mountains. After an hour or so in Colorado I could see the dark outlines of the mountains off to the West. As we got closer and closer to Denver, they got bigger, but still far off on the horizon. I was waiting for them to just be like a huge wall of rock jutting high up into the sky that would look like an awesome impenetrable-looking mountain range just waiting to be explored. I was rather disappointed that when we got to Denver, they were bigger, distant and those snowcapped peaks were still far-off. Often in my life, when going somewhere, I get a picture in my head of what something will be like, and many times it is not quite as impressive as it is in my mind's eye. It is like reading a good book and having a vivid picture in your head of what the scene looks like, then seeing the movie and the scene is nothing like you imagined and not nearly as good. This was one of those times.

We stayed with a friend of mine who was living near the University of Denver where his girlfriend was going to school. We lasted there just a few days until the girlfriend accused Bob of pilfering some of her stuff. We had a bit of a row, packed up our gear and headed out to Boulder looking for other accommodations. I felt sorry for my friend.

Boulder was a little more like how I had pictured Colorado. The Flatirons were quite impressive-looking from town and I was happy to be there. We stayed with friends of Bob's, Peter and his wife Sherri. They had a house on the edge of a bluff just to the East of Boulder which overlooked the whole Boulder valley and the mountains beyond. This was more like it. Peter was one of those guys who was likely to strike it rich with one of his schemes.

He sold used cars out of his large yard and his biggest score was renting the CU Auditorium one time to show the porno flick Behind the Green Door which was sold out making him a bundle. Peter and Sherri took us up to their foothills cabin in the Ponderosa Forest outside of Nederland for a day. He had a little 125cc dirt bike and we took turns riding it down the dirt roads. On my turn, I immediately felt comfortable and cruised down the road at a thrilling speed feeling confident of my abilities. That is until I approached a not so gentle turn to the right. I banked the bike into the turn and started skidding until I laid the bike down and slid off the road into a large tough Mountain Mahogany bush. I scraped up my hands, scratched my face, ripped my pants and broke off the right rearview mirror bending the brake. After licking my wounds and bending back the brake lever, I slowly rode back to the cabin, defeated by this dirt bike and with the knowledge that this would never be a sport for me. I ended up getting a dirt bike years later in spite of this earlier experience, and broke my leg doing a whisky throttle in Utah. I did not even know what a whisky throttle was! Learning from your experience is a good thing no matter how far in the past it occurred.

Bob and I immediately got to work looking for jobs, a summer job for him and a more permanent job for me. The four of us took several trips up to the high country near Indian Peaks and went four-wheeling and exploring. We were all impressed how well that old Scout made it up the steep slopes to the remote lakes and creeks. I spent most of every day calling help-wanted ads in the Boulder Daily Camera and dropping off resumes. After a couple of weeks, Bob and I found a place to live for the summer at a flophouse on Broadway called Cloud Nine. It was a hippy kind of place, not that dissimilar to my first dorm with two twin beds and cement block walls. We rented the cheap room with a bathroom down the hall and a dis-functional swimming pool out back with a bench and a rusty set of barbells that I thought would be useful, but I quickly joined the YMCA which had my favorite Universal weight machine. It was filled with kids mostly our age, lots of whom would lie around naked sunning by the empty pool. It was perfect and we were lucky to find it. There were lots of kids staying at Cloud Nine, new arrivals like us, college kids spending the summer in Boulder and just hippy types. Bob and I made friends with several of them, it being easy in this dorm-like environment. Now that I was living in Colorado, I was again two years away from the legal drinking age and would once again need to sneak into any bars.

Bob and I decided to go out one night with a couple of our new friends Craig and Steve. We headed downtown to a rougher biker-bar place called Shannons on W Pearl Street where we figured they would be less stringent in checking IDs and we would be more likely to get in. A huge long haired, red-headed angry looking dude was at the door checking IDs and with a bit of trepidation we handed our doctored drivers licenses to him and were waved through into the party inside. We hung out listening to the music and bumping into everyone dancing. I was dancing in the middle of the crowd and there was a cute biker chick in front of me, and with a wild hair, I reached around the guy in front of me and pinched her ass.

She swiveled around and with fire in her eyes, slugged the guy in front of me yelling, "You fucking pig, keep your hands to yourself!".

I was as shocked at her reaction as the guy that she hit, so I wandered back over to where my friends were and wormed my way up to the bar. As I was yelling to the bartender for another Pabst Blue Ribbon, I noticed a sign taped to the wall behind the bar saying "Help Wanted". When he brought back my beer, I asked him if they still had a job opening since I was definitely interested. He yelled back to me, "Have you ever washed dishes?". I yelled back "Have I ever! Yes, for years". He told me to come back tomorrow during the day. Well I was excited to have my first job interview lined up and was happy partying with my boys in the bar for the rest of the night.

The next morning, I went back to Shannons and it was quiet and smelled like stale beer. There was a guy stocking the bar and he directed me to the back to talk to the owner. The owner was a hard-nosed grandmother type Jewish woman that I thought was curious since I figured a bar named Shannons would be owned by some crusty red-nosed Irishman. Of course, she knew nothing about my job interview. We talked and sort of hit it off and she hired me on the spot to start right away. I never filled out any paperwork which I was glad of, since I was worried that I would not be hired if she found out that I was only 19. I waited around for a while for the cook to show up to prepare for the lunch crowd. The cook was a tall, stringy haired, skinny hippy kid in his late 20's with a bad attitude like being a cook was his punishment in life. I was thinking he had a better job than I did and at least he was working, which was why I was so happy and excited. He ran through how to use the sprayer to clean off the dishes with the spray nozzle before putting them into the steam hood and what I could do to help him prepare the food. It was pretty straight-forward. We were pretty busy for the lunch crowd and I was working hard to keep the dishes and the kitchen clean and help making salads and preparing the plates for sandwiches and burgers. I fell into a groove in a couple of days and would work while the cook would complain about being stuck in Boulder. He really wanted to wander around Mexico and told me that he had a secret that allowed him to eat the local food and drink the local water without ever getting sick. His secret was to eat a whole fresh garlic clove every day and that would kill any germs and bacteria, keep his blood pressure down since he was pretty highly strung and basically keep his immune system strong. I was thinking that he was never going to meet any cute Mexican girls down there with his industrial strength garlic breath. True to his word, he quit without any warning about 2 weeks later and I was promoted to cook!

I spent a couple of days training as a cook with the owner and I was on my own. Luckily the menu was basically pub fare and did not require too much culinary expertise. I learned to cook burgers and steaks to rare, medium and well done, the sandwiches just needed to be grilled, the salads just had to look nice, the deep fryer had a timer on it so that was pretty easy as well. I settled in. My favorite time at work was the quiet period in the afternoon between lunch and dinner. I would make a nice cheeseburger with a thick slice of onion and fries or a hot turkey sandwich with mashers and lots of gravy, sit at the back bar and relax for an hour eating my lunch and watching Groucho Marx Hosting You Bet Your Life. A big benefit of working here is that they supplied lunch and usually dinner so that I did not need to purchase many groceries or have to cook so much at the community kitchen at Cloud Nine. Another benefit is that I always had a place to drink without sneaking in, since they knew me there. I could go with my friends and they would usually not get carded either.

The owner, who I really liked even if she was a tough boss being very picky about how clean I would leave the kitchen and that I would consistently make each order in the "Shannon way" ordered a Rubin sandwich for lunch not long after I had taken over as cook. I made my best sandwich and fries and had the dishwasher, a cool Mexican guy they hired not too long after I was promoted, take the lunch plate to her in the back office. Almost immediately she came back with my lunch since it was not up to her high standards. We would weight the individual portions so they were always the same size and I would carefully spread the meat on it so that the patrons would get the same quantity of meat in every bite. She was quite upset and told me to pile the meat into the middle of the sandwich with almost none at the edges. Then when the cut sandwich was on the plate and it was set before the hungry customer, the meat would be piled high and would look like twice as much meat as was really there. I made her another lunch plate just the way she wanted it even if it seemed like false advertising to me. I made all my sandwiches like that from then on. I suppose that is the difference between a cook and a chef. Part of being a chef is the presentation of the food, and this was just making the presentation of my sandwiches look as tasty as possible, even if I never did feel right about it.

Bob and I would take the Scout up into the high country and drive up the 4WD roads as far as we could until the truck could go no farther. Sometimes the truck would just lose power on these timberline dirt roads and we would have to turn the Scout around and back up the hills to get that little bit of extra power from the slightly lower reverse gear. We would then hike up to the Cirque basins and jump into the cold tarn lakes and just be amazed at what a beautiful place we were in. I had finally found the Colorado that I had imagined when I was driving out. Laying in the grass and looking up at the tall cliffs surrounding these lakes was very satisfying to me. I almost wore the Vibram soles off of my boots that summer with all the hiking and scrambling that we did.

Not long after I started at Shannons, I got a letter from BesTop, a company making Jeep convertible tops in East Boulder where I had dropped off a resume a couple of weeks earlier. It was not a job offer, but an appointment for a real interview in a few days. At the time Bob was still looking for work and had not had any luck. I read this letter and it sounded like a better long-term job than working as a cook. Bob also needed to make some money this summer to have back at FDU in the Fall. I already knew that I would be working in Boulder for a couple of years, since it would take at least a year of living here to become a resident to afford the tuition at a state school here. This seemed like the perfect long-term job but I knew Bob needed this job also. We discussed our options and decided that Bob should take the job, even if it was just for the summer. He went to the job interview with my letter and explained to them that I was already working, we both had similar qualifications, he was even a harder worker than I and that he would be an excellent candidate. He ended up getting the job and I felt good about helping him find employment and he was glad to be able to start working at last.

My brother Matt came out for a few weeks and stayed with me at Cloud Nine before heading off to Macalester College in St Paul, MN to start his freshman year. He was really enjoying his time away from home and loved the outdoors as much as I did, so we went camping and hiking quite a bit. We decided to take a couple of days and go backpacking so after looking at maps, we found a long trail up to a lake above timberline that looked perfect. We took the Scout up to the trailhead, loaded up our packs and headed out up the trail in the middle of the afternoon. We were hiking on the trail for about an hour or two when the sky got dark, but we continued on since we were not up to the lake yet. Well the rain started falling in huge drops, so Matt and I threw our packs down and setup our tent. I had found a discarded tent next to a dumpster in Boulder. Finding stuff like this was pretty common there with all the students coming and going and leaving stuff that they no longer had a use for. It was a simple A-Frame tent with no fly, but the fabric was waterproof. Our campsite was only 10' off the trail since we did not have time to find the perfect spot, but it was pretty level and a little grassy and we were lucky to find it so quickly. We threw ourselves and our gear into the tent and were already fairly wet, but we dried off with tee shirts in our packs. Matt and I were sitting there looking at each other and I was seeing Matt's hair standing straight out towards the walls of the tent. I was feeling prickly with my hair standing out with the intense static electricity and we looked at each other knowing what was coming. There was a tremendous clap of thunder and flash of light that sounded like it was right on top of us and that was it. We were still alive and not fried into human egg rolls wrapped in the melted nylon of the tent. It really started raining then and the thunder and lightning continued, but never as close as that first strike. We got out Matt's Svea 123 stove and made dinner in the tent. That food tasted so good after hiking with heavy packs, even if it was freeze-dried and we were eating it from a pouch. After dinner, we heated up some more water and made tea as it was getting dark. We lit a couple of candle lanterns and I pulled a copy of the Rocky Mountain News from my backpack that we got when getting last minute supplies on the way up to the trailhead. We were laying back using our backpacks as recliners, reading the paper by candlelight and sipping our tea with our feet inside our sleeping bags, snug, warm, fed and entertained, while the wind and rain of the storm was still carrying on outside. I had been backpacking before, but this singular moment of being totally comfortable in the wilderness during adverse conditions made me a lifelong convert to backpacking. That feeling of being totally self-sufficient ranks right up there with the amazing country that can be seen when out hiking for several days to seldom seen places.

Matt was wanting to go climbing while he was here and had brought some of his climbing gear. The obvious place to climb was one of the five Flatirons that loom over Boulder from the edge of the mountains. We decided on the second Flatiron, so we hiked up from Chautauqua to the base of this large rock face that was angled back about 45 degrees from the vertical. Matt pulled out his EB rock climbing shoes from his pack for the ascent and I was wearing my standard Boulder footgear of Vasque leather hiking boots. I had my trusty bota bag for water and a couple of granola bars. The face is pretty long and totally exposed, but offers pretty good hand holds on the solid Fountain Formation rough conglomerate sandstone. We talked about fourth classing the route where we would only lift a single arm or leg off the rock face at a time to maintain maximum contact since we did not have a rope. We started up the route, Matt leading since he was the experienced rock climber. It was pretty exhilarating to be up high on the rock face with the view of Boulder far off below us, as well as the ground where we left the pack. We made it to near the halfway point where the first large slab ended with a little ledge below the top-most slab and stopped for a bite to eat and some water and enjoyed the view. The second pitch to the top was a little steeper and seemed much more exposed, but was nothing that we could not handle although the feeling of being so high up was a bit unnerving. I would think that if I slipped and fell, I would not free-fall through the air, but would bounce down head over heels dozens of times until one of them would crack me on the head hard enough to knock me unconscious before the final killing blow. Bidwell, put that thought out of your head! As we were nearing the apex of the flatiron, I was looking forward to walking off the backside and enjoying the hike down with a successful climb under our belt. We go to the top and the view was amazing looking down the long rock face to the ground and the entire town of Boulder literally just below us. My daydream of hiking off the back was dashed when we saw that there was a near vertical climb off the back-side for a good 50 feet to the ground. This was a much more difficult climb than we had just come up, plus it was down-climbing which is much harder since you have to feel for footholds with your boots. The rock looked rougher on the back side, offering more holds and Matt was sure we could make it down, I was not so sure, this being my maiden rock-climbing voyage after all. We backed down the rock, again Matt leading with nice bucket holds for our hands, but with the scary feeling of lowering down and feeling for a foot-hold. Slowly we made our way towards the ground. There was an aspen tree next to the cliff when I was about 20 feet from the ground and I jumped the 5 feet to the tree and grabbed it in a bear hug and shimmied the rest of the way down, safe on the ground! Matt made it down climbing the whole way. We were really going to enjoy the hike down since a fall on the trail would not be fatal. We stopped at the bottom to get Matt's pack that we had stashed behind a rock and it was gone. Perhaps someone had discovered it and thought it was lost, but we never found it again. I was bummed for Matt losing his pack and his hiking boots, me being his host and all but he seemed to take it in stride. It was just "Stuff" and we had had a grand adventure. The summer went by pretty quickly, working, throwing frisbee, tubing in Boulder Creek, hanging out with friends, hiking in the high country, skateboarding, backpacking and Exploring Boulder Canyon. Eventually Matt went off to college, Bob flew back to FDU and I moved into the Varsity Townhouses with Craig and Steve my friends from Cloud Nine, into a 3-bedroom apartment together. Craig from Rochester NY was starting his second year at CU in the Engineering department, Steve was a full-bearded, hard-scrabble Vermonter working at a Structural concrete plant out on 55th Avenue and I was enjoying my break from school. We were an interesting crew, but we meshed well and this seemed like we were becoming more permanent Boulderites living right in the midst of the College Hill.

I am really glad to have your story which fills in a lot of questions about your trip west. I never realized that Matt was such a climber. I think he told me that he had climbed the Devils Tower in Wyoming. You both prevailed in survival mode. We are now in a different kind of survival mode. You are lucky to have found Mona, as I am with Robin. She helps me with my showers and a pesky psoriasis condition which my dermatologist says is with me for life. Stay safe.
Love Dad

Haha, great story and as I remember it too! Also, between you and me: first time I saw a naked woman lol.
Matthew

22 Boulder part 2 - Construction Work

I had finished up work one evening and was hanging out at Shannons having a couple of beers before going home since I did not have to work the next day, when a big fight broke out near the front door. A tough long-haired Native American warrior-looking dude was extremely irate and was violently fighting a couple of patrons and was getting backed into the wall when he grabbed a beer bottle and smashed it on the table and held out the jagged end of the bottle as a weapon in front of him. I had never seen anything like this ferocity and he was not backing down one bit. The big red-headed bouncer that guarded the door strolled into the room, looking every bit as scary as this wild-haired Indian. I had got to know Magnus, the bouncer and he was a very serious fellow, seldom cracking a smile and not one to mess with either. Magnus quickly made it over to the Indian dude and told him loudly to put the bottle down right now. The Indian was not calmed down one little bit and Magnus repeated his command, but this time a little louder and more forceful with his burning eyes drilling into the fighter. The Indian could see that even with his bottle he was outclassed as Magnus could subdue him without ever needing to use the large hunting knife on his belt. The two of them walked towards the front door as the crowd parted for them in case some spark would set them off again. I was standing next to a guy that I had gotten to know named Mike that often hung out at the bar and mentioned that that had escalated quickly, and we were lucky to have Magnus at the front door. Mike told me that when he was in Vietnam, Magnus was under his command and after the war, they had both come to Boulder together. I could see that they had a bond forged in war and would be friends forever and their relationship fell into place for me. It was September and I had been working as a cook all summer and Mike mentioned that he was putting a crew together to do miscellaneous construction jobs and asked if I would be interested in joining his crew. That question was a no-brainer and in a couple of weeks I started working with him. Magnus never did work with us. He was happy being stationed at the front door of Shannons Restaurant and Bar guarding the place like an Army base.

My first day of work Mike introduced me to the crew he had put together. We would basically be contract construction workers working for a couple of young semi-corporate guys that were putting together jobs for us but under the command of Mike. This is not too dissimilar to a Driller hiring his crew of roughnecks but reporting to the Tool Pusher who was in charge of the Rig, but more on this later. We were at an old motel out on 28th street. Our job was to demolish the motel, saving as much of the lumber, bricks, cement blocks, and anything else that could be useful in future jobs where we would be building something. We started working pulling the hardware, doors, cabinets, bathroom fixtures out of the motel and loading it into a truck owned by a guy Mike had hired as a turnkey worker who was not much older than me that was trying to start a trucking business, but so far just had one old dump truck and he was the driver. He would haul this stuff off to the dump. Eventually we took the roof off, throwing away the shingles and saving as much of the lumber of the rafters and joists as we could, but much of it would split off or be rotten and could not be reused by us. We were recycling before recycling was cool! At noon, we would all take lunch together and tell stories and get to know each other. Sometimes Cooper and I would go out to lunch to eat at Uncle Joes Plantation Barbecue on Arapaho street. Old Joe would be there and his BBQ was very spicy hot. Cooper and I had become the type of friends that would compete in everything. His dad owned a construction company back in Indiana and he thought he was the shit when it came to building and working construction and it made me want to work as hard as I could to be better than him at everything. We would order the BBQ rib baskets with a couple of cokes and sit at the barstools in front of the grill and eat without taking a drink, at least as long as we could, trying to outlast each other. Such was our relationship.

I got to know Tom Leathers and his best friend Kevin Little. Tom was a quick witted, big burly red-haired biker with a thick beard and a heart of gold. Kevin had accompanied Tom from Missouri and was about my age, easy going and laid back. Tom and Kevin always drove to the worksite together in an old Chevy sedan and soon became my best friends outside of my roommates. Our crew would be pulling nails out of the boards and stacking and sorting the lumber while others of us worked at dismantling the place and knocking down the walls. This was just the type of work that Frank Cilley at the Bidwell Hardware Company had prepared me for. There was work to be done everywhere, and no one had to tell me what to do as I could see the tasks at hand without needing to be micro-managed. Eventually we got the entire Motel down to just the floor and we worked with pry bars and crow bars to get the plywood up from the floor, saving any we could. Several days later, all that was left was the floor joists, several feet above the dirt of the crawl space. I grabbed a sledgehammer and stood in the dirt and pounded up on the end of the joist, working it free from the foundation timber. There was a hundred feet or more of these joists going down towards 28th street, then the foundation turned left for another 100 feet. Mike had figured it would take most of the week to pound all these joists out, it being just hard work pounding up with a sledgehammer. Well Cooper grabbed the other sledgehammer and pounded the other end of the joist up and out from his end. The race was on. The two of us sweated and pounded and worked all day at the joists, not letting anyone else take a turn. I was enjoying the feeling of working my muscles and knew that I would totally best Cooper at this. He turned out to be very handy with a sledgehammer from working with dad and it was a most excellent competition. We made it all the way down that first 100' run of the Motel that day keeping up with each other and the crew hauling the joists away as fast as we could pull them out of the building. It was not an "official" competition, but Cooper and I totally understood it as such and the other guys on the crew eventually did as well and left us to our sledges. We basically finished the day on the same last joist, the competition being a tie, but the prize was that we became part of the core of Mike's crew with Tom, Kevin and Peter.

My non-work life was back at the Varsity Townhouses on the college hill only a block from the CU campus. It was all kids living there, most of them going to school, including my roommate Craig. I was saving my receipts for rent and soon got my Colorado driver's license and was saving all my working pay stubs as documentation to prove that I was a Colorado resident when I would eventually go back to school. We had three college girls living next to us, Karen from Littleton that was studying business and wanted to start a tee-shirt business, Kathleen from Northglenn and Jane from Alaska. Jane had worked with her Dad the previous summer up in Alaska and made enough money to cover all her college costs and purchase a new Ford Granada with all the gold that they had dredged. Those three girls were the exception to almost everyone in the apartment complex getting high every day. CU was living up to its reputation as a party school. We made friends with a guy down the hall named Cleve from Chicago who always wore PhotoGrey prescription that made it seem like he was wearing sunglasses all the time. He was studying business management and his parents should be so proud of him putting his degree to work before he even graduated. He would take the money that his parents would send for school and use it as investment capital, using it to purchase a large quantity of pot which he would turn around and sell in nickel, dime and ounce bags to the other kids for a profit. He would pay the late payment fee at CU for tuition and pay it back as he was selling his product, having extra spending money and free weed while he was at school. All the construction guys that I was working with smoked pot, I think that was part of how they dealt with life after war and Cleve's supply would help them stay in weed as well. Craig, Steve, Cleve and I would often go backpacking and hiking up on the mountains on the weekends.

After work one Saturday Big Tom and Kevin asked me if I wanted to go on a road trip with them up to Helena Montana. We had been trying to finish up a job and got some overtime for working on the weekend. They had just decided on the trip while talking over lunch, it was a true spur of the moment adventure. It sounded like a fun trip but they wanted to leave right away, not even going home to gather stuff for the drive since it would take 12 hours to get there and they wanted to get going. I had never been to Montana before and thinking "there's only one way to do it and that's to do it", I was in. I dropped the Scout off at home and we headed out in their Chevy sedan. It was a long drive up the interstate through Cheyenne, where I had been a couple of times to go drinking, since the legal age was 18 there and we could drink wherever we wanted. It was dark when we passed Casper, then past Buffalo, still on the interstate when the car started sputtering and we noticed that the red low-fuel indicator light was on. Luckily, there was an exit right up ahead with a gas station and we cruised on fumes up to the pumps. There were no lights on and this was before pumps that would take credit cards, so our only option was to spend the night in the car. I had a thick leather fringed Indian-looking jacket that I got out of the lost and found basket at Shannons and pulled it around me for the cold night in the car here in Northern Wyoming. As soon as the sun peeked over the plains to the East, we got out of the car and in the window of the gas station was a sign, "Closed Sunday". Damn! We did the rock, paper, scissors or as the NorCal's call it roshambo to see who would hitchhike back to Buffalo. The least likely one of us to get picked up hitchhiking lost. Big Tom stood up on the other side of the interstate with a huge shit-eating grin plastered on his face until eventually a pickup stopped and he got a ride. An hour to two later he showed up with an empty windshield washer fluid container filled with gasoline and we were back on our way. We made it up to Carroll College in Helena that afternoon to meet Cynthia, a friend of Tom & Kevin's who was going to school there. We ate in the school cafeteria with Cynthia and her boyfriend and were a bit of a spectacle to the other students, with Tom looking like a scary biker dude, Kevin all disheveled from driving 12 hours and sleeping in the car and me looking like a mountain man that had just crawled out of a cave. We enjoyed the attention and really enjoyed that steam-table food. We slept on the floor of Cynthia's boyfriend's dorm room after showering and cleaning up in the community bathroom down the hall. On the drive back, we stopped and took pictures with our little 110 Kodak pocket cameras at spots of interest. In a cartridge of 20 pictures, you would be lucky to get just a couple that would turn out OK and I still have a good one of Kevin and I leaning into the wind in Montana with the mountains in the background and our grubby jeans on and my fringes blowing back. My one memento.

There was a pretty good skateboarding community in Boulder at the time, even though there were no skateparks, since they had not been invented yet except for the occasional empty swimming pool. The college hill where we were living was excellent for skateboarding and I would go out often. In fact, not too far away was a street that was the closest we had to a skate park. Columbine Avenue is a quiet tree-lined street that parallels the much busier Baseline Avenue, both being on the hill that leads up to be base of the Flatirons. The street was marked up with spray paint making a slalom course down for a couple of blocks and there would usually be at least a dozen guys skating there, working on their slalom moves. We rarely did tricks, mostly just riding and working to stay on the course on the hill all the way to the bottom. The cops never bothered us there and the neighbors seemed to like having the kids out playing on the street.

I ended up building a sweet slalom board out of a piece of oak with a curved kick-flip tail, wide California slalom trucks and the new Kryptonics urethane sealed bearing wheels that were made right here in Louisville. This board gave me tremendous grip on the street and kept me up riding the course with the best of them. I would ride this board all over town as well. When Craig got his 650 Yamaha bike, we would take turns pulling each other up to the top of "the hill" near Chautauqua Park like waterskiing behind the bike. We would then turn around and skateboard the six or eight blocks back down on different streets each time. This long board was perfect for that type of riding. Craig would ride a little bit, but my main riding partner was Cleve. This riding evolved into mountain pass riding where Cleve and I would pack our skateboards into the trunk of his car, when we would go backpacking with Craig and Steve. On our way back from our camping trip, when we would get to a long downhill we would jump out of the car onto our skateboards and have these great long rides. Our best ride was one time when we were coming back from Rocky Mountain Park and we got dropped off near the top of Trail Ridge Road, heading down the Eastern slope. Cleve and I got on our boards and rode down the rough asphalt while Craig drove behind us in the car. The cars had made very smooth tracks in the road, two going up and two going down that we would use to crank our turns on. Sometimes we could ride off the main road and skate through the scenic vista turnoffs while any cars behind us could pass and we would skate back onto the road without ever jumping off our boards. A one point a car passed Cleve and I taking a super 8 movie from the car window. We eventually rode to a stop just past the Hidden Valley ski area and according to Craig who had followed us the entire way, we had ridden for 9.6 miles!

Our next construction job was building a foundation for a house that had been moved to a quiet neighborhood in East Boulder from an area under construction. Boulder has a strict growth ordinance and the house had been in the way of a re-development area and had been spared the wrecking ball. It provided our crew with a couple more months of work. Tom went back to Missouri and rode back on his massively chopped Harley with a big fat friend of his Tony, also riding his own Harley. Tony would be our mason and mentor for building the foundation out of cement blocks. I was a hod carrier for a big part of this job as well as working on fixing the outside of the house and repairing parts of the inside for eventual resale. We were taking a lunch break one day and Mike was telling us about being a Green Beret in Vietnam. The Army would drop his crew off behind enemy lines where they would do reconnaissance and capture/kill any Vietcong that they encountered. They would wrap det-cord around their necks after showing the det-cord blowing a stump apart and walk them out of the jungle for interrogation. They also used the det-cord in creative ways to setup ambushes. All this dangerous fighting did not seem to give him PTSD, as he was a good serious leader for our crew and we all liked and respected him. The last guy rounding out our crew was Peter, a frail-looking hippy guy, also a vet with a chip on his shoulder against the police since his sister had been shot in the face by the riot police during the Kent State riots which had disfigured her. Peter had a girlfriend that I really liked hanging out with, since she reminded me of my aunt Gussie being funny and open and had made their little apartment amazingly homey and inviting. She made up for Peter being hard to get along with.

I was trying to be frugal to save money and had come to the conclusion that I should sell the Scout and get a motorcycle. In a weird coincidence, I went to Johns 4WD Shop and sold them my truck. Just across the street was a used car lot that had a motorcycle for sale that was about the same price as the Scout I had just sold. It was a Kawasaki 500 three cylinder two-stroke motorcycle that looked perfect and cheap. I purchased the bike on the spot. The bike was fairly light, extremely fast and was a blast to ride. I figured it would be cheap on gas and low on maintenance and would be a money-saver. That was semi-true. I had to add oil to the engine every time I filled the tank, since that is how a two-stroke engine works and I would foul a spark plug every couple of weeks. I took my riding test several weeks later, negotiating through the cones and got my motorcycle endorsement. The first time I rode it to the job site, Mike came up and looked at the bike and asked me why I got rid of the Scout, since it had gotten me to work on time every day. I had a momentary twinge of regret since I respected his opinion, but then I thought of my reasoning for swapping the truck for the bike and my regret vanished. It was part of my long-term plan, even though sometimes going back to school would occasionally seem like a pipe dream.

I was hanging out one weekend with my work friends at the apartment of an electrician friend of Tom's. He had a beautiful wife and a bunch of us were sitting on the front step and talking and admiring the custom chopper sitting out front that Tom's friend had just purchased. The front wheel was raked way out in front of the bike making it look cool, but also hard to ride until you got used to the steering geometry. The electrician had a friend that was a skinny tweaker-looking dude that really wanted to ride the bike, so he relented and let him take the bike for a ride. We were watching as he tried several times to kick the bike over and eventually it roared impressively to life. He rode it down the street, goosing the throttle to enjoy the loud pipes and promptly crashed hard into a car at the end of the street as he could not negotiate the turn. The bike frame was ruined and the engine had been smashed as well. I learned a valuable lesson that day to never loan out anything, especially a Harley, that you cannot afford to lose. I never did loan out my H1 500 motorcycle, since it could be hard to ride with the very sensitive throttle and I could not afford to lose my only means of transportation. Later that afternoon, Tom and the electrician went out to find some psilocybin mushrooms while I hung out with his wife, smoking a joint and talking in their apartment. She remarked that I was the only friend of her husband that had never hit on her. I was a little embarrassed and took it as a compliment since I was not "that type of guy". She must have thought I was attractive also and I wondered just a little bit if she was hitting on me or why would she have said it. I felt a little closer to her since she told me something so personal, but it did not make me want to bone her.

The guys got back with a baggy of wet mushrooms that looked disgusting to me. At the time I still did not like eating mushrooms and in fact had never successfully eaten an entire shroom. It would be the next summer when I read the Hobbit and was totally sucked in, feeling like I had the heart and soul of one of the little guys and was really relating to them as they were leaving the Shire on their grand adventure. Bilbo and his crew had stopped at farmer Maggot's house on their first night and his wife had fed them dinner in their farm house which was unusual since Hobbits usually lived in comfy holes in the ground. When they left, Mrs. Maggot gave them a gift basket of mushrooms which they could smell the scent of as they crossed the farmer's fields and promptly devoured them as soon as they reached the woods, making them sound unbelievably delicious. After reading that story a girlfriend Pam who I really liked and whose parents owned the Aristocrat Steak house downtown, not 2 blocks from Shannons, took me to her parents' restaurant for a mushroom omelet and I did not just like it, I loved it!

This was before I loved mushrooms, so I ran out to McDonalds and got a half-dozen chocolate milkshakes and brought them back for all of us. We chopped up the magic mushrooms and put them in our milkshakes and drank them down, not tasting them the slightest bit, although I felt that I could feel the disgusting slimy mushroom texture going down my throat. I was not hesitant about taking the Shrooms since I had taken them before in college at a Steve Miller concert at the Spectrum in Philadelphia. I remember hallucinating during the concert and enjoying the light show as much as the music of the Space Cowboy and being glad I was not having to communicate during the show, but just enjoying my head trip. This trip was just as enjoyable, running around with my friends and being crazy, but most of the craziness was in our own minds.

We had other construction jobs roofing houses but the jobs started getting spotty and I would fill in the gaps working with my roommate Steve at Winfreys Structural Concrete Company pouring pre-stressed concrete panels used for building large warehouses and bridges. There were several long steel beds that were basically the forms used to mold the panels. Steel cables would be pulled the length of these beds that were about 150 feet long, then we would tie rebar into the bed as reinforcement. The concrete trucks would drive slowly down pouring the cement into the beds as we would walk down with shovels and spread it out. A couple of the experienced guys would walk down the beds with these giant vibrators called stingers that would literally turn the concrete into a liquid state and it would settle into the deep ribs of the bed where the steel cables resided. There would be headers bolted into the beds that would separate the pre-stressed panels from one another and we would work until the cement was poured all the way down to the end of the long beds. After all the concrete had been poured, a large machine would pull all the cables to about ten thousand pounds per square inch. Then the bed would be left alone for a couple of days to cure. We were warned to never walk past the end of any of the beds that were curing, since occasionally the chocks that held these high-tension cables in place would break and a cable would shoot out of the end of the bed like a gun going off. During this curing time I would work as a concrete finisher, making the ends of the finished slabs look pretty by cutting the cable off the ends flush with the concrete using a chain saw with a metal-cutting disc on the end. I would then spray paint the end of the cable to keep it from rusting, then using a trowel I would work to make a beautiful finished end using a wheelbarrow of mixed cement. This was the part of the job that required the most skill.

It was during this time of basically working 2 part-time jobs that one of the resume's that I had dropped off earlier at Wickes Lumber Company had caught the attention of the company manager and his secretary gave me a call.

    I had no idea of your varied work career before Wickes Lumber. Thank you Frank Cilley. (Since deceased}. I am impressed by the number of friends that you made and with your acute memory of events. Robin and I have just added Netflix and I just watched the Irishman which is a history of Hoffa and his rise and fall.
    Love Dad.

23 Boulder part 3 - Wickes Lumber

I was hired at the Wickes Lumberyard at 28th and Pearl as the warehouse foreman due to my experience working in the warehouse at the Bidwell company with Frank doing shipping and receiving. This was just a block away from the YMCA where I was already working out with weights, so now it would be really handy. The job would involve receiving all the shipments to the yard, taking inventory, stocking and helping customers who come into the yard as well. I would unload the trucks and train cars (we were right next to the tracks) and verify that the items we ordered were on the bill of lading and were included in everything we unloaded. Sometimes a large train car filled with lumber would arrive and I would spend the entire morning unloading it with the railroad man and we would be short something like a bundle of Redwood 2x6s. I would know this since I would check off the items as we unloaded them. I would make sure they would put it on a back-order slip that I would take up to the bookkeeper upstairs in the front office so they could track it. There were a couple of girls working up there and I could get a little break and chit chat and get the real scoop as to what was brewing up in the managerial office. I would keep the warehouse in shipshape using a forklift. It was a great job and I was lucky to have it. There was an old guy, Ed, that was the yard manager and mostly drove around in a larger forklift managing the larger stacks of lumber out back. He would try to boss me around, but I would ignore him, since we had our own domains and he was not my boss.

We had a large saw next to the warehouse and I would use it mostly for the "birdhousers" who would swarm the warehouse on Saturday mornings for their home projects and would often need the lumber and plywood cut to their specifications. Once a week we would have team meetings up in the storefront area to discuss lumberyard stuff. We would talk about stuff like trying to sell a pile of returned lumber that had been in a corner of the yard for a year and they wanted to get rid of. I would usually be the one in the best position to sell this, since I had dealings with our customers in the yard and could broach the subject of trying to sell this to them. We would get "lumber points" for completing tasks like this.

They were like Green Stamps and I would use them to purchase things like Buck Knives, folding chairs, kitchen pots and pans and other incentives to keep us motivated.

I got 15-minute breaks in the morning and the afternoon and would usually sit outside on the loading dock of the warehouse looking out into the back of the yard and occasionally Ed would come cruising by on his forklift and yell out, "Get back to work Bidwell."

I would ignore him since he was not the boss of me. I was looking out into the yard and just musing on my day and wondered if old Ed would talk to Mr. Richards the manager about what a lazy kid he had hired on, since I was always sitting out the loading dock doing nothing. I was probably just being paranoid, but perhaps I was onto something. I liked Mr. Richards and the feeling was mutual I could tell and wanted our relationship to continue like that. I came up with a solution. On the way to work the next day, I stopped by the gas station and picked up a pack of Marlboro lights to feed my "fiendish habit". At work that day, at 10:00, like every day I sat down on the loading dock for my break and lit up a fag, sometimes I got Vantages to mix it up. Since I am not a smoker, my one suck on the cancer stick was to light it up. Well old Ed was a fairly heavy smoker and it was part of his persona. If you were talking to him and he did not have a cigarette in his mouth, he would step back, pull one out of his pack and light up.

This day, like most days, Ed putted by on his fork lift and looked at me sitting on the loading dock staring off, lost in my thoughts and I heard him start with the "Bidwell, what..."

I cut him off by raising my hand up into the air with the smoking cigarette. He smiled like he had made a mistake and waved in acknowledgement of my legitimate smoking break. I "smoked" 2 cigarettes a day from then on and I'll be damned if he did not warm up to me just a little bit, us both being smokers and all.

One weekend day I was exploring East of Boulder, where I had spent very little time as we would usually head out West into the mountains. I was on the back roads and spotted a little gas station with the old-fashioned pumps and pulled in for gas and a refreshing beverage. An old guy came hobbling out to fill the little tank on my H1 bike.

I asked him "Do you have a soda machine?"

He looked at me and said "What?"

I repeated my question again and he looked at me with a blank face and said, "A sewing machine?"

I repeated it a third time and he said "Son, I haven't the faintest notion what you are talking about.".

Then the light came on. I asked him, "Do you have a pop machine?"

Then his light came on, he understood my query and informed me that they did not have one. I guess I'm not assimilating to being a local as fast as I thought I was. I just hoped that the University would consider me a local so that I could afford to finance my education when and if I got accepted into college.

That next summer Craig, Steve, Dan a high school friend of Craig's, and I moved into a stone house with a big porch right at the edge of the beautiful little Beach Park just a block or two from the Varsity Townhouses. We could hang on the porch when our friends came over and play frisbee in the park next to the house. We started our own Ultimate frisbee team and we would play other teams after work at the sports fields on the CU Campus. I would usually do the "kickoffs" since I had a very strong throw and snap of the frisbee, much unlike my snappy throw of a baseball.

One weekend when Cleve had a couple of girls that he knew from Chicago over to visit for a few weeks, he and I took a road trip with them to the Strawberry Hot Springs outside of the town of Steamboat Springs. It was in August, and the four of us drove out there to spend the night soaking in the two-foot-deep pools. We drove down the dirt road to the springs, which were just scattered around in a lightly forested, undeveloped area. We got there just at dark and found a pool that we had to ourselves, peeled off our clothes and soaked on our backs, looking at the sky as the Perseid meteor shower put on a show for us the entire night. We floated, talked, passed a couple of joints around and saw more meteors than I had ever seen in my life. We never noticed the chill of the night with the steamy warm pools and no one bothered us all night. It was a surreal night and I've never done anything like it before or since. In fact, I can probably count on one hand all the nights that I just stayed up until the morning.

I never got hurt working at the lumberyard, even working with the large circular lumber saw, but I did break my right pinky one time unloading a huge beam we had ordered for a contractor. The truck driver tipped up the bed of the truck and the beam slid off the back to the ground on a large steel roller mounted in the back of the flatbed. Then he pulled forward as the beam was sliding off the back. When the beam came off, like an idiot, I put my hand on the beam to steady it as it dropped to the ground, like I could do anything to steady it. It somehow bounced onto my little finger breaking my right pinky. The doctor put my finger in a bent aluminum brace taped on my hand and I wore that for a month until the doctor told me it was healed and to take it easy for another month. About a week later, I was heading out to the store with my roommate Dave in his VW bug. We got to the store and without thinking, I put my right pinky into the inside latch and pulled sideways to open the door, giving it a good yank since it was an old car. I immediately knew what I had done was against doctor's orders but low and behold, my finger did not snap. I knew at that moment that if my finger could survive that, then it could survive anything, and I never thought about my finger again.

I did break my wrist skateboarding back on Columbine Street when I swapped boards with another knuckle-dragger and his board slid out from under me on a sharp slalom turn and I slammed my left hand down on the asphalt. It stung bad, but I kept skateboarding. It was not until later that evening when I was sleeping and rolled over onto my hand and the shooting pain woke me up that I realized that it was broken. I was lucky that I had insurance from Wickes lumber and went to the doctor for a waterproof fiberglass cast since it was summer, and I wanted to be able to go swimming. The doc asked how it happened and I told him that I broke it diving for a frisbee that I caught on the edge of the road, hence the black tar lodged into the scrape on my hand. I'm sure he never believed me, but I did not want to give skateboarding a bad name.

One other time I almost got hurt, but not quite. I was climbing around the large boulders in Eldorado Canyon with my roommates and there was one about 15' above a deep pool in South Boulder creek that looked perfect for jumping into. My hand was still in a cast so this was the type of activity I could still do for a thrill, plus the water was extremely inviting on the hot summer day. I could see a large rock in the pool, so I was going to jump just next to it. I leapt off the boulder and into the pool when the rock struck my right leg just below the knee with a glancing blow. Unlike the skateboarding accident, I immediately thought I had broken my leg. I swam to the side and just sat in the cold water for 5 or 10 minutes since the cold felt good and I thought it might numb it. I figured the refraction looking through the water must have made the boulder look just a little farther away than it actually was. When I got up out of the pool, I found that I could stand on it and limped up to the dirt road of the park and was so relieved. I could work with a broken wrist or pinky, but there was no way I would be able to work with a broken leg.

Sometimes to break up the work, I would go out on Sheetrock jobs with another yard worker, often a CU Football player that we would hire for the summer to help out on this demanding work. We would drive out to a house under construction with two huge stacks of 4-foot by 12-foot bundles of 1/2" sheetrock. These bundles weighed about 150 pounds each and we would carry them from the truck into the house and stack them where the sheet rockers would put notes on the studs of how many bundles they wanted at each location. Occasionally we would have to carry them upstairs, which was very grueling work but if we could, we would use the hydraulic scissor-jack bed on our big flatbed truck and jack it up even with the 2nd floor. We would run an aluminum plank from the truck to the house and carry in the sheetrock, bypassing the stairs. We did many of these jobs and never had an injury, even with the lack of any type of safety equipment. The hardest part of the job was keeping a grip on the edges of the bundles and it took me several weeks to get my grip strong and comfortable enough to unload an entire truck without taking a break. We would alternate the teams of 2 guys since this was backbreaking work. Luckily, I would just use it as a break from the warehouse and I never did it full time. My favorite days would be when we would get a new shipment of wallboard straight from the factory in Gypsum on the Western Slope and haul it straight out to a job site. The wallboard bundles would still be warm against our skin on chilly days and would be exuding a little bit of steamy mist.

Wickes hired Rick, a long-haired blonde surfer dude from Huntington Beach CA to install our garage doors. He would work out of his little Toyota pickup truck and I would occasionally help him out installing custom doors where we would nail and glue cedar siding to the outside of the door, making it match the houses perfectly. Usually Rick would install alone, but these custom doors were so heavy that he would need assistance. Rick, his girlfriend Jill, and I became good friends and at the end of the summer Rick's friend Dave, also from CA, moved in with Craig, Dan and I to an Apartment out in Gunbarrel.

Ed had hired Hector, a stout Mexican fellow to help out in the yard. Hector thought he was the tough guy in the yard. We were about the same size, but I was a couple of inches taller than him. I think he had "little guy" syndrome, where he had to make up for his stature by exuding an air of toughness. He was OK to work with, but I did not like his pretentiousness. One day he came up to me and was in my face about something I cannot remember and grabbed me by the front of my blue Wickes lumber shirt and pulled it towards him, unsnapping my shirt down the front. I'm not a person to get mad easily, but this time I was immediately pissed off and slugged him pretty hard in the stomach. I did not go for the face since I did not want to hurt him and get fired, but Hector did not have the same qualms and reflexively struck out with his right fist catching me with a glancing blow on the side of my head on his way down. I was as surprised at him hitting me, as he was when I hit him.

He stood back very surprised and said, "I did not take you for a fighter." which I am not, but he never came near me after that and would make a big deal of giving me a wide swath when our paths crossed.

It turns out that he was a golden gloves boxer in his past, which explained how he could instinctively hit like that.

Right across Pearl Street from the lumberyard was a large prairie dog field where we would watch them chirping and see the occasional hawk munching on one. One day some construction equipment was dropped off in the middle of this field and over the course of the next several days, they flattened that entire field of prairie dog mounds. Each morning, the prairie dogs would dig back out to the surface in their new flat, grass-less home. It looked like a draw, prairie dogs 1, construction equipment 1. I remember standing there looking across Pearl Street zoning out about what was happening across the street when a guy on a bicycle came barreling down the street heading East with his head down and peddling hard and went right into the back of a car parked on the side of the street. He flew off his bike through the back window and into the back seat of the car, literally right in front of me. Things were going to hell in a handbag quickly. We got an ambulance out and the guy was quite shaken up when they took him away leaving his mangled European racing bike behind. That weekend the construction company came in and laid asphalt across the top of the entire prairie dog village, building a parking lot for a new Target department store that was going in. I often wondered how the little dogs dealt with being buried alive. I was a little shocked that something like this would happen in a progressive and environmentally friendly town like Boulder. About a month later the bike guy wandered back into the yard asking about his bike that I had stashed in the warehouse. He had hurt his neck in the crash which is why it took him a month to come looking for it. After he left, I wondered what would've happened if I had not been standing there in front of the crash since he may have laid in the back seat of that car for hours before somebody noticed him.

I rode my Kawasaki 500 to work every day and would park it in the yard by the warehouse out of the way and protected. There was a guy Eric, that worked with Ed in the yard as the other forklift operator and he pulled into the yard one day with a brand-new Kawasaki 650 four-stroke motorcycle. Everyone in the yard was standing around his shiny new bike. He thought it must be faster than my bike, since his was 150cc's larger, but I knew better. My bike was the fastest production motorcycle when it came out in 1972 and was still a barn burner. One thing led to another and we agreed to race down that 2-block length of the lumberyard that stretched from 28th street to 30th street after work. I had another advantage since I was used to shifting my bike as well, so I was not worried a bit. After work, we closed the chain link fence gate leading out of the yard and lined the two bikes up next to each other aiming down the pavement between the warehouse on one side and the row of lumber sheds on the other side. We were revving our bikes and making a bit of a show of it when Ed from the yard dropped his arm. I had the bike revved pretty hard when I dumped the clutch and the front wheel came right up off the ground into a high impressive wheelie, scaring the crap out of me and did not come back down for quite a ways until I regained my composure and shifted up through the gears, down to the end of the yard. My heart was pounding from the near spectacular crash that I had narrowly avoided, but I had left Eric in the dust. We rode back to the starting line where the rest of the lumbermen were waiting and turned off the bikes to talk about the race. Eric and a couple of the other guys called me a show-off for starting the race with such a large wheelie and then smoking him down the line like I was rubbing it in. I managed to hold my tongue about it not being premeditated and scaring the shit out of myself. I made like that was my plan all along, like I was an Evel Knievel in the making. Little did they know. Often times in life things are not as they appear and something spectacular may be just a lucky quirk of fate but it's best to take advantage of these things with a smile on your face like you meant it!

I had not really considered commuting in the wintertime when I sold the Scout but riding the bike in below freezing temperatures became the norm for me in the winter. I was glad that I was saving money on insurance, gas and maintenance, but the downside was the weather. If it was cold and raining, I would be riding. If it was cold and snowy but the roads were clear, I would be riding, I just needed to be vigilant to avoid the inevitable patches of snow or ice on the road. I could catch rides with my roommates and after we had moved out to Gunbarrel, I would jump on the Gunbarrel Express, an hourly bus from our apartment complex for the 6-mile ride into town.

That Christmas, I did not fly home to Connecticut like I would normally do, and I stayed in the apartment working weekdays at the lumberyard. Dave flew back to California, Craig and Dan flew back to Rochester NY, leaving me to relax in the apartment by myself. In fact, my friend Rick, from work asked me to watch and water his pot plants while he went back to CA with Dave. That turned out to be a bad idea, when a woman with a little boy were walking past our apartment unit and saw the pot plant in my bedroom window and called the cops. I was in the living room, working on a bar that I was making using a big piece of rough-sawn beetle kill pine which I had purchased from a bearded hippy dude selling the planks out of the back of his truck. I opened the door and there were 4 cops standing there, demanding to come in, since they had also seen the pot plant in the window and had probable cause for a search of the premises. I thought that I was screwed, since there was a bong on the coffee table, a little pot in an album next to it and a roach or two in the ash tray, not to mention the pot plant in my bedroom. The cops walked in, three of them went into the back to checkout and search the bedrooms and I stayed in the living room with the big woman cop. She headed into the kitchen and started searching the drawers. I had moment of panic when I remembered that Craig had two paper shopping bags in the freezer with a pound of pot in each! I did not know what I could do, when providence came to my aid. The woman officer searched the fridge, nothing. She then opened the top freezer compartment and there were the two paper bags of pot, staring us both in the face. I was totally screwed. Her eyes lit on a plastic baggie with 5 Thai Sticks right at the front of the freezer compartment. Her eyes lit up and she picked up the bag and brought it over to me and asked me what it was. I nonchalantly closed the freezer, ostensibly to keep the cold from pouring out and saw my opportunity to distract her. I launched into the most detailed description ever done on a Thai Stick.

I said, "It is extremely potent marijuana that grows around a stick in Thailand. It curls around the stick like a vine, increasing the potency and then the pot is tied to the stick with thread to keep it together for the long journey to Boulder. In fact, due to its extreme potency we would keep it on the stick and just pinch off a few parts of the bud and put it into the bong for a single hit, which would usually be enough to get high. It glistens with silver highlights due to the strong THC weeping out of the buds."

I kept talking about how rare it is, etc. when the other cops came out of the bedrooms. None of them knew about Thai Sticks either. The female cop took the lead, showing them the Thai Stick that she was still holding in her hand and talking about it to the other officers like show and tell in school, telling them all the facts about it that I had just told her. That was the big score, this new type of weed and the female officer had gained some respect from the other officers since she had been the one to find it. One officer took all the loose joints, roaches, little baggies they had found in the bedrooms, another took the plants growing in my bedroom and the woman brought the Thai sticks out to the patrol cars. The officer in charge stayed behind and told me that what they had found, excluding the young plants which did not have any THC in them, measured less than an ounce and was only a misdemeanor crime in Boulder. He wrote me up a ticket going on to explain that if I was not arrested for any other crime in Boulder for another two years, then this episode would be expunged from my record. When the cops left, I could have fainted. Getting arrested would probably screwup my chances of getting accepted to the University, not to mention having a drug record. I sat down on the couch trying to calm my racing heart, knowing how close I had come to disaster. It just goes to show, when shit hits the fan, just keep a cool head, and see if an opportunity presents itself to help you extract yourself from the situation. It could be blind good luck. This was really a total combination of the two and I knew I had dodged a bullet big time. Perhaps it was my superpower that allowed me to remain calm in an otherwise very shaky situation.

The franchise general manager of our lumberyard called me into the office after I had been working there for a year and I wondered what was up. I liked him and would talk to him during work occasionally about how things were going out in the warehouse and I figured he just wanted to talk about any issues that I was having. He laid out a plan for me for the future that started with him recommending that I be accepted to the Wickes lumber school in Saginaw Michigan for a year to learn the ins and outs of being a general manager of a Wickes lumber franchise. I was flattered and honored that he thought that highly of me and listened intently to his pitch. After he was done, I explained to him that I really enjoyed working as the warehouse foreman, but my dream was to be a Geologist, and I told him that I was planning to go back to school. He was disappointed and had treated me well which I really appreciated, and I felt a little bad about letting him down. Not long after that meeting I was accepted to the Geology program at CSU up in Ft Collins. I gave my notice at the lumber yard even though it would be a couple of months before I had to leave for school so that they would have time to find a replacement.

Your Bidwell Hardware training certainly paid off at Wickes and the offer of Wickes's training. I'm impressed also with your physical stamina on the job. It's great to have this snapshot of your life. On to Geology!
Dad

I had been looking for accommodations during my last few weeks working at Wickes and had ridden up to Ft Collins to look for apartments in the want ads in the Coloradoan and had visited a few places. I checked out one place on South Columbine Street, just 2 blocks West of campus. Tracy, a serious outdoor rec major and Dave a tall joking Forestry major nicknamed Norton for his habit of wearing a vest over his white tee shirt were living in the basement apartment of a ranch house. They liked the fact that I would be in the same Natural Resources college as them. They were straight as an arrow and would be perfect roommates. They had both finished up their freshman year in the dorms and had moved off campus for their second year. They asked me if I smoked pot and I told them "Never". This was true, since part of my plan when leaving Boulder was to quit smoking weed cold turkey and concentrate totally on my studies. I had long hair with a wispy mustache and was tan as a nut from working outside. They told me months later that they thought I was a Mexican and I told them that it's a good thing they were not prejudiced. I moved my few possessions up a couple of weeks later, the pine bar top, and a desk. I had acquired the desk from an alcoholic Vietnam vet friend of mine in Boulder who drove an electricians pickup and had been hired by the Boulderado Hotel to haul off old furniture and junk to the dump as part of the remodeling. He had a beautiful old antique desk with a folding top and a couple of little pencil drawers that I purchased from him on his way to the dump for $25. This would be my main work surface for studying and reading.

I talked with the financial aid people and got a 2.5% national direct student loan and a Pell grant to help me finance my first year back. Back then the semester cost for tuition and fees was $215 plus the cost of the 16 credit hours of classes, another $2500, so about $6000 with text books for the school year plus $150/month rent. I was assigned an advisor, Dr Tommy Thompson a serious Hard-Rock Geology professor to help me get started and choose my classes. After looking at my transcript, he explained that it would take me 3 years to graduate, since I had so many Psychology and liberal arts classes under my belt that would be far more than the allowed elective classes for a hard-science Geology major. I had suspected as much, but I was so excited to be finally studying about the earth.

I used to worry about going back to college when I was in Boulder that I would be putting my life on hold for several years while I completed getting my degree. I wanted to get on with the business of life, not the work of school. My mom, being a professional psychologist explained to me that being in school is life, perhaps at its best. In fact, I might look back on it as the best time of my life. Just enjoy school since there would be plenty of time for work. Life would continue and I would be living it to the fullest, in the moment and not worrying about things like marriage, mortgages, money, vacations, which was also life, just not so much in the moment. I had also learned the secret to college, other than buckling down and studying hard was to study something you loved and were interested in, so that you looked forward to learning and enjoyed it. Between these two things, the extra year was just extra life.

I had to take a remedial class to catch back up with Trigonometry which would be needed for my Structural Geology class and would be needed for the one semester of calculus that was required. I jumped into Geology with both feet and sucked up everything that I was studying, as I wanted to know everything I could and be the best professional when I graduated. The structural geology class was excellent using surface bedding clues and trigonometry to determine the sub-surface structure of the sedimentary rock beds. The funny thing is that most of the non-geology required classes were classes I had not taken at FDU. I took one class in public speaking and a girl in the class gave a talk about hot dogs and went into so much detail about them that I have never had a hot dog since, except the occasional one at the ballpark where it is just tradition. I hoped she got an "A", since she deserved it. Another girl in my class gave a very confusing speech about euthanasia. The whole time I thought she was talking about ending the lives of "youth in Asia", since I was not familiar with the term and she never explained it. She probably got a "C", haha.

Norton was about 6'4" and skinny and he liked to work out with weights, so we became lifting partners as well at the school rec gym and he was about as strong as me, so we were a good match. He and Tracy got along well, sort of like how water and oil get along. Norton was a practical joker and his main target was Tracy. He would go to elaborate lengths since Tracy would get so upset that it would totally encourage him to keep doing it. Tracy came home from classes one afternoon and I was sitting at the kitchen table taking notes from my Paleontology textbook and I asked him to please grab a paper in the trash can in Norton's bedroom, since I did not want to lose my train of thought and I needed some notes that I had thrown out. He dumped his backpack on the kitchen chair and got the paper for me. Norton used a paper supermarket bag as a trash can. He had cut out the bottom and part of the side and was lying under his bed with just his head sticking out, but in the bottom of the bag under a single sheet of paper. When Tracy reached into the bag in the dark bedroom, Norton let out a blood-curdling scream and Tracy about shit himself he was so shocked and upset. It was exactly the type of reaction Norton was hoping for and I felt a little guilty for helping him with this prank, but just a little bit.

One of my favorite Classes was physics. I like learning about how the natural world worked from a mathematical and surprisingly practical standpoint. My professor was a bit of a flake, he knew his stuff but he would sometimes get confused. One time he held up his hand during a lecture and said "Hold it, I have this completely backwards", after talking about a concept for 15 minutes. In the midterm, there was a question about this topic and I could not remember which way that he had explained it was correct. I guessed wrong, damn. I really liked the practical labs where we would do experiments and take quizzes as part of our grade. The best part was the recitation labs where we would meet with a grad student in a lab setting and could ask any questions we had and this is where I really learned the hard concepts. Well when the final rolled around, the professor said that it was optional and I could just take the midterm and the quiz scores as my grade. I had an 89% in the class, just one point from an "A". I met with the professor and asked if there was any type of extra-credit project that I could do to get an "A". He told me to just take the final and hope for a 93% or better and I would earn the grade I wanted, but if I screwed up the final, my grade could be knocked down since the final was optional. I liked Physics and really understood the concepts, so much so that I had considered a double major, but that would have added even more time to my schooling. I took what I considered a safe bet and took the final exam, getting the 94 that I needed and getting an "A" for the class!

We went to a party with friends of my roommates, mostly kids I also knew from our co-ed mud-football team. The school would dig pits about 20 feet wide by 60 feet long in the dirt, then fill them up with water and let them sit for a couple of weeks before mud football season. It was flag-football but tackling was prevalent and we would get so covered in mud that we could not see. After a play we would often slosh thought the mud to our side of the "field" to get our eyes spray-bottled off to be able to see. We had a ringer on our team Spencer, who was a cowboy studying Range Science that had been a high school quarterback, so when I would go out for a pass, the ball would come zinging into my chest making it so easy to catch, even with the slippery mud. Well 4 of the girls from our team were throwing a party after the game that evening, after we had all hosed off and cleaned up. I was drinking a beer and a sturdy smooth-skinned, lovely, full-bodied girl wearing jeans and a dancers black leotard top was checking me out. I wandered over, so suave with the confidence of our mutual checking each other out and since I was an older guy by a couple of years. We talked and hung out getting to know each other a little bit. I'm a light-weight when it comes to drinking and we sat down at a table to play a drinking game where you had to do a shot of vodka every time you lost. I don't remember the details of the game, obviously. We were all getting drunk and eventually when I would lose, I would make a big deal of taking my shot, picking the shot glass off the table throwing my head back as I threw the shot into my open mouth with gusto. At least that is what it looked like I was doing when in actuality I was throwing the shot over my shoulder and onto the wall and carpet behind me. No one noticed, except probably the girls the next day when they had to clean up the apartment. It beat throwing up from too much drinking and I could talk with Debbie after the game was over with the smooth confidence that drinking gives you. It turns out she lived in that apartment; she played on the girl's rugby team at CSU which was why she was so good on our mud football team. Spence and Tom, our two cowboy friends, would get us together for trips out to a cowboy bar east of town with Debbie, myself and our respective roommates. We would go cowboy dancing at Bruces Bar in Severance where I learned to cowboy dance with spins and twirls to the country music. The place would be so packed with mostly cowboys and cowgirls that there were two lines into the men's bathroom to pee. One line went to the toilet and the other to the sink. No hand washing allowed! Bruces Bar was also locally famous for having the freshest and best tasting Rocky Mountain Oysters that I loved, living so far from the ocean and all. Debbie and I went out for a couple of months until our relationship basically faded away, due to factors beyond our control.

If I was late for class, I could ride my motorcycle over to the Natural Resources Building where the Geology department occupied the top floor and the basement for the rock lab. Usually, I would either ride my bicycle to class, walk or take my skateboard, depending on my mood and the weather. My roommates got to calling me Skate for my habit of skating to class since I could take it in with me and not have to lock it up outside.

Tracy and I were talking about what we would do for jobs this coming summer. Norton was joining a fraternity and was moving out as soon as classes were over. We both wanted to have jobs in our area of study, him working for a park somewhere and me being out in the field doing Geology. We decided that if we wanted jobs other than working at a fast-food restaurant, doing yard work or selling encyclopedias, we would have to work hard looking. We both went to the Morgan library and I got several reference books and geologic periodicals with information on mining companies. Tracy got parks and recreation literature that we brought home. My parents had given me an electric typewriter when I graduated from High School to use for writing papers in college and Tracy and I took turns using it. I came up with a form letter explaining my burning desire to do geologic field work, that I was an extremely dedicated, hard worker and blah, blah, blah... I wrote a total of 63 letters, signed, stamped and mailed, as did Tracy. The summer was approaching and I had actually gone to a seminar on selling encyclopedias door-to-door in the Midwest, when I got a letter from Western Nuclear offering me a summer job doing field work in Oregon. The offer was $650 per month with housing, food and transportation included. I was ecstatic about having my dream job, getting some experience in my future career and I would be able to save most of my money as well.

I loaded up my pack with clothes I would need for the summer and considered my options. I did not have much money left when the semester ended so I decided to hitchhike out to Oregon. I got on Hwy 287 and caught a ride up to Laramie and I had the guy drop me off as we were crossing I-80. I picked a spot on the entrance ramp and watched cars pass me for an hour before one stopped. Unfortunately, the car that stopped was a state cop and he informed me that it was illegal to hitchhike on the interstate. I explained that I had very little money to get to Oregon for a job and he compromised and drove me to the bus station. I only had enough money to get a ticket to Reno with five dollars left over and I was soon on the bus. In Reno, I considered my options, I would need a map to figure out a hitchhiking route to Lakeview and it was late in the day. Instead, I went to a nearby casino to hang out for a bit and checkout the scene and experience a casino, since I had never been in one and I was on a travel adventure. I was sitting in the area of one-armed-bandits and watching a little old lady with a metal bucket playing the nickel slots. She would put in 3 or 4 nickels and get 4 or 5 nickels back consistently. It wasn't much, but she was making money, so I changed my five-dollar bill for 100 nickels and sat back down and watched the grey-haired money maker at her slot machine and considered which machine I should try. I was quite surprised when the woman picked up her bucket and wandered off to another machine. I guess she was getting tired of just making a nickel here and there. I immediately jumped up and took her place and started putting nickels in. I was making a little money like the woman before, and at least I was now a legitimate gambler, perhaps get a free drink and double my money if I was lucky. I had gone through a dollar or two when the one-armed-bandit lit up and started flashing. Some of the gamblers around me came over to congratulate me and checkout my winnings. I had just been putting in single nickels and one gambler said, "Shoot, if you had been putting in 4 nickels, you would have won $6500! Sixty-five hundred, sixty-five, I didn't care, I was flush with some much-needed cash when I went to the window and the cashier gave me $65!!! This was a game changer for me, a travel voucher from God. I was done gambling; it had served its purpose and now I was going to put the money to work. I got a prime rib dinner at the same casino for the $2 special which really beat getting a map and a hotdog at the gas station. I went back to the bus station and purchased a ticket to take me the rest of the way to Lakeview Oregon. I had just enough money for a room for the night at my favorite casino where I could stretch out, relax and take a shower and have a good night's rest in this strange city before hopping on the bus the next morning. Life was really good and I was ecstatic about my good fortune. The next morning, I took the bus up to Klamath Falls where we transferred to a van for the final leg to Lakeview. I had them stop at the turn-off to the old Navy Air base and walked the two miles to my new home for the summer. We would be living in the officers' quarters in the old WWII base which had been idle for at least 25 years, but was still in pretty good shape. You could still faintly see the painting of the decks of different aircraft carriers on the tarmac where the pilots could safely practice landings before heading out to sea for the real thing. I met my boss Terry and he showed me to the room where I would be staying and I dumped my stuff on the bed. There was a large bathroom down the hall with a couple of toilets out in the middle with open showers and a line of sinks along the wall. Well so much for privacy this summer!

Terry took me into town the next day and introduced me to the owner of the local gas station where we would have a tab to fill up our trucks, and we toured the little town. The next day Toby arrived. He was also a geology student at the University of South Carolina and was a real southern dude, with a perfectly manicured beard and a natty metro-sexual sense of Style. Terry had an office out at the air base where we were staying with maps laid out on the tables and he went over our plan for the summer. We would be doing a Track-etch survey in the mountains just East of Lakeview looking for uranium deposits. He showed us a place on the map where we would start our reconnaissance work and the three of us headed out to the spot for a little training. He had a topo map that he had overlain with a grid with points about 100 yards apart. We would navigate the grid and dig a hole about 18" deep at every point, take a soil sample at the dark platinum/palladium layer about 10" down, then bury a plastic track-etch cup upside down, fill in the hole and plant a little flag on top of it. A uranium deposit will emit radon gas. This gas permeates up through the soil and gets trapped in the cup, since plastic is an impermeable barrier to the gas. The radon gas emits alpha particles that will leave a little etch on a piece of film that is taped to the bottom of the plastic cup. Two weeks later we go back over the same grid, digging up our plastic cups. Terry had each one numbered and would send them off to a lab where technicians would look at each piece of film and manually count the etches. Sometimes there would be close to a thousand of them in the little one-inch piece of film. Finally, when all the cups had been processed by us and the lab, Terry would get the results and create a contour map of where the hotspots were, as locations for future core-drilling, looking for a viable deposit for mining. We would repeat this process every couple of weeks in different locations in the mountains.

The next day, we went to the gas station and met the 2 high school kids who would be Toby and my assistants for the summer. We would be carrying picks and shovels and have packs with soil samples and our other gear. Sometimes we would carry a portable but heavy magnetometer to help us identify cross-cutting structures in the volcanic rock as well, so extra muscle was welcome. I would be working with the gas station owner's son Brian a long-distance runner and Toby would be working with Brian's friend a tough high school wrestler. We piled into the pickup truck and headed out to what us geologists call the "field". In this case a rugged part of the mountains, where there had been quite a bit of logging in the past. Brian and I got oriented and we started at the first grid point, dug the hole, taking a soil sample that we put into a little screw-top aluminum cylinder, then buried the cup, marking the number on the map, filled in the hole, planted a little red flag and using a compass, would navigate to the next station.

Up to this point in my life, I had always carried, at least in my bag, Grandpa Noss's pocket compass with a crack in the bezel but it worked perfectly. We were using these new Silva Ranger compasses that were much more accurate and not much bigger than my pocket compass. You could adjust the bezel to offset for the magnetic declination, then hold the compass out at arm's length using the folding mirror built into the cover to align with the heading in the exact direction of travel. Then using the little gun-sight on the top of the cover, mark a tree, rock or some other topographic feature as far away as possible and hike towards it. It was an extremely accurate way to navigate and we could always correct our course with the topographic maps if we got a little off course. To keep track of the distance, we used a foresters hip chain. This is a box you can attach to your belt that spools out biodegradable mason line. The line would be tied off at the station where we dug the hole and an odometer on the box would tell you the exact feet you had traveled, then knowing the distance between the points on the grid, we could go exactly that far to the next station. Sometime we would be in open country, sometimes on a steep slope, or crossing a creek. Occasionally we would have to climb down into a big pile of slash leftover from the lumberjacks and dig a hole at the bottom, if we could get through it. This is what we did all summer, and I loved every minute of it. The string would be useful to follow when we came back in a couple of weeks to dig up and collect the cups.

We could usually do a dozen, perhaps 20 stations in a normal day of work. One day, I suggested to Brian that we work extra hard and see how many we could do in a day if we worked at maximum speed. I told Brian that if he tripped, just make sure to fall into your work so we don't lose any time. Well, we were working at a fast pace, enjoying ourselves and were on track to set ourselves a new record.

We were on a steep slope that afternoon, working hard when I heard Toby yell from down in a little valley below us, "How are you doing, how many have you done today?"

We were on station 25 and still had an hour or two to go so I yelled back "We are finishing up number 25!"

It was quiet for a minute, then we heard Toby yell back "Fuck you!!".

We smiled and continued on our way. We were doing this to set a personal record to see what we could accomplish, but Toby did not see it that way. He liked to work at a comfortable pace and did not want us setting a new precedent.

That summer, I worked every day at sticking my thumb and middle fingers into my mouth and trying to whistle. It would be useful for calling out to Toby and Josey, his high school assistant. Eventually, almost 6 weeks into the summer, I blew into my fingers and a whistle came out. Not long after that I refined my technique so that I could blow out an ear-shattering clear whistle that could be heard from miles away. I've never lost this valuable skill, although I mostly use it nowadays to call my dog or signal that I loved a song that had just played at the Telluride Bluegrass festival.

Another time, just Toby and I were out finishing up a grid when storm clouds blew in and we got caught in a thunderstorm. We were sitting under a huge Douglas Fir out of the rain and the thunder and lightning were hitting all around us. I've always enjoyed being out in in a thunderstorm, the loud crashing would be thrilling and the lightening added an edge of danger, but not something to seriously worry about. We were under this large tree, up on a steep slope and we could see our Ford F-150 sitting on the edge of the logging road way below. Toby was too frightened to make a run for it, but was also too frightened to sit under the tree.

I knew I had to light a fire under him to get him going, so I looked up at the dark sky and shouted as loud as I could, "Mother Mary queen of grace, send a lightning bolt from space!"

Toby shouted "Shit, shit, shit", and took off running down that hill as fast as he could with me right behind and we made it to the truck without being singed.

He was not happy with me. We would have been dry had we stayed under the tree up on the hill but we were in a precarious spot. We were now soaking wet but safe in the truck. He did not care. We never did really bond together that summer, even though we had geology in common. I could not understand how he could spend an hour in front of the mirror in the morning trimming his beard to be just so, and he could not understand how I would do 300 pushups and 300 sit-ups after work when we had just spent the day busting our asses in the hills.

Sometimes we would stop by the local bar in downtown Lakeview on our way back from working. We would be covered in dust and fit right in with the other working folks of the town. We became friends with a burly bushy-bearded sheepherder that would come into town occasionally and have a couple beers with us at the bar. He would talk about how once a month he would drive the 200 miles over to Winnemucca to visit his favorite whore house there. It was the highlight of his month and we would politely decline when he offered to take us there. I always wondered why he would go to so much trouble getting to the house of ill repute, when he had a whole herd of sheep at his disposal.

Brian's family invited me over one evening for a fried chicken dinner and to participate in their family tradition of watching A Man Called Nobody, the funny cowboy movie. I had never even heard of it, but I loved it, laughing and enjoying the family watching my reactions as their favorite scenes would come on. One scene sums up the movie. A little kid and his dad are standing watching two gunslingers having a dual out on the street, when one gets a jump on the draw and shoots the other.

The little kid looks up and asks "Dad, is he the fastest gunfighter in the West?"

The dad thinks a bit and replies, "Son, Nobody's faster"

Brian's mom told me about a friend of theirs that owned a rock shop in town and thought I might be interested, being a Geologist and all. I visited the shop and ended up working there a little bit after work and on a few weekends sawing open geodes and polishing up the black obsidian and just helping out. I ended up bringing home a couple of the ones I had worked on as a souvenir of this summer. Several days after the movie night, Brian and I were out in a field with some cattle wandering around and were digging a track-etch hole and going about our work. When we looked up, there were about 20 cows and a couple of young bulls, perhaps steers, standing around us pretty close just staring at us. We are not cowboys, so I was trying to decide if we should just start walking through the herd to our next station when I wondered if my new skill could help us out in this situation.

I looked at Brian, then at the herd, put my thumb and middle finger into my mouth and blew out the loudest whistle I could muster, then shouted "Yee haw" like a cowboy would do.

We did not know if we would get trampled or charged or if they would run the other direction. Luckily, the entire herd bolted off in a cloud of dust away from us. I had learned a little something about cows stampeding from just a loud noise and I was just glad the bulls went away with the cows. One day we were working down a steep slope towards a creek and noticed weird waves in a pool. It was a large black bear swimming and splashing around, not paying us any mind. The most surprising thing was when we were down in a marshy draw one morning and heard what sounded like a couple of dinosaurs shrieking at each other. Brian and I snuck off from where we were working to check it out. It was a pair of beautiful Sand Hill Cranes making the eerie calls. It gave me goosebumps.

At the end of the summer, Terry my boss had much of the mapping done and we looked at the likely spots to start a drilling project at the hot spots we had found. Our work would pay off for the Western Nuclear drilling program next year. At about that time, a private jet with a few of the Vice Presidents flew in to check out our work. Terry showed them the maps and areas that we had narrowed down to be the most likely spots for a drilling project. When they were finished with their assessment and were getting ready to fly home, I jumped on their plane with them, since the main office was in Denver, just an hour away from Ft Collins where I was headed. The cool thing is when the VPs, who were also geologists wanted to see some mountain, or cool geographic feature they would have the pilot circle around and take pictures out the window. My trip home was just as amazing as my trip out.

Your work with Western Nuclear is very interesting. You worked hard in Geology. Your recall is amazing. Dad

25 CSU Geology & Homestake Mining

After landing at Stapleton Airport from Oregon with the Geologist VPs I took a bus up to Ft Collins. I was dropped off downtown in front of the Northern Hotel with my bags. I went across the street to an old dive bar to consider how to get to my apartment with my bag. I had been in this bar previously with Norton when the old bartender had offered him a free beer if he would drink it out of the dirty glass sitting on the bar in front of him. I knew Norton would do it. One time he and Tracy were home and arguing how clean the water was in the toilet. Tracy was saying it was filthy, Norton was saying that we were flushing the toilet with clean drinking water so Tracy offered him $5 if he would drink a glass of it. Norton accepted, proceeded to flush the toilet twice, then dipped in a little juice glass, filling it with the toilet water and drank it down. He never had any ill effects from this bad decision of his.

The old bartender was there and I ordered a Pabst and asked to use the phone. I called Tracy and he came out and picked me up in his old restored Chevy pickup. We talked about our cool summer jobs on the way back to the house and he told me that the cops had been to the house twice to pick me up, since they had a warrant for my arrest. I was a little concerned, but not too worried since I had not committed any criminal acts that I could remember. Just before I left for Oregon, I had been working on my 500 H1 sport bike and had finally got it running smoothly, so I took it out for a test drive. It was late in the evening, I was on College Avenue heading back, the bike was running perfectly and I goosed the throttle all the way to check the performance under full power. In just a few seconds I was up over 100 MPH. I let off the gas, slowing down and turning up Laurel Street next to the campus and slowly cruising back home. I heard some commotion behind me, looking back in my mirrors there were a couple of cop cars bearing down on me fast. They pulled me over and gave me a ticket. They had no idea how fast I was going, since they were off on a parking lot talking to each other in their separate cars like cops do when they spotted an orange flash speeding by with a scream of the three chainsaw motors at full revs. They made up some number to put on the ticket, well under the 100+ I was going, but still more than double the speed limit. Before I had left for Oregon I had mailed in the fine, but they had no record of it. I ended up going to court and the Judge apologized for their clerical error and threw out the case. I ended up moving about a block away to another basement apartment on W Plum Street with some friends, Darrel, a plant pathology major and Steve, an accounting major for the upcoming school year. There were three girls upstairs, Julie, Ilene and Mary who we got to know well. I traded in my Kawasaki H1 for a Honda 360 scrambler, a less temperamental 4-stroke motorcycle.

This year I was getting into the meat of my Geology classes and took the class that I had been waiting for and looking forward to, since to me it was the defining class to become a geologist, Mineralogy. This class taught me to identify over 60 different minerals by looking at the mineral color, crystal shape, comparing the hardness on Mohs scale (Dr Burns had already taught us a dirty little saying to remember the acronym TGCFAOQTCD) , checking for carbonates with the acid test, using a flame on the scale of fusibility, looking at the flame colorations. Mostly it was looking at the minerals with a hand lens like a jeweler's loop, which by the way I added to my little trifecta arsenal that I always carry with me. We would use that skill to identify rocks based on the composition of minerals they contained. I was totally ready for this class and made big cards with all the information on each of the minerals. Not only was mineralogy my defining class to be a geologist, it was the "weed-out" class used by Dr Thompson to decide who was serious about this major and who was not. In addition to identifying all the minerals, we had to learn the chemical composition of each of them as well, which was rote memorization. You could get a clue of the composition once you learned which of the roughly 17 mineral families they belonged to, such as silicates, carbonates, sulfates, phosphates, oxides, etc. An easy example is quartz SiO_2 or cinnabar HgS. Harder examples include Hornblende or epidote, that pistachio green mineral which have chemical formulas that would take up most of a line of text. We needed to memorize the periodic table as well since that was key to learning these formulas. The first day of mineralogy class was in a large lecture hall with over 100 students.

Dr Thompson talked about what would be required for this class and that only serious geology students should be taking it. The second lecture had noticeably less kids in the class and after the midterm we had less than 30 students in the classroom virtually all of us geology majors.

We had a kegger at our house with all our friends over. We made a temporary bar with my big piece of beetle-kill pine on a couple of boxes and cranked The Who and the Stones on Darrel's kick-ass stereo. I noticed a very attractive girl at the party and managed to work over to her and talk with her. She became my girlfriend for a semester, such is the nature of college romances and we would hang out at her apartment since it had a swimming pool that we could play in. On one of our dates, I took her back to my place.

As we were walking into the living room downstairs, I turned on the lights and Pam said "Oh my god"

My roommates had plastered the walls with centerfolds from their collections of Penthouse and Playboy. Literally the entire back wall had titty wallpaper. Pam could hold her own with any of them, but we decided to retire back to her place where it would not be in our faces. I yelled at my roommates the next day, since this was early in my relationship with Pam and we were still feeling each other out, literally.

Sometimes, we would crank vinyl on Darrel's kick-ass stereo system and dance around the living room of our basement apartment. My roommates and I would sing at the top of our lungs to these songs that we knew. Occasionally when we were really getting into the music, and The Who would come on, Darrel would get crazy and like Pete Townsend at the end of a concert, smashing his electric guitar to pieces on stage, Darrel would pick up whatever was handy, a chair, a side table, anything and smash it to bits with a crazy look on his face like he was a rock-star. Speaking of smashing things, Steve's mom had given him a set of Corelleware dishes and was bragging about how they were totally unbreakable, even though they looked like china. We bet him that if he just dropped one, it would surely break. He had the confidence of his mom's words about these plates and picked one up to drop it at waist height. I said, "Wait, hold it up over your head sideways, not flat.". He said that was not fair, but I reminded him that they were unbreakable, and the floor had carpet as cushioning over the cement as well. Steve held the plate over his head and dropped it. When it hit, it broke into a thousand little pieces that flew all over the kitchen and Darrel and I had free beer that night from our little bet.

Ever since I had left home for Colorado 5 years ago, I had usually visited once a year on Christmas over my winter break to see the family for a couple of weeks. The other holidays would just be celebrated with my friends. Well on this, my 2nd year back at CSU, my roommate Darrel invited us for Thanksgiving dinner at his parent's house. Steve and I accepted. I was looking forward to a family holiday with a nice home-cooked meal with friends and family. On Thanksgiving Day, we drove down to Lakewood and met Darrel's family and relaxed for an hour or two with them before dinner was ready just snacking on Hors d'oeuvres The big dining room table was all set and Darrel's mom brought out the turkey and stuffing with green bean casserole and mashed potatoes and gravy, salad, French bread and other little goodies that were a family tradition, followed by apple and pumpkin pie and ice cream. It was awesome. I got seconds on absolutely everything including dessert since I was a starving college student and having probably my best meal of the year. We sat around after dinner enjoying a beer before heading out at about 5 or 6 totally satiated and happy.

Steve needed to pick up some stuff at his parents' house in nearby Littleton so we made a pit stop there to meet his parents and get his stuff. His mom was very nice and invited us into their house and said that the timing was perfect, dinner was almost ready. Steve graciously thanked his mom as Darrel and I looked at each other and followed his lead and thanked her for waiting for us. I was wondering how we were going to be able to consume probably the largest meal of the year twice! We met Steve's family and almost immediately sat down to dinner with them. She had made a feast, no less wonderful than the meal we had at Darrel's house. We loaded up our plates with a little helping of everything on the table but even a little helping added up to an overflowing plate. Unlike our earlier meal, I did not get any seconds even though Steve's mom kept offering. I did relent and get a second helping on one of the side dishes that was her specialty and knew it would make her happy. After dinner, Steve gathered up his things that he needed and we bade his family farewell as we were headed back up to Ft Collins. As we pulled down the street from Steve's house, we were moaning about how stuffed we were, we thought we might barf, our stomachs were bloated and uncomfortable, so we pulled over at a park nearby. We all laid down on our backs on the grass which was more comfortable than sitting in the car, compressing our stomachs. We laid there comparing notes on who ate the most, what was the best dish, who was going to barf, and that we should try to enjoy the painful feeling of being over-stuffed since we might never experience it to this degree ever again. We all managed to hold down everything and after that 20 or 30 minutes of male bonding on the grass on our backs staring up at the sky, we piled back into the car for the ride up to Ft Collins.

I took a rock-climbing class from the outdoor recreation department which was held on the Dakota sandstone hogback up at Horsetooth reservoir. We learned how to tie knots, use a climbing harness, setup a top-rope for safety and how to scale the 30' rock faces. I was hooked and ended up getting a pair of EB climbing shoes like Matt had used on our Flatiron ascent. I just made a harness out of webbing that I could clip into. Rock climbing became my passion and I would do it as often as possible. It was probably the combination of testing your strength on the rock, learning the techniques such as mantling, heel hooks, stuffing hands into cracks, the thrill of safely being in such a precarious situation and just being so intimate with the rocks that I was studying that attracted me to the sport so much. In this case we were climbing on an arkosic arenite sandstone from the Cretaceous period overlying the much softer Morrison shale that formed the basin of the reservoir. Matt stopped by for a visit when he was on a break from Macalester College and we went rock climbing with his rope and gear. He was studying Biology and one day when I was away at class, he was hanging out in the house and was looking at my geology textbooks. When I got back, he told me that what I was studying looked far more interesting than what he was studying. When he went back to college, he changed his major to geology like I had done, a good choice in retrospect since his geology career turned out to be much longer and more fruitful than mine.

My roommates, plus Tracy my old roommate and I decided to take Steve's large station wagon on a trip to San Diego for Spring Break. We loaded up the car and headed out to a Beach just south of San Clemente with little campsites perfect for our tents. We swam in the ocean and I looked to rent a surfboard, but the shops were still closed for the season. The water was a little chilly, but certainly swim-able so we consoled ourselves with body surfing. There were some other girls at the campsite and it turned out they were also from CSU and Steve knew them. We spent a night or two sitting around the campfire with them, passing a bottle of whisky around and talking. I was nursing a bad sunburn on my face. It had been so hazy out that the sun was just a big spot in the haze like it was a cloudy day, but it turned out to be very strong and burned me up pretty good. We ended up camping down the beach to San Diego and after visiting the world-class zoo there, we went body surfing in Mission Bay. The waves were pretty large and were breaking pretty far out. I would swim out on the rip tide, then work over to the sandbar where the waves were breaking and body surf them on several rides all the way back into the beach. Tracy went out with me for one surfing session and the rip tide freaked him out so bad that he would not get back into the water. On our way home, we stopped by Las Vegas and parked out back of Caesars Palace and changed out of our beach clothes to some nice clothes we had packed for just this occasion. We went into the casino and I had earmarked just $5 to gamble with, since I was already up $65 from my trip out to Western Nuclear last year and I wanted to stay in the casino black. We were in there gambling on the one-armed bandits and I was actually up a bit when the other guys wanted to check out another casino. I was reluctant, since I was on a winning streak, but they insisted and we wanted to stay together so I begrudgingly left my machine, already becoming a gambling addict and I did not know it. Thank you, my crew, for saving me!

In early 1979 during the end of my Junior year at CSU I was working in the basement of the Geology building in a lab cutting thin sections with a rock saw for the optical mineralogy lab classes. A thin section is a slice of rock, cut and polished to a standard thickness of 3 micrometers and glued with epoxy to a microscope slide. Once the epoxy has hardened, it is polished a second time to get the exact thickness. I would look at the finished slide with a jeweler's hand lens that I kept around my neck and then with a polarizing microscope to verify the thickness, typically by looking at any quartz in the sample and making sure it looked correct. It is messy and exacting work to get each slide done, since the thickness is important and you get covered in rock dust. I felt lucky to have this job since I liked the work and it was helping to pay for my schooling. This particular afternoon I had an interview for a summer job with the Homestake Mining company, doing uranium exploration in Wyoming. The head Geologist, Jim Puckett had come down from Casper to Ft Collins to interview students for the single job opening. My interview was in the middle of my work in the geology lab so I took a break and walked up to the office that was being used for the interview. In the hall outside of the office were several seniors, dressed in suits and sports jackets and a couple with brief cases looking all professional. I was just dressed in jeans and a tee shirt with rock dust on my shirt and in my hair, but I did splash water on my face to freshen up. I had my interview with Mr. Puckett and it seemed to go pretty well. I told him about my work the previous summer with the Western Nuclear Mining company in Oregon also doing uranium exploration. I knew there was a slim chance of getting the job since the seniors had an extra year of geology study under their belt. I went back to work after the interview and put it out of my mind. Several weeks later I got a call from Jim at Homestake offering me the position of Summer Geologist with a salary of $850/month with all work-related meal, lodging and transportation being paid. Jim also told me that I would be furnished with a 4-wheel drive vehicle and he would reimburse me for transportation to Casper. I was ecstatic and accepted the position on the phone. This would be an awesome way to spend the summer, doing something that I really enjoyed, learning more about exploration and would really help me to pay for my senior year of school. I could save almost 100% of my salary.

The weekend after school got out, I took a bus up to Casper and got a room at the Best Western. That Monday I walked to the office and met Jim again and he showed me around the place. There was a storage area in the back with racks and racks of core sections from exploratory drilling they had been doing. There were maps lying around everywhere and Doris worked at a desk in the front office. It was not a huge office, in fact the only other geologist was a Ron, an adventurous guy about my age that was doing exploration work year-round. That first week, Jim went over everything that the job entailed and what he expected of me. I would be hiking around the high desert of northern Wyoming looking for surface clues for uranium and doing geologic mapping of the rock formations, mostly the uplifted Dakota and Morrison formations that I was already familiar with from rock climbing up at Horsetooth reservoir in Ft Collins. The idea is that over millions of years, the granitic mountains that were being pushed up from below would also push up the sedimentary layers above it at an angle as the entire sediments and granite would also be eroded and worn down. The minerals of the granite, including the disseminated uranium would be dissolved into the oxygenated water that would seep down through the tilted porous sandstone and would travel for miles underground. This water would travel down though the rock formation until it hit a geochemical barrier called an oxidation-reduction front, also called the redox front, where the uranium would drop out of solution and be concentrated in the porous sandstone, often resulting in a large uranium deposit suitable for mining. My classes in mineralogy and structural geology would come in handy for sure!

We went down to the local Ford dealer and Jim had leased a big, brand-new Ford F-250 4WD truck for me to use for the summer. It was a huge step up from my old Scout, but just did not have the same functional hard-core off-road feeling that I loved about the old Scout. I had been looking at the topographic maps in the office and the next weekend I drove over to the huge Deer Creek canyon, not too far south of Casper and got to try out the four-wheel drive, going up a steep dirt road towards the heart of the canyon. I spent the day hiking down into the canyon and encountered my first ever rattlesnake climbing over a huge talus slope to get a better look at the creek. It was down in the rocks and I could hear it rattling, but I never saw it. I thought I might come back here in the future and try my hand at paddling this steep creek as it looked boat-able and was definitely fishable.

My first task was to help Ron with a survey up in Jeffrey City, a town that used to be called Home on the Range. The work would be a lot like what I had done last summer for Western Nuclear. It is interesting that a wealthy guy name Dr CW Jeffrey financed a prospector to open a uranium mine here. The prospector, Bob Adams then started a mining company, Western Nuclear, the same company that I worked for last year! There was a huge mine on one side, a uranium mill on the other side and the boom town of the newly named Jeffrey City between the two. There were about 2000 people living here, 90% of them working for the mining company and all of them living in mobile homes or trailers. In fact, the motel that Ron and I stayed at was just eight or ten mobile homes attached end to end and divided into little motel rooms. The only permanent buildings that I saw were the post office, a high school and the Split Rock Bar and Cafe where we retired to every day after work. Ron and I sat at the bar and carved our names into it, me with the large Buck knife that I had purchased with "lumber points" from Wickes. Ron and I were the same age, he just got into the workforce sooner than I since he did not take a break in the middle of college like I did. We would sometimes go bouldering after work on the large sandstone boulders and outcroppings around town. It was an exciting bustling town with huge trucks constantly rumbling through with loads of ore for the mill. Ron's roommate Barry had worked here as a flagman in the giant open pit, setting flags at the boundary of the ore deposit to demarcate the boundary for the large front-end loaders to know which gets loaded onto the trucks and which gets dumped. On the way home, Ron and I stopped to look at some gnarly rapids below the Pathfinder dam on the North Platte River. Ron was putting together an order for some Perception whitewater canoes to be delivered to Casper and wanted to know if I was interested. I was definitely interested since I love canoeing and had not done much on rivers, let alone these big tough western rivers, but alas, I was still in school and had not a penny to spare since I would be spending it all on completing my education. I would end up meeting and hooking up with Ron again 7 or 8 years later when I was putting onto the Delores River for a 3-day paddle in the sandstone canyons of Southwestern Colorado with my Mad River Whitewater canoe and he was doing the same with his Perception canoe. We had many adventures together after that which were yet to come.

A week later Ron and I were back in Casper, I was finishing up my preparations for my exploration work and Ron was working on the data from our survey. Memorial Day weekend was coming up, I was hanging out at Ron's house having a beer talking about backpacking and Ron's roommate Barry and I decided to go up to the rugged Wind River Range for a few days. We drove up to the Big Sandy trailhead, our staging area and hiked up into the wilderness. It was only 5 miles into the large cirque basin where we had decided to camp, but it was 1600' up to the top of Jackass Pass before dropping back down 600' to our camp overlooking Lonesome Lake and the huge massif of Pingora Peak rising as a pure granite cone almost straight up another 1600' from our camp. We had split up our combined gear, Barry had a nice tent and I had cooking gear so that we carried no duplicate gear, but our packs were still pretty heavy with food, photography equipment, sleeping gear, etc. That night we sat around sipping whiskey and looking at the stars and milky way galaxy. The next morning Barry woke up to a moose just outside our tent. We brewed up coffee and breakfast before hiking and exploring all day Sunday. We got back to Casper the next day and Ron told me later that Barry had a crush on him. Boy, I really do not have gaydar at all, but I'm glad that I did not know, since I was totally comfortable with him, sleeping together in the little tent and sharing coffee and talking openly with each other in the dusk with our tin cups of whiskey. Well, I guess not totally openly, ha-ha.

My base camp for much of the summer was a little Motel on the outskirts of town as you were driving into Lovell. A nice Mormon couple owned the motel, in fact most of the town of Lovell was Mormons. The largest building in town was the grain/sugar beet elevator next to the railroad tracks and the second largest building in town was the Mormon church. I would be doing field mapping from Lovell down to Greybull. There were a couple of cafes in town where I ate all my meals and I would read the Lovell Chronicle. I became a local in these cafes, getting to know all the waitresses. Most of the locals wore cowboy boots and ball caps or cowboy hats. My trusty Vasque hiking boots had worn out, so I had taken my tough Frye boots from high school that were tall like cowboy boots and had replaced the leather soles with rugged Vibram hiking soles for use outdoors. I was pretty much dressed like a local with my boots and ball cap, but everyone knew I was not from there. I had been working for about a week in the scrub area following the hogbacks, taking readings with my Scintillator detector that is like a more powerful Geiger counter, to get a measure of the background radiation that I would mark on my map as well as taking an inclination of the rock beds of interest. The angle of the beds was important since the redox front could be much deeper if the beds were at a sharper angle. I was hiking along and stepped over a large sage brush when I heard a rattle and immediately jumped away from it. It was a coiled-up Prairie Rattlesnake looking at me with his tongue flickering out of his mouth and his tail rattling. It was the first that I had actually seen and my heart was racing. I had been working hard to set a good pace to cover as much ground as I could. I decided to get out of the sage area and work over to the rocky ridge since they must like this scrubby desert area. I was walking on the rocks when again I was startled by another snake. It had also started rattling before I spotted it and I veered around it thinking no place here was safe. I went to the top of the ridge, took off my pack, pulled my lunch and water out and sat down with my back to the rock. After I finished my lunch, I was just enjoying the beauty of the surrounding country and quietly relaxing, thinking about the two snakes when I noticed some movement several feet off to my right. I looked and it was a triangular head poking out of the crack below the same rock I was leaning against. Damn, I jumped up right away and stood there looking at the snake. I was pretty shaken up at this point and was working slowly for the rest of the afternoon looking for snakes. For the rest of the week, I was working slowly doing my work, but so busy looking for snakes that I was on about half speed of my normal work output. During that week I did see several others, sometimes stretched out looking like a stick, or sometimes coiled up looking like one of the cow pies that were everywhere also. One time, when I got into my truck and slammed the door closed, there was a rattling outside and a snake was coiled up just under my truck and he could not have been 6 inches from where I was standing just moments before. I was thinking about it the next weekend. How was I going to get to full speed working again? I decided two things. One, I had been very close to perhaps a dozen of them that week and none of them had struck at me even though I was close enough several times. The second thing was that they probably would not bite me if I did not step on them. I made a rule so I would not have to think about it so much when hiking around. The rule was to never step on a stick or a cow pie. The rule did get me back up to speed and I did see dozens of them during the rest of the summer and I never got bit.

I became friends with Jack, a guy about my age who was a reporter for the Chronicle since we both ate at the same cafes and got to know each other. I think the thing we had in common that bonded us immediately was that we were the same age and we had both been born in Hartford Hospital during the same week. I thought that I had recognized him when I first saw him in the cafe! We started hanging out and would go to the local horseshoe bend beach down in the Bighorn canyon at the Yellowtail Reservoir to go swimming and check out the women sunbathing there. It is a beautiful sandy beach with the canyon cliffs behind us and across the water with good swimming as well. Lots of the locals would come down here and spread their towels out on the sand and spend the day here, not that dissimilar from the beaches at Cape Cod, just on a much smaller scale and in a totally different setting. Jack explained to me that all the single women here were one of two types. Mormon girls just out of high school and looking to get married and young Mormon women, perhaps with a kid or two, recently divorced also looking to get married. That kind of took some of the wind out of my sails, since my life plan was to stay single until I was 32, enjoying life and going on adventures and having girlfriends, but not settling down for another decade. That was also why geology was such a good career for me since it was perfect for the single adventure lifestyle.

Pouring over maps I found a couple of large wild canyons worthy of exploring on my weekends off. One was Cottonwood Canyon, just 10 miles east of Lovell. I took the truck up a 4wd road as far as I could and hiked up into the canyon. I was following the stream up for about a mile when I could smell something foul. As I got closer, I encountered a couple of piles of bear scat, but I was not too worried, since the Big Horns only have black bears, not grizzlies. I found a dark little cave opening which was the bear den, at the base of a large canyon cliff not too far from the creek I was following. I was like a hobbit, hiking quietly and on the lookout for the bear that I never saw. I continued exploring the canyon up for several miles. The canyon never opened up but was less impressive going from about 1000 feet deep at the mouth to about 500 feet where I ended up turning back around. The other canyon is Devil's canyon where I did a tentative exploration and swore I would come back to again for a more in-depth hike. On the 4WD road into the top of the canyon from up in the Big Horn Mountains I parked at the end of the road and hiked through the most beautiful wildflower meadow I had ever been in. Not only was the meadow gorgeous with exploding colors of flowers and golden tasseled grasses gently swaying in the breeze, but the bluebird sky and crystal-clear air backed by the mountains made it a place of dreams. I could have just laid down in this meadow for the weekend. When I'm relaxing with a meditation guide and they say to think of a beautiful place to get you in the relaxation zone, I always come back to this meadow.

I had decided to go backpacking on Independence Day weekend that was coming up. Looking at my stash of topo maps that Jim had provided, the Northwest corner of the park looked like a good wild area to explore. I took the big pickup and drove up into Yellowstone Park, rocking out to tunes on my boombox that I had picked up in Billings, Montana at a local department store. My one luxury that I had brought with me was a box of cassette tapes with music like the Stones, Loggins & Messina, The Who, the Dead, Clapton, etc. I kept the boombox on the front bench seat next to me and it would be great on the long drives in this lonely state although it was only a couple hours to the park. I was just a bit apprehensive about the area I was heading into, since a hiker had been mauled by a grizzly just the week before, but I was not to be deterred. All I had for defense was my handy Buck Folding Hunter and my back was protected by the large pack. I would not be running, but running is the worst thing to do anyway. I started at the Pack Trailhead (good name huh) and soon crossed the huge Yellowstone River on a footbridge at the mouth of the Black Canyon. Once across the river I ran into a baby moose at the edge of some Aspens, but I never saw the mom. I setup camp at the junction of Hellroaring and Coyote creeks under some large Ponderosas as my base for exploring. Each night I would take my food bag about 200 yards from my camp, throw my parachute cord over a branch about 25 feet up and hoist it up into the air, out of the reach of bears, while keeping the smell of food away from camp. That first night in the tent, as I was laying on my sleeping pad in my bag listening to the loud sounds of rushing water, every so often I would think I heard a bear and would poke my head out of the tent and look around, but no bear.

I did this for an hour or two but it was preventing me from sleeping when I just decided "The hell with it, I'm going to sleep" and fell off into a deep slumber for the rest of the night.

One weekend, Jack and I decided to go dancing at a cowboy bar about an hour away across the Bighorn Basin in Cody. We were going to meet his brother there who would be getting off of work about the time we got there. He was a Wyoming state patrolman and it started making sense why Jack had been working in the little town of Lovell. I got dressed up in my cowboy gear, basically my work boots with a pair of jeans and a western shirt and we took Jack's car for the hour drive or as the locals would call it, a two-beer drive since it would take two beers to get there. This was before MADD when drinking and driving was just a thing, especially in Wyoming. As we left town, we stopped at the drive-up window of the bar and Jack got a rum and coke and I got a beer, both in a plastic to-go Coors cup and we headed west on highway 14 to Cody. Halfway there, we passed through the town of Powell, which had a community college that a lot of the kids from Lovell went to. We pulled up to the drive-up window of a bar that Jack knew and he got another mixed drink and I got my favorite vodka tonic on ice. When pulling up to the window, we were basically pulling up to the bar and could see the patrons drinking behind the bartender who was making our drinks. We both drank them in the car on the rest of the drive to Cody. We met Jack's brother there and spent a few hours dancing with the cowgirls and listening to the live music and just relaxing together. Eventually we had to leave since Jack's brother had to get home to his family, so we followed him closely in his state patrol car back to Lovell going about 90 MPH the entire way! I had dinner another time at Jack's brother's house with his wife and we had Moose steaks, which I had never had before and it was wonderful, tender and not too gamey.

Jim came up to Lovell a month later to check up on me, get a report and have me show him around some of the hot spots I had identified. I took him out to one place where I had been walking across the Morrison shale when my scintillator detector just pegged off the scale then dropped back to normal. I turned around and walked back till it pegged off the scale and just stayed there. I turned the attenuator up to 2x, then 5x, then 10x and finally up to near 100x before the needle started going down. I dug down a little bit and pulled out a 20lb dinosaur vertebrae fossil that was filled with the yellow uranium mineral carnotite. In fact, I had carried the fossil back to my truck and put it in the bed as far from the cab as I could. With the scintillator detector in the cab, I could get the needle to peg out with a lower more sensitive setting. When I got back to the motel, I had put the fossil out near the motel sign next to the highway to keep it away from me, the maid and anyone else in the motel. I took Jim out to the site and the overlying Dakota sandstone was at a favorable angle for a fairly shallow redox front. It would be a good spot for a drilling project next year. A day or two later, after I had showed him some other spots that had promise, he went back to the main office in Casper taking the fossil vertebrae with him. I would sometimes just walk downtown from my motel for dinner and on one of these walks I ran into Mike who I had known at school. He was a geology MS graduate student who had just graduated and was working for the Wyoming highway department doing rock mitigation on the steep, winding highway 14 that was being worked on in the mountains east of town. We had a couple of beers together; he was still dating a co-ed from CSU who was staying up here with him for the summer. We went out several times fossil collecting for prehistoric horse teeth in an area that he knew about and in a quirk of fate we came across their modern-day ancestors when a herd of wild horses that Lovell is known for, ran across in front of us kicking up dust like they owned the place, as we were hiking up a fossil filled gulch in a little badlands area. The area we were exploring was devoid of any vegetation, just a pebbly clay soil. We were looking for little triangles poking up out of the ground which were indicative of the large fossil teeth we were looking for. I found several that I kept on the table of my motel room as my only real decoration, other than my dusty field gear.

In August I took the truck out to the Black Hills, the home ground of Homestake Mining since they operated the largest gold mine in the US in Lead, South Dakota. This was a gold claim job, so a Geologist in Lead had called my boss Jim, and asked him if he had an intern that could do this.

He said, "I have a real go-getter! I bet he could do the whole job in a week; I'll send him up to the Black Hills".

Homestake was the first mining company ever listed on the New York Stock exchange in 1879. I spent several days updating close to one hundred, 20-acre mining claims. To be legal, the claims have to be staked out with wooden posts at each of the 4 corners, with the #1 North-East corner post containing the claim notice, rolled up and placed in a drilled-out hollow of the post. I spent a good week with a pack of claim notices and a shovel to shore up any falling posts and replaced all the old notices with the new notices. Not a bad job, but a bit tedious if you were to do it for more than the week I was at it.

After that I headed up to Libby MT for a couple of weeks to work at an abandoned vermiculite mine they had. Libby was a small little town and had a couple of "Modern" Motels, at least according to their signs. I had learned from a summer of staying in motels and hotels that the word Modern must have been very popular in the early 50's and those motels tended to be run-down. I went to the local bar, ordered a beer and talked to the bartender since it was the afternoon and the place was almost empty. I asked him if there were any places to stay other than the couple of motels. He knew of a guy in town that rented out his nice little travel trailer in his back yard. I ended up staying in that trailer for the couple of weeks that I was up there. The weekend I was off, I drove through Glacier National Park, where my grandfather had taken Grandma Noss for a multi-week backpacking trip back in the 40's. My visit was not nearly as adventurous, driving on the beautiful Going to the Sun Road to lake McDonald to take pictures, but the park was beautiful and totally worthy of a return visit. Jim actually came up here to review the results of my work and was surprised when I told him I was not staying in a local motel.

At the end of the summer, I was back in Casper and walked into the office. I greeted Doris at the front desk and as I was talking to her, I noticed that she had my dinosaur vertebrae sitting on the corner of her desk. I asked her about it and she said she liked the little square yellow crystals and was using it as decoration.

Those yellow crystals were radioactive autunite. I said "Hang on, I'll be right back". I ran out to my truck and got my scintillation detector and placed it on the desk in front of Doris. I had it on the most sensitive setting and turned it on. It pegged out the meter with the electronic buzzing sound indicating the presence of radioactivity. I turned up the attenuator several clicks before it started going down a little and recommended that she place it in the core sample room in the back. She replied that there was so much radiation from the core samples and the misc. rock samples in Ron and Jim's offices that she was not worried. I was a bit flabbergasted, realizing that if pegging the scintillator on her desk had not fazed her, nothing I could say would change her mind. I wondered if working there basically getting a low-level radiation treatment would prevent her from ever getting cancer. I hoped so, as I really liked this tough older Wyomingite woman. I went back to Jim's office to talk with him about the work we had done over the last few months. He was very happy with all that we had accomplished and he offered me a full-time job after I graduated. Again, I was ecstatic since this was exactly what I wanted to do. We were chatting about what some of the future goals would be and what he wanted to accomplish and I asked him why he hired me over all the seniors and other students applying for this job. I just assumed it was because of my experience doing uranium exploration the previous summer, but I was curious about what he thought. He told me that of all the kids that came in for the interviews, I was the only one that looked like a field geologist with my jeans and rock dust everywhere and the hand lens around my neck. He said that I looked like I could handle hiking and bushwhacking around the back country and my experience was a definite plus. It just goes to show what I have always thought about cowboys, that 80% of being a cowboy is the outfit. Well I guess that applies to geologists too!

The Three Mile Island disaster had happened March 28, 1979, just two months before my summer job at Homestake mining, but the repercussions had built up. I got a call from Jim during my senior year that all domestic uranium exploration had been halted and Homestake was getting rid of their uranium exploration division and I no longer had a job when I graduated. Damn, my dream job was gone, in fact the entire industry was gone. It was the best job I ever had, doing exactly what I had hoped a geology career would be all about. Little did I know that the oil boom was just starting. In the year or two that followed, Jeffrey City went bust and the town lost 90% of its population. People were selling their appliances on the side of the road, as Ron told me a couple of years later, before hooking up their mobile homes and trailers and moving away, probably to the oil patch that was just starting up, such is the cycle of boom and bust.

One good thing about my job was that it had fostered in me a love for the wild areas of Wyoming and the independent people that live there. Wyoming's relationship to Colorado is analogous to New Hampshire's relationship to Connecticut, a wild state that is fun to visit North of a more civilized state with more job opportunities.

TGCFAOQTCD – Texas Girls Can F*#@ And Other Queer Things Can Do (Talc, Gypsum, Corundum, Fluorite, Apatite, Orthoclase, Quartz, Topaz, Corundum, Diamond)

The anecdotes (Thanksgiving dinner) make me want to barf. However, most of your anecdotes are very interesting and generally unknown to me. I wish Mom could read your story.
Love Dad
Love it! Had me guffawing! -Gussie

26 CSU Geology & Field Camp ('79 –'80)

I got back from Casper to start my senior year at CSU in the same basement apartment. Pretty much all my classes were Geology, which I needed to finish up the requirements for my degree. I decided to take a programming class since it seemed like there would be a lot of number crunching of all the geologic data we would be finding in exploration and this would be a useful class. I took a class on FORTRAN, which is short for Formula Translation and would be perfect for scientific and numeric computations. Most of our programs that we wrote for this class were pretty basic, just enough to give an overview of programming and how this procedural language worked. The data structures were very primitive, basically just a shared "common block" that could be accessed from any part of the program. I realized when I wrote my first program why the assignments were fairly simple. I would write my program out on a piece of paper since this was before we had computer monitors to edit with. We would go to the school bookstore and purchase a box of cards to use at the card puncher machine. The basement of the mathematics department had all the computer equipment. There were four card punchers, so we would wait in line to get access to a machine. Once on the machine, we would put our cards into the input feeder and type out our program, one card per line. When you hit return on the keyboard, the card would be ejected to the output bin and a new card would take its place for the next line. This would continue until I had typed in the entire program from my notes. I would pick up my punched cards and walk over to the card-reader machine and put them into the hopper. This would be a shorter line. This machine would read all the cards that I had programmed, sort of like a money counter, then submit the program to the mainframe computer to be run. After executing the program, the mainframe would output the results to the print queue of one of the two large printers. Then we would all wait for our results to be printed out to see how the program worked. Waiting for the printer output would be the most tedious part of the process. Your name would be on the beginning of the page and whoever was looking at the printer would call out the name, or just rip off the output from the huge sheets of perforated printer paper and put it in the pile by the printer. The first several times would usually say something like "Syntax error on line 12". This meant that you had made an error on the 12th card, so I would need to go back to the card punch machine, put in a fresh card, retype the 12th card in my stack with this new card. Then go back to the card reader and try again. Every once in a while, you would hear a scream or moan when someone was putting their cards into the reader and would drop their stack. We would help them pick up all the cards, and they would have to put them back in the proper order. Needless to say, I decided that computer programming was definitely NOT something I liked, and would not be a career path for me. Straight geology was the way to go!

My roommates and I were on an inner-tube water polo team with the girls upstairs and a number of our other friends. We would play this game in the big swimming pool in Moby gym, named after the whale. Really. It was great fun. We had played the year before as well with basically the same team.

We had a team meeting upstairs in the girl's apartment just before this second season was starting and I overheard Jane, a girl on our team talking to some of the other girls on the team and saying, "Wait till you see Chris' body".

I took it as a little compliment, but mostly it just served to make me feel a bit self-conscious later, when walking out to the pool from our locker room. Too bad Jane was not my type. I got over that soon, as it was amazingly fun to play this coed game from the comfort of a black inner tube and I was a natural paddler, even if it was just using our hands.

I liked paleontology, which was like zoology for dinosaurs. It was interesting and I liked learning the skeletal structure of these creatures and how the day-to-day life of them could be inferred from the scant clues in the sedimentary rock beds. There was not too much commercial use for this knowledge, other than knowing that these creatures were the basis for oil, along with all the tropical vegetation that was around at the time. That, and just the sheer interest as the field was starting to change from slow-moving lizard like creatures to fast moving warm-blooded creatures as Professor Robert Bakker was promoting. In fact, he was the model for one of the scientists in Jurassic Park decades later that just missed getting eaten by a T-Rex. Paleontology was like a liberal-arts class that you would take for the sheer joy of learning something interesting, but not much practical application in the job market.

I became friends with Dennis since he was over at the house upstairs quite a bit hanging out with his girlfriend Julie. Dennis was working as a doorman at Washingtons bar and grill which sounded like a perfect job for this last school year. I had a National-Direct Student Loan rather than a work-study job this year, so I had free time for a part-time job. He recommended me and I was soon a doorman at Washingtons. It was a big student hangout, with three floors, a disco and dancing area with a bar backed by a constantly moving steampunk sculpture of cogs, wheels, chains and pulleys downstairs. The main floor had a big bar next to the kitchen window for ordering mostly burgers and fries, a smaller bar in the back and an upstairs game area with another bar. The work crew was comprised of several doormen mostly students, several bartenders and their bar-back helpers, a couple of bouncers usually large linemen from the CSU football team and a couple of managers. The bar was filled with props from a Hollywood warehouse that the company had purchased. We had a streetcar from A Streetcar Named Desire, a huge 1800's hearse hanging from the ceiling above the balcony that looked over the dance floor below. There was a large machine gun hanging in the air pointing directly at anyone standing by the cash register at the main bar and hundreds of other props hanging from the ceiling and on the walls so the place had its own sort of character and was extremely popular on the weekends. I would work at the door, carding everyone that entered since the drinking age was 21. That was part of the reason that I got the job since I was 23 and most undergrads would graduate before reaching the legal drinking age. When not carding at the door, we would wander around the bar in our red Washingtons polo shirts picking up bottles, glasses, leftover plates and basically keeping an eye on whatever was happening. If a fight broke out, we would jump into the melee and try to break it up, or at least keep them apart until the bouncers arrived.

Our code word for a fight was "sassafras". A manager or bartender would say over the loudspeaker "Sassafras at station 4" and anyone near would go and help break up the fight. After closing time and cleaning up the bar, we would get together and the Manager would sort out who had got hit breaking up a fight, since we would get $5 for any punch that we did not punch back.

For instance, Dennis would say, "Chris, you saw me get hit" and I would concur and the manager would examine Dennis's face for any signs of a punch and decide if it was worthy of $5.

There were not a lot of fights but one or two on the weekends was fairly normal and it would usually be drunk college kids that would not be too much trouble. I liked the job, I liked the burgers, I liked the loud music, I liked that they worked around our schedule of tests and assignments at school and liked making some extra cash.

My roommate Darrel worked down in Longmont at the Great Western Sugar factory doing plant pathology work in the lab on sugar beet samples from the many farms near there. In the lab were the "Toad Ladies" who would work counting the nematodes, that can reduce crop yield by sucking nutrients from the beet and stunting the growth in an industry where the percentage of sugar in the beet must be high to make a profit. Darrel became friends with one of these Toad Ladies and he invited her up to a party we were having at our house. It was a big party with loud music and lots of beer and I noticed this attractive blonde girl who was not afraid to smile and grin, even with braces on her teeth. Her looks and her confidence pulled me in and we started talking and dancing a bit. She told me that her step-dad worked at the Great Western Factory in Scottsbluff and got her the job working in Longmont where his brother and family lived and that is where she was staying. We joked with each other about having the same first name and what other similarities we might have in common. I ended up getting pulled into some party activities and talking with all my friends that had shown up. After a bit I looked around for that cute girl. She was still there but was getting ready to leave so I walked her outside the house as the party was winding down and I got her phone number. I noticed the bumper sticker on her car as she was pulling away, "Single and loving it!".

The next weekend I rode my motorcycle the 40 miles down to Longmont to visit her at her uncle's place. I was excited to see her and jumped off my bike when she walked out of the house. We took her car up the Big Thompson canyon and sat on a large rock on the edge of the river and talked, soaking in the beauty of the place. She had been there when she was little and they had stayed in a motel not too far up the canyon and had fond memories of the place, especially since it was one of her dad's favorite places to go on vacation. Her dad had passed away when she was little. He had worked as a foreman in a bean factory in Morrell NE and she suspected that he died from the chemicals they used on the beans. We got into talking about some heavy stuff on this first date and I liked how open she was. Her first impression of me was not so good as I had left the motorcycle ignition on, and my battery was dead. The good thing was that she knew that I was a bit flummoxed when she walked out looking all cute and any thought of turning the bike off was gone from my head. We pushed that bike down the slight incline of her road and I jump-started it. The alternator on that 360 Honda was just strong enough to provide a spark for the engine and a slight trickle to the battery. As I got about 10 miles from home, the bike could not keep up the 60 MPH pace and slowed down to 50, then 40 and eventually slowed to a crawl before dying. I was probably 4 miles from home and ended up pushing that 350-pound bike all the way to my house along the side of the road in the dark. I really had to work hard for that first date!

Our first "dinner date" was going through the drive-thru at a Jack-in-the-Box where we got drinks, burgers and fries. We were sitting in the car discussing the cost of this meal for some reason. While talking about the cost, I was adding it up in my head and came up with a total for our bill. I then factored in the 3% sales tax and came up with an exact cost of our meal. When we got to the drive-up window, the bill was exactly, to the penny what I had computed and she thought I was a math genius. That was a step in the right direction. We took our burgers up to Horsetooth reservoir and climbed up the hogback looking over the town and ate our cold burgers and they tasted amazingly good, like a sub-standard dinner on a camping trip always tastes great. We made out on the grassy slope under the stunted ponderosas with the nice view. The town below looked pretty good too! It turned out that Chris had a full-ride scholarship to Chadron State college in western Nebraska and had a teaching degree in English. Her mother had insisted that she get a teaching degree so that she would always have a job. Chris had worked a couple of years teaching out in North Platte NE where things were pretty strict. She had a Chevelle with a huge V8 motor in it at the time for blasting across the flat countryside that I wished she still had since it sounded so cool. After she was hired, the principal laid down the law and told her that she was not allowed to go into any of the bars in town and she was not allowed to date any of the railroad men, as North Platte was known as a railroad town. Being an English teacher meant reading a lot of papers and one was a disturbing paper written by a boy in one of her classes. He ended up acting on the impulse that he had written about in the paper. Somehow the court found out about this paper and she was called in to testify. That was the end of any interest she had in teaching high school, since she was not all fired up about it to begin with. That had led to her becoming a Toad Lady and without that little hiccup in her life, we never would have met.

That Christmas, we had been together for a couple of months and she invited me to her parents' house. I had noticed her stumbling around in the snow with her flat soled cold shoes and got her what I considered the perfect gift. A pair of SOREL insulated boots with a rubber footbed and laced leather uppers. They were not cheap since they were very warm and comfy. Chris really liked them when I gave them to her. I learned later that her mom and sister-in-law had both expected me to give her a ring! I had never heard of this tradition and had no idea that anyone would have this expectation. They were really jumping the gun. That winter, Chris was laid off from her job, since there were no fresh sugar beet samples for the Toad Ladies to examine and she was needing to leave her uncle's home. We had been dating pretty steadily and her only option was to move back to Scottsbluff where her parents lived. We talked about it and decided that she could just move into my apartment, since we all had our own bedrooms and it would not be much of an imposition on my roommates. She moved in with her meager belongings and became a part of our crew, even if my roommates were not 100% keen on the idea. The person that was definitely not 100% was our landlord and he came over to talk to me. I explained that Chris was not working and kept this apartment so much cleaner than it would be otherwise. He wanted to kick her out, but I insisted and she stayed with me until the end of my final semester at school. It turned out that he was my calculus professor the next semester and I was worried that he might take his frustration out on me with my grades, so I switched to another calculus class with another professor. It was at about this time that I noticed that Chris no longer had the bumper sticker on her car! She ended up having no problem getting a job at the local Perkins restaurant on College Avenue, about 6 blocks up from downtown where I worked evenings at Washingtons. Sometimes after work, we would go to the Perkins at 2:30 in the morning and have loud fun in our booth in Chris' section. She might have been a little irked when we came in, but she loved the tips that the bar manager would leave. She drove a Dodge Aspen, probably the car that coined the acronym POS! Her car often was not running and I would take her to work on the back of my Honda Scrambler. Even when there was six inches of snow on the ground, the two of us would get on that bike and ride slowly down the back roads to the restaurant and I would drop her off, looking all cute in her Perkins outfit. We never did dump that bike, although I came close a couple times when riding in the snow by myself.

That Spring I attended graduation and got my degree. Actually, I was in the procession where the dean would hand out the green case that held the diploma and I walked up with all my classmates and after they called my name, I got the diploma. What I received was just the case for the diploma since I still had to complete the 8-week geology field camp which was my final requirement to get the actual degree, but this way I could graduate with all my friends and classmates.

After "graduation", I had 2 weeks of pre-field camp at the big 11,000-acre Maxwell Ranch on the Colorado-Wyoming border that had been donated to CSU several years before by the old rancher that owned the place. We called it the Maxwell Tick and

Rattlesnake Ranch for obvious reasons. We met with the Maxwell children and they talked about closing fences to keep the cows in and that type of stuff. I always thought they were not happy with 30 college kids running all around their ranch practicing mapping, sample taking, scaring their cows and probably harbored a little resentment that the ranch that they loved was not under their control any longer. Here we learned to use a Brunton compass clinometer for navigating and measuring bedding planes, use a plane table for drawing geologic and topographic maps with an alidade for measuring distance. We had two 15 passenger vans and in the overview meeting with Dr Burns and all 30 of us students, he asked for volunteers to be drivers. The stipulation is that you had to be certified to drive a 15-passenger van which required a bus license. I immediately shot up my hand to be a driver, since I had to be in the van anyway, and I may as well get paid to drive and have a good view through the windshield. That afternoon I went down to the DMV and took the test, waited around for my results and of course I failed it. I then got the driver's test book and sat down right there in the DMV and read the entire booklet. I took the test a second time and passed. I was going to be one of the two drivers! Every morning, on the way to the ranch, we stopped at the 100-year-old Forks Cafe for coffee and a chat before heading out into the hogbacks and rangeland of the ranch. By then I was an old hand in dealing with rattlesnakes and ticks. Occasionally, on the way to the field, someone in the van would have a tick embedded in their neck or somewhere and would be mildly freaking out. The secret to taking a tick out is to use a fine pair of tweezers and to grab it by the little head, and pull it straight out, usually with a bit of skin as well. The idea is to never grab it by the body since that can make the tick inject its bodily fluids into your body like a hypodermic needle. You already know the secret to not getting bit by a rattlesnake!

After we had learned our skills, the real field camp began. Dr. Burns went over the list of things we would need for our 6-week trip to southwestern Colorado, a place that I had never been to before.

The main piece of advice he told us was "The whole idea is not to 'Rough it', the idea is to 'Ease it'", easy for him to say with his car all loaded up with his stuff, while we had just a big duffle bag, a little backpack, a cooler and a folding chair that was in a large box truck that dropped off our gear.

I suppose the folding chair and cooler were my tools for easing it. Our first stop was a couple of days outside of Leadville where there were numerous mining prospect pits, usually from eight to fifteen deep from the old-timers searching for gold. These were scattered throughout the mountains east of Leadville almost everywhere. We would basically hike from prospect pit to prospect pit, looking at the rocks at the bottom and putting our mineralogy skills to work to recognize the minerals and mark them on our maps. This was by far the ugliest part of Colorado that I had seen, since the pits were scattered everywhere for miles around and had really scarred the ground in this otherwise beautiful place. I put together my map and submitted it to the professors and the main problem is that I drew the extent of the mineral deposits much bigger than they were, probably since I was used to the huge redux uranium deposits I had been looking for the previous summers. I quickly learned that less is more when mapping out sub-surface ore deposits from just samples pulled from these pits.

Next, we stayed in the dorms at Western State University in Gunnison, where later my son Coulter would go to school. We mapped around that area and up at the old mining town of Tincup. The mine had quit running around the turn of the century, and had been a rough place to live back in the day with Indian (Native American) attacks and gunfights out in the streets. After mapping in the field, we would draw our final maps back in our dorm rooms.

The last month was spent up in the high country in the San Juan mountains just above the top of Molas pass at 11,000', outside of Silverton. Here we would actually be camping in our tents for several weeks. When the big box truck pulled up to our camp, we all gathered around the back as the door was pulled up and the driver would call out the names written on the gear. Sue, Mark, John, "I love you Chris Bidwell" as I walked up and they threw down my duffle bag. Then more names, then another "I love you Chris Bidwell" as my folding chair was thrown down, and finally a third time when I went up to get my cooler. By then everyone in the camp knew that I had a girlfriend!   I took a bit of a good-natured ribbing about it, and took it as a compliment that René thought I was so desirable that the 4 or so women that were in camp might want to jump my bones.

The area on the South side of Molas pass is absolutely stunning, as are the volcanic range of the San Juans and I had never seen such beauty. I hiked around the steep hills and canyons, crossing raging creeks on big logs and mapping quite a large area every day. We would stand below a culvert pipe sticking out from under highway 550 and take icy showers in the snowmelt pouring from the pipe 10' over our heads. You could literally rinse the shampoo from your hair in 5 seconds. I had a crew of 3 other guys that I knew from school. We always mapped together and compared our notes. We would sit in our folding chairs by the campfire every night and tell stories over beers as the entire universe would open up above our heads like I had never seen before.

After field camp was over, and I was back in Ft Collins, we stayed at the house since our lease was not up till the end of the Summer. Matt came to visit and we went rock climbing quite often up on the Dakota hogbacks. Really, we were bouldering and top-roping. One time Matt and I headed down to Boulder Canyon to climb on the Dome. It is a smooth granite outcropping towards the bottom of the canyon, but it required fording the creek to get to the rock face. Matt and I had our packs with our ropes and climbing gear and we took off our pants and shoes to wade the fast-moving water. We were holding our pants and shoes over our head, and I was following him gingerly feeling the bottom with bare feet to gain a good footing before taking the next step. About halfway across the creek I yelled, "Matt, your wallet!", as I saw his wallet slowly sliding out of the back pocket of his upside-down pants over his head. He looked back just as the wallet fell free and we both watched it splash into the creek in horror. We could have made a lunge for it, but then we probably would have fallen into the water ourselves, probably losing our pants and shoes as well and possibly our heavy packs of climbing gear. A good day of climbing ensued, but the loss of the wallet was in the back of our minds to take the edge off of the joy we felt when we got back to the truck.

René and I ended up renting a mobile home on the north edge of town just off of Hwy 287 for the last month of the summer. The price was right and the rent was month-to-month as I did not have a job yet. We got along well and I enjoyed the loving feeling of being a family of just two together. The trailer turned out to have a lot of mice, since there was a hay yard behind the house where the ranchers would load up their hay onto semi-trucks. We would often hear the snap of a trap going off just as we were getting ready for bed. Sometimes the trap would just snap shut on their tail and they would make an incredible racket running around the kitchen, knocking everything with the trap flying around behind them. I was looking for geology jobs in the paper and found a couple of leads, but nothing solid yet although I did get my old job back as a doorman at Washingtons. One day I rode the Honda into town and was walking around just thinking about how I loved René. I was looking at engagement rings in the window of a jewelry store, but I did not go in. I loved René and was considering my options and was just lost in thought looking at the different engagement rings and wedding bands. That was the first time that I had seriously considered getting married. Up to then it was the normal fun and games of having a girlfriend. I realized that if I did get a job soon, that job would probably be in the oil patch somewhere and I might not be around for much longer, plus we had been together now for almost a year and the time was ripe. If I wanted to stay with René, I should really get engaged to her. I got home and I was so happy to see her and she lit up when I came in and our love was in the air. We were talking and she asked me what I had done downtown. I was telling her about just walking around town and the time was right so I told her about looking in the windows of different shops and looking at rings. She knew exactly what I was talking about and she exploded with yelling and laughing and kissing as I was just smiling at her. It was probably the easiest proposal in the history of romance although I missed the experience of getting on one knee in public and embarrassing us both with a more formal proposal. I already knew she would accept, and not because of the missing bumper sticker on her car.

Matt had headed back to school in St Paul and I ended up getting a job as a mudlogger from a classified ad in the Denver Post for a company called Xpert Logging. I would be training for a couple of weeks down in Denver out East in an industrial park with other recent college geology graduates. I commuted from Ft Collins to Denver for a couple of weeks. Meanwhile on the weekends we took all of our belongings to René's parents' house in Scottsbluff. On the last trip she followed me as I rode the little Honda to Scottsbluff as well. I had been talking to Pete, Chris's stepdad about keeping his eyes out for a Toyota pickup. I had been so impressed with my friend Rick's little Toyota that I knew that was what I wanted. In the training class, we learned about the workings of a hotwire and a gas chromatograph, how they work, how to interpret the results, how to clean and fix all the equipment and how to hook up our drilling log output to the rapidograph up in the dog house on the rig. We also learned how to hook up our gas sensors, basically plastic tubing that was connected to the shale shaker on the rig to our equipment in the mud logging trailer. At least half of the training was learning all about how oil rigs work, what all the parts of the rig are named, what the roughnecks would be doing and how to work with the other supporting people such as the Schlumberger E-loggers, Haliburton Drill stem testers, mud engineers, Tool pushers, Company men and wellsite geologists. The latter is the entire reason I was doing this, since I wanted to be a professional geologist as soon as possible.

I was talking with Chris and saying, "Being married will be a trip, I will then introduce you as my wife. We will be Mr. and Mrs. Bidwell. That will take some getting used to."

Chris replied with "What! I'm not taking your name. My name has always been Christie René Walker and I don't plan to change it. If I did change it, then we would both have the same name. That would be confusing."

"But I usually call you René anyway, so that won't matter".

"Yeah, but other people don't call me that".

This led into our first big argument about her taking my last name. It's funny that it never occurred to me that she would want to keep her name. This was our first real argument and it happened after we got engaged.

Towards the end she said, "You probably would not marry me if I don't change my name".

I thought about that statement. Yeah, we were both mad about this and I had not really thought deeply about it since the idea had blindsided me and led to the fight. My answer to her was not to say anything, since I needed to think about it. It turned out that that was really the end of the argument.

When a new roughneck is hired on at a rig, he is the most junior worker and is called the worm. The worm is hired by the driller who in turn is hired by the toolpusher, the drilling company's top representative at the drilling site. The toolpusher usually would hire three drillers, who would manage their own crews in either 8 or 12 hour "towers". A tower being a work shift. The driller would typically hire a derrickhand, a chainhand, a floorhand and a worm to work the rig with him. Everyone at the rig ultimately reported to the Company Man, who worked for the oil company that had leased the rig. I was basically the worm of the geologists, learning the ropes of being a professional out at the rig while trying to do as much geology as possible.

René had green eyes and I had a couple of pet names for her. One was Sweet Pea and the other was Emerald Eyes, both a nod towards the color green. Sweet Pea came about one time when René was climbing into bed and I noticed she had a bruise on her leg. When she fell asleep, I slipped a pea under her mattress and climbed into bed myself. The next morning when she got up, I made a big deal about the bruise on her leg, telling her that she was a princess, like the story about the princess and the pea. In fact, there was probably a pea under her mattress and she just laughed. I reached under the mattress and pulled out the pea and showed it to her. She laughed some more, perhaps a bit sarcastically, but after that she was my princess and the nickname was switched from Princess Pea to Sweet Pea since I liked the sound of that better. Anyway, it was a good thing that I did not purchase an engagement ring and give it to her since she wanted a green diamond in her engagement ring. We searched around and found a diamond that had been irradiated turning it green and that was the stone in her engagement ring. We had decided to get married at the end of October after my training when I had several free weeks to prepare for working in the oil fields. Pete had found an almost new Toyota Sport pickup. He had also sold my Honda scrambler to a local farmer who was going to use it to check on his irrigation lines, so I had a down payment for the bank loan. We went to look at it and the truck was a peppy little 2WD with a 5 speed. It had a little racing stripe, I immediately liked it and it was really fun to drive, hence the sport. We bought a used topper and installed that on the truck as well and I was set for transportation for work. I knew this little truck would be able to handle anything I could throw at it.

Chris and I did marriage counseling with the young pastor of the Morrell, Nebraska Presbyterian church. He was a young fellow, probably mid-30s, never married and not a wealth of information on what to expect when we are married. I would meet with him one-on-one and my main question was about love. Was it supposed to be an all-encompassing, knock your socks off, true love experience that trumped everything else in your life, or was that something that would naturally happen as part of being married and falling deeper into love and getting to know your spouse better than anyone had ever known her before. How could you be sure that she was the "one"? I knew we were in love. It is just that this is a lifetime commitment and I wanted some assurances from this counselor that I was just experiencing the pre-marital jitters that everyone experiences, or if I was uniquely experiencing my own personal doubts. He never could help me, since he could not grasp the depth of my desire to understand my own feelings and my understanding of our love together. He would give me some general Christian platitudes that we had read in a guide to marriage counseling. You cannot be an expert in anything without having any experience in the field and that was his problem. My problem was that I could not get an in-depth philosophical discussion with him about the nature of love, the nature of life and the nature of the universe, all things that I was dying to know about in gory detail. Just telling me that Jesus would look after me, but only if I believed in him, was useless advice at the time since my revelation that God did not exist had occurred 12 years earlier.

That's the thing with love, it is just something you cannot plan. I had a life plan to get married when I was 32, so I would have my 20s to do crazy single guy stuff. I did not plan to meet Chris Walker and fall in love with her, it just happened, and it happened when I was 24. You don't walk away from love since it does not fit into your plan which was part of the reason that I wanted to ascertain that I was truly in the type of love that would keep the two of us together for the rest of our lives. When October 25th rolled around, my parents, siblings, Grandma and Grandpa Bidwell who had flown out from Connecticut, my friends from college had driven out from Ft Collins and Chris' family and friends were all there as well. The wedding and reception were being held in the church; the organ was playing the type of background music that gets people in the mood as they are ushered to their seats. Matt, the minister and I were sitting together in the little room that grooms sit in before the ceremony, like that Green room that rock stars wait in before walking out on stage. When the time came the minster looked at me and told me to take my pick of doors. One lead outside to the parking lot where my pickup was waiting for a quick getaway to the freedom of single life and the other door lead to the alter of the church where we would be married. The minister had interpreted my quest for knowledge about love to mean that I did not love Chris and I was looking for a way out and he was finally able to be of real service to me. Perhaps he was making a joke, one he made to every groom to get a smile out of them like the salesmen with only one joke about getting up in the world when I was doing inventory up on a big ladder in the Bidwell company warehouse. Whatever his reason was, Matt and the Minster followed me up onto the alter to await the bride's procession down the aisle.

It was interesting to learn about mudlogging. I remember your wedding well. I think we had fried chicken for the rehearsal dinner. It was very reasonable which was good since I was unemployed at the time. The brown tuxedos were very stylish. I never talked with

Chris René *that much but I still keep in touch with her mother in Scottsbluff.*

Love Dad

WOW IS ALL I CAN SAY! I THINK THE MINISTER WAS PATHETIC WITH A CAPITOL P! - Gussie

27 Oil Patch – Mud Logging '80 – '81

After I had finished my training, but for the six weeks before we were married, I headed up to North Dakota for my first mud logging job. I took René's Dodge Aspen up to Dickinson and spent a day in the company condo before meeting up with Jim, the lead logger and heading out to the rig with our gear in my car. The roughnecks had just finished setting the casing, installing the Christmas tree of blowout preventers and bypass valves and had nippled up to the drilling rig. They had already drilled down several thousand feet by the time we arrived on site. Xpert logging had delivered the mud logging trailer and it was just sitting by its lonesome about one hundred feet from the rig, across from the shale shaker.

If mudloggers are the worms of Geologists, then I was the worm of Mudloggers, since there was the lead logger and me. Armed with a full head of geologic knowledge, but almost no knowledge of oil rigs I was fired up to be the best logger the Williston basin had ever seen. First, we went over to the toolpusher's trailer and introduced ourselves, then we went up to the doghouse, which sat just off the drilling floor where the roughnecks would hang out eating lunch, grabbing some coffee and doing paperwork for the drilling company. The driller and derrickhand were in there having a cup of coffee as the rotary table was spinning just on the floor, turning the pipe that was drilling away. We introduced ourselves as the Mudloggers that they would be seeing running around gathering samples, hooking up our gear and checking the drilling progress. We were interested in the doghouse since it contained the geolograph, basically a printer that would output a Perforated paper log of the drilling speed and the depth, both of which are very important parameters to everyone on the rig, especially us and the geologist that we had not yet met. Jim and I then carried the long power cord over to the generator shed, a large steel shed on skids next to the rig with a big diesel generator that was powering the whole rig and plugged in. We then had lights and power to our equipment in the little trailer, and most importantly power to our trailer furnace. Next, we pulled our water line out to the water tank and hooked it up. Finally, we hooked up our gas sniffer line to the shale shaker where the drilling cuttings from the rig get shifted out from the drilling mud and also where we would be grabbing our samples. Back in the little 30' mud logging trailer, we calibrated the hotwire and the gas chromatograph.

We had to compute the lag time it takes for the rock cuttings to come up from the drill bit to the shale shaker so we loaded up an envelope with carbide and headed up to the rig floor. When the last 30-foot section of drill pipe had worked its way down to the floor, the driller would pull up the Kelly, until the top of the drill string is exposed. The Kelly is basically a swivel connected to a square section of pipe that fits into the rotary table into a square hole. When the rotary table turns, it turns the Kelly that in turn turns the entire drill string down to the bottom of the hole, in turn turning the drill bit that is cutting into the earth. The chainhand will then drag over the heavy "slips" and drop them into the rotary table. The slips are basically large metal wedges hinged together and when dropped into the rotary table will wedge the entire drill string to the floor so the drill string can be pulled apart and another 30-foot section of pipe can be added. Then the roughnecks will attach some large tongs to the Kelly to hold it still and the driller then spins the rotary table, unscrewing the top section of pipe from the Kelly. Tongs are basically 200-pound pipe wrenches suspended on cables which clamp to each section of pipe so that the driller, standing at his controls like a ship Captain standing at the helm of a ship, would then pull down on the lever that would use the power of the rig to pull on a cable attached to the end of the tongs and break the pipe sections apart. At this point Jim walked out on the floor and stuffed the carbide envelope into the top of the open drill string.   The end of the Kelly is then moved over to the mouse hole in the floor, where a fresh 30-foot section of drill pipe is waiting, with the end several feet above the floor. The chainhand throws the chain around the new drill pipe while the floorhand guides the threaded end of the Kelly into the top of the pipe. The driller then pulls hard on the chain with one of the levers on his console that then spins the bottom pipe counter-clockwise, tightening it up to the Kelly. The whole time the chainhand is holding the end of the chain as it is being pulled to maintain tension on the chain. Sometimes the chainhand will hold the chain in place on the drill pipe with both hands and fingers splayed apart. All of the jobs on the rig are dangerous, but this is a good place to lose a finger if it gets too close to the pipe or a glove gets caught in a chain link. The tongs are attached to the bottom of the Kelly and the top of the new pipe and the driller pulls another lever and uses the power of the rig to tighten up the connection so it won't come apart. The Kelly is then pulled up the derrick with the new pipe and the process is repeated to attach the new pipe to the top of the drill string being held onto the floor with the slips. Finally, the whole drill string is pulled up a foot and the floorhand grabs the handles of the large slips and muscles them out of the rotary table. Then the pipe is lowered until the Kelly slips into the square hole in the rotary table and drilling commences. Jim and I then set our watches and headed back to the Mudlogging trailer and watched the Hotwire waiting for a spike. What happens is that the carbide envelope that we put into the drill string will just take several minutes to reach the drill bit, but it could take up to several hours for the cuttings and drilling mud to work its way up the outside of the drill string to the surface. As the rig is drilling, it is pumping drilling mud, basically water, bentonite and salt down through the Kelly and down the entire drill string and out the bottom of the drill bit. This very viscous mud will carry all the drill cutting back up to the surface on the outside of the drill string. When the carbide that we put into the drill string gets wet, it reacts with water and gives off acetylene gas that we can measure with our Hotwire. When the Hotwire spikes, we know the lag time of samples that we pull off the shale shaker and can accurately determine the depth the cuttings are coming from.

A big part of the job is to periodically walk out to the shale shaker and grab a sample of cuttings, then clean them up, look at them with a microscope and describe the lithology, the porosity and any show that is visible from our fluoroscope that indicates the presence of oil. We would also use HCL acid to help separate carbonate rock formations such as limestone from other rock types.

Another part of the job is to monitor the Hotwire and the gas chromatograph. In a nutshell, the Hotwire is an accurate way to measure the total amount of all gases, using a hot glowing coiled platinum wire which gets hotter when it comes in contact with the various hydrocarbons thus changing the electrical resistance which is plotted on a graph that spools out of our equipment console. The gas chromatograph on the other hand, break out the various hydrocarbons into its components of methane, ethane, propane, iso-butane, and normal butane. We take all this information and laboriously write it onto a log by hand using rapidiograph pens and straight-edges to create a professional-looking log for the well site geologist and the oil company that is paying for the drilling. We also save all the cuttings into boxes that can be examined by the well-site geologist and will be sent to the oil company at the end of the job by the lead mudlogger, in this case Jim. Jim and I each worked 12 hours towers, Jim mostly during the day and me mostly at night. After a week, we got a break for a day when the drill bit needed to be changed, requiring tripping out of the hole, three pipe segments at a time, called a stand, to change the bit with a new one.

We headed back to Dickenson to cleanup at the company condo, wash some clothes and get a good meal. Dale, one of the owners of Xpert Logging was there to checkup on things, but mostly to sell the condo since it was too hard to maintain, being so far from the company headquarters in Denver. A bunch of us, including Dale headed out to a local bar for dinner and drinks, I ended up sitting next to Dale at the bar, and we got more and more loose and talked into the evening. He was about 40 and had been a mudlogger for his entire life and had now hit the big-time with the oil boom and starting this new company with 2 of his partners. In fact, they had agreed that Dale could purchase a car and he had a brand-new Cadillac with all the bells and whistles that he was very proud of and probably explained why he was willing to take the ten hour drive up from Denver. It turned out that Dale was checking out the condo to see what it needed, before Xpert Logging was going to sell it. I told Dale that I was getting married soon and wanted to move my lovely bride up closer to where I am working and would like to rent out the condo before it was sold. Chris and I would not have too many belongings and could keep it in good shape for any showing eventually. Dale agreed, we shook on it sitting right there at the bar and I had procured our "honeymoon home"!

Dale and I talked about married life, mostly Dale, since he was an experienced husband and he gave me one piece of advice that has served me well for my entire life. "You are going to be tired whenever you get home and your wife will be wanting to go out and do things with you when you are there. No matter how tired you are, always pay attention to her and go out and do things while you are home such as eating out, shopping, visiting cool places around town, exploring the nearby countryside, bowling, shooting pool and just driving around and talking. Just make yourself do it! You can always sleep for 12 hours if needed back at the trailer between towers, but don't neglect the valuable time at home with your wife".

This is good advice even if you are not a mudlogger. René had a wedding gown from a place called Gunny Sax, which was funny since a gunny sack was the absolute furthest thing from a wedding dress, but this dress was very nice and flattering and looked great on her. We had a wedding night at a local Scottsbluff motel, with the little Toyota pickup pulling a line of cans down the street curtesy of my siblings. At this time, I switched from calling her Chris (she hated being called Christie) to calling her René. I liked the way it sounded and it would be less confusing.

She later told me, "Only people who love me call me René."

Our honeymoon was yet to come when I was a consulting geologist, but for now we loaded the truck and a little U-Haul trailer and headed north to the oil fields, stopping and having lunch at the base of Bear Butte in South Dakota on the way up. We got settled into the Xpert Logging condo. Xpert Logging was in the process of changing the company name to Analex. I thought this was a curious name since we were working with mud being output from the rig at the shale shaker, which could be considered the anus of the rig. I'm sure the owners thought it sounded very professional, just like I thought I looked very professional with my full mustache, but we were probably both wrong.

I would work out at the rig 24 hours a day until either the hole was completed, the drill bit needed to be replaced, a hole was discovered in the drill pipe, or a cone from the drill bit fell off and needed to be fished for, then replaced. For any of these things, the roughnecks would need to trip out of the hole, a "stand" of 3 sections of pipe at a time to sped up the process. They would be collected on the rig floor, tied off near the top of the derrick. This is when the derrickhand would really earn his money. Hanging off the diving board, throwing a rope around the top of the string, hauling it into the side of the Derrick and securing each one. While the rig workers were working their butts off, us Mudloggers would get a break for a day and would go home to our wives. That sounded so alien to me. "My wife". Jim and I would talk about our wives and it was really a big deal and a weird skew to my world view. It was several months before talking about my wife was as normal as talking about my girlfriend had been. Hanging out with René was just as normal and as comfortable as ever however.

It was getting very cold and we would walk around the Dickinson Mall. Just a small mall for a small town, but it was nice to have a place to go for a stroll without needing to fight the cold and snow. Occasionally René would come out to the rig and stay for a couple of days. It did not take long for me to become a lead logger and get the good towers to work and be responsible for the output. I was a stickler for doing very detailed rock analysis' and would insist on detailed descriptions. We were all geologists after all. The business model for Analex was to hire recent college geology graduates to work for them in the oil fields. I got to be pretty good friends with several of them and we had a few "couple friends", such as Bill and Sandra that we could hang out with and have fun socially. René actually spent quite a bit of time with me out at the rig, since I was the boss. We would sleep in the tiny bunk bed together, but we were newlyweds and did not mind one bit. It was better than being married and being apart.

I did one job in the ND badlands that first winter as the lead on a job with Chuck. It was extremely cold, well below freezing every day. We ran the trailer heater constantly and kept the sink faucet running just a trickle to help prevent it from freezing. The job was over, we were wrapping up and disconnecting the lines from the rig. We were in the "basement" near the Christmas tree of blowout preventers, I was coiling up the water line and Chuck was in front of me coiling up the sample gas line. It was a little warmer under the rig and we were sloshing through an inch or two of muddy water, with splotches of grey grease floating on top from the pipe connections that would fall down from the floor. As Chuck was walking near the borehole he just disappeared. Poof, gone, like a magic trick. He came sputtering up from the mud with a panicked look and I helped him to his feet. He was soaked in drilling mud and his winter coat, now very heavy had grey streaks of grease on it and his hair was matted down and his hat was lost. He looked like I did after a game of mud football back in college. I helped him to the trailer; he was so pathetic looking that I was having a hard time keeping from laughing at the absurdity of the situation. We had already scrubbed and cleaned the trailer, but Chuck and I did not care and it would not have mattered since he needed to warm up. I finished bringing in the water and gas lines and then we sat together and commiserated for a while before I disconnected the power cord and turned off the propane so we could go. I felt bad for him as he got into his nice Subaru like a filthy Sasquatch and had to drive back to Dickinson all wet and dirty.

In April, things were warming up and René and I celebrated our 6-month anniversary by going to the Badlands Park during a break in work when they were running a DST (Drill Stem Test) at the rig and I got off for a day. Most of these jobs would terminate at the Red River Formation, typically about twelve thousand feet down. At the end of May, a year after me, Matt graduated from college with a geology degree and 2 days later he arrived at our house in Dickinson. I was nearing the end of a job, so Matt came out to the rig with me and we played chess as we waited for the results of the test. Matt had been playing chess since high school and was a strong player. I had purchased a chess board after about a month working on the rigs and would play with the other logger, the toolpusher, the company man, the geologist, a roughneck that was not working the floor or anyone that was free for a game. I had picked up a couple of books on opening gambits and had learned a few of the more well-known "named" opening moves and was getting much better at the game. I was currently studying the French Defense. It was a good way to pass the time without smartphones, iPads, computers or televisions. The latter was invented then obviously, but just no analog service way out in the sticks where these rigs were located. Thank God for books! This current job was going to be a production well, so no more drilling was needed and I was released from the job after another day. About this time, in early June, I was hired by GX Consultants to be a well-site geologist, to start after my next mudlogging job finished! This was an arm of my logging company Analex and they had one last logging job scheduled for me in the Powder River basin. René, Matt and I took a break for two weeks and drove to Nebraska to see her parents, then to Denver to see old friends from Boulder, college friends from Ft. Collins and catchup. Matt and I went rock climbing with Eric, a geologist friend from ND that I had worked with and we had hit it off. I turned in the rock samples and the mud-log to the oil company and met my new bosses at GX, and had a belated official job interview.

My last mudlogging job was on a rig outside of Kaycee, Wyoming. I really liked Wyoming, the prairie seemed wilder, there were mountains in the distance with lots of creeks for fishing and exploring and rock outcrops for climbing. The well-site geologist was an old hand, and had been working outside of Casper for 40 years. He had met his wife after serving in WWII in Italy, falling in love with her, marrying her and bringing her back to the USA with him. She did not speak a lick of English at the time and he no Italian. It must have been an interesting time for them both. We hit it off immediately and spent many hours out at the rig talking, playing chess and working. Chris came out to the rig a couple of times to visit since we were 400 miles from Dickinson and it was too far for me to run home when tripping out of the hole. We would run into Casper to purchase a little stack of paperbacks to read back in the trailer. We would swap books and read each other's, then talk about them like a little 2-person book club. This job lasted for over 6 weeks and was my deepest hole at 15,185 feet. I bade farewell to John and hoped to run into him some other time, which I never did, but he enriched my life and for that I was glad.

René and I took three weeks off, mostly in August and we drove out to Connecticut with Matt to see my family and for René to visit New England for the first time. We left in the trusty pickup, stopping in St Paul for Matt to get some things, then beelined East on the interstate, stopping only at Perkins for food and in NJ for fresh clam rolls that I had been craving. We arrived at Terry Rd at 2:00 in the morning after 1900 miles and 37 hours and crashed for 10 more hours before having a BBQ with everyone. That evening we all hung out in Mom and Dad's bedroom and talked and BSed well into the night, catching up and exchanging belated Christmas gifts. We ate lots of lobster, clams, swordfish, scallops and bluefish whenever we could and René got the tour, going to the beach in Long Island sound and sailing a sunfish at a cottage of one of Mom's co-workers. We also went with Julie, her friend Arlene and Mom out on the ferry to Block Island for the day riding to different beaches on rented bikes while Dad was working and Matt was seeing his college girlfriend in NYC. Matt, Jerry and I went rock climbing at Ragged Mountain. We all went up to New Hampshire to "the cabin" on my grandparents' property with all my siblings. We jumped off the rocks at the potholes while the girls took naps, and then hung out and swam at Swift River on the smooth granite by Picnic Rock. We played scrabble well into the night in the cozy cabin and had dinner with Grandma Noss at Valley Farm the next day. We visited Dad's parents for dinner in Avon and watched slides with them. Grandpa's advice to me on photography was to only save the really good slides and get rid of the rest so you don't bore your audience to death, good advice. Jerry and I went rock hounding for tourmaline crystals and jumped off the high cliffs at Strickland's Quarry. We visited cousins at Westport (the BM club, minus Susan who was away at "horsey camp") for BBQ, swimming and sailing. René and I went with my siblings and Barb, Matt's girlfriend, to the beach at Watch Hill, Rhode Island for bodysurfing and frisbee, the site of my nocturnal drinking adventures in high school. It was a great whirlwind tour and we drove back home on my birthday with Julie, dropping her off in Chicago and met her boyfriend, Tunny.

I started working as a geologist at GX Consultants two days after we got back home to Dickinson.

Technically impressive, but beyond my ken. I most enjoyed your story of the trip back East. I never knew Matt had a high school girlfriend. We did enjoy the sea food from City Fish. Strickland's quarry is now a big water park with zip lines and the whole bit. We are enjoying take out from the Blue Plate. No indoor dining yet. We are lucky to be living in CT. I could not manage without Robin. She helps me with my shower and wonderful back massage. I suffer from "reverse psoriasis which my dermatologist says I will have forever. It has led to painful outbreaks in the groin and the pits. We now have this under control with medication. I am comfortable but now am on oxygen 100% to help with breathing. We got our absentee ballots and my immediate goal is to hang on till the election and after 92, who knows. We await the inevitable.

Love Dad and Robin

Bruce loves getting the next installment of Chris's "tome". Love, Robin

28 Oil Patch - Consulting Geologist '82

Our life was about to get better now that I was a geologist. I would no longer need to live in a trailer out at the rig when working. I got a raise from $75/day to $200/day so that was one better thing. I also was now a Geologist, a Well-site Consulting Geologist to be precise. This had been my goal all along and I was very happy and excited. The best thing however was that I had per-diem for housing, meals and gas which meant that I would be staying at hotels close to the rig and René could go along with me on all my jobs. This was the "honeymoon" I mentioned earlier. We would be traveling and living together, going out for most of our meals to the local cafes and diners, but sometimes there would be a really nice restaurant and we could just split an expensive dinner and still be under the meal cost cap for the day.

The other part of the job is that I would now go into Denver to help procure the next consulting gig by meeting with the Oil Company geologists to help sell the jobs. This entailed finding out which formations we would be targeting, how deep they were expecting to drill and any other details. After a job was over, I would usually meet with the Geologist back in Denver who was in charge of the drilling job and turn in my report, usually about 40 pages that we would discuss and review. During the job, I would also do "Morning Reports", where I would go out to the rig early in the morning to get the drilling status, then drive back to the hotel to call in a status report to the Oil Company geologist at 8 or 9 in the morning. After a successful job, especially when the drilling resulted in a production well, the Company geologist would then be assured of my competency and I would get subsequent jobs from them.

My first job was a series of 3 shallow drilling projects looking for gas for Total Petroleum. I drove down to Belle Fourche, South Dakota and checked into the local Sunset motel. I then headed out to the rig in the afternoon and met the toolpusher of the rig and talked with the driller and his crew. We would be drilling down about 2000' to the Shannon Sandstone looking for gas, but were currently a long way from there. I looked at the drilling log and the rock cuttings and determined that we had a good half dozen more rock formations to go through before we got close to the potential production zone, plus we were still pretty close to the surface, and it would take several days to get close. I got out to the rig early the next morning at 5:00 and was checking out the drilling progress. I was in the doghouse of this little rig and was talking to the morning tower crew, which was mostly Mexican roughnecks. The whole crew was in the doghouse since they were waiting for the casing cement to dry. They asked me if I wanted a cup of coffee and I gladly accepted, since I had just hopped out of bed and came straight out to the rig. The driller grabbed the only mug there, and filled it with coffee. This mug looked like it had been in the doghouse for a year and had never been washed. They looked at this young white boy to see what he would do and side glanced at each other as well.

I knew this was partly a practical joke, but mostly a test of how well I would accept them so I picked up the mug and took a nice loud slurpy sip, put the mug down and said "Thank you, that really hits the spot", like I drink out of dirty dishes all the time.

The crew was disappointed and accepting at the same time and we worked well for the rest of the job. I monitored the drilling closely and the next day I called the top of the Shannon Formation and we drilled several feet into the sandstone at just over 1300 feet down. I had the driller stop drilling and trip out of the hole. I had the Company Man call Halliburton to come out and run a Drill Stem Test (DST) that day. Basically, a DST is when a tool is screwed onto the end of the drill string instead of a drill bit. The tool is lowered down to the bottom of the drill hole and two expandable packers are inflated that seal off the potential production zone, essentially making it a production well just for several hours. This is done to see how much gas and/or oil it can produce during the test. We got nothing on this test, so we continued down, drilling another 1200 feet to the Niobrara formation and just circulated on the bottom looking for a gas show. The gas was enough that we got the Schlumberger truck to come out and run their electric logging probe down the hole to get an idea of the porosity of the rock. A check for me in the plus column for bringing in a production well!

After this short 7-day job, I dropped off my report and some rock samples at the Rapid City airport and headed up to Dickinson to get René on the 2-days off before my next job back in Belle Fourche. This time we upgraded to the Super 8, a better motel. We ate lunch and dinner out at the local diner. I finished the next two wells, then immediately got another 3 more shallow gas wells just like this, mostly a week on and then a couple of of days off to move the little rig. Sometimes we would drive to Sundance to The Sluice restaurant. It looked like a mine adit outside, with railroad tracks and ore carts going into the front of the building and a very nice first-class restaurant inside with a soup & salad bar in some more ore carts inside. We loved this place and I gained about 8 pounds in the two months here, up from my ideal climbing weight of 165 lbs. Sometimes on our couple of days off, we would go into nearby Rapid City and do some shopping. It just turned out that the end of my last job in Belle Fourche was on René's birthday. We leased a Bronco to help me get out to the rigs on the muddy rough rig roads. Then we went to the Rushmore mall to get some birthday presents and finally went for a blow-out crab leg birthday dinner at the Sluice. It was a really good way to kick off my Consulting Geology career. We both loved our new lifestyle!

I was off for the rest of the month and we went to Denver to visit friends and family and check in with GX Consultants at their office in downtown Denver. While we were there, we decided to move back to Ft Collins, since I would be coming to Denver quite often between jobs and René would be going on all my jobs with me from now on. We signed a lease on a Tri-plex apartment on Edora Street. This required driving up to Dickinson, loading up a U-Haul, driving back to Ft Collins and unloading with help from my college friends, then heading back up to Sidney, Montana to start my next job back in the Williston Basin. Many of my friends from school were still living here so we had a pretty good social scene, plus friends I had made up in Dickinson would stop by as well to visit and sometimes to take a shower if they were still mudlogging.

The next job was to be more typical. We were drilling clear down to the Red River Formation and we would be in the same place for 8 weeks. On big jobs like this, the drillers mostly know each other, especially those that worked for the same drilling company. They would have informal competitions to see who could get to the Red River formation the fastest. My job as a geologist was to make sure they stop and look for oil in the way down to TD!   A big reason that I spent time up in the dog house getting to know the drillers, is that I would have to work so closely with them when we got to a production zone. I would pick the tops of all the rock formations on the way down and knowing the stratigraphy layers could very accurately predict when we would be approaching a rock formation with production potential that may only be 20 feet thick. The different types of rock will drill at different rates. The rig might be drilling shale, then slow down when hitting limestone and then slow down more when reaching some dolomite and might pick up much faster when reaching some porous sandstone. As a result, the Rate of Penetration (ROP) logs of the geolograph tend to indirectly reflect the lithology of the formations.   When approaching a potential production rock formation, I would only drill about ten feet in to the top before signaling the driller to stop drilling. It was easy to tell when you hit the porous rock of the production zone, since the drilling speed would pick up from perhaps 10 minutes per foot to 2 minutes per foot. I would mark on the geolograph where the speed picked up and have the rig quit drilling after 10 feet of fast going. Now an oil rig is a very noisy place, but when a production zone is hit, the drilling gets so fast the brake on the rig, controlled by the driller, will start squealing loudly as well, like an alarm that we would pay attention to. We would continue pumping mud, but not drilling for several hours until the rock samples would come to the surface where I could examine them. I would usually go to the mudlogger's trailer and wait to see if we got a gas spike on their equipment. I would look at the samples under my microscope for any oil shows in the rocks as well. Our main target would be the bottom-most Red River Formation, but often there would be another production layer at an intermediate location that could create a production well, even if the Red River formation did not pan out.

René and I would play Panhandle Rummy and Pitch, two card games that would keep us entertained. I could occasionally talk her into a game of backgammon and we would bet on silly things, but never a game of chess. We continued reading several books a week as well and I would take a paperback out to the rig to pass the time as I was waiting in the doghouse for a drilling break. We knew all the restaurants, diners and cafes in Sidney and would go out and shoot pool and have bar food at the local Corner Pocket, a bar/pool hall that had locations in most of the oilfield towns. René had a sewing machine that I had got her for her birthday from Monkey Wards in Rapid City that she would use to help pass the time when I was at the rig. She spent many happy hours fighting with the bobbin and foot tension trying to make clothing. I saw a friend from CSU at the post office one time and we talked about how a lot of us that graduated in 1980 were now working up here. René actually purchased a male Pomeranian named Diablo while we were here to breed with Muffy, her little female who she had brought up here. I would throw dumbbells around, do dips in the corner of the kitchen counters with a dumbbell tied to my waist, push-ups and sit-ups on the floor and pull-ups on the door trim to keep in shape for bouldering in the Spring. People had told us that we would get sick of living in motels and eating out, but in the three years we spent together in the oil patch, we never tired of either one, or each other! This was our 3-year honeymoon.

It was January towards the end of the job when it was below zero every night and below freezing every day! The Semi trucks parked in Sidney at our motel would be outside our room around the large park where the old guys would play horseshoes during warmer weather and would keep their engines running all night long so they would not freeze up. I would drive my truck out to the rig at 4:00am, typically the coldest part of the day and plug in my truck's block heater to the rig to keep the engine a little warm. Sometimes, even doing this, the battery would be too weak to crank the engine so I would need to get a jump start. We had one stretch where it hit 40 degrees below zero for 4 days in a row. I would drive out to the rig in the early morning and could see the little cloud bank surrounding the rig from the steam coming off the hot mud in the tanks below the shale shaker. It would cover the iron rig in a rime of ice everywhere. You could get a bloody nose from just rubbing it and the frozen hairs in your nose would crack the skin, making you bleed. The roughnecks had a hard time keeping warm. When we got close to the Red River Formation, I spent 2 days out on the rig, closely monitoring our drilling progress and being careful to quit drilling at precisely the correct spot. If we drilled too far into the rock formation, then our DST test would be ruined with salt water that would overpower the oil in our tests. The oil sits on top of the water so I had to be careful not to drill below the oil zone. I spent the last couple of nights napping in the company man's trailer while monitoring the drilling, picking the formation tops and running the DSTs. I drove back to the hotel, pulling the mudlogger's Subaru Brat with my Bronco, since it had been sitting in the brutal cold for too long and would not start. René and I left Sidney for Colorado as they were setting casing to make this hole a production well. Another check in the plus column!

We were back in Ft Collins for 4 months and I just did one job in the DJ basin, just north of Denver. I would drive out to the rig from our apartment in Ft Collins to work and come home at night. This was only a week-long job. Matt was staying with us at this time. Jerry came out for a couple of weeks to hang out with his brothers and have an interview with CSU to be accepted into the Chemistry department in the Fall. René and I would play tennis occasionally, grab ice cream at Dairy Queen, read to each other from things like the Book of Lists, walk the dogs in Edora Park directly behind the apartment and play cards. We had now graduated to playing poker with chips. Muffy gave birth to a couple of stillborn pups which was very sad for us.

Jerry told me that our parents were getting a divorce! That was news to me and I was surprised. I knew that Dad still loved mom, so I figured that Mom was the one that wanted out. I called home and talked with them and they were planning on having a huge "tag sale" as they call it back East. I probably could have flown out to get the scoop first-hand but my brothers were here and I had the promise of another consulting gig that I wanted to be ready for. Dad never said anything bad about Mom ever, even after the divorce, but Mom was quick to blame dad for not telling her when he lost his job. She said that dad would get dressed and leave the house for the day, just as if he had a job. She did not notice that anything was wrong until several months later when she saw that all the silverware was missing. I suppose I need dad to refute this story with his version. Dad?

We went climbing with Jerry almost every day for the couple of weeks he was here, always up at Horsetooth reservoir, usually at rotary park and the torture chamber areas. The torture chamber was a long hogback cliff that went for almost 100 yards, and we would boulder on it doing long traverses. Jerry was really good at doing upside-down heel hooks to give his fingers a break when they would get pumped up trying to make the entire traverse without stopping. None of the traverse was more than 12' above the ground. It was great fun climbing with each other and seeing how much we could push our young bodies before hitting our limit on the rock.

I had my eye on a discounted Mad River Explorer canoe being sold at a bike shop. René and I would drive around Ft Collins and I would have her stop at the bike/boat shop and look at the canoe. Every couple of weeks I would pull the truck over and run in to look at the boat and hope the price had gone down. Like my first canoe, this shop had decided to quit selling boats and just focus on bikes. Finally, one time I ran into the shop and the price had dropped low, so I bought it, just a little bit to René's chagrin. I could now continue my paddling heritage and would once again be at it after an 8-year break!

Finally, I got another consulting job at the end of May for Southland Royalty up in Kaycee, Wyoming in the middle of the Powder River basin. I was more than ready to start working again on a real job. I knew I liked this area from my last mud logging Job and was glad to be heading back. We drove up to Buffalo, the nearest town with a motel even though it would be a 50 mile drive out to the rig and checked into the Z-bar motel, the perfect cowboy name for a place to stay. I went out to the rig the next day and they were at 7000'. The next day they tripped out to replace the bit and René and I went hiking at the Bob Love wildlife reserve. She had talked with the motel manager where we were staying and got a job working at the motel, mostly doing maid work, but it would be something to do and make a little money as well. It was a long dirt road from Kaycee out to the rig which was in the middle of a huge ranch with thousands of jackrabbits. There was some kind of rabbit boom and there would be hundreds of them running across in front of my truck as I was headed down the dirt road to the rig. I love bunnies, but eventually it got to the point that I just had to drive, just at a normal speed and every once in a while, my heart would drop as I heard the thump of another bunny under my tire.

The toolpusher was a big survivalist with an Armageddon place up in the upper peninsula and was a gun nut. When I went up to talk with him at his trailer, he yelled for me to come in. He was standing at his sink with the window open and his elbow on the counter sighting in at a prairie dog probably 150 yards out with his hunting rifle and a powerful scope. He told me that the rancher was all for the roughnecks killing prairie dogs. He took me out back of the trailer to shoot his big 44 magnum 6-shooter for some target practice. It was great fun, even with the kick of the gun. My steady hand did not help me much in hitting the beer can we were shooting at. One of the drillers would change the oil on his crew truck by draining the oil pan directly down a prairie dog hole. I liked the mudloggers on this job. Debby was an experienced logger who lived on the Wind River Reservation on the other side of the Big Horn Mountains. Early was a kid that worked for Debby from Riverton. One day I was several miles from the rig, heading home on the dirt rig road and there was the driller's Chevy Suburban sitting in the middle of the road with 2 barrels sticking out of both sides of the truck. They had stopped to shoot prairie dogs from the comfort of the vehicle and I had to hold down on my horn when passing them to avoid getting shot. In fact, once on I-25, the highway signs were pretty much peppered with bullet holes getting less and less as it got closer to Buffalo. I had a pretty good idea of how that had happened!

When René got her first paycheck, we went up to Sheridan and had a fun day with her shopping and spending all of her paycheck on books, clothes, candles and other things that made us smile. René and I also spent a day driving up into Middle fork of the Powder River to the Outlaw canyon. We had fun four-wheeling up the washed-out jeeping trail in the Bronco to the rim of the canyon, and climbed down the 1000' of limestone and dolomite switchbacks to the canyon bottom and went swimming there. I went skinny-dipping in the cool water and René waded and splashed in her terrycloth short shorts. It was a great way to explore and cool off on a hot summer day.

This job was having lots of trouble. They often get stuck in the hole from deviating from too much WOB (Weight on Bit). They would also lose drill cones and would have to go "fishing" with a magnet to get them out. An iffy proposition at best. I dropped off René at Casper one weekend to meet her parents who were at a dog show there, showing Pete's Pomeranians. We ended up getting a lot of time off whenever there was a rig problem. I taught René spin fishing with Mepps and Panther Martin lures and we would go fishing, me mostly fishing dry flies, my personal favorite way to fish creeks. We fished Clear Creek outside of Buffalo, Crazy Woman Canyon and other little very productive trout streams in the Big Horn Mountains. I joined the local YMCA to lift weights and we would go to the local drive-in to watch movies every week when I was not working. We ate out most days, even though we had a kitchenette. Debby and Early would stop by the motel to take showers in our room and relax away from the rig for a bit and I was glad that we could help them out. Buffalo is really a tourist town with more hotel rooms than houses so there were some good places to eat, but our favorite was the little Busy Bee Cafe, situated right on the banks of Clear Creek on Main Street in Downtown Buffalo. René and I would pull on our hiking boots and often go hiking up the numerous paths heading up towards the Cloud Peak Wilderness for a day of fun and exercise. Matt came up to visit and we would scout out top-roping climbing areas for first ascents. The three of us went fishing. Back then we kept all we caught so it was not long before we literally had the freezer in the motel filled with brook and brown trout. We were eating trout one evening for dinner and I got a bone stuck way down in my throat and could not get it out, until the local doctor pulled it out with a very long pair of forceps. Ever since then I've not been so keen on eating trout, but still loved catching them and that is when I made the transition to a mostly catch and release fisherman. The biggest fish of the summer was caught by René on a shallow rocky section of the South Fork of Clear Creek. I watched her cast into this section of water thinking that it was not a promising part of the creek, when she hooked into a lunker. She skillfully played the fish in, tiring it out before pulling it in close to shore where I netted it for her, a 12-inch Brown. On these little creeks a foot-long fish was a trophy.

Back at the rig, I was having trouble picking formation tops since the company geologist had estimated where our target formation would be hit. I was puzzling on the stratigraphy and it looked like we were almost 1000' deeper than we should be. I mentioned this to Jim, the sharp owner of the mud logging company who happened to be on site and he agreed. I knew where we were, but I needed the confidence of someone else who concurred with me before I could call the company geologist with this information. I was worried about how he would take this bad news of him modeling this area of the Powder River basin, but having his geologic model being so far off from the actual geology. I called him the next morning and told him that instead of drilling into an anticline (a dome of the rock formations that traps the oil), we were drilling into a much deeper syncline and our odds of striking oil was slim and we might want to pull the plug on this job and cut our losses. Not only that but this job was having lots of problems from the severely deviated hole which was why I was getting so many days when I did not need to go out to the rig. He was not deterred and wanted to keep drilling anyway, doggedly determined to stick to his guns.

Pete and Betty came up for a couple of days and we showed them around. I put two folding lounge chairs in the back of the Bronco and they rode back there when we went exploring up the Middle Fork of the Power River, not far from the Hole in the Wall of Butch Cassidy Fame. On the way back we were hit with a huge powerful thunderstorm and I pulled over to let it rain itself out. When we got going again there were brown waterfalls pouring down the cliffs all around us in a spectacular fashion. Eventually we got to a place where a little tributary went through a couple of 6-foot-high steel culvert pipes under the road. The brown water was about a foot over the road, with the road acting like a dam, even with the large pipes under the road. There was a large whirlpool above the road and we saw small trees floating down towards the road, get stood straight up and sucked under the water, then blown out the other side. We watched in amazement at the power of the water for 20 or 30 minutes until the water subsided well below the road. The downstream side of the road was about half washed away and we manage to cross on the single remaining lane. On the other side a pickup pulled up with a rancher that was looking for a tractor he had parked next to the creek and it had washed away and he still had not found it.

At the beginning of August, I was put on stand-by due to the many problems the rig was having drilling. We had drilled down to 13,629 feet and I had circulated up the Lakota formation with no shows. I was not surprised, since this job had turned out to be more of a vacation than a work trip due to the problems the rig was having. The drilling company was going to try and re-drill much of the well and would call me to come back when they got back to the Lakota formation again. We drove back to Ft Collins and celebrated being home by purchasing a waterbed and setting it up on top of the 12-drawer underdresser that we needed since there was no room for our dressers any longer. Matt came to visit and he and I took the Mad River Canoe for a maiden voyage out to Horsetooth reservoir, after purchasing two paddles on the way. We did not go fishing but saw a couple of Great Horned Owls sitting not too far from shore. I finished working on my report and went into Denver to deliver it to the oil company. We talked about the hole being so much deeper that it was expected to be, but again, they were committed to reaching TD on this drilling project. Matt and I scouted the lower Poudre River and did our maiden river trip down and through Mad Dog Rapids in the canoe, paddling straight as fast as we could, since that seemed to be the best approach. Jerry came out for a visit with Julie. We showed her around town. The three of us paddled down the reservoir and went swimming. Jerry registered for school and got a room in the dorms.

Three days after they arrived, René and I decided that we would like to have a kid (August 26, 1982), so we quit using the diaphragm, unbeknownst to everyone else! We hiked and climbed around the hogbacks of Horsetooth reservoir, went canoe fishing and threw the frisbee quite a bit. We took a trip to Kimball to visit Mom Jones, René's grandmother. She is a hoot and very fun to hang out with. She loved to play cards, watch the Home Shopping Network, chain smoke and sip her whiskey. My kind of woman. She and her husband had run a speak-easy over in Scottsbluff back in the day. Later she ran a small cafe back in Kimball which all the locals loved. She would bad-mouth him occasionally and told René's mom that she did not want to be buried next to him. Betty told her that that was impossible since he had bought 2 plots for each of them, right next to each other.

Mom Jones replied, "Well if I have to be buried next to him, then I want to be buried with my back to him!"

I would get updates from SRC since they were re-drilling the bottom half of the hole to straighten it out and when they got back to 13,000 feet, I would be called back to the rig.

A couple of weeks later Julie, René and I went to downtown Denver to wander around before going to Stapleton Airport to pick up Dad. He was happy to be here, especially since all his kids were here as well. Matt, Jerry and I took dad up to the hogbacks for an afternoon of bouldering on the rocks. We had been working on the routes with little white arrows on them, usually painted at the bottom of a huge boulder. These were little climbing routes that had been put up by John Gill, the "Master of Rock", probably the best boulderer in the world at the time. We might work for several days, trying to figure out the moves to get to the top of the rock and often it would be so difficult that only John Gill had the ability to climb them. Dad spent a happy afternoon with us wandering among the boulders and hogbacks with us as we climbed and explored.

Matt, Julie, Dad and I headed out on Labor Day to the Forks Cafe near Virginia Dale for breakfast, site of our morning Field Camp coffee meetings. We then went over the beautiful Snowy range, stopping in Saratoga for fishing gear and licenses, finally arriving on the North Platte River at 6-mile gap for three days of camping and fishing. Julie slept in the back of the Bronco and us men slept outside in the tent. The highlight of the trip for me was when I was fishing up above camp in stovepipe rapid out on a big boulder when I hooked into a nice sized trout. I played it hard for a while until it started tiring out. I put my food down toward the bottom of the rock to net the fish, when I slithered into the water.

I was about in the middle of the rapid and swam, holding my rod but trying to get to shore. Eventually I swam and scrambled my way into an eddy and stood up, I noticed that I still had the fish on the line and pulled him in and successfully got him into the net this time. That section of river is a Blue-Ribbon Trout stream, meaning that any fish under 18" had to be thrown back. My fish was 17", but I had gone through so much to catch it that I ended up keeping it for dinner that night. We all caught fish with Matt catching the most of course, being a natural-born fisherman.

I was called back to the Southland Royalty job at the last week of November, so René and I headed back up to Buffalo. We got a 17-pound turkey, invited the Mudloggers, Jim, Early and Debby to have Thanksgiving dinner with us in our motel room, since their home base was on the other side of the Big Horn mountains in Riverton, Wyoming. In mid-December, I went out to the rig with René while we circulated up the Minnelusa Formation. We had an antelope and venison dinner with the Mudloggers, dining on animals they had hunted for themselves over on the Rez. Neither of us had eaten antelope before and I just remember it as being lean, leaner than buffalo even. We got no show on the circulation, but I was not surprised.

We had a quiet romantic Christmas together. Well at least a romantic morning with opening presents and having egg rolls for lunch, since I was out to the rig at 2:00 that afternoon and spent the night sleeping in the company man – Bill's trailer. We hit TD (Total Depth) not long after this and I was released from the job after Schlumberger attempted to run Neutron/Induction logs and got their e-logging tool stuck in the hole. I hoped for the sake of SRC, the oil company, that this drilling job was being done turnkey. I was just disappointed that it was a dry hole since it would lower my percentage of rigs that I sat on that became production wells, but I already knew that it would be so. Bringing in a production well is a collaboration between the company geologist and the well-site geologist. We both need to be good at our jobs, they at picking the location for the well, and me at making sure that I skillfully choose the formation tops and the DST locations to maximize any return of oil and not miss any potential production zones. A check in the minus column.

I will send a lengthy reply in a few days. Dad

29 Oil Patch – Mudlogging Redux '83

We went to Scottsbluff for an after-Christmas get together with René's family. We took Pete and Betty out for an anniversary dinner at the Moon Lake Supper Club which was her parents first time back there since they had their marriage reception 12 years earlier. Betty hooked me up with the high school shop teacher where she worked and I got "friend" prices on 44 feet of 1x10 oak boards and some oak plywood. The shop teacher and I ran it through a planer and ripped it to size. The next day, Pete and I notched the side boards on his circular table saw and I spent a day sanding down all the wood for the bookcase. The third day, Pete and I assembled the entire bookcase. It was special since It was just the right size to hold paperback books with little wasted space.

In the second week of January, Mom called to tell us that Jerry had wrecked his car, crashing off a small bridge going into Mom's Highlands neighborhood in Avon, Connecticut and smashing his foot pretty good when the floor of the car buckled. A couple days later, we picked him up at the airport for his Spring semester at CSU and dropped him off at his apartment that he shared with his friend Andy and his pit bull that wore diapers in the apartment. After Jerry was acclimatized for a few days, he, Matt and I climbed the Greyrock dome up the Poudre Canyon using some climbing gear of mine and Matt's rope. It took a couple of hours for us to get to the top where we ate M&Ms, smoked cigars, drank water, took pictures and relaxed for almost an hour admiring the view as the sun was setting over the mountains. We down climbed in the gathering dusk and hiked back to the truck in the dark. I dropped them off at Washingtons Bar and took René out to dinner at Tico's, our favorite Mexican restaurant where we consumed a large quantity of margaritas. René and I were talking about names if we had a boy and came up with Stanley "Bud" Elliot Bidwell.

I would typically workout in our spare guest bedroom with a weight set that I had, most often at about midnight since we were night owls at the time. René would workout at Gloria Stevens, but I had not joined a gym. We lived in the middle of three units in our Tri-plex and one night I was working out doing military shoulder overhead presses. I had the barbell loaded with a couple of 25lb plates on each side of the bar. I would always workout to failure, since I figured that of all the sets and repetitions that I was lifting, the final rep, that pushed your muscles to the maximum was the best of them all for muscle building. I was on this last rep on my last set, struggling to get the bar up above my head, when my slightly stronger right arm pushed the bar a bit higher and a 25-pound plate slid off the other end of the bar. That lightened up that side making my left arm go to full extension, sliding a 25 pounder off the right side of the bar. This then continued as the last two 25 pounders slid off the left, then right, crashing to the floor from seven feet up. My arms were too pumped to stop this cascading failure and it made a tremendous racket. As it turned out, our guest bedroom was right next to our next-door neighbor's master bedroom and this tremendous crashing at midnight jolted the two of them out of a deep slumber, scaring the crap out of both of them. They came running out saying "Good God! What happened? It sounded like an earthquake!". I explained what had happened and they eventually went back to bed, not quite believing my sheepish explanation. I was just glad that I had not given one of them a heart attack. A couple of days later I dismantled the weight bench and joined the Fitness Forum.

Jerry and I would go climbing up on the Dakota Sandstone above Horsetooth reservoir and René would sometimes go with us and take photos, since one of us would be climbing and the other would be holding the end of the rope on belay. A couple of days later, René baked a cake and made my favorite Mexican Haystacks for Jerry's birthday at our house. I got him a figure-8 that he could use for repelling and to belay me when climbing. We watched a movie and then went back to Washingtons for a couple of hours to conclude the birthday bash!

Mom flew out a week later for a visit and we had a Mom/Engagement party with Jerry, John & Di, Darrell and Eileen the next day. It was a little different seeing my parents now, but always separately. We took Mom up hiking at the wild rock formations of Vedawoo for a day. This area is magical to hike and climb at. The Arapahoe name means "Land of the Earthborn

Spirits." We also went hiking up in Rocky Mountain Park to Bear Lake and I got a really good picture or mom on the hiking trail. At the end of her 2-week visit, we took mom to the airport and walked out to her gate with her where Mom got a box of chocolates for Dad, even though they had separated 9 months earlier. I was a bit surprised.

On the way home, we picked up a Basenji puppy that we named Nicco and by an unhappy coincidence when we got home Muffy had passed away from congenital heart failure, probably from the Greyrock hike we had taken with Mom the day before. It was a mix of emotions, especially for René. The silver lining is that Nicco was a show dog, unlike Muffy and René started going to dog shows on the weekends and would meet Pete who was showing Pomeranians. I went to quite a few of these shows and learned to identify all the dogs that were recognized by the American Kennel Club.

Jerry and I climbed a couple of times a week, after his classes had finished for the day. We made up names for a lot of the routes that we discovered, such as Lollypop Kids and Sticky Buns. We must have climbed hungry a lot! The Psycho Two Roof was one of our favorite climbs. Jerry, Matt and I spent many happy afternoons working out the moves to get out below the ten-foot overhang and over the lip to complete the climb. When you dropped off trying to work out the moves, the top rope would swing you out into the air for an exhilarating ride.

I had a Nikon 35mm film camera that had a switch which would allow you to stay on the same frame of film when spooling for the next shot. I wanted to get a picture of Jerry standing there with himself leaning on his own shoulder. We had to do this in the total darkness with the flash to prevent over exposing the shot. I setup a tripod in the grassy area between our Tri-plex and the building next door one evening after dark. I had Jerry stand there, then remembering his position, move over and pose as if he were leaning on his own shoulder. This required many takes since we would not know if we got a good shot until the pictures came back from the developer. People would often take a short cut into the park by cutting through the grassy strip between the buildings. It just so happened that a couple of girls were cutting through that night while Jerry and I were working on this double exposure and happened upon us in the darkness. They both let out loud screams of surprise and fear. We tried to calm them down by telling them we were just taking pictures.

One of the girls said "In the dark!"

Neither of them believed Jerry and I, so they turned around and took the long way around. I think Jerry and I were just as shaken up as they were! BTW, one of the pictures came out perfectly and when Dad saw the shot, I remember him asking who the other guy was. At that point I was very proud of the picture and that made it all worth it.

We went to one party at our friends Darrell and Eileen's house. John and Di were there as well as my old roommate, friend and workout partner Norton. What makes this party standout in my memory was that Darrell had discovered home-brewing and we drank a couple of his beers. It turned out that they were quite high in alcohol content and I got very good and buzzed on just two of them. It made me want to start brewing my own tasty concoctions someday. Tracy came to stay with us just before we all went up to the Stanley hotel in Estes Park where John and Di got married. René and I danced the night away and she had never looked better!

I would paddle out at the reservoir for exercise, fun and to practice my paddling strokes, often bringing René, Jerry or a friend. About this time, I also started river canoeing which was even more fun. I joined the Rocky Mountain Canoe Club and learned to outfit my canoe with knee pads, thigh straps and flotation air bags at a clinic where we paddled the South Platte River from Chatfield to Bowles Ave. I would practice on the Poudre River, paddling solo with other boaters, mostly kayakers, to work on my skills. My first real trip was in May when we did a 3-day paddle on the Delores River from Slickrock to Bedrock at a very high 6000 CFS. This was before the McPhee Dam was built and changed this warm brown-water river to a much smaller trout stream with the cold water coming from the bottom of the reservoir. As I was unloading my boat and camping gear, I hear a familiar voice from the other group that was also paddling this section. I yelled "Ron" and we re-connected, since the last time I had seen him was up in Casper working for Homestake. We exchanged numbers so that we could start canoeing together. Our group paddled through the paradox valley and camped at the head of Bull canyon for the night. The second day had pretty good rapids and we had 3 canoes and 2 kayaks flip and swim. My bracing practice with people I would meet-up with on the Poudre River to run shuttles had helped me to keep the canoe upright this entire trip! On the last day there were two quite large rapids that flipped a raft right before us. We made it through by picking a good line in the rapid, although I had 4 inches of water in the boat at the bottom of the drop.

I did another paddling trip with the club on the North Platte River for an overnight trip where Dad, Matt, Julie and I had gone fishing earlier. I would also paddle easier parts of the NF of the Poudre down to Halligan reservoir, beefing up my boating skills. I was hooked on River canoeing and just wanted to do it all the time. Later that summer, Ron and I hooked up and we pushed our skills paddling the Foxton run on the North Fork of the South Platte which was flowing at a nice intermediate level. We paddled with Ron's best friend Bob, another geologist who was paddling a decked canoe. We put in just above the "rock garden" and paddled down to the confluence of the South Platte, all. Having clean runs and I then counted myself as a solid class III paddler!

Just before my birthday in mid-August, Ron, his girlfriend Brenda and I took a long day trip up to run the North Platte through Northgate Canyon which was still flowing at over 1000 CFS. We saw a raft at the put-in and they told us that this was a remote canyon with large rapids and that we would not be able to run it. Ron and I were not fazed, but Brenda was having second-thoughts. We appeased her with descriptions of our amazing paddling prowess and she agreed to go. We scouted the 5 major rapids down in the canyon as we approached them in our canoes, starting with Windy Hole and the crux rapid in the middle called Narrow Falls. As with any other class IV rapid, there were lines to hit and paddling moves to make to stay on line, but we cleaned all the rapids and at the end, I was a fledging Class IV boater. That was my birthday present to myself. Two days later on my birthday, René invited our friends over and we had a party where I got several gifts from her, but my favorite, that she saved for after the party was some lingerie!

GX Consultants had dropped the ball, as I did not work this Spring and Summer, just living on the money from my previous jobs. GX had teased me about jobs that did not materialize, so I went to Analex in Denver for a week, staying in the company condo with other trainees, several of which I knew from working in the Williston basin. We were trained on the new Flame Ionization (FID) gas chromatographs that were being fitted into the mudlogging trailers. Finally, I took a mud logging job at the end of August. René had got a job at Nancy's Mini Maids for a couple of months to help us until my next job came through. This was enough that she decided to re-apply for a Colorado Teaching License. One of the things I had learned about getting a college degree is that it is worthless unless you can get a job in your field of study and René was finding this out to be true as well; otherwise, the degree was just good to make you a more interesting person with the additional knowledge stored in your brain, but that will not pay the bills!

The mudlogging job lasted a month outside of Watford City, ND. We started at 8900 ft and drilled down to the Red River Formation. On September first, it hit 102 degrees F and I would throw around my 50lb dumbbells to keep in shape for boating and climbing and to keep in shape for my bride. I was friends with Kim, the well site geologist and would take showers and call René from her hotel room occasionally. She, Mike and I would go out to dinner sometimes, us all being geologists and all. Mike and I would go to Duffy's Bar to shoot pool and drink beer when tripping out of the hole. I would write letters to René, a couple a week and she would reply. One day I got two letters, the first she was down on herself and the second was her at her sexy best! I read the second one a bunch of times! The job ended towards the end of September, and by then it had been snowing and our water lines to the trailer had frozen a couple of times. One of the reasons I remember this job fondly is not so much the job, but after the job ended, on September 24, 1983 I arrived from ND to Scottsbluff where René was at her parents' house with her cousins. We had a big family dinner together. René and I went to bed early and in our excitement, we broke her parent's waterbed. Hello Coulter!!!

I went into Denver and talked with Dale. He had another mud logging job for me up in Lame Deer, Montana. We talked about my work and he agreed to bump up my pay to "Frontier Pay" which was $100/day, a $25/day raise! I also went to Arco and met the Company geologists, Paul and Cori. They would be acting as the well-site geologists and were happy that I was already experienced at that and could help them pick the tops and decide on the DSTs. They warned me to stay out of Lame Deer since it was a rough reservation town where whites were not welcome, but to go to Ashland, just outside of the Rez. Of course, that just motivated me to go into Lame Deer, since I had been warned away from places before that turned out to be the highlight of a trip and I had no fear of being treated badly. Right after René's birthday which we celebrated with German chocolate cake, mint chip ice cream and Taylor pink champagne, I left for Lame Deer. I stopped at Crow Agency where I saw the Analex mudlogging trailer parked by the side of the road, so I continued on to Ashland, Montana and got a room for the night. I was going to be doing the first part of this mudlogging job, about 2 weeks, alone.

The next morning, I headed out to the rig where Jay & Glenn were on location setting up the mudlogging trailer. I had them move it much closer to the rig, since I would be working alone and wanted the shortest walk to the Shale shaker as possible. I met Richard, the toolpusher and we got power hooked up to the trailer which I then cleaned up and got ready for logging. I then went into Lame Deer to get a "trespass permit" since I was going to be spending the month on the res on my days off, then spent a cool evening in the trailer since the heater was malfunctioning. The next morning, I called in my morning report, basically being the well-site geologist until the Arco folks would get up here in 2 weeks. I set up our extractor and hooked up the poly flow line back to the trailer. I had to wait to hook up our geolograph switch, since the rig was getting a newer geolograph tomorrow. I worked on the logging until 2:00am then went to bed for 3 hours before calling in the morning report to Arco. I was getting very low gas readings on my equipment, so Richard and I pulled one of the screens off of the shale shaker to get better readings. That helped a little bit. I called Dale back in Denver and he suggested bad power, so I hooked up to another generator and everything started working perfectly. I was behind on my log and had a moment of frustration, basically doing three jobs simultaneously, the mudlogger, the 2nd tower mudlogger and the consulting geologist. I was thinking that this whole job was a crock of shit and not worth my time. The real reason was that I was behind on my log, but the problem resolved itself about then, when the rig lost circulation and they had to trip out of the hole to find the perforation in the pipe. I got a reprieve for a day to get caught up. After that the job ran smooth.

One of the requirements the Reservation put on Arco was that was that there had to be two Native Americans from the tribe working with each of the towers of roughnecks on the rig. At the start of each tower a Rez truck would drop off two workers to help out. They would be working the rig like day work for a job agency, in this case the reservation. Working safely on a rig requires that you know exactly what to do, especially when tripping out of the hole so you don't get injured, hurt or worse. These temp workers were the inexperienced worms of the rig, and the toolpusher would keep them away from the actual drilling rig where they could get hurt by putting them to work painting. They mostly painted the steel outlying sheds that were part of the rig support, housing generators, pumps, spare parts, mud shed, out house, etc. That meant that each tower was down a hand or two, which was OK, except for when the hard work of tripping out of the hole was required. I was up in the doghouse talking with one of the drillers and they were getting ready to trip out of the hole to replace the Hughes drill bit. He saw that I knew my way around a rig and that I knew exactly what was involved in tripping out of the hole. He asked me if I would like to work the floor for this tower since they were short-handed. That is a filthy job with mud splashing on you every time a pipe connection is broken apart and then the big grease stick that is used to slap grease on the pipe threads prior to connecting them gets on everything. I just had my work clothes. I agreed, since I liked hard physical work, if they would give me a pair of coveralls and gloves to work in. I ended up working a few towers for the different crews when they were tripping out. Part of the reason was that I would have nothing to do during these periods of time and was glad to be able to help out and put my muscles to good use, like a cross-training workout for me. In all the laundries in the oil patch, there would be one set of machines for the roughnecks and another set for everyone else. The bentonitic mud and tenacious grey thread grease would be very difficult to get out and would get those laundry machines filthy.

Well true to form, I spent most of my off-time in the little town of Lame Deer. I could get groceries there, search for a good book, look at art and wander around relaxing in town. The Native Americans living there welcomed me or ignored me, but either way, I liked the town. The town of Ashland was just off the Rez and there were bars and pool halls and was in fact a much rougher place than Lame Deer. The pool hall where I occasionally liked to hang out and drink beer, had windows on the second floor painted with topless ladies dressed like whores. I never did go upstairs, but I think it was just for show and to get the attention of passers-by.

We reached the casing point at 3100' after 2 weeks when I got a day or two reprieve while they set casing and cemented it in place. Dave, my second Mudlogger showed up the evening before we resumed drilling and the job became more relaxing. Two days after that, Mary-Ellen a green geologist from Arco Denver arrived to be the well-side geologist and we had a bit of a run-in, not seeing eye-to-eye on things. I would call René from the Phone booth in Ashland (they had a better grocery store and laundry), and send lots of letters. Eventually I would call from Mary-Ellen's trailer and on one of the calls, René told me that she might be pregnant. As we were approaching the Niobrara Formation, I was working and called the formation top and had the driller stop and circulate, while I went over to Mary-Ellen's trailer and woke her up for the test zone. After about a week Mary-Ellen went back home to Denver and the next two geologists from Arco showed up to tag-team the well-site geology tasks. I called René from the geologist's trailer and she has been having a lot of morning sickness and was not feeling well. Two days later, we hit the Muddy Sandstone and again I had the driller stop and circulate up the test zone before I went and woke up the two company geologists.

That night Dave and I went into Ashland to shoot pool, have a few beers and relax. We were playing against two large pony-tailed Indians from the Rez who were getting belligerent since we were kicking their asses pretty well. On our last game, Dave scratched on the 8-ball on purpose losing this game.

I was like "Dave, What the fuck!"

He replied "Hey, although we are kicking their asses, I do not want them to do the same to us after the game is over."

I could not argue with that, other than to tell him "They are so drunk they could never catch us if it came down to that."

The next day I wandered off the rig for a hike till I got to a nice overlook, sat down under a tree and wrote René a letter and enjoyed my quiet Zen moment. We were having nice summer-like weather here at the end of October. Arco swapped out the geologists for a 3rd time with Peggy and Linda, just before we hit the Tensleep Formation. We picked the top of the formation and tripped out of the hole to take a 50-foot core sample of the production zone, something that I had never done before. Dave and I had been trading stickers with the roughnecks. We had them plastered on our hardhats and on our tool boxes and I gave a few for the geologists to put on their virgin hard-hats so they might get a modicum of respect from the roughnecks. After over 6 weeks on this job, we hit TD and I should count this as a check in the plus column for me, but I was not the geologist so it just made me feel good.

I headed home in my old Bronco, having traded in my new leased Bronco for this square little big-tired older one with a hefty 302 V8. I had been up all the last night, so I only made it 90 minutes to Ranchester, WY where I got a motel and called René. The next morning, it started snowing and by the time I reached Buffalo I was in a full-on blizzard, heading south on I-25. Between Buffalo and Kaycee, I hit a patch of ice and the Bronco swung right 90 degrees (at 60 MPH), then swung left 180 degrees, still on the road and finally got turned back the other way 270 degrees and was then heading off the right side of the highway probably doing about 30 MPH. I managed to keep the truck lined up as I went off the highway backwards and down the steep embankment only stopping when the snow was piled half way up my rear window. I climbed out to lock the hubs and put the truck into 4WD and rocked it out of the snow bank I had made. I then drove the truck back and forth next to the snow pile I had created, making a packed track that I used to get a running start back up to the highway. With the V8 screaming I made it up to the interstate and stopped in the middle of the highway sideways, blocking both lanes of traffic, but the highway was empty. I got home to Ft Collins in the late afternoon and snuggled close to René while we talked and got caught up.

Together, we called our families and told them that we were pregnant, making it official. We had Thanksgiving dinner with just the two of us, since in the two weeks from my last job we had visited Chris' folks, grandmother, cousins, etc. being so excited about our pregnancy. We had a few dinner parties at our house and at friends' houses, and I liked the ones with Darrell & Eileen since our dogs could play together and they had that awesome home-brew. Remember this was before the micro-brew revolution and these tasty ales were very hard to come by. I called my geologist friend Eric since he would hang out with us often between his mudlogging jobs but he had had enough of the oil patch and had gone home to the East coast.

I got called out to another job, just 2 days after Thanksgiving. I took the old Bronco up to Wyoming in a blizzard and when I got to Cheyenne, the truck was sputtering. I filled up with gas and put a can of heat into the gas tank and the truck started running fine. When I got to HWY 85 there were over 100 semi-trucks parked at the side of the road since there were blizzard conditions and the highway was closed. I drove that tough little Bronco around the gate with the warning lights that the road was closed and continued on seeing several cops, but they were all busy with cars that had slid off the road. I continued with little visibility due to the blowing snow, clear to Spearfish where I ate dinner. When I got to Bowman, ND and gassed up, the truck would not start so I got a jump from a friendly cop and made it all the way up to Belfield without a heater. I was so cold that I went into the gas station convenience store and stood under the heater for 20 minutes to warm up talking with the girl at the cash register, mostly about the weather. I arrived at the rig at 4:00am after 17 hours of driving! I got 2 hours of sleep in the trailer before hooking everything up to the rig and worked until after midnight. My logger never showed up, but I was not too surprised. I asked the roughnecks to catch samples for me that night so I could get a little sleep. My 2nd Mudlogger Steve showed up the next day just as we were tripping out, so we went to the Cattlemen's restaurant for dinner, after I took a shower at the truck stop. A couple of days later I went into town from the rig and my truck overheated since the engine was mostly frozen and got a tow into the truck stop by a roughneck from another rig. I left it there to thaw out, replace the water pump, put in a new thermostat and block heater and caught a ride back to the rig where I was dropped off and hiked across a foot of snow in a sunflower field to my rig.

One day at the rig, Clifford and Slim working the current tower asked me if I would work for them as a floorhand since they were shorthanded. I borrowed some coveralls and helped them trip out of the hole. The next day, when they were tripping back into the hole, I roughnecked for them again to help them out. My only injury was a slightly mashed toe when we dropped the heavy slips on my non-steel-toed boots. The mudlogging job was finished about 10 days before Christmas, so after we rigged down the trailer, I got into the Bronco and went to put the "Three on the Tree" transmission into gear. I heard plastic in the steering column shattering from the extreme cold. I had lost two of my gears, reverse and second. This was fortunate for me, since I could get out the rough rig road in first, then shift directly to third when on the highway. I drove straight back home this way, being careful not to stop anywhere that required backing up. I got home in the early evening, just after dark and hugged René in the driveway for a long time, then looked up and said "Hi" to Matt. We had my favorite cabbage rolls for dinner and I got the Bronco fixed the next day for just over $100!

I was only back for one day before Dale called with another shallow job in Liberal, Kansas where I worked my last mudlogging job in a dry county in the heart of the bible belt where the rig was located. The only places to drink were these clubs that you would join, like a members-only bar. You would give the bartender a bottle of your favorite hard liquor (from out of the county) and they would sell you a setup to drink your own alcohol. We ended up taking our breaks at the local bowling alley where you could drink beer and eat pizza. This was a cold, windy location and I called Dale to tell him that this would be my last mudlogging job. I got home just in time for Christmas to end the year with family and friends.

I did not realize how much time you and Jeremy and Matt spent together and how extensive your climbing was. I never understood what Jeremy's situation was at CSU. Our lack of money for him didn't help. I am working on Addendum 2 of personal family financial history.
Dad

30 Ft Collins - Coulter, Consulting Geologist Redux

By January 1984, we had moved up to a winterized vacation house on the West side of Horsetooth reservoir. I could hike 1600 feet up from the house to the top of Horsetooth rock. I could carry the canoe down to the water for paddling and fishing. Often, we would see groups of Great Horned owls sitting on the rocks at the North end of the reservoir where they would be nesting. Nicco, our basenji, had a nice steep backyard that he could tear around at 90 miles per hour to burn off his energy. René, Matt and I would hang out on the deck overlooking the reservoir with the Dakota sandstone, our personal playground, stretching for miles along the hogback as the backdrop. It was our first time living in the foothills and we loved it. Jerry was going to school at CSU and would come up often to hang out with his brothers and sister-in-law.

The oil boom had really started two years before I graduated, overlapping with the uranium exploration boom for a couple of years before uranium busted. The oil boom peaked up in North Dakota around 1981 with about 120 oil rigs actively drilling and by this time was tapering off just as fast as it started. We were down to about half that many rigs, but I was not aware at the time that the bust part of the oil patch boom & bust cycle was in full swing. I had started working again as a well-site consulting geologist with Summit Consulting with a boost in salary to $250 per day. I had got the job when Summit had called me asking if I wanted to work for them which was excellent timing since I had quit working for Analex and GX consulting. Now René could start going on jobs with me again. I was thinking that life was easy, I was at the top of my career, making good money and was set for life. I was about to be blind-sided by the crash of the oil boom and after that I never took for granted my position in life, the things I have and thinking that it would be smooth sailing from here on out. Since then, I've continued to work hard, but now I realize how lucky I am and that things could change in an instant. I should have already learned this lesson from Westledge when Val Hart taught us how life is about change, and we need to accept and embrace the changes it brings. Things will change in ways that we have no way of predicting. We just need to go with the flow and not stubbornly cling to the past. An example of this is when Henry Ford asked people what they most wanted. The overwhelming answer was "A faster horse". They could not conceive of the automobile and the change it would bring to their lives. I no longer take my great job I have currently for granted, there may not be a boom and bust cycle in the computer industry, but things like corona-19 could change life quickly also.

I worked a couple of jobs back up in the Williston basin for Summit. We did one job outside of Terry, Montana where we stayed in an old historic hotel with a bathroom down the hall. We would take our robes and towels down to the bathroom and lock the door for an hour while we took showers and baths, cleaned up, dressed and basically made it like a little spa for a relaxing hour. Back out at the rig, the company man was a big old Texas oilman that thought he was the shit. I realized right off that he was an ornery old bastard that wanted to do everything his way and I would have to take a hard line with him. Whenever I saw him, usually in his trailer out at the rig I would look him straight in the eye with a non-blinking and hard-nosed stare like Henry Stamper. He was an old man in his 60's, a big guy, but I was in my prime, full of the vim and vigor of youth, bench pressing sets of 260 and feeling up for anything. I did not back down and neither did he. He was upset that I was testing zones on the way to the Red River and would slow down his numbers as compared with the other rigs. This was usually a competition that would be done by the toolpushers and not the company man, but he had not totally moved on from his previous toolpusher mentality, now that he was working for the Oil Company. We would discuss things while staring at each other like we were sizing each other up for a fight. It was a good thing that we never got physical since he outweighed me by 70 lbs. and I did not know about "Old-Man strength" at the time. He got the last laugh on me when the job ended and I was heading home and realized that I left the very cool yellow rain slicker from the Bidwell Company in his trailer. I've never found a rain jacket that I liked as much as that one.

I worked another job for Total Petroleum for a couple of weeks outside of Bowman, North Dakota where we stayed at the Northwinds Lodge and would eat really good Walleye dinners at the Hunter Restaurant in Rhame. René and I packed up from this job at the beginning of April and drove straight home to Ft Collins and were glad to see Matt and Jerry just hanging out when we got there.

The next day, the three of us went climbing on the southern ridge that we could see from the house and spent the afternoon climbing into dusk on new routes that we had scouted out. After the sun went down and the air started cooling down quickly, these West-facing rocks would be glowing from the light of the sky over the mountains and our climbing holds would still be warm from the heat of the day. I had collected rocks since I was a kid, I studied rocks, I climbed on rocks, I made my living with rocks. The warm rock with our climbing chalk on it seemed almost alive at this magical time of day. We were climbing on it like the Oxpecker birds climb on the backs of Rhinos. It was from climbs like these that dusk became (and still is) my favorite time of the day.

After I finished my logs and writing the report from the last job, Matt and I went into Denver. He checked jobs at Tooke Logging and I talked with my bosses at Summit Consulting. We picked up René back at home and left for Scottsbluff to help Pete tear down an outside wall of his house to open it up to the porch which was going to become a huge family room. We pulled wires through the ceiling for lights and power, sheet-rocked the ceiling and left one wall open for the mason to build a large brick fireplace. During our visits to René's parents, there would usually be a box of donuts to have with our morning coffee, a big mid-western dinner and football on the TV if the season was right. On other visits to Scottsbluff, I would jump into Pete's pickup and we would drive around looking at cows and bulls on the farms in the area. He was especially interested in breeding quality bulls since he was a farmer at heart, but his career was managing the beet harvest at the Great Western Sugar factory. I always enjoyed these diversions and I would be having that Woolly Bully song going on in my head and would be tapping my fingers on the door, keeping the beat with my feet while humming and singing it. He would look at me sideways like "what the fuck". He very rarely swore, but I'm sure that is what was going on in his head. Everyone liked Pete, all the farmers and Mexican workers that he saw at the factory and when visiting the fields loved him. I never saw a black person in Scottsbluff, which was good for Pete since something bad had happened to him in Korea when he was in the service that turned him off to them due to some teasing or tormenting that he never talked about.

We were back at our house by Easter when I got a nice check from Summit for $1650, but Matt bought our Easter turkey and Jerry, René and my brothers played pitch and panhandle rummy into the evening. I would go into Denver and talk with the Oil Companies, sometimes we would meet at the Denver Petroleum Club, which seemed like the kind of place to sip cognac, smoke cigars and discuss events in the far-off oil patch, which is exactly what we did. Other times I would meet at places like the Total Petroleum offices and would talk with the geologists for a couple of hours about the jobs I had completed, and future jobs coming up. René continued meeting Pete to show dogs together in the surrounding towns like Laramie, Cheyenne, Longmont and even Ft Collins.

I took a training class to be certified by the American Canoe Association to teach canoe paddling for the Rocky Mountain Canoe Club. I learned more from training to be an instructor than any of the students ever learned from me in the class, at least it seemed that way to me. I met with a State Farm agent to purchase health insurance, something I had never done before, just in case there would be any complications with the delivery. The normal birth charges would be paid by us. I got to know people in the canoe club from classroom training, on-water training and evaluations including a final party where we concluded the instructor's course.

We went to a big party at Darrel & Eileen's where about 25 people I knew from school were. Most were still hanging around in Ft Collins, where we had graduated almost 4 years earlier. René and I had kept in touch with a lot of them and it is always nice to catch up and share stories of being out in the world after school.

In early May, Matt and I took his VW Rabbit and my Mad River Canoe and we headed down to southern Colorado to paddle the Rio Grande from Lobatos Bridge in the San Luis valley Colorado, to the Lee Trail in Northern New Mexico in the Taos Box canyon. We were with a group of 20 other paddlers from the club. It was a beautiful river with geese, mergansers, vultures, red-tailed hawks, falcons, ospreys, swallows, herons and beavers swimming. We practiced peel-outs, eddy turns and ferries in the current of the class II river. We sat around the campfire talking for a couple of hours, sipping whiskey while Gary, an older paddler, would occasionally read poems from Robert Service about life in the far North during the gold boom in the 1800's. Gary and I became good friends in the ensuing years, him being an accountant that did my taxes for years. We would meet at tax-time at the end of the day, where we would spend most of our visit comparing stories of our adventures, well past the allotted time. The next day we paddled a couple of class III rapids to the take-out as we entered the Taos Box proper. The canyon walls got higher and higher. We then carried our canoe and gear up the 200' trail to the canyon rim. A cool part of this trip was that I had never been to New Mexico before and I entered it for the first time by canoe on a legendary western river.

We would often pick up Jerry at his Ramblewood apartment to go climbing. Matt, Jerry, René and I would hike up from the house on the lower trail to look at the waterfall that would be flowing over the cliffs into Spring Canyon. René and I were going to Lamaze breathing training in preparation for the delivery. "He, He, He, Ho" was the chant to control the pain with timed breaths. Jerry, Matt and I were climbing one time in June below the Torture Chamber and we all got the 5.10 climb called The Swing. We then moved up-ridge to climb the Timber Crack which required an awkward hip-lock move to complete. Jerry and I had done it the year before and we worked with Matt until we all got it again, but it took so long that we did not get back home until after 9:00 pm and René was not happy. She was probably worried about us being hurt or something and then when we showed up late and happily talking about the climbs, she was mad about worrying for nothing. I love her. We did all stay up late however eating stir-fried vegetables and working on crossword puzzles well into the night. Often, I would paddle solo on the reservoir when no-one else at the house was in the mood. I would relax and get into a good paddling rhythm and could put down the miles and get into the zone where my mind would wander and come up with cool thoughts and answers to life's problems. I would sometimes troll a Mepps spinner way back behind the canoe and would occasionally catch a nice trout as a bonus.

Jerry left Ft Collins after finishing his Spring semester at CSU and left for CT on May 18, 1984. He never came back to school and our best bonding time ever was over. When he was little, I was 6 years older than him, so when he was here in college, we could really connect and do fun things together and just hang out, eating dinner, having BBQs, watching movies, sucking down a few beers, climbing, joking around and just being guys together. I was sad to see him go, knowing that he was not planning to come back for the Fall semester.

One-night René, Matt and I talked and played cards after eating yummy taco salads until 4:00 in the morning, just not wanting the evening to end. We did not get up until 1:30 the next afternoon when Matt and I went climbing at the Psycho II roof and another overhanging climb for five and a half hours.

In late May, I went back to paddle the Delores River again, but this time with Matt. We stopped in Brighton at Varsity sports, René's cousin's sporting goods store to get wrestling sweat tops to use as paddle jackets. Kerry and Paulene were a little late because they had rolled their Land Cruiser off the loose shoulder of a dirt road. The truck rolled 360 degrees over the top of the canoe on the Yakama rack, just denting the truck a little, not hurting the canoe at all, but crushing the rack down to the top of the truck. On the first day we paddled down to Bull Canyon rapids where we set up our tent and I fell asleep on the sand outside next to the tent. I got up and Ron Singleton of our crew made Matt and I tasty gin & tonics that we sipped on as we climbed the rocks picking our lines through the long rapid in preparation for the next morning's paddle. We met my friend Ron (no surprise) while we were scouting and he was paddling with his own crew. All of our fresh veggies had gone bad in the 90-degree heat, but we made up for it by combining rice, cheese and canned oysters into an ad-hoc tasty meal. The second night we camped at Coyote Wash that was running sandy and shallow at 88 degrees, going into the colder 55-degree Delores River. I washed my hair, keeping my body in the Coyote Wash water and my head in the much colder but cleaner river water.

René and I would walk down to the Marina store to pick up minor groceries that we had run out of. Driving into town required driving around the end of the reservoir then to the spring canyon dam, so we would try to limit our trips if we just needed little things. We were taking classes on labor and delivery, and watching movies on the birthing process, visiting the maternity unit, but I could not wrap my mind around it and it remained a very scary and mysterious process. We had lots of BBQs on our deck with our friends from town. We would hike down to the North Fork of the Poudre to go trout fishing and Nicco would go tearing around everywhere.

On Tuesday evening, actually after midnight on the 20th, René and I were practicing our breathing exercises when at 1:00 she said to me, "I think my water just broke".

I followed her into the bathroom and we agreed that it had.

She said "But I'm not ready for this!"

We arrived at the hospital at 2:30 am and the contractions got more intense until 11:30 am when she was dilated to 8 cm and we started the transition breathing together. René would take a cleansing breath, then go right into the "He, he, he, ho". At 12:50, right in the middle of our last breathing pattern she screamed right in the middle and I held her face right in front of mine, to get her back on the breathing pattern.

At that point Dr Jessup told her to start pushing and that made her much more comfortable, although eventually René uttered, "I don't think the baby is ever going to deliver!"

The doctor gave René an episiotomy (a surgical cut made at the opening of the vagina, to aid a difficult delivery and prevent rupture of tissue) and on the next push, Coulter Stanley Bidwell was born! René held and talked to Coulter for 25 minutes as she was getting stitched up. The coolest thing was when Dr Jessup swung Coulter up after the delivery. He was completely full of life, beautiful and was basking in the attention everyone was focusing on him. It was fantastic seeing that and was truly life-changing for me. He was measured at 7lb 6 ½ oz and 20 ¾ inches. I then carried him to the nursery. I never took my eyes off of him, watching in wonder, even as they stamped his feet and gave him a little arm band since I wanted to make sure that the hospital did not mix him up with any of the other babies. A half hour later I brought Coulter back to René and the nurse told me we had a visitor. I let Matt into the room, even though it was against the rules and he was really excited. We checked out in the afternoon of the next day and René drove my little pickup home since the driver's seat was the most comfortable. Coulter was in his car-seat on the passenger seat and I rode the hump.

The next day I drilled out the floor of the old Bronco to put seat belts in the back seat for a child carrier. Matt left for Columbia, Missouri that morning. René was having trouble getting Coulter to take her nipple. We tried hot cloths, jelly on the nipple, holding a plastic nipple over Chris' nipple and were about to take him back to the hospital when he latched on just a little bit with the last trick. About then Betty arrived and René visibly relaxed and between the two of them got Coulter feeding pretty well on her breast. Matt's girlfriend Barb called and was excited that Matt had left. A couple of days later Pete and Mom Jones arrived, then René's cousins, aunts and uncles. Betty left after a week, telling me to just put up with René who was still not quite herself worrying about feeding and taking care of Coulter. That same day, René got Coulter to breastfeed on her left side and was pleased with herself and was more relaxed. Mom came out ten days after Coulter was born, the same day René got Coulter to suckle from the right breast, a milestone in breastfeeding for us! Mom held Coulter, we showed her lots of pictures, she told us about her recent trip to Mexico, had BBQs on the deck, played cards and just hung out together. A couple of days later, René and I took Coulter in for a checkup with our new pediatrician Dr Booth and he told René that she was producing a prodigious amount of milk, his words. That was good for Coulter and as it turned out good for me, since I enjoyed suckling just as much as he did when she produced more than Coulter could drink!

On Independence Day we drove to the Dixon dam and watched the fireworks in town from the car but were disappointed since they were small, far away and we could not hear them, so we left early to go home and watch All Creatures Great and Small on TV. I took Mom up to the Mishawaka Inn on the Poudre River for the day. We watched a kayak race there, then I paddled down from the bar in my canoe with Ron and Mike, hitting the biggest hole I had ever paddled through just a couple hundred yards down. The river was flowing around 2000 CFS and was pushy enough that we scouted 2 rapids down to Pineview Falls where Mom was watching the river and we pulled out.

René and I took Coulter to the Pine drive-in theater for a get-away. I got the Bronco all outfitted with pillows, we got pop and candy on the way. During The Natural, I had a beer and Coulter had a breast! Coulter slept through the Big Chill and we got home at 2:00 am. The next day, I took mom up for a hike in Glacier Gorge up to Mill Lake in Rocky Mountain Park. That evening, René took mom out for beers at Jack Daniels, our local bar in walking distance from our house. The following day, after 2-weeks I took mom to Stapleton Airport after a fun and relaxing visit. So far, this year has been 3 months on mostly working and 3 months off mostly relaxing.

In July we needed some money, so I sold the Bronco for $2600, the same price I had purchased it for and René was happy since we had money for rent and bills. A day or two later, I loaded the Mad River Explorer on top of my little pickup and drove up to Mishawaka on the Poudre and hooked up with a New Zealander named Brid on holiday. We paddled down to Pineview Falls at a lower 1000 CFS where we scouted the falls. I was uncertain about running it since there were 3 or 4 holes before the final lower drop. Brid ran it and a minute later I followed in the open canoe. I slid through the upper hole perfectly and stayed dry. On the second hole however, there was no easy slot and it hit it dead-on, taking a half a boatload of water before eddying out into a small eddy on the right and sticking my paddle into a rock to hold the boat in place. The current started pulling my boat backward downstream and bent my paddle snapping it in half. I was kneeling in a half-submerged canoe floating backwards towards the 2nd half of the rapid without a paddle, so I didn't think twice, jumping out, climbing up the bank and watching the canoe finish the rapid without me. I ran down the road, reaching the Bridges Put-in just as the canoe was floating by with the big truck tire inner tube that

I used as rear flotation floating behind the boat attached to a rope. I jumped into the river grabbing the inner tube and swam the boat to shore in a nice self-rescue, since my buddy Brid was helping another kayaker that swam the falls. My canoe had sustained no damage but I had lost my spare paddle. I had the feeling that something else was missing and immediately realized that my wedding band was gone, what rotten luck! It must have slid off my finger when I broke my paddle and fell into the middle of Pineview Rapid. Perhaps it was a good offering to the River Gods since I never got hurt in almost 40 years of whitewater paddling and none of my friends got hurt or killed except for the occasional dislocated shoulder, but René sure did not see it that way! By a happy coincidence, I saw my friend Craig that I had lived with in Boulder there at the Bridges put-in with a couple of inflatable ducky kayaks. I borrowed a canoe paddle from him and we continued on downstream, doing the Bridges run together to finish up a long fun afternoon of boating and catching up.

Finally, at the end of July, I got another consulting job with Summit for Total Petroleum. I left for Bowman, ND early in the morning and took Nicco with me. He slept in the passenger seat for the nine-hour drive. Heading up through southern North Dakota, I looked up and saw one of the wonders of the high plains, a flock of White Pelicans with their distinctive black wing bars, way up high circling down like a funnel cloud to a pond far below. The next morning, I got up at 4:00 and got out to the rig which was at 8000' and did the usual of meeting the company man, toolpusher, driller, Mudloggers and got caught up. Scotty was the Company man and we talked for a good hour getting caught up since we had become friends on a prior job. I ran back to the Northwinds Lodge to call in my morning report by 8:00, and was then back out doing the 70-mile round trip to the rig where Nicco and I spent the night checking every hour for the Duperow production zone. This was a busy job, picking the Interlake top the next day and circulating up. A day later Nicco and I headed out to the rig to pick the Stony Mountain formation top and we got stuck in the mud in the driving rain so we walked in the mud out to the rig. Scotty, who was older drove us back to my truck to pull us out and got a flat tire, that I changed for him in the mud while he stayed dry in his truck. A few days later we hit the Red River and I circulated up the "A" porosity zone. I headed out to the rig with Scotty's patched tire and spent 3 days at the rig doing DSTs picking the "B" and the next day the "C" porosity zones. On the "C" zone, the DST was showing good blows and looked very encouraging. A couple of days later, near TD, I headed out with groceries for Scotty. We had to wait to drill the last 100' before running the E-logs. I talked with Scotty for a couple of hours and he told me about his first two wives, both of whom had died of cancer and a bunch of oil patch stories. I threw horseshoes with Scotty and the Mudlogger Mike until we reached TD and the e-loggers arrived in their big truck. Nicco and I drove home the next day after putting a check in the plus column for this job!

We drove through Sturgis, this being the first week of August and weaved in and out of the thousands of motorcycles on the way to Scottsbluff to see René and Coulter. After a quick visit with René's parents, they piled in the little pickup truck with Nicco and I in the back. I slept until 4:00 am when we arrived at home in Ft Collins. Two hours after we were back, I ran into Denver to deliver the e-logs to Chuck, the company geologist at Total Petroleum and discussed the job. I later went to Summit to talk about the job and gave Steve and Gary some leads on future jobs I had learned about up in ND.

In René's stint with Nancy's Mini Maids, she became friends with Nancy, so I watched Coulter while they had an evening together. René and I went to Boulder the next day and I was looking to rent a C-1 decked whitewater canoe and ended up giving Eric Bader, the owner of Boulder Outdoor Center $50 as a deposit on the most beautiful (too me) Pewter-grey Hydra Centaur used boat. I went into Denver to get my paycheck and Steve did not have the money yet. That should have been an indication that we were in the middle of the bust phase of the oil boom. It is sometimes hard to see the forest through the trees.

I have just finished shucking five ears of corn. Robin goes to Anderson's Farm in old Windsor where the best corn is grown in the fertile CT River bottom land. Your story continues to be so interesting. I am glad that you and Matt and Jeremy spent so much time climbing and hanging out. My best wish is that you and Jeremy patch things up. Julie is another story. Robin and I are working on Addendum #2. It addresses things that I never dared discuss before, but that are important to understanding our family.

Love Dad

31 Yuma – Farming & Teaching '84

On my birthday in mid-August, we went to Greeley to meet Dr. Kortmeyer, the principal of Yuma High School. René had renewed her teaching license and Yuma was looking for an excellent English teacher to fill in the void so we were there for an interview for the position. He more or less offered René the job right there, while Coulter and I waited in the car doing crossword puzzles from the Denver Post. We discussed the job on the way back home. René did not initially want the job since it meant teaching a couple of English classes that she had never taught before and that meant a lot of time creating lesson plans, grading tests and homework. I did not like the job since it meant moving three hours East to Yuma, away from the mountains that I love. We both liked the prospect of extra money, since the oil patch work was kind of spotty. We had a BBQ with our friends Darrel and Eileen when we got back and discussed our options with them.

The next morning, we got up and discussed the job for a couple of hours before deciding that morning not to take the job. In a fortuitous quirk of fate, when she called the High School to turn down the job, no one was in. Then René's stepdad Pete called and we discussed it with him a bit and decided to drive out to Yuma and check out the school before making a final decision. We left for Yuma at noon, both convinced that she wouldn't take the job. The principal showed René around and she liked the school and liked it even more when Dr. Kortmeyer told her that she would not have to do the school play, which was part of the original job description. That was the clincher and she took the job. We met with Lawrence, the realtor and he showed us the two places that were available in town, an apartment and a house. We took the house and René really liked it.

The next day on Friday, I went into Denver to pick up my last check from Summit Consulting and on the way home I paid the rest of the $200 for the Hydra Centaur decked C-1 whitewater canoe and brought it home. On Saturday, I rented a 24-foot U-Haul truck and Pete and I spent all morning loading it up. Most of my friends were busy getting ready for the wedding. That afternoon René and her folks went to a dog show in nearby

Longmont and I went to my friend Tom Taylor's wedding to Donna and saw many of my college friends there.

On Sunday, after eating breakfast out at the Farmers Table, we spent the rest of the morning loading up the truck, cleaned the house and left for Yuma, arriving in mid-afternoon. Lawrence showed up to help us unload, and a little later a dozen teachers showed up and we had the truck unloaded in about 30 minutes. They had also brought all sorts of things for dinner. Pete and Betty were bushed, but had supper with us before heading back to Scottsbluff. We had just enough energy to get the bed and the crib setup and went to sleep. Three days later, René had her first school day and was back in the work force, while I became a househusband, looking after Coulter.

A week later, Grandma and Grandpa Bidwell arrived from Connecticut in a car they had rented at the airport. They were thrilled and excited to see their first great grandson and to see how we were doing in this western farming town out on the high plains. They were both 82 years old, but were spry, although Grandpa's eyesight was not what it was used to be. They were interested in exploring the little town of Yuma, so we took their large rental car around town. Now Yuma does not have storm sewers but instead has little dips in the road where there were intersections to allow the rain water to run off. Grandpa was driving and did not notice these dips in the road and as we drove over them, first on one side of the road, then the other, the car would bounce over these dips, scraping the back bumper and on each, Grandpa would say "Thank you ma'am!". This was not a term that either René or I were familiar with and we were giggling in the back seat. Grandma told him to slow down, but he was enjoying himself and kept up the pace, while we lost count of the "Thank you ma'ams". Back at the house, while Grandma was holding Coulter, I showed Grandpa the growth charts where I was tracking Coulter's height and weight. He was well into the 90th percentile for large size and I was sure that he would be a great big man someday. He was unbelievably cute with his rolls of healthy fat everywhere and Grandma did not want to put him down. They left for the airport the next day after their brief visit, having caught up with us and getting to know their happy great grandson just a little bit.

Normally, René would take care of Coulter when he got fussy in the middle of the night, but now that she was working, I would get up. He was a very easy baby and most of the time I just had to gently turn him over from one side to the other and he would go right back to sleep, as would I. I went to visit the high school after classes had got out and talked with Dr. Kortmeyer about working out in the school weight room in the evenings and he agreed, giving me a key to the gym. I talked with the wrestling coach to let him know that on Monday, Wednesday and Friday evenings after dinner I would be working out with weights for an hour and he was fine with that as well. I would go there and turn on the minimal lights and lift weights for an hour, stretching out on the wrestling mats and keeping in shape. I have always enjoyed weightlifting. I like the way it makes my body feel and enjoy the movement of my muscles when going about day-to-day activities. It was also a good way for me to relieve stress and my mind would wander, helping me to solve any issues and get into that mental zone of contentment. It was also good for keeping in shape for rock climbing and C-1 kayaking, neither of which I could do in Yuma.

The day after my grandparents left, Dad arrived for a week bearing mementos from Valley Farm, my maternal grandparents house after Grandma Noss had passed away. He had Grandpa Noss' straw hat, an embroidered foot-stool and other things, including a selection of books from their library. He also brought some of my things from the sale of our family home on Terry Rd in Hartford, such as my High School Diploma and more books. Dad took us out to dinner at Murfs and we all had meat; ribs and steak since we were in grain country, although René's meat was Rocky Mountain Oysters. When René went to work the next day, Dad and I went to get a large county map from the courthouse in the county seat of Wray. I love maps and like to know what is around us geographically for possible future exploration. The most interesting thing was the sand hills that I was eager to check out. We took Coulter to see Dr. Dallow and he got his 4-in-1 baby shot which he did NOT like at all! Like father like son and probably like grandfather like grandson as well.

I was enjoying hanging out with Coulter and Dad, although I was missing working and keeping busy. On a break in the teachers' lounge, another teacher asked Chris if her husband would be interested in helping with the harvest for a local farmer. Based on that tip, I called the farmer, Gary Koenig and he asked me about hard work, driving large trucks, tractors and helping to finish-up the wheat harvest. I had always enjoyed driving trucks, both for my dad at the hardware company and driving the sheet-rock trucks at the lumberyard, and was excited about the prospect of driving a large tractor. He offered me a job, working with his son Kevin whose wife Jean would also be able to watch Coulter while I was working. After the call, I turned around and told Dad that I was going to be a farm-hand making $6/hour! He knew that I had been looking for some work to keep busy and supplement our income. This would also be another life experience and in his dad-way he was encouraging. Dad looked at me and smiled and we talked a little bit about getting busy working again. We both knew that I was a Geologist, I had a professional career, even if I had not had a job in several months. The bust of the oil patch was almost in death mode. For Dad, education and career were the most important things to define a life and they were and are his most important things to discuss and find meaning in. For me education was a way to learn about things that interest you and then work in that field. It had worked so far. Little did he know that my future path would be more education, but this time to find a more stable career. I did not even know this yet since I had still not given up on Geology. I relished the opportunity to do some physical work, learn about farming which by the way was one of my 2 career choices when I took the aptitude test for the best career match back at FDU, along with being a writer. Time to find out if the test was accurate!

On Wednesday after Labor Day, René left for school at 7:30, Dad left for the airport 10 minutes later, then I took Coulter to drop him off with Jean, Kevin's wife. They lived in a nice little ranch house, just several blocks from us and had a little boy Travis, just a little older than Coulter, so he could get some socialization as well. I met Kevin there, a big slow-talking farmer with a smile and an easy manner that I liked right off the bat. We drove out to the farm after stopping at the bakery for a couple of bear claws and some coffee. The farm was quite an operation with several grain silos and a scale, a barn with tractors, combines, and grain carts. Gary had built a newer house closer to the airport and no longer lived out here. Kevin showed me the operation and then we drove out to the Bartlett Elevator to show me what we would be doing there, when dropping off our loads. Kevin and I took the first load together, weighing the empty truck, turning on the auger of the silo at the farm to fill up the large farm truck, then weigh the full truck, fill out the books, drive to the elevator, get weighed there, dump the grain, re-weigh, get a ticket, etc... I ended up doing the round trips for the rest of the week, which I really enjoyed although I would get my lungs full of wheat dust, but even that seemed healthy. When the week was over, Kevin paid me and Jean would not take any money for watching Coulter, so René and I took them out for pizza that night. That was the end of the wheat harvest and my work.

Coulter and I would wrestle in the living room of the large house that we were renting. I would put him in the C-1 kayak on the floor of the living room, kneeling on the small foot-stool dad had given me from Valley Farm and practice my canoeing strokes. The house was on Main Street just a few blocks from downtown and Coulter and I would sit on the front steps and I would put my arm around him with my hand cupped on his unbelievably cute shoulder and we would watch the goings on around town. A week later, the Koenig's stopped by and Kevin offered me a job doing the corn harvest. I did not know it, but the end of the wheat harvest was a test to see if I was up to the much bigger task of helping with the entire corn harvest. Of course, I accepted and they took us out for a steak dinner in Wray as a way of celebrating.

The house we were renting had originally been a Mortuary. The large living room had been the casket salesroom. There was a bedroom upstairs with a large loft area where Coulter slept just outside of our bedroom door. The kitchen had a fridge with an ice-maker, which at the time was a big-deal. There was an old elevator in the back where they would take the bodies down to the basement for embalming and cremating. It sounds creepy, but the owners had done an excellent job of turning it into a residence and we always felt at home there.

We would walk around town, and it seemed that everyone in town knew that Chris (René) was the new English teacher and would stop and say "Hi" and welcome us to town.

They would ask us if we knew what our house used to be, and I would reply, "Why yes, it was a mortuary".

They would look at us for a moment, say it was good to meet us and walk off.

I soon learned to say "No, what about it", when they would ask the question.

Their eyes would light up and they would be so happy to be the ones to tell us that it had been a mortuary, just to watch our expressions and that would often lead to a longer conversation about the history of the town. I was happy to do my part to brighten up their day.

Kevin and I started preparing for the corn harvest. Kevin had two and a half center pivot irrigation circles that his dad had given him so that he could learn about the total start to finish tasks of managing his own crop circle, plus he could learn about the market prices, hail insurance, running pigs or cows and get some more personal experience on his own. He took a tractor out to his circle near Akron and I followed in the farm pickup. We went out to his circle and Kevin showed me how the tractor worked as we practiced disking under the wheat stubble and loose hay in the bottoms. We would be using one of Gary's (Kevin's dad) large John Deere 4440 4WD tractors. We spent the day as I got used to driving the tractor, trying to get the widest swathe possible with the 20-foot-wide disk array being pulled behind. I got used to the 8-speeds, using the turning brakes, manipulating the 3 hydraulic controls and operating the rear PTO. The tractor was sweet with an enclosed air-conditioned cab, cassette stereo and a cushy air-ride seat. The rest of the week we practiced on Gary's circles. For as long as I can remember, I have been a bird-watcher and I was surprised at the literal flock of red-tailed, Swainson and other hawks that would follow the tractor as the mice would run out from behind as we were disking under the soil. They just generically called them chicken hawks, because standing on the ground eating mice, they were about the size of a chicken.

The next weekend, René had a bit of a cold, but she was happy since it got her out of taking tickets for the gymnastics meet at the high school. Jean and Kevin came over to the Mortuary for a BBQ. Jean was talking about a farm auction taking place later that afternoon. I considered going to the auction, but decided to stay home since René was much more enticing. I definitely made the correct choice! At dusk, I took Nicco, now a fully-grown Basenji out to the Koenig's farm for a run off the leash through the corn fields. I love the way when dogs are panting after a good run, it just looks like they are grinning and having the time of their lives. What we could learn from dogs about living in the moment! When we got home, René was finishing up grading papers and I helped her out by averaging all the grades for her.

Kevin and I were working on the equipment, lubing up the combines, tractors and grain carts by pumping grease into the zerk nipples (pretty much a daily task) changing out sprockets and chains on the combines and adjusting the width of the corn heads on the two combines; a JD 7700 and an 8820, preparing for the corn harvest. Gary came into the equipment barn where we were working one morning and announced that we would start the corn harvest at noon today. Gary and Kevin drove the two wide combines down the road, followed by me in the tractor pulling a large grain cart. I quickly fell into the rhythm of the harvest and we filled 5 semi-trucks and one farm truck that afternoon, quitting at 8:00 pm. The way to get the maximum harvesting is to keep the combines moving all the time. If a combine is not moving, then it is not harvesting. My job was to plant myself in a harvested part of the field and keep an eye on the combines. When they started getting full, the corn will start filling the top of the bin and you can see the yellow color, which is appropriate, since this is like gold to the farmers. I would motor across the field and match speed with the combine, then Kevin would pull the auger arm out away from the combine and over the grain cart and dump his load into the cart. When full I would head over to Gary's combine and he would dump his load into the cart. There would be a semi-truck parked on the road at the edge of the irrigation circle and I would pull up to the truck, swing out my auger arm and put my load of corn into the semi. The truck driver would wave me forward slowly as the truck was filling up. My grain cart would hold several combine loads of corn and the semi-truck would hold several loads from my grain cart. When everything was running smoothly and in sync, it was a beautiful process to be a part of, and made me feel very productive and helpful, knowing that we were harvesting as fast and efficiently as possible. Sometimes work can be very satisfying.

Gary picked me up one afternoon and we went driving out to an oil rig that was working several miles away. I showed him around the rig for an hour. On the way back, we checked on a couple of his circles to see how his winter wheat crop was coming along. He told me a lot about farming from his perspective, about the town of Yuma and other stories. He had been a pilot in WW2 and had lost an eye. He had a piper super-cub crop duster that he used to spray his dozen irrigation circles and I wondered how he could do that safely without the depth perception that two eyes give you. The thing that surprised me was that farming was all about keeping the equipment in good working order for planting, amending the soil and harvesting. Gary would keep an eye on the markets (literally) and kept his three dryer bins (silos) full of corn for speculating. He would hold it for months until the market took an upturn so he could sell it at a larger profit. He was basically a very successful small businessman. The thing that surprised me the most about farming was that I was not working in the dirt with the crops, but was basically a large equipment operator and a minor mechanic. It is very expensive to take the equipment into the John Deere Dealer for maintenance, so we did as much as we could on our own, such as the time the auger arm broke on one of the grain carts and Gary welded it back together.

René and I met with Kent Haruf the other English teacher several times at school and around town. He was a gentle man with a soft voice and a bit aloof in his own thoughts. When I met him, my first impression was that he was not motivated or really focused. I had learned in life that my first impression of a person means nothing. I am only correct about half the time, meaning that it is completely random and this was one of those cases where I misjudged him. In future get-togethers with him I realized that he really did have a focus on writing, in fact his dream and goal was to be a published author but he did not talk about it for quite a while. I suspect because people would judge him for being unrealistic. I had changed my opinion of him and respected him more for not giving up on his dream even if I also thought it was a bit unrealistic. When we left Yuma, years later, I ran into him again, but this time not in person, but on the leaf of his first published book, The Tie That Binds. It was all about life in the Eastern Plains of Colorado, his subject being the place that he taught, lived and loved. I was happy that he had followed his dream and I now have several of his excellent books in my bookcase.

We worked hard harvesting the rest of Kevin and Gary's circles. When we were finished, Gary had lined up a number of local farms, that did not have the luxury of owning their own harvesting equipment, and started a few weeks of custom combining. I had seen these custom combine crews on the roads in North Dakota, going from farm to farm to harvest crops for the farmers up there and we would be doing the same. This kept us busy for most of a month. On one farm, Gary knew a women Mary-Ellen and he told me that her husband had been amending the soil with nitrogen a couple of years earlier, disking under ammonia. On one of his passes, he turned the tractor around and the ammonia line broke, rendering him unconscious as the tractor continued disking in circles and killing him. We would be harvesting her #2 feed corn from her crop circle. In fact, all the farms out in Yuma were growing this #2 feed corn that would be for livestock. We started in the morning, Kevin and Gary in the combines, I was driving the tractor and grain cart. We actually drove a couple of Gary's large farm trucks to the elevator before the semi's arrived and I hauled a couple of grain cart loads down to her barn for feeding for her pigs. We worked straight through lunch eating burgers on the run from Mary-Ellen. It was a normal hard day for us and Mary-Ellen paid us with the proceeds from 18 piglets that she had sold for the sole purpose of covering the cost of the harvest. I'm sure Gary had given her a screaming deal on this job. The big joke for the rest of the season was this.

"Man, that was a tough 20-piglet day", or "That was nice to have just a 15-piglet day".

We measured our work in piglets from then on, similar to how the locals up Northern Wyoming measured distance by the number of beers consumed.

One day Kevin and I went out to his dad Gary's circle in the town of Eckley. We put up an electric fence around it so that a local rancher could graze his cattle on the corn stocks for the low price of $1200 for the winter. We fenced another circle and were there when the 2 semi-trucks arrived with 70 head of cattle and we stuck around to ensure that our electric fence would hold. It was just another way to make income on the farm. Kevin had 2 and a half irrigation circles and one of his dilemmas each year was how much hail insurance to put on his crops. The insurance was so expensive that the cost was about the same as the amount of money he could make from the entire circle. What he did this year was to insure one entire crop circle and leave the other two un-insured so that he would not lose everything. The thunderstorms would typically roll through the plains in the late afternoon and if it was a hail storm, could completely flatten all the corn to the ground, rendering it useless to be harvested with a combine. I don't know how much the profits were from one circle, but Gary had told me that one of his three drying silos which held 2700 bushels of corn would be worth $65,000 at the day's market price for corn. We put up a lot of electric fences and this was the closest I got to getting my fingers in the soil, since we were working with a pickup truck and walking the edges of the field fencing, again more hard work.

René and I headed into Denver one weekend just a week before the corn harvest was finished. Things were slowing down and I had the Saturday off. We needed to replace her Dodge Aspen POS. We had decided on a Ford Escort wagon. It had enough room for groceries and luggage for our travel to Scottsbluff to visit her parents. I've had Ford F-150, a Ford F-250, a couple of Ford Broncos and liked their trucks. We went to Formby's Ford and a new escort wagon was $6800. We then went to O'Meara Ford at 4:00 PM and they did not have any new Escort Wagons, but they did have a 3-year-old Mercury Lynx with 32,000 miles which was basically the same car. The problem was that they wanted $6300 which was way overpriced. We played the game where the salesman for the dealership would go and talk to the manager over and over as we negotiated down the price. They switched to another salesman after a while with their strategy to wear us down. Their ace in the hole was that it was Chris, Coulter and I and they knew that it would be hard with a baby.

The new sales man said to us, "OK, let's stop talking price and talk payments."

I was reluctant to try this strategy and told him so. He came up with a price for a 3-year plan to pay off the car. I thought about it and realized that he had made an error and the price for the car would be under $4000, so I agreed. We drew up the paperwork, and were almost done when we went to the finance guy to finalize the bank paperwork. He looked at the contract and said, "Wait, how did you get this car for this price? We won't make anything on this car.". The good thing was that we had been there for almost 5 hours and he was tired too and we ended up getting the car for $3600. In hindsight, that was not such a good deal since that car was a piece of shit, we had wasted our afternoon and missed going out for dinner that night. That car was bad enough that I never purchased another Ford again.

Kevin and I had cleaned out the 3 dryer bins at the farm before we filled them up with some of Gary's corn. There were some gaps under the eaves of the bins where moisture could get in. I ran home and got my climbing gear and climbed to the top of the 40' bins, checked the metal structures carefully for any sharp metal edges, then repelled from the top, patching up all the gaps in the bins that they could not reach. It was a nice break from farming and was as close to climbing that I had in several months. The next day we filled up the 3 drying silos to the eves which would also seal up the cracks and keep any future snow out. We had the bin filled up and climbed into the silo with a hatch on the bottom of the roof. We climbed up top and pushed the corn down tight into the eves, being careful to leave a little free on the side where the hatch was. We then slid down the hatch with the corn falling all around us and just managed to get out before being buried. It's a good thing I'm not claustrophobic! Talk about getting corn in your boots, pockets, hair and underwear!

On our anniversary, I sent René 10 red and 5 yellow roses and had them delivered to school. When I was driving home, I saw her walking back from school with the flowers and picked her up to go home for a bottle of pink champagne and a candle-lit dinner with a cake that René baked.

Two months after I started, in mid-November, I was done working for the Koenig's we were finished with the corn harvest. On that same day, Coulter took his first walk around the kitchen in his walker for an hour! That next week, I went into Denver, met my friend Tom Taylor for lunch at Fins on the mall, then walked to the Total Petroleum office to discuss future drilling projects for about an hour. I then went to the Denver Library to look at maps and read back issues of American Whitewater, before heading back to Yuma for an excellent Mexican dinner with René and Coulter at the Indian Station. Back at home now, Coulter was zooming around the tile floor in his walker and I was back spending time with him. A week after I stopped being a farm hand, Coulter and I were walking back from the bakery where we had a coffee/milk and donut breakfast. Gary stopped by after we got back. He gave me my final paycheck and also gave me a gold corn kernel that he had cast from one of the corn kernels we had harvested. I was touched and very appreciative.

Thanks so much for this installment! I am going to see Bruce after lunch and will bring it. I can't remember who I've told what. I found out last night they had to remove fluid from his bladder. Did I tell you that? He was very encouraged. This morning he had diarrhea so he's discouraged but said it was medication related. How exciting to know that you met Kent Harouf. I have read at least several of his books and think he's a very special author. Thanks again, and we'll be talking with you soon. Love, Robin (Dad's wife)

I am glad to know more about Mom and Dad's visit in Yuma. I also learned more about René. I AM CONSTANTLY IMPRESSED ON HOW YOU HANDLE NEW CALLENGES LIKE FARMING. - Dad

Just more than a week after I was finished farming, at the very end of November in '84, I bought some chains for the pickup and headed up to Bowman ND and checked into the 4-U Motel. You can tell from the name that this was a very upscale Motel, catering for me! I worked out with the 50 lb. dumbbells before going to bed since I had missed my workout at the high school earlier in the week. The next morning, I headed out to the rig, but it had been recently bulldozed with a big D-9 Caterpillar and I missed the road. I spotted the rig and ended up hiking a half mile across some fields out to the Total Petroleum Harding West State drilling operation. They were at the Duperow @ 8250 feet, so there would not be much to do today. The next day was a long one. I left for the rig at 3:30 AM and spent the day out there waiting for the Duperow formation which we did not hit, so I spent the night in the extra bunk in my friend Scotty's trailer which was on-site. In fact, I spent several more nights out there since we seemed to be hitting all the production zones in the middle of the night. Several days later, we hit the Red River "A" zone where I stopped the rig and we circulated up the cuttings which came up with 600 feet of oil and 400' of salt water. I called in my morning report and the company geologists wanted to drill further down to the "C" zone. We got a hole in the pipe so it took a couple of days to get down there, where we ran an actual Drill Stem Test and circulated up 600 feet of oil, but over 4000 feet of salt water! Everyone was happy and we would be making this a production well. The rancher stopped by and saw all the oil coming up and into the reserve pit and knew that the lean times growing sunflowers on the high plains would be a thing of the past. I headed home in my tough little pickup after being out on this job for 11 short but productive days. Another check in the plus column!

One of the nice things about teaching is that you get the holidays off that the kids get off, so we had a really nice break in our big house for Coulter's first Christmas. I was thinking hard that winter about what I would do for a career. Matt had gone back to school in Missouri at the same time we moved to Yuma, since the oil patch was not really his thing as his true love was hard-rock geology. I had been through the Uranium exploration crash and now the oil boom bust. With a little family, I was needing a more stable career and being a part-time farm hand would not cut it.

The joke was "Do you know which company has the best oil exploration department?"

"The shoe department at Penny's".

I had plenty of time to do a little soul-searching with Coulter while René was teaching English at the high school. Coulter and I would talk about it and explore our options during the day, and I could discuss it in more detail in the evenings when René was home. I considered opening a gym, first here in Yuma, but I realized that that the farmers would not be likely to go to the gym after a hard day working, although I continued working out while I was working for the Koenigs. But that was me, and I'm not like most other people. Then I thought about opening one in Ft Collins, but it was just too much of a gamble and I abandoned the idea, but not after I had spent quite a bit of time researching gym equipment. Home computers were not a thing yet, so I had ordered catalogs from Nautilus, Universal Equipment and others to see what was available and get an idea of the cost.

Hey, speaking of computers, perhaps I should get in on the new computer craze. Large mainframes were being used by the Fortune 500 companies and I was pretty sure that they would be a key part of any geologic exploration department. Then I could combine my experience and knowledge of geology with software development, writing computer programs for oil and mining companies. The big problem with this idea was that I did not have any programming skills. I had taken that Fortran class back in college and I did not like it with the old hardware, but now people were using green-screen monitors hooked up to mainframes and it was a much more appealing prospect. This meant that I would need to go back to school to get a Computer Science degree. There were a lot of out of work Geologists and I would need an edge. The problem was that I was now 30 years old, but this seemed like a little detail since I was barely working now. I knew René did not want to be a career HS English teacher, in fact she did not want to teach much longer anyway and this would be good for her as well. I applied to CSU again, but this time to the Computer Science department and waited to hear from them.

I was learning to use the Centaur C-1 kayak and switched from running rivers in my Explorer open canoe to the C-1. By this time, I had already paddled over 40 whitewater river runs in the open canoe, all of them solo, except the two overnight runs on the Delores River. I did runs on the Poudre River, some with friends from town and most with friends that I met through the RMCC (Rocky Mountain Canoe Club). I had been practicing my roll in the Ft Collins pool when I was there, and had it down pretty solid before I ventured out onto a river. On my first run, I was kneeling in the Centaur, strapped in with the thigh straps tight on my upper thighs to hold me in tight with my sprayskirt against my stomach under my life jacket. I was sitting in an eddy watching the other boaters and turned as they paddled past and flipped over. I hit the cold water, water flushed up my nose, I was disoriented and before I knew what I was doing, I pulled the strap on my sprayskirt and wet exited the boat. I was still in the relatively calm eddy and had all my gear and learned an important boating lesson to keep your wits about you when it seems like shit is hitting the fan, because your skills can keep an uncomfortable situation from becoming a bad situation. In this case I dumped the water out of my boat and climbed back in. The funny thing is that the main reason I went from a canoe to a C-1 kayak was to have a dry boat at the bottom of a rapid and not need to pull over to the side and dump water out of my boat every time. I ended up getting accustomed to the lack of initial stability in this boat, which is what caused me to capsize in the first place, and use my strong canoeing brace to keep upright. I got better fast, as I already knew all the canoeing strokes that I would need from my years paddling whitewater in my open canoe.

This year I really upped my game, from paddling the Poudre River on the Bridges run, the upper and lower Mishawaka runs and the upper river from Rustic to Kelly Flats Campground above the narrows. I rarely missed my roll since the C-1 canoe roll is extremely strong and powerful with the leverage gained from a kneeling position. This gave me confidence to paddle the

Arkansas River where I started on Browns canyon several times. In fact, on my second run, I flipped over in the middle of the first big rapid called Zoom Flume and did my first real combat roll! There was a photographer there and I stopped by the photo shop in Buena Vista and purchased a picture of me just completing the roll with water dripping from my mustache. I also did the milk run with the RMCC, the Texas Creek run with a couple friends and finally capped the season in August doing the Royal gorge at 800 CFS with some of the other strong boaters in the RMCC which is where I met my friend Don Clark that became a key member of my crew for decades.

That summer, I got the letter that I had been accepted into the Computer Science department! I had been accepted with a caveat; the CS department was full, so I was accepted into the mathematics department. The acceptance letter also said that at the end of my first semester I could apply to transfer from the Math department into the CS department and they would accept only three transfers, those with the highest GPAs. That meant that I would need to get straight A's that first semester. Nothing like a challenge and of course I accepted. Good news, our plan was starting to fall into place. René and I discussed our current living situation and we decided that she would teach for her second year at Yuma High School. I would find some cheap living accommodations in Ft Collins

In September, just a year after we had moved to Yuma, I rented a room from a young couple that were in graduate School at CSU and needed some extra income. It had a bed and a desk in a wing just off of the main house, so they would not see me too much, just when I would microwave up something for dinner. It was also good since it was quiet, it did not have a TV for a distraction and I really had nothing else to do there but study. The mathematics requirements for Computer Science were almost as much as a Mathematics major would need to take. Linear Algebra, discrete mathematics, 2 more semesters of calculus and a semester or two of differential equations. It was starting to make sense why I was accepted into the mathematics department. I was living like a traveling salesman, going to classes and studying at night, then driving the three hours to Yuma every Friday afternoon and spending the weekends with René and Coulter. We were already semi-used to this schedule from my days as a Mudlogger when I would be away at the oil rigs, but that really did not make it any easier. I put a lot of miles on my little Toyota pickup commuting to home and back. It was just part of the plan for a better life for us. That Fall, while I was in the middle of my first semester back at school, we found out that René was pregnant again. She was getting weary of teaching, she did not want to have the baby in Yuma, so we decided that she would move back to Ft Collins with me. I managed to get us living accommodations in Married Student housing just a couple of blocks off campus and over Christmas break we moved. When we first got the keys to our apartment, we opened the door and there was a hall in front and a kitchen off to the side. We walked down the wide hallway and realized that it did not go anywhere; it was the living room! We were used to the casket sales room of the mortuary as our huge living room and this had not much more room than a couch would fit in. There were 2 bedrooms upstairs and we would be able to make due here until graduation. At least moving in was going to be very easy.

Spring 1986 School & Cori born
Life was about to get easier and more relaxing for the three of us. René would not have to teach and could take care of Coulter mostly by herself. Coulter would have both his parents together and with him every day, not just on the weekends, at least for me. I would no longer need to commute to Yuma on the weekends and could spent that time studying and hanging with the family. We would have another child this spring but two kids would not be much different than one; little did we know! I was also accepted into the Computer Science Department after the grades were in from my last semester. My hard work had paid off! It was only later that I discovered that only three of us had applied to transfer into the Computer Science department!

I continued with the mathematics classes with more CS classes sprinkled in, spending lots of time working in the Computer Lab on my programming assignments, working at home on my math problems, working out in the weight room at the Moby Gym and climbing and kayaking to blow off steam.

Halfway through the semester René gave me an ultimatum, "Between going to school, working in the computer lab, rock climbing, kayaking and me, something has to give!"

I thought about it and knew that she had a good point and told her that I would give up rock climbing. I did love the fun times my brothers and I had climbing and cherished those memories. Kayaking and canoeing were nearer and dearer to my heart and I knew that I could be a much better boater that I would ever be a climber. I never really climbed again after that, but it was not a loss as I had so many other activities to fill the void.

On May 8th, just a week before finals, René went into labor and we went back to the Poudre Valley Hospital where Colt was born. We had not done the Lamaze classes this time around, since we both remembered the breathing techniques. The labor and delivery, although long and painful was smoother the second time around with a lot of "He, he, he, hos". I was standing right next to her during the delivery and she was breathing and concentrating hard on my belt buckle, which was a rock climber with an ice axe climbing a cliff, molded in 3-d bronze. When Cori was born, she was delivered into the doctor's hands and I looked over and was a little shocked at how different she looked than Coulter. Cori was bright red, angry and screaming like an alien from another scary planet. I was immediately in love with her! I never took my eyes off of her, following her into the incubator room, watching them put the wrist band on her with her name, Corrine Marie Bidwell. Then I could relax a bit more, knowing that my beautiful baby could not be mixed up with another in the hospital. I did not trust anyone not to make a mix-up. We sure were lucky to have 2 very healthy children! I helped out as much as I could for the next two weeks, although I was quite busy studying for finals the next week and then taking my exams the following week.

Summer 1986

I was signed up to take Discrete Mathematics and a scientific Fortran class in summer school. I attended for a couple of weeks when I got mononucleosis and had to drop out of classes to rest and help out for a month with the kids as I was recovering. I was surprised that I caught Mono, as I had it as a child, along with the other typical childhood diseases in the 60's, chicken pox, mumps, measles and German measles, all of which I contracted.

Matt had started working on his Geology PHD in Laramie and would come down occasionally later that summer to go kayaking with me and my Ft Collins paddling friends on the Poudre River. René would go to visit her folks in Scottsbluff and go to dog shows. I went to a lot of these dog shows, especially when it was not boating season and knew the names and conformation standards for all of the registered AKC dog breeds. On Labor Day, after registering for classes and attending a Computer Lab Operators meeting, I took Julie to Stapleton airport after her late summer visit with us. Fall '86 semester was just starting. The next weekend I took my last paddling trip of the season going to Westwater Canyon for a couple of days of boating with my good friends Mike and Terry. We took Terry's old Scout II and the alternator fell off in Glenwood Springs. Being boaters, we had a lot of cam straps and rope which we used to tie it back into place on the engine, not getting to our campsite till 1:30am where we slept outside during a beautiful starry night that we don't get to see in Ft. Collins. We had a great day of boating in the hot Utah desert, catching rides back to our car with rafters that we hooked up with at the take-out. On Sunday, we had a long day paddling, since we were surfing and playing on the water so much and ended up getting back home at 2:30 the next morning!

Fall 1986

The University had purchased a private student housing building and converted it into the computer Science department, just a block North of campus across from Laurel Street. I now had a job working in the computer lab, sitting at a desk right by the front door to the main computer lab on the third floor, which was a room with terminals into the school's mainframes, plus quite a few stand-along computers, basically pre-PCs with 8" floppy disks with Borland Turbo-Pascal running on them for writing programs. Most of the classes were taught in Pascal. I had scanned the Denver Post classified job listings and seen that what companies were looking for mostly were C programmers that knew the Unix operating system. The Computer Science department had close ties to Hewlett-Packard which had a large factory in neighboring Loveland and had donated all the HP terminals that we used in the lab and a few of the main-frame computers which we did our assignments on. They were running the HP-UX operating system which was basically Unix. I decided before I took a single programming class that I would do all my programs in all my classes in the C programming language and NOT in the Pascal teaching language, since the companies were looking for C programmers. Other than my first introduction to programming class that was in Pascal, I did all my assignments for all my classes in the C programming language. The professors would always warn me that any template code that they would give out would be in Pascal and I would be at a disadvantage. I agreed to this limitation. It turned out that all the professors ever gave out was pseudo-code. This is a language-agnostic overview of the algorithm that they wanted us to write, so I was never at a disadvantage. I was always a bit paranoid that there would be large amounts of Pascal that would be given to us students, so I was always working on my programs immediately, never putting them off in case I would need to catchup. This helped me in several other ways as well. Many of the students that were studying in the lab and writing programs that had been assigned by the professors were in my classes. They would be working on an assignment and ask me if I had started on it. Usually, I would tell them that I had already finished the assignment, like I was some sort of frigging computer whiz, but the truth is that I just wanted to be ahead of the curve. They would ask me questions about the assignment and would often ask to see my code. Well, this was a no-no, but I could agree and show them my C code and they would look at it like it was some foreign language that they did not understand and they would just walk away since it was of no help to them. I may have had to cram at the last minute for a mid-term or a final, but I rarely was one of those kids in the lab furiously trying to finish their programming assignments.

The campus was truly integrated with international students. René and I were walking around the loop with Cori in a stroller when a Saudi woman came walking down the sidewalk towards us.

As she approached, Coulter stopped and looked at her in amazement, pointed at her and yelled as us, "What is that animal! What is that animal!"

She had on a full burka outfit with even her eyes covered in slightly lighter fabric. She just walked by without missing a beat and I hoped she was a non-English speaking spouse of her student husband.

On Christmas break we had realized that having two kids is not just the same amount of work as one, but was literally more than twice the work as they both want attention and Cori was too small to entertain Coulter, although she already knew how to get under his skin. We decided that we need a more permanent solution to birth control and I decided to get a vasectomy.

My friend Mike asked me "Are you sure? What if something happened and you wanted to get married again and the woman wanted kids"

I replied, "If that was ever the case, she had better already have her own kids; Plus, I am happily married to René."

It was described as just a little snip, snip in the doctor's office and then on home, no big deal. When the day came, we went to the office and René stayed in the waiting room while I went back to get my balls shaved, then was numbed up with a shot to each testicle! No one told me about that part! The doctor made a little cut and tied off each of the vas deferent tubes, then sewed me up and we were done. I walked out to the waiting room, just a bit pale, smiled weakly to René and walked to the counter to check out. As I was standing there, the whole world went black and I was completely out for 5 seconds or so, enough that the woman at the desk asked if I was OK. That was the second time in my life that I almost fainted, I don't know how I remained standing, other than I had my hands supporting myself on the counter. As fate would have it, Dad called that evening and asked me how things were going. I told him that I had just had a vasectomy that very day. The phone was very quiet for a few moments and Dad asked me how school was going. That was the only conversation we had about the subject although I was a bit curious of how his experience compared to mine and I never managed to steer the conversation back. I was pretty fragile for the next couple of days, and right as I was feeling better, René drove us to the market and when I was getting into the car, my balls swung down and hit the seat as I was getting in and put me right back into fragile mode.

Spring 1987 Graduation

During my final Spring semester, I started interviewing with companies such as Hughes, Auto-trol and others, including visits to the actual companies if they were interested after the initial interview. I was preparing for life after graduation. I stayed up late many nights studying and finishing up programming assignments, often staying in the computer lab after hours to work in the dark and quiet, sometimes sleeping on the floor under my computer desk in the lab.

Over Spring break, René took the kids to her folk's house for a week and I went on a kayaking trip with my friends Mike & Rick to New Mexico to paddle the Taos Box, the Gila Box and the Salt River Canyon. I had pulled an all-nighter the night before, finishing a tough programming assignment, so I was a bit tired as the three of us piled into my little Pickup and headed south for a week of paddling. I climbed into the back of my little truck in Denver and slept all the way to our camp spot next to the Rio Grande River. When we got back from our spring break kayaking trip, I drove to Kimball, NE to escort René and the kids home in the snow.

The kids were starting to interact more with each other and were fun to be around. Coulter, when he was mad would say "Ever, ever, ever, ever". On March 23rd, a few days after we got back to our apartment, Cori started really crawling. She and Coulter would sit and "Pfff..." To each other in their secret language. Coulter's favorite movies are Little Kids and Mary Poppins. Cori's favorite is the Singing Bears. A week later Cori climbed her first stair step. Coulter would take me upstairs to hunt for lions, tigers, bears and gators. I started reading to him and his sister at night. Sometimes I would sleep with Coulter since Cori would be up for half the night, she was so different than her brother that way. By early April, Cori can walk while holding hands.

Coulter says "No!"

Cori says "Dyaa!"

Coulter then says "No!", etc...

Cori has a great time and Coulter gets angry. "No! Dyaa, no, dyaa, ..."

Coulter had become friends with Katrina, a little girl his age who lived in a little married student apartment just across from ours. In mid-April, he had learned to peddle his trike with help from his mom. There was a large sidewalk that circled around the inside of all the married student housing buildings that was perfect for the two of them. He and Katrina would tear around in their plastic Big Wheel trikes. At this same time Cori has 3 teeth and a couple more coming in. By now, Coulter's favorite movie is Merlin, the animated sword in the stone story.

He would also lay down pretending to be helpless and yell, "Lassie, save me!".

He calls a tummy ache a tummy egg. On May 4th, the adventurous Cori climbed to the top of the stairs with no help from anyone. When Coulter goes to bed, he says to keep the door quite cracked.

I graduated on May 16th, at 31 years of age, a Saturday, with René's parents and my mom in attendance. We celebrated on Sunday and I started work the next day at Auto-trol Technology in Broomfield as a Software Engineer.

It is dedication how you worked to become a better boater... - Dad

33 Staycation - Oct 17, 2020 - Back to the Present

Mona and I were planning a trip to Grey Reef up on the North Platte just 40 minutes upstream of Casper. As the time for our vacation got closer, we checked the weather and it would be in the 40s and windy during the day and well below freezing at night for the week we would be there. We considered our options, considering the Utah desert, southern Colorado and Northern New Mexico and finally settled on going to San Diego, stopping on the way in Phoenix to see Kamari, Yesi and Colt. On Friday, a day before we were leaving, as we were getting ready for vacation while Mona was packing her clothes, she headed downstairs to do some more packing when she fell on the landing of the stairs. I was working in my office downstairs and heard the crash of falling down the stairs and jumped up, heading to the stairs expecting to see Dillon lying there since he sometimes will drop down the last couple with his weak hips and legs (Just like the old grey mare, she ain't what she used to be!), but instead I found Mona lying there and quietly moaning. She did not know if she had injured herself since she was hurting everywhere so I helped her down to the bed and noticed that her left arm seemed a bit off, not normal, bending a little in an unnatural direction. She just wanted to lay there, perhaps take a nap and evaluate herself later, but I insisted that we go to the hospital. After getting some clothes on, since she was basically in Walmart attire being at home and all. I loaded her into the car to take her to urgent care, but on the way down the canyon I changed my mind and decided to take her directly to the St Anthony's Hospital Emergency room for X-rays. I knew from my hip that if we went to the urgent care, the wait would probably be longer than the emergency room, plus they would refer her to the hospital anyway, insisting that she take an ambulance there further wasting several hours. It was the right call as the X-rays showed she had a displaced spiral fracture of her left humorus bone in her upper arm. They cat-scanned her head and neck as she had a bruise over her left eyebrow, then put a compression splint on her upper arm and a wrist sling with a prescription for some Percocet that we filled on the way home. Needless to say, we were not going to San Diego but I was committed to taking a break from work, as I was committed to taking care of Mona, so a week-long Staycation it is! Mona relaxed as best as she could in the living room recliner and I spent the night on the couch keeping ahead of her pain by giving her a Percocet every 4 hours.

The next day we worked on getting Mona's Medicare card and Mona guided me through all the steps of making a tossed salad with romaine lettuce, iceberg lettuce, cherry tomatoes, red onion, fresh baby bella mushroom caps, blue cheese crumbles and homemade Thousand Island dressing with a four-bean salad on the side. I thought that this staycation would be a good indicator of what it would be like if I was to retire and would be at home all the time. So far it looked like I would be making all the meals and cleaning up the kitchen afterwards every day and working was not looking so bad! We binged watched some Trains from Hell and The Bly Hell House. It was a hell of a night!

I had purchased some sweet Bose speakers for the workout room to replace some cheap ones that I had blown several weeks earlier. I did my first workout with the music blasting as loud as I could take it and it was a spectacular weight-lifting experience dancing around between sets and being pumped up from the music. This staycation was looking up. Later, Mona setup in the mezzanine while I was shooting several sets of pool in the adjacent Coyote Beach Lounge. On my last game, playing 8-ball where the final ball needs to be a bank shot, I had the cue ball on the rail behind the 8-ball, meaning that I had to shoot to the opposite rail with a hard spin to the left so the cue would arc back to the 8-ball. The shot was perfect and the 8-ball sunk for my final shot of the day. Vacation was looking good.

On Monday, I cooked us up a 4-egg, 4-cheese ham & cheese omelet with toasted, buttered English Muffins, the first time I had ever made us breakfast other than Honey Nut Cheerios with sliced bananas, hand crushed walnuts and lots of sweet blueberries. We spent the rest of the day lounging around doing mostly nothing other than taking care of Red. She had been giving him antibiotics with an eye dropper, but since she broke her arm, I had been giving him water the same way. He is 15 years old, based on getting him in 2005, but he was full grown already and could actually be a year or two older than that. He has lost a lot of weight and finally this morning I had searched the house for him and finally found him sleeping in the litter box where he had just run out of energy after doing his business. He was resting comfortably on the rug in the bathroom but is just fur and bones so we have been helping him eat and drink.

Dillon and I went on several hikes to help him with his leg strength and make sure that when he leaves a trail of poop, it is outside and not in the house.

We went in to see the orthopedic surgeon and ended up seeing his assistant that took X-rays and her arm still looked the same. Our options are to just leave her arm in the plastic and Velcro compression sleeve with her wrist resting in the splint and let the bones find each other and heal up. The other option is to get the bones pinned together and have them heal perfectly straight. They said that for these types of fractures the treatment is about 50/50 either way. Mona is leaning towards natural healing, but we have 10 days to change our minds. I heated up some lobster bisque for us before we binged a couple of movies until after midnight again before heading to our respective recliner and couch. The doctor's assistant did tell us that smoking, even a quarter pack of cigarettes a day would slow down the normal healing process of 10-12 weeks.

The next day, we worked on social security, surfed the net and I spent the morning watching videos on tying the leader to the tippet with a Surgeons knot and tying a fly onto the tippet with a Clinch knot. I had been using my own made-up knots since I was a kid and decided to start using proven knots especially since on our last vacation, I had tied my tippet onto my leader with a knot that put a kink in my line and was really messing up my casting. After a couple of hours, I had the knots down, with some helpful kibitzing from Mona when I was getting frustrated and was about ready to quit.

I rigged up Dad's old carbon-fiber Quiet-Sport 7.5' rod in the living room with the little Orvis Battenkill II reel to try both out. I hopped in the truck after disconnecting it from the trailer since it was still in camping mode and headed down below the house to do some fishing. I went up to the wild loop around tunnel #6 and spent an hour throwing a brown dry fly from one of dad's old fly boxes into the river. At the pool just below Double-knife rapid, a class 4+ drop that I had kayaked many times, I floated my fly into a seam at the head of the eddy and immediately hooked and landed a nice little 9 1/2" brownie. I had left my phone in the car so no picture, I just released him back into the water after pulling out the fly that he had mangled. Walking back down the creek to my truck I put my still rigged rod in the back and drove up through the tunnel and to the bottom of another little waterfall called Beaver Drop #2, again a fun kayaking rapid. There I worked my way up the long pool, this time with a wet fly with a little gold head. I was not having any luck, but saw a little 4' wide eddy just across the pool and after several casts, managed to land the little fly in the center of that eddy and my fly was hit hard after just a second or two. I played the fish for about 40 seconds with her running up and across the pool, but never jumping and on my second try got her into the net. A very nice and plump brown trout just under a foot long at 11.5 inches. I took a quick picture of her and let her go back into the pool so that I could perhaps catch her again next year when she was a little bigger.

Mona is excited about learning how to fly fish. She is already an accomplished spinning rod fisherwoman!

At the end of the picture book that I published on our San Juan Boondocking camping trip a month ago, I was wondering how the fish in Clear Creek stacked up to the fish from this last vacation up on Cebolla and Henson creeks as well as the Arkansas River. The consensus is that nothing beats the beauty of the Henson Brookies, but this nice brown on my home stretch of Clear Creek was bigger than any I caught up on the other three creeks and was similar-looking to the nice browns we caught on Cebolla creek. You cannot beat the spots on the Arkansas River Browns however. They are all fun to catch and the ones on Clear Creek have the definite advantage of being just 10 minutes away, as well as a little size advantage! Beauty vs size. I think that beauty wins! If that book had an addendum or a postscript, this would be it.

When I got back from fishing, Mona was relaxing in her recliner, feeling pretty good and in no pain although I know she felt bad for changing our vacation plans. I told her that this staycation was the best vacation I had ever had! I really meant it in the moment since it was all about how good I was feeling, not about what exotic locales and exciting adventures we were having. I still have a few more little adventures in mind for the 2nd half of our staycation. Not only that, but I have 2 six-packs of my favorite craft-beer IPAs and I don't have to share them with anybody, not even Mona since she is on pain killers. Life is good.

Mona says that "Sometimes life kicks you in the ass, but it is good."

On Wednesday, we relaxed in the living room for most of the morning, reading, talking and drinking a pot of coffee. I made us grilled ham & cheese sandwiches on the Foreman Grill before heading up to Idaho Springs to get some wood pellets for our stove and some Coke since Mona wanted something fizzy. I went to the Clear Creek Outdoors fly shop and picked up some fishing supplies as well as a cool beaded fishing necklace for Mona which has a retractable line cutter, fly pad, tippet spool holder, an alligator clip and a couple of swivels that hang from the necklace. After cleaning up the kitchen I headed back up Clear Creek to drop a line in the river across from the 2 Bears Tap House, owned and run by some friends of ours. I fished a pretty dry fly for a while, but the fish were not feeding on the surface so I switched to a wet fly and put a foam strike indicator on the end of my leader, something I had never used before. I fished with this setup for about 10 minutes with no action before my tippet got so tangled up in the strike indicator that I had to cut off all my tippet. I pulled off the foam indicator from the tail end of my leader and then spent 5 minutes getting the glue off my leader with my fingernail. That test was a failure and I am not a fan of these temporary foam indicators. I'm working on fishing wet flies and nymphs, something I've not done much of in the past.

I sat down and cut off several feet of tippet from the spool, tying it on my leader, then tied on a little beaded nymph fly. I walked down the river a quarter mile to a spot across the road from the rock quarry and not far above the Beaver Drop #1 kayak rapid and threw in that fly for about 15 minutes with no strikes. I saw a little eddy across the river about 20 yards away and worked my line out until I could see the backing in my reel, trying to get the fly across the river. That is when I got a good strong strike and

I set the hook, playing him across the river to my side. I almost lost the fish trying to get him into the net as I was in the river on a little rock and missed him twice before netting him. This was the first rainbow I had caught, so I have a trifecta of trout this fall between these two vacations.

I may have to go up towards the headwaters of Clear Creek to catch a brook trout also making the trifecta in my local home river. I am extremely fortunate to be able to be out fishing in 10 minutes on a beautiful river, in fact the same river that is in the print I sent to Dad and Robin this summer of Dad fishing the last time he visited us.

The stretch of water directly below our house is called the "Golden Mile" for the numerous trout spawning pools and excellent fishing. It has become my training ground for fly fishing. I'll save the spinners for lakes and ocean fishing, something I would like to do in my ocean-going fishing kayak, probably when I retire someday, perhaps a year from January. That is the current plan anyway.

Like on our last vacation, our Clear Creek neighbors had come out to greet me at the end of a friendly line.

I've always really been just a dry fly fisherman, but these wet flies are mostly what they are going for this late in the season. This staycation is also a fishing vacation, even if I'm only getting out for a couple of hours in the afternoon. I do have two more days to explore the creek for some more fish before the weather drops below freezing this weekend.

On the last Saturday of my Staycation, it was a bit warmer and I met Matt across from the gravel quarry to do a little fly fishing together. We compared trucks, as we had modified both of our trucks to be better off-road for Boondock camping and overlanding. I showed him the little 3-weight rod that I've been using on the creek. We gave each other fly fishing tips. His was to double back your line to keep the leader from going into the rod-tip Ferrell when hiking, to make subsequent casts easier. I gave him a tip about using a Clinch knot to tie a fly onto the end of your tippet using hemostats.

We climbed down to the pool above Beaver #1 with no luck, we then climbed to the pool below Beaver #2, again with no luck.

We decided to go up to the highway bridge and fish in the big hole below the East-bound Lane of the highway with no luck. On our way back to the truck, I jumped down to fish the pool below the West-bound Lane and Matt was watching from above when he quietly said "There's a big fish just two feet above the aspen leaf floating in the pool". I cast there with no strike and after that I saw the fish and did perhaps a dozen casts for it and he never chased the fly. Matt tried and I fished the other side of the bridge and we had no luck. Not the loveliest place to fish anyway. We then went to the big climbing area between tunnels 5 & 6. We fished our way down to the undercut pool below the main climbing face across the river and Matt caught a pretty little Brown trout. Finally… That turned out to be the only fish of the day.

Matt texted me a couple of days after our fishing excursion and we compared Prescription meds that Dr. Tanaka, the physician that we both use, had prescribed for us. The doc was putting him on BP Meds and I'm already on Cholesterol meds so we agreed that between the two of us we have the drug thing covered.

This made me think about my last checkup, which was a video call with Dr Tanaka, we started off the virtual exam with a little discussion of what I was doing to keep in shape. He was impressed with the weights that I was lifting at the gym, especially for an old guy like me. For a doctor he did not seem to know much about old-man-strength. We then talked about cardio and he did not believe that I had hiked my trail at least 2-3 times a week. He believed that I hiked often, just not so much, since I think most of his patients exaggerate how much exercise they do. I pulled out my iPhone health app and showed him the total flights of stairs I've climbs in the last 12 months which was 68,000 feet of vertical, more than 2 Everest climbs from sea level. That averages out to just over 3 hikes a week on my mile round-trip, 400' climb on the Dillon Trail. He told me that that trail would be a lot easier to hike at 175 lbs. after losing 10 pounds. At 5'11" and 185 lbs., I'm near the top of the healthy range for my BMI, but I agreed with him that it would be a good goal. He kept me on my cholesterol medication, probably for two reasons.

One, he cannot take and test a blood sample virtually and secondly and probably the biggest reason was on my last visit, I told him, "My cholesterol might be up a bit because I have a new girlfriend... and she loves bacon!"

Yes, I threw Mona under the bus for this exam.

At the end of the exam, I told him, "You know what I like best about these virtual physical exams?".

What?" he replied.

"The fact that you don't get to stick your finger up my butt at the end!"

After a good laugh together, the exam was over with a promise that I would monitor my BP.

During the week, I was working and helping Mona with tasks that are difficult with one hand. Mona was helping me with things like making tacos and salads. She would pull out two types of lettuce, tomatoes, avocado, onion, green pepper, artichoke hearts, three-bean salad and other veggies secreted away in the fridge and lay them out for me to chop up. Eventually it would turn into something that we could eat. When I look in the kitchen, there is almost nothing other than chips, crackers and nuts that I can munch on quickly. There is nothing that is just heat and eat. I'm looking in the cupboards, pantry and fridge, like I'm searching for a climber in a blizzard on Everest that I really have no hope of spotting, no exaggeration (I just finished reading Into Thin Air). There is nothing that does not require some serious mentoring from Mona to make something edible. No frozen pizzas, burritos, pre-made salads and other things I used to stock the kitchen, pre-Mona. In other words, all we have in the kitchen is ingredients. After dinner, Mona came walking up to me with her arm outstretched with her sippy-cup (suck-jug) in her right hand.

I had just cracked open a Coors light and as I was walking by, I toasted her mug with my can and headed into the living room when she said "Hey".

I turned around and she had just wanted me to unscrew the top of her mug so she could fill it with ice-water.

I hike the trail with Dillon after I'm done with work most days. These days now that he is older, about half the time he starts down the trail and turns around after the first switchback. Sometimes it is because the heat of the direct sun is too much for him, sometimes because Mona is cooking and he wants to be there, but mostly, these days it is because he is testing what support his hind-quarters will give him on this day. Today he was game for going on a hike to the bottom. We stopped on the way at Prayer Rock to say "Hi" to Red that I had buried under a huge Juniper after Mona and I had written our goodbyes on the burial box to him.

The best kitty cat I ever knew. Thanks for all the love and companionship. Thanks for all the mice. -Love Christopher

Goodbye "Red-headed coon hound". We had so many great conversations! :) I will miss you so much. - Love always Mona

Red had passed away peacefully on the rug in the upstairs bathroom where he had been mostly for the last 2 weeks. We have trapped 3 mice in the last few weeks as Red has been out of commission since we got back from our last Southern Colorado boondocking vacation.

Dillon and I also hiked past the 14 little Ponderosa pines that I had rescued from the edge of Coyote Spur. I actually had planted them several weeks before, hiking down several times a week with two large watering cans. Since then, all but two had died and on this day with Dillon they were all dead. So much for saving them! I think I may try later this fall when it looks like snow and transplant some Douglas firs that are also in danger from the snow plow since they are just at the edge of the Road. My neighbor Kerry had told me that they are a little more drought-resistant and hardy.

My friend Mike came over one evening this week with his brother-in-law Bill to talk and shoot some 8-ball. Bill was going in for hip-replacement surgery soon and wanted to talk to me about it. We ended up talking for almost two hours while drinking our IPAs and talking about all kinds of things including the hip surgery. He had been apprehensive about it and Mike thought that talking to me would be good for him since I'm now actively kayaking, hiking, riding motorcycles, fishing and doing heavy yard work. It really has not slowed me down and I think I made him feel better. We shot pool then for another couple of hours with the world series on the TV in the background, but listening to some blues and rock & roll music, dancing around between shots telling each other stories, discussing work and this weird world lately. Mona brought down a tray of munchies that we set on the bar before she retreated back upstairs so we could have our guy-talk. Eventually Bill had to go back home to Arvada. Mike and I then broke out the Rye whiskey and made a couple of old-fashions, shot some pool while cranking some Ziggy Stardust and talking about girls until 1:00 in the morning. My Philosophy on Billiards is that it is not only a fun game to play, but is more of a social thing since we listen to music and talk the entire time. A one-hour conversation will turn into a three-hour conversation with the distraction of the game and the discussions get much deeper and more meaningful.

Staycation has been gone for a week, and this weekend, Saturday turned into a warmer-than-forecast day so after lunch I headed out for a couple of hours of fishing. It's funny that I've lived here for over 11 years and this is the first time that I've gotten serious about fishing (mostly since for the last 35 years, whitewater kayaking has taken precedence over fishing). It really started because I want to perfect my casting, practice my knots and up my fishing game a bit. What better place than a river, and a river 5 minutes from home no less. Then I started catching fish, on both dry flies and nymphs alike and practice now feels like just fishing.

I parked my truck on the side of the road, just above tunnel 6, loaded up with my rod, a Nano-puff windbreaker, fishing pack and rod and headed down river past the rock-climbing area where there were 3 or 4 groups of people top-roping along the cliff. As I passed a guy in pajamas standing next to his girlfriend I said "I like your outfit!" and we all chuckled briefly as I continued on. I was up here a week ago and hooked a brown just upstream. On that day, I was fishing a dry fly on the surface, but was having no luck. Then on one of my casts I cast just into the current going into the pool. A little crease in the current as it entered the pool pulled my dry fly underwater and I immediately got a strike. I realized then that the only reason he took the fly, was that it was underwater and that is where they were feeding. After that catch last weekend, I took off the dry fly and put on a little gold-beaded Copper John nymph and have been fishing with that ever since. I worked up to a pool not far below the climbing area and hooked a nice Brown trout that put up a pretty good fight on my light tackle until I got him into my net. I'm getting good at netting them, getting a picture of them, pulling the fly off their lip, swishing them in the water with my hand before they slowly swim off or dart off depending on the attitude of the fish.

I continued walking down the old railroad grade on this wild part of the river, since Hwy 6 now goes through a long curving tunnel, leaving this stretch quiet and wild. I stopped for a bit to watch a Red Tail hawk flying across the river with his shadow on the huge cliffs like he was a pair of birds, eventually circling around and landing in the middle of a large pine. I stopped at an open area next to the water to practice casting my fly across the water over and over to try to get to the back of an eddy behind a rock towards the other side of the creek. I hit with my fly in the current to the left, to the slack water to the right, to the front of the eddy, on the rock behind the eddy and even the middle of the eddy. I finally got the fly to drop exactly where I wanted it to be and involuntarily let out a little "Yes". By this time with all the practicing, I had scared any fish out of the eddy, but it is important to hit the eddy in the perfect spot, especially if it is across the river. When the little nymph hits the slack water, there is only a second or two when a trout can see the fly and dart up and grab it. After that, the current will yank that part of the line in the middle of the current, pulling the fly quickly out of the eddy and into the current. I suppose that if a fish grabs the fly like that, the line itself will set the hook without needing any help from me. I think this has happened when I feel a fish on the line and I never set the hook.

I caught a second smaller brown at the apex of the Tunnel 6 trail. I'm starting to get a feel for where to cast the nymphs for the best luck. Typically, into the fold of current going into a pool that will pull the fly down just to where they lay waiting for things like my nymph. I'm still not used to fishing nymphs and get surprised when I feel a tug thinking I'm hitting a rock on the bottom and tug my line so it won't get stuck. This is fortunate since it happened on both fish today and I ended up setting the hook into their lip both times. This last fish grabbed the nymph in the ripply runout from the pool where I was surprised to get a hit. I really thought that I let it float too far down past the pool into the shallower water and hooked on a rock, but the tug to get my fly off the rock, hooked the fish and being smaller, was just as long of a fight since I needed to work her upstream into the pool and my net. I guess there are some carry-overs to fly fishing from fishing treble-hooked panther martins which will hook on the bottom. It is interesting today, since not long after unhooking each fish, I lost the fly I had caught them with just casting into the river. I think perhaps their sharp little teeth had weakened my tippet line. I'm tying the fly on with a clinch knot, one of the strongest so I don't think that is it.

I had switched out ball caps from last weekend's fishing since the weight of the flip-up magnifier that attaches to the brim of my hat was pulling the hat off my head. This magnifier was another tip from Matt to help get the fine tippet line through the eyelet of the tiny #14 flies I'm using. I was wearing a bigger cap today which fit my large head better but I had not noticed that it had a smaller bill. I did not realize that the bill on the ballcaps was not a standard size and I could not flip my magnifier inward into the brim under the bill like my previous hat. Instead, I had to push it out forward, obscuring my upward vision a bit and looking a bit goofy since it stuck out in front of the bill. We have to look serious you know! Towards the end of my fishing, while I was working my way upstream back to the truck, I noticed that my lips and sometimes my cheek were getting hot. I figured my lips were just chapped and my cheeks were getting warm from the afternoon sun. I finally realized that I was burning my lips with the magnifying glass hanging over the hat! Time to look for a third hat that fits my head and has a longer brim. I suppose I could start fishing with my felt cowboy hat, boy howdy.

When I was passing the climbing area, I smiled at the woman with the pajamas guy and she asked me if I caught any. I replied truthfully, "A couple."

In these days of COVID and all, some conversations are brief, ha-ha. This reminded me of when Mona and I drove our rig to a parking lot at the end of a dirt road on the Arkansas River while looking for a camping spot. As we pulled in, a surly looking older local was walking up with his fishing gear from the river. I had my window down and asked him if he had any luck.

He grunted "Yeah", and I could totally tell from his look and attitude that he had been skunked and he was not going to let on in front of some stupid "Front Ranger".

Fishermen lie about more than just the size of a fish!

I was out today for 2 hours, caught 2 fish, talked (outside) to two people. Not bad for these COVID times. I did not see another fisherman today, just lots of climbers social distancing way up on the rock faces above me.

I took an edible when I got back, just cause it's Saturday night and I wanted my creative brain to come out. I was looking for my favorite pair of sketchers. I was in socks since I just took my hiking boots off and remembered I had left them in the passenger seat floor of the Tundra. I walked out, limping around in my thin socks on the rough pavement, unlocked the truck on the driver's side since there is no key on the passenger side. This is weird since I used to be such a gentleman with Mona, opening the car door when she got in or out. I never carry the remote with me since I'm a minimalist when it comes to stuff in my pockets and a single key per car seems like enough. With my old truck, I would walk her to the passenger door, unlock it with my key and open it for her. Now I walk over to the passenger door in my newer Tundra, I realize that I cannot open it on this side so I have to go around and then about half the time I just hop in and hit the unlock button on my door. Not very gentlemanly of me! Well anyway, I opened the passenger door, got my sketchers out and stood there looking back at the house and not wanting to walk back in my thin socks. That's when I realized that the edible had kicked in and also that I was holding a pair of shoes in my hands. I put on the Sketchers and got my keys out of the other side of the truck and went back to the house.

That evening, just at midnight, I went out back on our "infinity patio" overlooking the canyon for my ritual of howling at the full moon. This was a special full moon, not just because it fell on Halloween, which has not happened for the last 76 years! It was also a "Blue Moon" meaning that we had two full moons this October. I usually go out back and howl at the full moon, not always at midnight. It takes me about a dozen good long howls before I get the perfect, non-voice cracking smooth howl that I'm looking for. A good howl I can hear reverberate down the canyon, not really an echo, just that the howl continues for a few seconds after I'm done, kind of like holding down the sustaining pedal on a piano after hitting a key. I sometimes wonder what my other canyon-living neighbors think when they hear it, but none of them ever howl back. My friend Mike did mention that he heard a coyote howling last month and I now wonder if it was just me he was hearing. When Dillon was younger, he would sit and howl with me, but now he just looks at me sideways as he wanders off to pee.

It turns out that this fishing story of our staycation is the last story in my series of <u>Stories for Dad</u> that he got to read before he passed away, so this is a special chapter for me.

Beautiful Brown and perfect sunset. Glad Mona is feeling better. Interesting decision on the best approach to healing.
Love Dad and Robin

I never used wet flies and nymphs much. My best fish were caught on bucktails, which the rainbows loved. Dry flies are a reason to be a fly fishman.   I probably would have done a lot better on the Farmington if I had learned to properly handle flies below the surface. There is nothing more interesting than studying the surface waters, fluid dynamics hiding who knows what in that crease.
Dad

Wow! What a treat to read this! I love the detail and am sure your dad loves that you are using his gear. I so enjoyed reading the section on fly fishing in your dad's book. Good healing to Mona.
I tripped and we got a concussion so Bob has taken up my cooking duties, just as you have. Enjoy the IPA!
Love to you and Mona!
-Gussie

Dad's Final Reflections

Bruce Bidwell - 5/20/2019

Consider this an addendum to my book <u>Reflections</u>. This does not contain interesting anecdotes, but rather my attempt to express my inner thoughts on life, living, aging and letting go as life nears an end.

I found pleasure in writing my book, Reflections. Having completed that magnum opus, I realized that I needed to have a continuing project to occupy my time and keep my mind active. I decided to keep writing. With the mistakes in my previous work, I vowed that I would take a more considered approach, to writing such as outlined in William Strunk's, <u>The Elements of Style</u>. The first time I plowed aggressively ahead, heedless of continuity and chronology. When the first draft was finished, this resulted in the need to drastically reorder paragraphs to make sense of the story line. This reordering was only accomplished, because fortunately my son, Christopher, a skilled computer software developer, made himself available at intervals when he could visit from his home in Golden, Colorado. Now I am embarking on the unknown, continuing the exciting work of writing a new work of personal reflection about my life and the act of writing. Experienced authors describe the hard work of writing and the dry periods when you do not achieve marvelous insight. I know that this is bound to happen, but I find such satisfaction and excitement in starting again, that this takes over and gives me energy. I would be perfectly happy to just rest in my arm chair observing life outside my window. But I must push myself to finish this project.

Health issues occupy more and more of my time. They certainly occupy Robin, my wife and personal caregiver. I could not live independently without her help. Robin has meticulously built up my medical file which encompasses several binders with records of my many specialists (approx. 12), Hospitals and urgent care (4). Plus, she has to drive me everywhere. I don't know how a single person can handle this, especially if like me their eyesight is diminishing, and poor hearing garbles many telephone messages. It is imperative to have a friend or loved one to accompany you to the physician's office to help interpret the instructions. I am very fortunate to be able to enjoy a comfortable lifestyle in our cottage. We are also lucky to be surrounded by nature, with wildlife which emerges from the neighboring woods, which are a virtual untracked jungle of state-owned land. Robin has been transfixed for the last weeks by observing the pair of great Blue Herons who occupy a nest high in a tree next to the swamp which is next to Hartmeadow. They have returned for a second season in their old nest. With this introduction, I believe I am ready to start my continuing narrative.

I have been reading Stephen King's <u>On Writing</u>, which is a study by this author of the horrors which we love to fear. He talks about the hard work of writing and says that it helps to write in a comfortable setting, free from distraction. Do not be afraid to start writing, just start!

But then I must have something to write about. This was one of my fears before I got started.
Will I have anything to say. Have I shot my bolt in writing Reflections? Robert Frost in his book <u>Speaking on Campus</u>, said the whole act of writing is learning to have something to say. After the accumulation of ninety years, I must have something worth saying! This accumulation in my mind could be like coming on an attic which is a tangle of junk but hopefully my mind can sort the past thoughts into understandable bits, ready for the written page.
"Reflections" was finished after four proof readings, just in time for a large family gathering cerebrating my 90th and Robin's 80th birthday. I had included the reflections of family members in the book, some mundane and some more dramatic such as cousin Alan Tobie's description of being drafted at the age of nineteen and his account of the Battle of The Bulge. The family celebration brought relatives from around the country. Some had not seen each other for thirty years and some met family members for the first time. Bidwell/Noss, Lockwood / Higgins and Mutter families got to better know each other. This was much more fun than attending a funeral. Robin and I were excited as we distributed copies of <u>Reflections</u> to the family. It was very satisfying when the publisher delivered four cases of books on our porch. I was actually a published author! Now the process of distribution begins. The relatives, and church friends receive copies as well as the local colleges, libraries and historical societies make up a list that will take months to cover. This

gives me added impetus to remain well and strong. It helps to have some immediate goals to strive for and which help to keep me enthusiastic about writing.

Now that people have had time to read my book, their reactions are interesting. Some will comment on certain sections and I am not sure they have read the whole book. As the serious lifetime reader has a better chance of being a good writer, so I prize the critical and perhaps enthusiastic response of such readers to validate what I have written. It helps give me the confidence in their opinion to continue what I have started and that it is indeed worth reading. I have received supportive letters from some of these serious readers and none more so than an E-mail from my son Cristopher. He said that he enjoyed the addendum as being more personal than "Reflections" and that I should continue to write, not worrying about publication. This changes my whole thought process regarding the Addendum. Until his E-mail, I thought that I was wrapping up my writing and ready for Robin to do the editing. I know that I want to continue writing and his message gives me the reason to do so.

About Writing

Stephen King said that the act of writing has the positive effect of not only enriching your life, but that of your readers. This is certainly one reason to keep writing. Atul Gawande, in <u>Writing</u> says "You should not underestimate the power of the act of writing itself". He says that my reflections introduce my thoughts to the larger world. Christopher first asked me to write <u>Reflections</u> in order to preserve the family memories for future generations, but the past is also in my thoughts. It is only a flash in time, back ten generations or so to John Bidwell and the founding of Hartford in 1636. I cannot imagine the stresses that occupied their lives in a new land and how they captured their thoughts in writing or more probably in conversation since paper was very scarce. Christopher concluded his book with this scripture which is a reminder of our temporary life on earth. This gives me incentive to continue to write while I am able.

We are here for only a moment visitors and strangers in the land as our ancestors were before us. Chronicles 29 :15

My memoir, Reflections, takes on a life of its own as I continue to remember things from my past. A memoir is a story of one's own life, while an autobiography is history which requires research. Gore Vidal, selected <u>Palimpsest</u> as the name of his memoir. Palimpsest: discrete archeological layers of a life be excavated like the different levels of old Troy. His memoir which covers only the first thirty-nine years of his life, is over four hundred pages. He writes "A memoir is set off by a thousand associations, often by objects in a certain room." I write in my study, surrounded by my books, which in themselves offer chapters in my life. I have the crimson volumes of Harvard College five-year class reports. There is a brief section of religious books featuring, <u>Man's Religions</u>, by John B. Noss and books by the Reverend Peter Gomes. A book that probably had the most impact on me is <u>The Language of God</u>, by the eminent scientist Francis S. Collins who unraveled the double helix.

Then there is an extensive section on the U.S. Navy highlighted by the autobiography of Admiral Chester Nimitz, a particular hero of mine. Then numerous books on WWII including <u>Citizen Soldiers </u>by Stephen E. Ambrose. My father republished <u>The Colonial History of Hartford</u> and books on Hartford and Connecticut include <u>Connecticut Yankee</u> an autobiography of Governor Wilbur L. Cross, who was a friend of my grandfather Bidwell. Then there is the Kennedy era with the histories written by Arthur M. Schlesinger, Jr. and on to several volumes about FDR and Churchill. I have a few books on fishing, including the beautiful watercolors by James Prosek in his <u>Trout Of The World</u>. There is an extensive section on art and architecture featuring <u>Architecture</u> by Vincent Scully, the longtime dean at Yale. The <u>Hitchcock Chair</u> is a fascinating study of early woodworking manufacturing by the banks of the Farmington River. And then there is a potpourri of books on the West. <u>Up On the River</u> by John Madson. A particularly meaningful book for me is <u>The Meadow</u> by James Galvin, which describes the life in a section of Colorado/Wyoming that I know well defined by the Platte River. These books offer a clue to my interests. I have been doing further reading about what established authors have to say about writing. Anna Quindlen, in <u>How Reading Changed My Life</u> said "Books are the greatest purveyor of the truth." and that books are the pathway to the world. Wallace Stegner in <u>Where The Bluebird Sings In The Lemonade Springs</u> writes of living and writing in the West. He says that a writer absorbs everything he has ever read or known and transmits it to the written page. Stegner opens up the world of the West, to which he always returns. I also have come to love the West, especially Colorado, from family visits and fishing trips in Colorado and Wyoming. At least getting dirty in stream-side mud gives you a feeling for the land and its beauty beyond that which a tourist experiences looking out a window. The West is truly a land beyond and unique. From the Front Range to the San Luis valley, from the Snowy Range in Wyoming to Sand Dunes National Monument near New Mexico, The West was challenging to the early settlers and today the West must meet the challenge of dividing up a finite source water that is fought over by the various states.

To return to writing, I realize how my book serves as an ambassador for me. Authorship has opened up a larger world to me. People initially come up to discuss my book, many of whom I would never have spoken with otherwise. This meeting allows us to develop a deeper conversation. Recently at a family gathering, the conversation started about writing the book, but then my friend said how she had dreaded the task of writing her dissertation, but that once she got started, she was surprised how pleasurable the writing experience was. This same feeling surprised me. Writing is universal in its ability to transport you to worlds that you never knew existed and that enthrall you as you experience them for the first time. Writing draws on your accumulated life experiences, your memories and ideas developed over a lifetime which are part of your unconscious that was so closely examined by the psychiatrist Carl Jung. The unconscious is the unexpected memory that pops up when you are not expecting. It pops up when I am dozing, it pops up when I am fully awake. It pops up particularly when I am walking outside and enjoying the freedom and beauty that living in Hartmeadow affords. Like my friend, Van Parker, I stumbled into writing late in life and as he says in the preface to his book of poetry, <u>Connected</u>, "I am always surprised how the writing turns out." This is true for me and I am also pleased at how eager I am to start writing. Writing the Addendum now consists of a number of constant revisions and rewrites which all serve to improve the story. The computer makes writing easier although I have to constantly correct spelling mistakes and typos. How did I ever handle crypto work in the Navy?

Another of my errant thoughts: Thank you Andrew Carnegie for your vision investing in some 1500 libraries across America. The library is a haven for the whole spectrum of society. It is a resource for the scholar and a lifesaving home for the homeless who have been turned out of a shelter in the middle of winter. The library is an energy source more lasting than nuclear power. It does not diminish in strength over the years and has no half-life. It gives the life of the mind fertile ground to reach an expanding audience. The reference librarian can find an answer to almost any question to expand your world. The library is a rich resource that expands your knowledge and helps you experience the joy of reading.

My Life

My life has been blessed. After my divorce and the bankruptcy of the Bidwell Hardware Company I had hit rock bottom… This is the story that I was afraid to tell in "Reflections". I was unmoored and unsure of myself. Fortunately, I had a job with Slater Publications of Newton, Massachusetts, selling advertising in their magazine and construction products directory. I also worked the booth in trade shows in Boston, which I enjoyed. Over the next couple of years, I tried a few diversions, cross country skiing at an inn in Vermont, taking a windjammer trip in Maine, canoeing in the northern Connecticut River. But then I had to return to reality. At first, I rented an apartment in a renovated mill complex in Glastonbury. Here there was a community of divorcees who reveled in the local bar scene. This was new to me and I found that I could not really make personal contact but then I wasn't ready and really did not want to. I used to go cross country skiing in Hurd State Park by the Connecticut River. I remember vividly driving by the stately homes in South Glastonbury and feeling such a sense of homelessness. But I dug down and decided that I wanted to live in Hartford. I moved to a sunny apartment overlooking the river in the renovated Brown Thomson building. At this time Hartford was in decline. G. Fox and Sage Allen, on both sides of my apartment closed. But my spirits improved with the sunny outlook from my abode. I joined historic Center Church which had managed to resist the ravages of time, and stood as an icon and beacon in the midst of the city. Center Church embraced me as someone who needed the security of acceptance. The congregation was welcoming and I enjoyed the very democratic feeling of people who were not judgmental. The church did not have the executive hierarchy of some congregations, but then it did not have their financial security. Here I found that my talents and construction background filled a need in the church. This led to a thirty-year program of volunteer property management and historic preservation. I had found my home. I also found a new friend, Robin Roy, a lifetime member of Center Church. We shared interests and trips, including the recreation of Thomas Hooker's pilgrimage from Cambridge to Hartford. We both traveled to London and Amsterdam on a historic trip led by our minister, Alan Mclean. This was an exploration of the history of the reverend Thomas Hooker as he hid from the conservative Archbishop Laud in Amsterdam before gathering his flock to set out for America. Robin and I enjoyed being together and shared our common interest in Center Church. Robin invited me to dinner at her big old Laurel Street Victorian. She served martinis and it all started from there. Ten years later we were married when the time was right and the strands of our personal lives had come together in a common bond. This is a very brief capsule outline of my life at that time. I may choose to enlarge on it in the future.

On Living

From my personal life, I transition to a more general discussion about living and the observations of writers and doctors who are writers. Sherwin B. Nuland, M.D. writes in <u>The Art</u> <u>of Aging</u>, "It is never too late to find tributaries that add vibrancy to our lives" A tributary for me has been the many strands of my life that flow into the main body. One tributary has been writing my book and enjoying the new people that I have met through it. Nuland also writes that age becomes a liberator, freeing us from the opinions and prejudices of others. This is what Van Parker, meant when he said that "you should be happy with who you are and not who you think you should be." I find this reality, late in life, which helps me not to be concerned about what other people are thinking about me, but allows me to be free to live a happy life!   The arc of life is different for each of us. Some lives light up in a blaze of glory like a wildfire, only to be extinguished at some cost. Others are more like a controlled burn, which requires a lot of work with pick and shovel and an occasional back fire to be controlled. My own arc has been reliably steady with some energy coming late in life from my book publishing and my reading and discussing books with Robin. She can recount a plot much better than I can. I am fortunate in what I can still do, much of it due to Robins help. We go to the library weekly to replenish our life-giving supply of new books. We go to church where I can sit quietly before the service and listen to the choir rehearse and glory in the power of the Austin organ. I can feel tears as a familiar hymn brings unexpected emotion bursting forth. I do not find this kind of emotion springing forth anywhere else.

There are many things that I can still enjoy and share. I can share a breakfast with my son and daughter at a local diner. I can discuss life with Robin. This shared life includes more intimate conversations because I am more mature in my outlook. This maturity is a shared experience which developed over a long marriage as we learned to respect each other's point of view. Fortunately, we both enjoy similar programs of travel and mystery from the quality of PBS television. Over the years we have followed the trials of Inspector Morse, and his protege Inspector Lewis. Then we watch the development of the buttoned-up Sergeant Hathaway. a sidekick to Lewis. Now we look forward to the prequel "Endeavor" which covers Morse's early career as he must prove himself against the established power structure. I like mysteries with foreign settings like Inspector Perez who keeps the peace in the Shetland Islands or the dour Welsh landscape in Hinterland. This interest brings out the heavy world atlas to better understand these locations. And of course, there is reading, although this now requires a strong Ottlight, assisted by a magnifying glass. Reliable authors such as Daniel Silva, Robert Harris, John Grisham and David McCullough are old friends. Without reading my life would have a large void that could not be filled otherwise. This summer I will watch the Yard Goats play in their impressive new stadium. I can walk around the beautiful grounds of Hartmeadow although I am no longer able to walk the meadows and watch the wild grasses grow and marvel in the wide expanse of sky at West Moor Park across the street. I have enjoyed talking with Doug Jackson, the naturalist at the park, and found out that like Robin and me, he spent time and enjoyed the Hill Country in Texas. A long way from the early settlements of Connecticut.

But things change. Now there are things that I can no longer do. I have just been diagnosed at the ST Francis Hospital coronary rehab program with the need for oxygen during the day, when I exercise, in addition to using it at night when I sleep. My oxygen level does not rebound as it used to after exercise. I will have to see how limiting this will be. As my doctor said, my life progression will be a series of ladder like steps with the inevitable drop or missed step. This is part of the slow decline in the arc of my life and every life. I believe that I have a good idea what the future will bring and face it unafraid. I give thanks for my faith and my belief in God. My God is a personal God who will care for me and offer support in times of need.

I look forward to my life that is left with faith, hope and love. My faith is solid. I am hopeful by nature. The love I find with Robin, with my family and with friends who offer their strength and understanding. Later in life, I now find that I am more open to accepting praise and its blessings. I am more open to expressing love and the ability to share it. I now better recognize compassion and appreciate the qualities in people who I might have previously written off as uninteresting. I am surprised to find out the secret assets that define them. This does open up new worlds and people in my life and makes me a more interesting and understanding person. I am constantly surprised by the kind words that friends have written me about my book and it is good to know that it was meaningful to them. Somehow, I hadn't been sure that the book had real value.

On Aging

I wrote about aging in my book Reflections, but that should not preclude a further study of this fact of life. Dr. Sherwin Nuland writes that "Successful aging is an art." It is an art that it is not easily mastered and must be worked at. Like brewing, it requires the lengthy time that a single malt requires to reach its perfection after years of aging in an oak cask. Hopefully the quality of our lives is not limited by the length of time spent in a wooden cask, but continue to be energized by new experiences. If we continue to embrace the new, it will help us to continue to be healthy and to age gracefully. I think it is right for me to continue to talk about aging because I continue to have new thoughts and experiences every day. New thoughts add to my personal knowledge of myself. As Dr Nuland says "Self-knowledge is often difficult to gage. Motive lies behind every decision we make and it is seldom pure." Wow! I had never realized that. Our decisions are quite often made with imperfect knowledge and like the politician who chooses the best apparent option, based on imperfect knowledge, at least we are acting on the knowledge that we have. Unfortunately, today many of our politicians are frozen by party loyalties, and no decisions are made because of a false fear that compromise shows weakness. Theodore Roosevelt, being a compromiser, became one of our best Presidents. Our country is not experiencing graceful aging with an ungraceful President at its head. **Transition**

Transition is defined in <u>Webster's Collegiate Dictionary</u>, eleventh edition as "A passage from one stage, state or place to another." This is a pretty thin definition. It seems to me that as our discussion about aging describes the downward slope that inevitably sets in, leading to death, that it is appropriate to delay this discussion until I have a more informed life view. This aging transition is determined in most cases by health issues. I am fortunate not to have suffered mental loss of acuity except that of short-term memory. Indeed, my sudden interest in writing at the age of ninety surprised me. It is an exciting gift that gives me an outlet for thoughtful consideration of my life. As a published author I can claim membership in a very exclusive club; a club not dependent on race, ethnic origin, economic status or the quiet vetting of members. Indeed, my writing seems to have released a sharper intellectual focus that transcends age. Let's hope that this focus continues for a while. It is certainly one marker among many that need to be watched in this transition period as a gauge for a sign of decline.

On Dying

The final chapter is as yet unclear. I had previously written that I was not afraid of death. Well, this is not really true. I am certainly terrified by the thought that I might eventually suffocate from the loss of breath due to increasing inelasticity of the lungs caused by Pulmonary Fibrosis, or that I would suffer the lingering end that so many suffer. Dr Patrick Coll, my primary physician and head of the Geriatric Department recommended that I wear a "do not resuscitate" band to alert the EMTS and I hope for a quick end without extreme measures being taken. I have the example of the English author George Orwell, who chose to finish his book <u>1984</u>, knowing that he chose between his health and finishing his masterwork. He died six months after the book was finished. Likewise, General Ulysses S. Grant, who was afraid of leaving his wife in poverty, opted to push on and finish his masterful autobiography despite increasing agony of his illness. I fortunately am not under this kind of stress as I work on this Addendum in comfort and with the loving concern of Robin and friends. However, I am aware that although my time left is unknown, it is limited. I try not to obsess over this unknown. We try so hard to nail everything down in our lives. I must try to use this time left as wisely as possible. One objective is to finish final tasks so they are not left for Robin to cope with. I have been writing the outline of the facts of my life which will help her develop my obituary. I always look forward to the New York Times obituaries of well-known people. The Times employs skilled writers who specialize in obits and their thoughtful biographies, written by skilled writers, bring forth a clear detailed picture of the person which is hard to find elsewhere.   Biographies are my favorite form of non-fiction. The best ones give you information not previously known or challenge accepted doctrine. A good example is the biography of General George C. Marshall by Leonard Mosley. Self-effacing, he did not write an autobiography like many contemporaries, and his epitaph could read "here lies an honest man". A new biography of Admiral William D. Leahy by Phillips P. O'Brien, challenges the notoriety given General Marshall and claims previously unknown authority for Admiral Leahy. However, calling Leahy "the second most important man in the world" is a vast overstatement.

My family memoir is a distinct genre. It offers connections to family and friends that otherwise might not happen. The memoir sheds light on past events and is unique in its ability to open up the mind to relate to family history and surprise us with forgotten stories. In the complex neural network of our mind, the neuron strands connected by synapses allow neurotransmitters to shunt electrical energy and form new connections that constantly expand our knowledge base. They enhance the new and clean out the distressed. How does our neural network compare to that of the robot's artificial intelligence? We watch IBM's Watson calling the shots at Wimbledon. We hear of a robot, after being programmed, that is able to beat a skilled poker player. But humans have moral intelligence which separates us from the apes (and the robot). It is impossible to know what the next thirty years will add to A.I. and whether we should be apprehensive. Henry Kissinger in the August, 2019 Atlantic wrote "AI has made it possible to automate an extraordinary range of tasks and has done so by enabling machines to draw an increasingly decisive role in drawing conclusions from data and then taking action. AI draws conclusions from its own experience unlike software which can only support human reasoning." Universities like M.I.T. are gearing up for serious study of this new frontier. I try to spend my time in relaxing pursuits and with a priority to use the time wisely. Our travel is now limited but we can still take day trips down the Connecticut River to Old

Lyme and the Florence Griswold Museum where we can enjoy a lovely lunch overlooking the lazy Lieutenant River. A priority is making a point of visiting with my children and friends. This is very important. The visit may be personal or it may have to be by E-mail. I am not familiar with the other host of "social media". This means it is easier spending "quality time" with Robin. This time spent can never be replaced and it is more life giving than "quality time" implies. The New York Times recently headlined an article, "The Reality of Death in Unreal Times", which reviewed the book Picnic Comma Lightning by Lawrence Scott. He writes that "Ours is an age of both endless data and limitless skepticism." When these unreal times meet the fact of our death, does this change how we approach our passing? I have to think about this, but with my skepticism and pragmatism, I do not think these "unreal times" will have an impact on my thinking.

The headstones are ordered and the cemetery will set them this spring. Mountainview Cemetery in Bloomfield sits on a crest affording a beautiful view West to the rolling hills leading to Talcott Mountain. Here my Welsh Jenkyn great grandparents and my Bidwell grandparents are buried with my Uncle Ken, LT USNR who was lost in a collision at sea in WW11. Robin and I will have our ashes interred in the Center Church memorial garden which blooms in the middle of the city as well as in the cemetery. We will be buried in the Bidwell plot, along with a stone for my brother John whose ashes were buried at sea by the US Navy. Mountainview also holds a tall, native brownstone monument, aging with the years, representing my Bidwell great grandparent Johnathan {1814-1902] and his brothers Cornelius, Cyrus and Nathaniel. The soft brownstone has eroded over the years, obscuring the names. The deep, old brownstone quarry in Portland, Connecticut is now home to a thriving ropes aquatic course which challenges the young daredevil. My son Jeremy loved to explore the shards along the edges of the quarry looking for garnets and other semi-precious stones. The old brownstone homes in Hartford and New York are a reminder of a gracious past that cannot be recreated. Other family members buried in Mountainview include Alan Tobie's wife Josie and his family. Earlier Bidwell ancestors going back to the Revolutionary War are buried in the Old North Cemetery in the center of Bloomfield. The restoration of this cemetery and installation of the memorial gate and fences was facilitated by my grandfather, F.C. Bidwell. Three historic events were commemorated by setting the plaques on the memorial gate in 1934. My father, Eliot N. Bidwell gave a dedicatory address and my brother John aged 1 and I aged 5, pulled the veils covering the new plaques. The three historic events were the 300th anniversary of the founding of the Colony of Connecticut in 1635, the establishment of Wintonbury parish in 1735 and the incorporation of the Town of Bloomfield in 1835. This is outlined in the first edition of <u>Over Tunxis Trails</u>, written by my grandfather F.C. Bidwell. Unfortunately, the Bloomfield Town public works budget does not seem to provide for serious maintenance and repair of the cemetery. The bronze plaques have lost their luster and await attention, the fences are rusted and weeds obscure many monuments. I would like to see the plaques restored and my grandsons, Nathaniel and Sam, could do the unveiling with a brief presentation by Jeremy. This would close the circle to when I was a five-year-old and renewed family history. After all, residents should take part in shaping a town's heritage. My grandfather certainly believed that. An upgrade of this historic site would be more meaningful than other proposed town improvements.

It is now time to stop avoiding the issue and discuss the serious business of dying. This is indeed serious for the husband in Middletown, who is accused of aiding in the suicide of his wife. Hopefully the legislature will revisit the aid-in-dying law which they recently refused to recognize. Other states including Vermont have such laws on the books. Sherwin B. Nuland, MD, writes in <u>How We Die</u>, that "modern dying takes place in the modern hospital, where it can be hidden, cleansed of its blight, and finally packaged for modern burial." This sounds dreadful and that it will be very difficult to have a "death with dignity." I think this is too antiseptic a description of the solace provided by the modern hospital. But more importantly for me, Nuland goes on to describe the basic symptoms which lead to a decrease of health and eventually death.

I have had questions regarding my developing symptoms and his discussion helps to describe where I am at. For the last few months, I have been afflicted by irritations and itches over my body, particularly in the groin area and the armpits. The armpits were surprisingly painful. Fortunately, my dermatologist was eventually able to prescribe the right ointment, and she diagnosed me with "inverse psoriasis" which would last my lifetime. My eyes also have become very itchy, which my retinologist is treating. I thought that I might have an immune system problem. Dr Nuland states "The immune system is the invisible force that allows us to respond to the assaults of potentially lethal enemies. When we get older, our immune system like everything else, increasingly fails us." So, my guess was right. As I have motioned previously, I have just been diagnosed at ST Francis Hospital, during my fitness classes, as being unable to bring my oxygen level up sufficiently after exercise. This means that I will need to carry a shoulder canister of oxygen when exercising and walking. One more in a line of life limiting decisions and actions. I will have to graduate to a walker to carry the canister. I am now getting used to the walker which allows me to walk more and get needed exercise. I will fight against eventually needing a wheel chair, but the fight can only last so long. When they end up carrying me, like the Pharaoh, it will be the end of the line. Dr Nuland states, "Death may be due to a wide variety of diseases, but in every case the underlying cause is a breakdown in the body's oxygen cycle." Problem two clarified. These symptoms contribute to the basic diagnosis of my cardiologist, Dr Kim, at UCONN Hospital of congestive heart failure. Dr Nuland writes, "This failure is the direct result of the scarred and weakened myocardium (muscle wall), that cannot contract with sufficient force to push out the necessary volume of blood with each stroke." This cursory list of my symptoms, pressures me to consider what tasks I have left. My book is published but needs to be distributed. I am heartened by the many kind responses to my book. I have pushed this addendum, as I felt pressure to complete it. As I work on it, I am developing an appreciation of this new compendium of thoughts, just as untrained as nature itself. This work stands by itself and is worth continuing. Thank you, Christopher, for encouraging me to continue to write, unhindered by a need to wrap this up. There are obviously other tasks left undone, many of a personal nature, which I must accomplish. Now I am experiencing changes in my health. This reduced energy level and increased problems of balance is partially due to my increased level of oxygen deficiency.

I read what Dr Nuland writes of "The futility of pursuing treatment against great odds that may seem like a heroic act to some but too commonly is a form of disservice to patients." The surgeon is tempted to operate using the startling advances of modern science, but this may lead to a terrible end of life for a patient who has only some months left at best. Medical schools are now starting to include end of life considerations in their curriculum. After ninety years, I hope I can feel that I have "lived a life worth living". I have been a visitor as well as a stranger in this land and my imprint will eventually be covered by the sands of time. I await my inevitable death, which rarely cooperates with the timeline that we think reasonable. My timeline is as yet unclear. I have been unsettled by my latest setbacks, but I feel well, so who knows what is in store? It is probably just as well that we cannot predict "when lightning strikes" but we don't have to stand under a tree in a storm. The very best that I can hope for is to die at the end of a brief, anguish free illness, surrounded by the people I love. By Robin and family and close friends.

www.ingramcontent.com/pod-product-compliance
Lightning Source LLC
Chambersburg PA
CBHW061129160726
48006CB00036B/1462